Memories in the Service of the Hindu Nation

Memories in the Service of the Hindu Nation is based on 14 months of ethnographic fieldwork in Delhi and its surroundings between 2017 and 2018 with Partition survivors from west Punjab and the North-West Frontier Province. It locates the global rise of far-right nationalism within globalisation and memories of victimhood. Focusing on Hindu nationalism in India, this book is an important and timely contribution to the literature on South Asian Partition Studies that shows how tragedy begets tragedy. It tries to answer an urgent, provocative but nevertheless necessary question: What does it mean to remember the Partition in the time of fascism?

The author shows what makes up cycles of violence by connecting the reinscription of trauma in Partition memories to the self-serving justifications of the contemporary violence of Hindu nationalism. It analyses how the hegemony of Hindu nationalism has structured the narratives of Hindu Partition survivors and recruited them in the service of a putative Hindu nation.

Pranav Kohli teaches sociology at Maynooth University, Ireland. He is a political anthropologist specialising in race, gender, conflict, authoritarianism and memory with an abiding interest in their intersections with the politics of health.

SOUTH ASIA IN THE SOCIAL SCIENCES

South Asia has become a laboratory for devising new institutions and practices of modern social life. Forms of capitalist enterprise, providing welfare and social services, the public role of religion, the management of ethnic conflict, popular culture and mass democracy in the countries of the region have shown a marked divergence from known patterns in other parts of the world. South Asia is now being studied for its relevance to the general theoretical understanding of modernity itself.

South Asia in the Social Sciences will feature books that offer innovative research on contemporary South Asia. It will focus on the place of the region in the various global disciplines of the social sciences and highlight research that uses unconventional sources of information and novel research methods. While recognising that most current research is focused on the larger countries, the series will attempt to showcase research on the smaller countries of the region.

General Editor

Partha Chatterjee
Columbia University

Editorial Board

Pranab Bardhan
University of California at Berkeley

Stuart Corbridge
Durham University

Satish Deshpande
University of Delhi

Christophe Jaffrelot
Centre d'etudes et de recherches internationales, Paris

Nivedita Menon
Jawaharlal Nehru University

Other books in the series:

Government as Practice: Democratic Left in a Transforming India
Dwaipayan Bhattacharyya

Courting the People: Public Interest Litigation in Post-Emergency India
Anuj Bhuwania

Development after Statism: Industrial Firms and the Political Economy of South Asia
Adnan Naseemullah

Politics of the Poor: Negotiating Democracy in Contemporary India
Indrajit Roy

Nationalism, Development and Ethnic Conflict in Sri Lanka
Rajesh Venugopal

Memories in the Service of the Hindu Nation

The Afterlife of the Partition of India

Pranav Kohli

Shaftesbury Road, Cambridge CB2 8EA, United Kingdom

One Liberty Plaza, 20th Floor, New York, NY 10006, USA

477 Williamstown Road, Port Melbourne, VIC 3207, Australia

314–321, 3rd Floor, Plot No. 3, Splendor Forum, Jasola District Centre, New Delhi 110025, India

103 Penang Road, #05–06/07, Visioncrest Commercial, Singapore 238467

Cambridge University Press is part of Cambridge University Press & Assessment, a department of the University of Cambridge.

We share the University's mission to contribute to society through the pursuit of education, learning and research at the highest international levels of excellence.

www.cambridge.org
Information on this title: www.cambridge.org/9781009318686

© Pranav Kohli 2023

First published 2023

Printed in India by Avantika Printers Pvt. Ltd.

A catalogue record for this publication is available from the British Library

ISBN 978-1-009-31868-6 Hardback

For my Nani, who carried the burden of a difficult past.

For my godson Anbu in the hope of an unburdened future.

Contents

Figures

Acknowledgements

There are a number of people to whom thanks are due. First and foremost, to my mom: thank you for being the best sociological mom ever! You are the best!

To Choti Nani and my family in Faridabad – Nani Masi, Tony *mamu*, Poonam *mami* and Sagar *bhaiya* – thank you for taking care of me during my fieldwork. None of this would have been possible without your kindness, hospitality, care and generosity. Thanks are also due to my extended family who helped me in various ways, including my search for informants.

To my informants, thank you for opening up your homes and hearts to me. You are my kin and ancestors, and I will always love and respect you. I will keep you alive in writing and memory. Thanks are also due to Mr and Mrs Adlakha for assisting me in my search for informants.

To my PhD supervisor, Thomas Strong, thank you for everything. You have been an inspiring mentor and role model, an exemplar of the kind of engaged anthropologist I aspire to be.

Thanks are also due to Chandana Mathur, Steve Coleman and Andrew Finlay for having been my supervisors at different stages of my academic journey. Your spirit animates this monograph. Thanks also to Peter van der Veer for his invaluable feedback as the external examiner of my PhD thesis. I bear the memory of passing my viva with zero corrections, with honour. Thanks are also due to my academic colleagues Eamonn Slater, John Brown and Barry Cannon for their advice and timely pep-talks at various stages of the publication process.

Thanks are also due to my whimsical Irish foster parents Ela and Michael Kennedy; to my friends Adeen Solaiman, Mahvish Khan, Miriam Teehan, Sara O'Rourke, Danielle Ng, Maire Ni Mhordha, and to my fellow Reading Room Rats (especially Gabriella for the lifetime free Dropbox space). A special thanks to Sherin and Nitin Williams – my family in Helsinki – for their feedback on the final draft of this manuscript.

Thanks also to Romila Thapar, Tanika Sarkar, Urvashi Butalia and Nonica Datta for taking the time to talk to me during my fieldwork. Thank you for inspiring me with your work and words.

Thanks are due to Maynooth University, whose John and Pat Hume Doctoral Studentship supported my PhD studies.

Last but not least, thanks to my editors Anwesha Rana and Qudsiya Ahmed, to series editor Partha Chatterjee, the members of the series editorial board and the three anonymous peer reviewers for believing in this project.

Prologue

The Linguistic Setting

The Partition of India remains the largest episode of retributive genocide and mass displacement in history (Aiyar 1995). It is estimated that between 200,000 and 2 million people were killed in the retributive violence that ensued, while between 10 and 17 million people were displaced in a haphazard transfer of population. In the process, approximately 3.4 million refugees went missing (Brass 2003b; Khwaja, Bharadwaj and Mian 2009). What began as a haphazard migration for safety – as people found themselves on the 'wrong' side of the border – was later formalised between India and Pakistan as a transfer of population (Bharadwaj and Mirza 2019).

This book is an ethnography of the memory of this historical rupture – its afterlife. It is based on 14 months of intensive fieldwork in Delhi and its surrounding National Capital Region where I located and worked with over 50 first-hand survivors of the 1947 Partition of India. My research specifically focuses on Hindu refugees from the north-western Pakistani districts of Mianwali, Dera Ghazi Khan, Dera Ismail Khan, Bannu, Quetta (Balochistan), Multan and Mianwali. Barring a brief trip to Dehradun, the overwhelming majority of Partition survivors I spoke to live in Delhi and its surroundings.

For the most part my fieldwork involved drinking copious amounts of tea with my informants as we discussed politics, history and their everyday lives. As a project that combines oral history with participant observation, this book relies heavily on the recording, transcription, interpretation and translation of the words of my informants. It is for this reason that detailing the ethnic and linguistic setting of my research gains added relevance.

Being a third-generation Partition migrant, my connection to the Partition is deeply intimate. Delhi was the obvious site for my fieldwork because my family's Partition survivors and their friends are settled there. This personal connection is visible throughout my research, shaping my search for informants as well as my engagement with theory. Due to the snowballing nature of my search for informants – that branched out into the kith and kin networks of my family's elders – all of my informants hail from the Derajat region and the North-West Frontier Province. All my informants were aged 80 and above at the time of interviews (2017–2018). Most of the people who find a mention in this book were close to 85 years of age. Roughly two-thirds of my informants happened to be men, an accident of social relations. All of my informants were upper-caste, middle-class and Hindu. They belonged to a mix of castes such as Khatri, Arora, Bhatia, Malik and Brahmin.[1] All of them came from well-off zamindar families. Quite a few even owned businesses in addition to hereditary land titles.

The stories I have documented here tell the story of the Partition as it unfolded in this north-western region of Pakistan. The Derajat region is located in the area where the Pakistani provinces of Punjab, Balochistan and Khyber-Pakhtunkhawa (formerly North-West Frontier Province) meet. The Derajat region is identified as a culturally distinct region, partly due to the fact that it is home to the Saraiki language. The historical districts of Dera Ghazi Khan, Dera Ismail Khan, Quetta, Mianwali and Multan are most closely associated with the Derajat region and the Saraiki language (Hashmi and Majeed 2014). However, as my informants continuously reminded me, Saraiki is something of an umbrella term for the closely related dialects of Derawali, Mianwali-*boli* (or Mianwali dialect) and Multani. These dialects also bear a close resemblance to Punjabi. Today, Saraiki is the major language of this region (in Pakistan) and is spoken by approximately 25–40 million people (Hashmi and Majeed 2014).

North-west of the Derajat region, in the North-West Frontier Province, the main languages spoken were Pashto, Persian and Urdu. My informants from Bannu and other remote parts of this province saw themselves as neither Saraiki nor Punjabi, but as Pashtuns and/or

Pathans. As my key informant Pooran Chand told me, in the years immediately following the Partition, the Frontier refugees asserted their ethnic identity partly through their refusal to marry into Punjabi families.

However, much has changed in the post-Independence, post-Partition context. Although remembered by the survivors of the Partition and some of their children, these regional identities have been subsumed within a larger Punjabi and Indian cultural identity. The grandchildren of Partition survivors, that is, the people of my generation, identify as Punjabi or Delhiites or whatever other local Indian identity they consider relevant. None of the people of my generation speak Saraiki or any of its dialects. Among the families of my informants, Hindi appeared to have replaced these dialects as the mother tongue. This is in contrast to Pakistan, where Saraiki has emerged as a slow-burning ethnic question, complete with the demand for a Saraiki province (Butt and Ahmed 2016).

The only settings where I observed an explicit emphasis on these (legacy) regional identities was in the activities of the organisations formed by Partition refugees, namely the All-India Mianwali District Association and the All-India Derawal Sahayak Sabha ('Volunteer Assembly'). These volunteer-based organisations were founded by Mianwali and Derawal Partition refugees in the 1950s with the explicit purpose of resettling their respective communities. However, by 2017 these organisations had become a mere shadow of their former selves. Almost all of their active members were aged 60 and above, with little to no involvement of young and middle-aged people. Although these organisations still organised annual meet-ups for their members, the general tone of these events can be best described by what Michael Herzfeld (2005) once referred to as a nostalgia for *real* community. Nevertheless, these organisations and their events were instrumental in my search for informants.

As a result of these transformations in culture and identity over the last 75 years since the Partition, my interviews and fieldwork interactions were almost entirely conducted in Hindi. However, given the diversity of the linguistic context of my research, other languages too often made an appearance in the speech of my informants. At times, either for dramatic effect or subconsciously, my informants spoke the occasional sentence or phrase in English, Urdu, Saraiki or Punjabi. Notwithstanding such instances, Hindi was predominantly the language in which my fieldwork was conducted.

Having been fluently bilingual in Hindi and English from an early age, I was able to transcribe and translate my informants' words with ease. My larger concern around translation in this context was not regarding my ability to convert words from one language into another. Rather, the challenge lay in confronting translation as an added layer of interpretation.

I have endeavoured to preserve the emic vocabulary of my informants as far as possible. Readers will observe numerous instances in this book where I have preserved the Hindi/Punjabi/Urdu words of my informants and explained their meanings in accompanying commentary. I have done this for words and phrases that do not have a direct English translation and to convey something of the literariness or emotive context of my informants' speech.

Paying attention to the literariness of my informants' speech has also informed my engagement with theory. This is most visible in Part II, where my analysis of the theodicical discourse of sacrifice partly hinges on the deconstruction of the gendered connotations of my informants' use of the word *purusharth*. The translation and interpretation of this word is part of a larger dialogue with my informants and their memories of the Partition.

In my transliterations of these vernacular words and phrases, I have strived for phonetic accuracy. Dispensing with the use of diacritics, I have written these words phonetically using the Roman alphabet. There is nothing novel or controversial about this. Almost every English-speaking Indian netizen would have encountered such transliterations in the form of mass-forwarded vernacular jokes. Wherever I was in doubt regarding the 'correct' transliteration of a word, I merely turned to the vast literature on South Asia for guidance. In this way, my transliteration of vernacular words follows colloquial linguistic practices and former scholarly transliterations. Occasionally, I also sought my mother and my grandaunt Anjali's advice on the translation and transliteration of particular words.

Ultimately, by preserving some of the literariness of the speech of my informants, I have tried to convey the individualised and personalised tone of these narratives. There is no master narrative of the Partition. What one finds instead is a constellation of independent voices that contextualise, organise, localise and mobilise their memory in relation to certain common frames of reference. As an ethnography of the last generation of Partition survivors, I consider the documentation of this polyphonous voicing an important scholarly objective. I hope that my work will sustain our ongoing dialogue with the suffering and violence in our past and present.

Note

1   I have not mentioned the specific castes of specific informants in their introductions as part of persistent efforts to preserve their anonymity. Some of my informants shared their last name with the name of their caste (for example, Arora and Bhatia). I have therefore used the somewhat generalising gloss of 'upper-caste' with a twofold objective: to make the caste dynamics at play intelligible to a larger non-South Asian non-specialist audience and to obscure biographical details.

Part I

The Past and the Present

Introduction

Death and the Problem of Theodicy

This book is primarily about death and suffering. It is an ethnography of the memory of the 1947 Partition of India and how its survivors make sense of the Partition's death and suffering decades after the fact. Although I worked with close to 50 informants while compiling this book, there was one person who was instrumental in the conceptualisation of this overarching theme: my late grandaunt Sneh.

My grandaunt Sneh died on the night of 7 June 2018. Her death came as a complete shock. Earlier that night, we had spoken on the phone and made plans for the following day. But it was not to be. She had a heart attack later that night and by the time her children drove her to the hospital, it was already too late. It was all over in a little less than an hour.

Through the course of my fieldwork, she and I had become quite close. She was the last surviving sibling of my late maternal grandmother. But growing up, I had not had the chance to spend much time with her. That year that I spent living in Delhi, she affectionately imposed a grandmotherly relationship on me. She would call me frequently to check up on me and would get annoyed if we went a week without talking on the phone. It was almost always my fault!

Sneh, or Nani Masi as I used to call her, was born in 1946 in Rajanpur, a small town in the district of Dera Ghazi Khan (now in Punjab, Pakistan). She was only an infant during the Partition. The youngest of four siblings (by quite a distance), she was relatively shielded from the chaos of the time. She remembered growing up in Kingsway Camp (Delhi) and later in the resettlement colony of Palwal, a satellite town 60 kilometres from Delhi. Her father – my great-grandfather – Chaudhry Pooran Chand[1] was a renowned lawyer in his time. He was even appointed the resettlement commissioner of this area. Until as late as 2018, a certain generation of people in Palwal still remembered how he had spearheaded the resettlement process in this area. As his last surviving child, Nani Masi quietly embodied his legacy.

In her youth, she had been something of a rebel. In contrast to the sheltered upbringing my grandmother had received, Nani Masi had enjoyed a degree of freedom and independence that was quite unusual in the context of its time. She was 11 years younger than my grandmother. This meant that Nani Masi was in school when my grandmother got married. Although only a teenager at the time, she would travel alone on public transport, from Palwal to Delhi, to visit them. As she described it, she had been fairly *chust* (street-smart) all through her life. Even after marriage, she often made her way on her own, sometimes even with a child or two on her hip. She and her husband had taken entire road trips on their motorcycle, often with their children balanced finely between them. She loved remembering the spontaneity and free-spiritedness of her younger days.

Ultimately, it was her failing health that changed everything. The last 10 years of her life were marked by a steady decline. The slide had begun soon after my grandmother's passing in 2006 and intensified after her husband's death in 2010. By 2017 her health was dire. Her stomach and face had swollen up alarmingly. She could barely walk now. And even with a stick for support, just hobbling around her home left her breathless. While she was still quite sharp, her near-complete bed rest had impacted her mental health.

Yet she did not let her failing health stop her from becoming a part of my fieldwork. She used her vast network of friends and family to find me a number of informants. And, whenever she put me in touch with a new informant, she insisted on accompanying me to our first meeting. So, as I made numerous trips to Delhi and Palwal, she came with me. She would not have it any other way.

Those long drives are some of the fondest memories I have of her. Away from the rest of the family, she spoke her mind, unfiltered. Nani Masi and I rarely saw eye to eye on anything, but it was through these conversations that we truly bonded. She told me about her quarrels with her children, and we gossiped ad infinitum about the petty politics of her household. She also shared her memories of my grandparents and of my mother's childhood. It was during one of those conversations that she told me that she saw a lot of my mother in me – that like her, I am self-reliant and independent. This was important to her.

Another time, she shared one of her best-kept secrets: she had a fondness for drinking. She told me that often after she and uncle (her husband) had put the kids to bed, they would have a glass of Scotch together. She had never touched alcohol outside the home or in anyone else's presence. Her 'transgressions' had remained safely ensconced within the four walls of her household. She still had a half bottle of Scotch hidden safely in her TV cabinet. After we got home that day, we had half a peg together, for old time's sake.

Looking back, I feel these trips were like the second coming of her younger days. They gave her an excuse to get out of the house and back on the road, to rekindle old friendships and acquaintances, to meet people one last time. They were a partial return to the restless rhythms of her youth. A final hurrah!

During my fieldwork in Faridabad I fell into a routine where, after having spent an evening talking to a group of informants in Rose Garden, I would drop by her house for a chat. Her house was a short drive from the park. True to form, she always had a box of sweets and lemonade ready for me. We would sit together, have a chat and I would make fun of whatever melodramatic soap opera she happened to be watching at the time. For her part, she would tease me about my receding hairline and warn me that no one would want to marry a bald man like me. Sometimes she would call on me for lifts to the market. But for the most part, we would just sit together, catch up, gossip, and then I would return to my aunt and uncle's house just in time for dinner.

Her sudden death was a profoundly dislocating experience. While her presence had had a great impact on my fieldwork, in death, she came to fundamentally structure my engagement with theory. On a basic level, her death reminded me of the fragility of life, especially that of my informants, the elderly – the last generation of Partition survivors. But on a deeper level, her death marked the beginning of my engagement with the philosophy of death and suffering: theodicy.

It was during her funerary rituals that I first observed theodicy at work. Everyone in my family had their own story about her death. Some of my relatives framed her death as the result of long-time neglect.

Her strained relations with her children, especially one of her sons, was common knowledge. She had also spent her last years visibly struggling with her health while no one appeared to have offered any substantial help. To them, her death was symptomatic of a larger social issue: the neglect of the elderly. Others found comfort in the fact that she had not suffered – that her death had been swift and relatively painless. Emphasising the alleged painlessness of her death – its lack of suffering – they contrasted her death with those of other relatives who had not been so 'fortunate'.

Others focused on the large number of mourners who had attended her *chautha*.[2] They found comfort in the way that this reinforced a sense of community – that she was loved by the community and that the community had turned out to pay their final respects. Through the recursive retelling of these stories in shared settings, they combined to create a narrative that sought to reconcile the life she had lived with the death she had suffered. On a deeper level, these narratives grappled with the overwhelming force of two related questions: 'why/how had she died?' and 'why do bad things happen to good people?'

This essentially is the problem of theodicy: the attempt to reconcile death and suffering with belief in a meaningful cosmos (a *nomos*: the order of things). Traditionally, theodicy comprised a body of knowledge that asked how evil can exist despite a truly universal, benevolent deity (Herzfeld 1992). Peter Berger, Berger and Kellner (1974: 166) define theodicy as 'any explanation of human events that bestows meaning upon the experiences of suffering and evil'. The term 'theodicy' was developed by Leibnez in his attempts to reconcile suffering, misfortune and death with belief in a just and benevolent deity (Simko 2012). Max Weber (1965) built on Leibnez's work to use the term in a sociological sense to 'describe interpretive vocabularies, religious or secular, that explain evil and suffering' (Simko 2012: 881).

Weber (1965) understood theodicy as a way of reifying belief despite one's lived experience of a flawed world. Weber posited that 'the social character of entire societies may be conditioned by repeated attempts to come to terms with "the experience of the irrationality of the world" as encountered in acute instances of human suffering' (Wilkinson 2013: 129). Building on Weber's largely religion-focused work on theodicy, Michael Herzfeld (1992: 7) argues that the goal of secular theodicy is somewhat more pragmatic. For Herzfeld, secular theodicy 'provides people with social means of coping with disappointment'.

According to Peter Berger (1967), every *nomos* implies theodicy. The term *nomos* refers to the order of things. In the context of religion, *nomos* is a 'sacred canopy' that provides a sense of what a meaningful existence is, what life on Earth is all about. We may consider belief in God (or any other such transcendent benevolent deities) as an example of a *nomos*. *Nomos* embodies the sense in which we live in a meaningful universe – one that provides a sense of purpose to our lives. The *nomos* makes sense of the world – or rather, it is the way in which the world *makes sense* and is *sensed*. That is, the *nomos* in Berger's terms is comparable to the 'episteme' (Foucault 2002) or 'paradigm' (Kuhn 1996).

However, *nomos* is not inherent in nature. It is an order or meaning that is imposed upon reality by human beings. Because the *nomos* is a human imposition, it inevitably fails. Certain events possess the potential to fracture the *nomos*. Events that defy the meaningful order assumed by the *nomos* – such as random, chaotic and asymmetrical experiences of death, suffering and misfortune – possess the potential to expose the *nomos* for what it is: an imagined reality.

Berger (1967: 53) understands theodicy as an institutionalised activity that protects the established *nomos* from 'recurrent intrusion into individual and collective experience of the anomic (or, if one prefers, denomising) phenomenon of suffering, evil and, above all, death'. Everyday phrases such as 'Nothing can happen without God's permission' and 'It is the will of God' represent basic theodicies that attempt to explain the randomness of death, suffering and misfortune by reference to a transcendental deity. In doing so, such theodicies attempt to rationalise the unequal distribution of suffering within the order of the *nomos* (Berger 1967). Yet, where the understanding of suffering as God's will represents a fatalistic acceptance of it, the modern approach to suffering is one that aims to minimise it (Wilkinson 2013). Wilkinson argues that this rejection of fatalism is visible in the philosophical tendency to characterise the violent atrocities and mass human suffering (which includes wars, genocides, poverty, droughts, famines and pandemics) of the last hundred years as one of 'useless suffering' (Levinas 1988). Where the uselessness of suffering implies the collapse of the meaningfulness of the cosmos – the fracturing of a *nomos* – theodicy attempts to rationalise suffering within interpretive frameworks to transcend the uselessness (or futility) of one's suffering.

The idea of transcendence is closely related to the need for theodicy. This is the idea that 'a moral principle, or a deity, could transcend the specifics of time and place' (Herzfeld 1992: 6). The issue of transcendence lies at the heart of the problem of theodicy. As Weber frames it:

> [T]he more the development [of religion] tends toward the conception of a transcendental unitary god who is universal, the more there arises the problem of how the extraordinary power of such a god may be reconciled with the imperfection of the world that he has created and rules over. (Weber 1965: 138–139)

Theodicies that explain suffering by reference to the unknowable will of God or the balancing of an invisible karmic account use transcendence to answer the question of theodicy. In Christianity, this takes the form of salvation (Herzfeld 1992).

The theodicies posited by my relatives were everyday theodicies that attempted to balance Nani Masi's suffering and misfortune against her 'fortunately' painless death. Stories allegedly evidencing her children's neglect were often followed by comments such as 'May God never show such days [or this fate] to anyone'. Against this, the fact that her death had been relatively quick and painless was seen as something of a heavenly reward. Death is inevitable, but a painful death (suffering) is not. While her death itself remained a singular misfortune, the manner of her dying was seen as a blessing of sorts. On more than one occasion, Poonam, my eldest aunt, said this is how she wished to die – that is, either through something 'major' and 'quick' or painlessly in her sleep. In this way, by balancing the misfortune of her last years against the 'fortune' of her sudden death, my relatives retrospectively resolved Nani Masi's karmic account.

This task of resolution was given increased urgency by the fact that her children's neglect of her health was seen as the primary cause of her untimely demise. By emphasising the painlessness of her death, as well as the fact that all of her funerary rituals had been well attended, they sought to rescue her from a 'bad', 'asocial' death.[3] Shoring up a sense of community also helped preserve belief in the inherent goodness of humanity – a *nomos*. Adding impetus to this task was also an implicit sense of their own guilt. After all, the very people who accused her children of neglect had rarely ever visited her themselves.

I watched this recursive and reflexive mobilisation of memory for the task of theodicy from a sceptical distance. But, in the midst of grieving my grandaunt, I found that I too had begun to subscribe to a form of theodicy. In the weeks and months that followed her death, I found myself repeatedly thinking about her. Unbidden, random snippets of conversations from the past, memories I had not considered particularly significant *became meaningful* as I struggled to frame her death against a larger philosophy of a meaningful existence. The theodicy to which I was adhering was fatalistically stoic – acknowledging the inherent meaninglessness of life, death and suffering. And, in support of this, I found myself repetitively recalling memories that confirmed Nani Masi's own acceptance of the inevitability of death. On more than one occasion, she had told me that she felt she had nothing left to live for. And on all of those occasions I had tried my best to remind her that she had much to look forward to: weddings, great-grandchildren and even my graduation. 'You have to live long enough to call me Dr Kohli', I would often remind her. But death is a funny thing. The very fatalism that had disturbed me at the time became a comfort in her death – that *she is at peace now*.

It was this intimate experience of death that brought my attention to the problem of theodicy in the context of the Partition. As South Asia moves towards a time when the Partition passes from a living memory to an archived history, the ensuing transition has given way to a boom of oral history. Starting from 1998, the last 25 years have seen the growth of a wave of oral historical work on the Partition, one that has included the establishment of online oral history archives such as the 1947 Partition Archive and even a Partition Museum in Amritsar. Just as Nani Masi's death led to a flood of memory, the inevitable death of the last generation of Partition survivors has similarly led to a wave of remembrance.

In this idea that the 'death' of memory evokes remembrance lies the implicit glimmer of French historian Pierre Nora. Writing in the 1990s, Pierre Nora (1992: 1) famously declared the death of memory by stating, 'Memory is constantly on our lips because it no longer exists.' Nora's pronouncement of the extinction of *milieu of memory* – environments where memory forms a meaningful part of everyday life – was accompanied, unrelatedly, by Francis Fukuyama (1992), who, that very year, proclaimed the *end of history* itself. Fukuyama was triumphant in his declaration, while Nora lamented (prematurely) the obliteration of 'memory' by the seemingly all-consuming tides of 'history'.

Read in 2023, these proclamations of the death of things seem less like insights on history and memory and more a reflection of the strangely dislocating global transformations of that time. The collapse of the Soviet Union, and with it the end of the Cold War, inaugurated a new world order almost overnight. These bold pronouncements seem to echo the dislocation produced by the swift collapse of political formations that had seemed as unshakeable as memory and history themselves.

In observing that the last two decades have produced a wave of oral history, I do not intend to proclaim the death or the end of anything. My point is entirely different. In pointing out that the inevitable death of the last generation of Partition survivors has sparked a public turn to remembrance, I argue that the vast body of literature on the Partition of India comprises a long ongoing search for theodicy. Just as the flood of memory provoked by Nani Masi's passing sought to reconcile her death with belief in a meaningful cosmos (a *nomos*), so too successive waves of literature on the Partition have sought to reconcile its death and suffering with the *nomos* that is the idea of India. Having delineated this theodicical arc of Partition Studies, I then position my own ethnography in relation to it. I argue that Hindu nationalism serves as a form of theodicy for my Hindu upper-caste informants' experience of the death and suffering of the Partition. Transcending the 'uselessness' of their suffering through its nationalist idioms of 'sacrifice' and 'martyrdom', Hindu nationalism helps rationalise death and suffering.

Partition Studies and the Search for Theodicy

South Asian Partition Studies has developed over successive waves. The first wave of Partition Studies focused entirely on the high politics of the

Partition (Dube 2015). Turning away from the human suffering of the Partition, these analyses focused primarily on archival research. This first wave of Partition Studies literature is noteworthy for the rhetoric of blame that it implicitly employs (G. Pandey 2001). Percival Spear's *India, Pakistan and the West* (1952) inaugurated the historiographical framework that became something of a common sense reading of the Partition (Dube 2015). Spear's (1962) analysis pitted the 'secular' nationalism of the Congress against the Muslim nationalism of the All-India Muslim League to argue that the Partition was the result of the irreconcilability of these twin nationalisms. This narrative presents the Muslim League as the driver of Partition and the Congress as the voice for unity. However, this simplistic mould of analysis has subsequently received heavy criticism for its binary juxtaposition and its backhanded voicing of the two-nation theory's logic (Dube 2015).

Spear's historiographical analysis was followed by Larry Collins and Dominique Lapierre (1975), David Page (1982), Ayesha Jalal (1985), Ian Talbot and Gurharpal Singh (2009), Rajmohan Gandhi (1986), H. M. Seervai (2005) and Stanley Wolpert (2006), to name a few. This body of literature represents a consistent attempt to understand the rupture that is the Partition through a study of the main organisations, institutions and personalities involved in the process. Seervai (2005) in particular focuses on the constitutional aspects of nation state formation that the Partition entailed. Another noteworthy piece of work in this area is Ramachandra Guha's (2018) recent biography of Mahatma Gandhi that tangentially touches on the latter's opposition to the Partition.

These causal examinations of the Partition represent a theodicical effort to make sense of the Partition. Deploying the rhetoric of blame, they examine the historical record to determine a guilty person or party and thereby the source of evil. Partition, from this perspective, is largely construed as a purely political event of nation state formation. In these analyses, the horrors of the Partition receive only tangential attention as the Partition itself is often inchoately framed as the unfortunate by-product of decolonisation. With the exception of Talbot and Singh (2009), these analyses largely neglect engagement with the specificity of Partition violence due to its 'complexity'. This is a symptom of most of the historiographical work on the Partition and is a consequence of its neat separation of archival history from the Partition's lived experience (G. Pandey 2001). As Gyanendra Pandey observes, the violence of the Partition has been 'othered' from Indian history as 'someone else's history – or even, not history at all' (6). These historiographical analyses of the Partition present its violence as an aberration to a *nomic* understanding of 'secular' India. And in so doing, they provide a theodicy of the 'secular' Indian state.

While early historiographical analyses occupied themselves with an examination of Partition high politics, the mantle of documenting the lived experience of the Partition was taken up by literature and cinema. In this way, a rich body of art sprung up articulating the 'small voice of history'. Anne Castaing (2018) describes fictional representations of the Partition as a form of subaltern memory. For many of these artists, the turn to the Partition was motivated by *Parrēsia* (Foucault 2019) – the desire to 'speak truth to power'. The overwhelming majority of these artists were themselves survivors of the Partition. In giving voice to their pain, they were the first – and for almost half a century – the only public tradition mourning the death and suffering of the Partition.

I use the phrase 'small voice of history' to deliberately invoke Ranajit Guha's (2002b) critique of the way history-writing is implicated in reproducing the rationality of the state.[4] This is evident in the treatment of the Partition as a 'political' or 'constitutional' event – to the neglect of the suffering of ordinary people – in much of the historiographical work on the Partition. Identifying this 'statist' bias as a central theme within most history-writing, Guha (2002a: 73) wrote, '[t]he noise of World-history and its statist concerns has made historiography insensitive to the sighs and whispers of everyday life'. Guha instead calls for a writing of history that in documenting the past pays attention to the rhythms of everyday life.

The legendary Urdu poet and communist thinker Faiz Ahmed Faiz was among the first to voice the ambiguousness of a freedom besmirched by the horrors of the Partition. First published in August 1947, Faiz's (2017) seminal poem "Subh-e Azadi" ("The Dawn of Freedom") juxtaposed the celebratory attainment of 'freedom' in South Asia with the denomising violence of the Partition. Faiz's poem begins by describing Independence as a 'smeared', 'spotted' and 'night-bitten dawn' that 'isn't surely the dawn we waited for so eagerly' (38).

Poetically describing how the ethnonational divide came to overshadow decolonisation, Faiz's poem ends on a mournful note, observing the incompleteness of a 'freedom' fraught with the violence of the Partition.

Contemporaneous with Faiz was Amrita Pritam's (2009) celebrated *nazm*[5] "Ajj Waris Shah Nu" ("An Ode to Waris Shah"). Pritam wrote the *nazm* on a piece of scrap paper while travelling on a refugee train to India (N. Datta 2017: 70–71). Channelling the depth of her despair at the violence she was witnessing, Pritam implored the eighteenth-century Punjabi Sufi poet Waris Shah – the writer of *Heer*[6] – to rise from his grave and address the suffering of a 'million daughters' of Punjab. Pritam's words resonated with people, such that refugees living in camps would cry while reading the *nazm* and some would even 'tie the *nazm* into a knot and wear it as a *taveez* (amulet)' (71). Her *nazm* continues to be sung, even today, at the Urs[7] of Waris Shah. By invoking the Sufi Waris Shah to observe the horrors of the Partition, Pritam's *nazm* speaks to the denomising character of the event, of the fracturing of the *nomos* of a syncretic India and Punjab. It is the death of a syncretic society which she calls Waris Shah to witness.

This denomising experience of the Partition was explored further by Saadat Hasan Manto in the unusual novella *Siyah Hashiye* (Black Marginalia). First published in October 1948, *Siyah Hashiye* describes the violence of the Partition through fragmentary vignettes of violence. Its title is a reference to the black margins within which the newspapers of the day enclosed pieces of bad news (Misri 2014). Sukeshi Kamra (2008: 100) notes that the brevity of Manto's vignettes recognises language as 'a casualty of this encounter with the unthinkable'. Manto's vignettes use irony, sarcasm and dark humour to convey the collapse of a moral universe. Deepti Misri (2014: 25) writes that in doing so, Manto hopes to evoke from his readers a 'cheerless laugh that resounds throughout the collection, as sketch after sketch dramatizes the cosmic irony of a bloody Partition that had been proposed as a solution to communal tensions [ethnonationalism]'.

Manto often expresses the denomising quality of the Partition through the theme of 'insanity'. Where the vignettes of *Siyah Hashiye* represent the violence of the Partition as 'madness', he takes this a step further in "Toba Tek Singh",[8] a short story about the Partition of the inmates in a Lahore asylum. "Toba Tek Singh" is a deeply affective tale that satirises the Partition as 'madness' by telling a story about the Partition of the 'insane' (Kala and Sarin 2018). Manto's satire ironically observes the 'insanity' of the time by conjuring a story where the only morally good characters to be found are those deemed 'clinically insane'. His prose prompts reflection on a world where violence and the impulse to partition have become so normative that peace seems a function of insanity. It is in these chiasmic juxtapositions – of the insanity of the Partition and the partition of 'insanity' – that Manto's prose articulates the fracturing of a *nomos*.

Manto's disavowal of the Partition as 'madness' also prompts reflection on a theodicical question that has been raised elsewhere by Veena Das (1997). Das has written forcefully about the profound contradiction of seeing meaning in suffering. Where the rigours of academia stipulate that we offer explanations for all social phenomena (including genocide), scholars such as Levinas (1988) have eloquently stated that the violent horrors of the twentieth century cannot be seen as comprising anything other than 'useless suffering'. Levinas argues that the sheer magnitude of violence, such as the Holocaust and the Second World War (and the Partition of India), puts an end to traditional theories of theodicy.

While sociologists like Zygmunt Bauman (1989) explain the Holocaust as the result of modernity – of extreme state fetishism, biopolitics, bureaucratic rationality, extreme objectivity and the nostalgia for holism (*lebensraum*, homogeneity, eugenics, *herrenvolk*) – Levinas (1988) argues that to study the testimonies of Holocaust survivors and conjure models which make sense of their suffering '"normalizes" that which cannot be normalized' (Das 1997: 568). Consequently, to see events such as the Partition as the failure of the state – as the collapse of law and order or the 'improper implementation' of the transfer and bifurcation of power – is to find theories of theodicy or salvational hopes in the very institutions which were responsible for creating the conditions of suffering.

Das (1997) argues that this merely comprises an exercise of subtle power that reifies the institution(s) while locking the victims in frozen positions. Through a fragmentary account of the Partition as madness and nothing but madness, Manto offers no such theodicy or salvational hope. In fact, Manto's irony and dark humour rely on an inherent understanding of the suffering of the Partition as 'useless'.

Khushwant Singh's *Train to Pakistan* (2009) and Bhisham Sahni's *Tamas* (Darkness) (2001) are two other noteworthy novels from this period for the way in which they depict the collapse of a social world. *Tamas* in fact goes a step further by critiquing the apathy of the bureaucratic (and historiographical) treatment of suffering through the character of Statistics Babu (Misri 2014). In a particularly stark dialogue, Statistics Babu chastises survivors of violence by telling them to give him 'figures, only figures, nothing but figures', as opposed to their 'endless tale of woe and suffering' (Sahni 2001: 316–317). This feeling of a perceived apathy towards their suffering continues to resonate with many Partition survivors. I explore this in Parts II and III through the theme of *ressentiment*.

Tamas was made into a television film in 1988 by director Govind Nihalani. This, however, was not Indian cinema's first engagement with the Partition. Other films such as *Chhalia* (1960), *Dharmputra* (1961), *Subarnarekha* (1965) and *Garam Hawa* (1974) had similarly depicted stories of the Partition on celluloid. Among these, *Garam Hawa* (*Hot Winds*) deserves a special mention for its portrayal of the anxieties and dilemmas of citizenship and belonging faced by north Indian Muslims[9] (*Deccan Herald* 2019).

Many of these early artistic endeavours served as precursors to the subsequent wave of Partition oral history. Here, Amrita Pritam's (2009) *Pinjar* (*The Skeleton*) merits a special mention. First published in Punjabi in the year 1950, *Pinjar* was a bold, pioneering novel that sought to document the plight of women during the Partition. *Pinjar* tells the story of Pooro, a Hindu girl, who is abducted and raped by Rashida, a Muslim man, sometime before the Partition. Pooro is subsequently shunned by her family and is forced to accept that Rashida, her abductor, has become her only relation in the world.

Pinjar articulates a damning critique of a woman's place in a patriarchal society, especially on the margins of competing ethnonationalist patriarchies. Pritam writes about Pooro's conflicted sense of belonging; a crisis she resolves by observing that she is nothing but a *pinjar*, a skeleton, an empty frame. Later in the novel, Pritam writes about Pooro's hatred for her own son in some detail. For Pooro, her son is a reminder of her abduction and rape, of a marriage in which she is literally held captive. Describing Pooro's thoughts while she breastfeeds her son, Pritam compares masculinity to a dog gnawing on the bone, consuming the essence of femininity.

The imprint of Pritam's (2009) scathing critique is visible in the oral historical/ethnographic works of Urvashi Butalia (2000), Ritu Menon and Kamla Bhasin (1998) and Veena Das (2007). Butalia's (2000) *The Other Side of Silence* and Menon and Bhasin's (1998) *Borders and Boundaries* emerged out of the same oral history project and decisively altered the course of South Asian Partition Studies. Documenting the experience of 'abducted' women as well as the Indian and Pakistani state's 'recovery' operations, Butalia (2000) and Menon and Bhasin (1998) – like Amrita Pritam – argued that in the cases of many 'abducted' women, returning them to unaccepting families often amounted to a second displacement. 'Recovery' in these contexts served only to assuage the patriarchal pride of the newly independent nation states while uprooting women from a home where – although not of their choosing – some had nevertheless managed to build a new life for themselves (Menon and Bhasin 1998).

Butalia (2000) and Menon and Bhasin's (1998) feminist perspective – a form of secular theodicy in itself – moved past mainstream understandings of the Partition as a purely religious conflict. Observing the plight of women as that of individuals caught in the crossfire of competing ethnonationalist patriarchies, they problematised common-sense understandings of the violence of the Partition. In particular, their work unsettled an established, common-sense theodicy of the death of women as 'sacrifice'. Their work showed that contrary to the popular memory of the alleged sacrificial 'suicide' of Hindu and Sikh women at Thoa Khalsa (and other sites), women did not go to these deaths willingly. Closer examinations of the surviving witnesses, especially women, revealed that in their memory, the men presented the honour killings of women of their own community in the hallowed terms of martyrdom and sacrifice (refer Chapter 4 for more). However, in (rightfully) problematising this theodicy, Butalia (2000) and Menon and Bhasin (1998) also implicitly confronted their readers with the uselessness of the Partition's suffering.

The publication of Menon and Bhasin's (1998) and Butalia's (2000) work signalled the beginning of the memory turn in Partition Studies. Anjali Gera Roy (2019) argues that this shift in scales was consonant with a larger crisis in history – that is, scepticism of history's claim to impartial truth (White 1966, 1984). Published a little over 50 years after the Partition, this turn to Partition oral history was driven by an implicit 'politics of recognition' (Wilkinson 2013) – that is, by the need to bear witness to and acknowledge suffering. The inchoate theodicical nature of their project can be grasped from their recognition of the fact that although the Partition remained a 'living memory', the Partition was also characterised by a complete lack of official commemoration and memorialisation (Butalia 2000). Through their oral history, Butalia and Menon and Bhasin (1998) sought to lift this veil of silence by prompting reflection on a troubled past.

Since the publication of their pioneering work, a growing body of oral historical and ethnographic literature has turned its attention to the Partition. Works by Gyanendra Pandey (2001), Veena Das (2007), Ravinder Kaur (2007), Yasmin Khan (2017a), Pippa Virdee (2013, 2018), Vanita Sharma (2009) and Vazira Zamindar's (2007) supplement archival research with oral historical methods to provide an ethnographic account of the Partition's human cost and memory. Meanwhile, the work of Jasodhara Bagchi and Subhoranjan Dasgupta (2003) and Manas Ray (2008) document stories of Partition in the East. Subsequent research such as the work of Mukulika Banerjee (2003), Nonica Datta (2009), Ananya Jahanara Kabir (2013), Rakesh Ankit (2019, 2020), Vazira Zamindar (2007), Veena Das (2007) and Ravinder Kaur (2007) have shown the Partition's ramifications beyond Bengal and Punjab, and even the year 1947. Churnjeet Mahn and Anne Murphy's (2018) and Anjali Gera Roy's (2019) recent work provides a comprehensive overview of how the Partition is remembered alongside its traumatic afterlife and post-memory.

These aforementioned academic oral historical and ethnographic examinations of the Partition's memory have been accompanied by a public tradition that has sought to preserve stories of the Partition. The realisation that with the passing of the last generation of survivors, the Partition is fast transitioning from a 'living memory' to 'history' has added impetus to the task. Alok Bhalla (1994, 2006), Cowasjee and

Duggal (1995), Mushirul Hasan (1995), Ahmad Salim (2003) and Vishwajyoti Ghosh's (2013) respective anthologies of Partition stories are good examples of this. Bringing together stories, poetry, memoirs and interviews with a variety of individuals, these volumes attempt a staccato, polyphonous narration of the Partition.

Aanchal Malhotra's (2017) *Remnants of a Separation* attempts something similar by documenting the material culture of the Partition. Malhotra compiles 21 stories of objects that connect Partition survivors to their stories of migration. These artefacts range from everyday objects that some refugees migrated with to prized treasures and family heirlooms that some retrieved after the fact. Malhotra's project has also led her to establish the Museum of Material Memory, a digital archive that uses material culture to record South Asian family histories. Malhotra's archive has emerged alongside older, well-established digital oral history archives such as the 1947 Partition Archive and the Indian Memory Project. Meanwhile, documentaries such as Mara Ahmed's *A Thin Wall* (2015), Gurinder Chadha's *India's Partition: The Forgotten Story* (2017) and Kavita Puri's (2017) *Partition Voices* have given documentary audio/visual form to oral histories of the Partition.

In this book, I attempt something different. This book compiles an ethnography of the way in which the Partition is remembered by the last generation of Partition survivors. Specifically, this book examines how Partition survivors make sense of the Partition's death and suffering. It pays attention to the organic, colloquial and vernacular ways in which people remember and rationalise their experience of the Partition – the theodicies to which they subscribe.

One of the major themes of this book is my discussion of my informant's use of the word *purusharth* to describe their hard work in the years immediately following the Partition. *Purusharth* occupies a central space within Hinduism and is intimately linked to the Brahmanical order of *varnashramadharma* (B. Singh 2020). The *varnashramadharma* connects a Hindu person's caste (*varna*) to the work and duties (*shrama* and *dharma*) they must perform in life. My discussion of *purusharth* in Part II contrasts the word's canonical meaning with its quotidian use by Partition survivors. Through detailed ethnography, I carefully pick apart the various ways in which Partition survivors sanctify physical labour, cleverness, hardship and suffering as *purusharth*. Their *purusharth* is seen by them as a form of sacrifice – a personal debt for which reparations are owed by the post-Independence state. My discussion of *purusharth* as sacrifice also deconstructs the gendered nature of the discourse. In doing so, it makes connections across the anthropology of memory, sacrifice and theodicy to illustrate the ways in which the masculine discourse of *purusharth* and sacrifice is mobilised in the service of the similarly gendered Hindu nation.

This discourse constitutes an organic form of theodicy. It rationalises the hardship and suffering caused by the Partition as a sacrifice to the nation. It reconstructs agency out of a denomising experience of helpless dispossession. It resolves their initial feelings of foreignness within the new nation by expressing ownership and belonging – re-framing the survivor refugee as a proud hard worker.

This discourse of self-making is accompanied by a vitriolic hatred – *ressentiment* – for those who are seen to have caused their suffering: political elites and Muslims. Using Hindu nationalism as a form of theodicy, they recast the suffering of the Partition as a contemporary manifestation of a 1,000-year-old history of 'Muslim invasions' of India. Secure in the victimhood derived from this Hindu nationalist understanding of history, they consistently voice the demand for reparations. The reparations my informants demand vary from demands for the official recognition of all Partition survivors as 'martyrs' and 'freedom fighters' to the retributive ethnic cleansing of India's Muslims. As I show in this book, the latter is consistently proposed by my informants as something of a 'final solution' to what they see as India's lingering 'Muslim problem'.

This book specifically examines the intervention of Hindu nationalism in the memories of Partition survivors. The fact that many Partition survivors remember their past through ethnonationalist lenses makes remembering the Partition a particularly tricky prospect. In the Indian context, remembering the Partition is made doubly difficult due to Modi and the Bharatiya Janata Party's (BJP) rise to high office. Here, narratives of a historically conceived Hindu victimhood license violence in the present.

In its treatment of hate speech, violence and ethnonationalism, my book continues the tradition of Shail Mayaram (1997), Butalia (2000), Menon and Bhasin (1998), G. Pandey (2001), Anders B. Hansen

(2002), Paul Brass (2003a, 2003b), Das (2007) and others who did not shy away from directly addressing the form and nature of violence and ethnonationalism. In this book, I mobilise a hermeneutics of suspicion (Ricoeur 1970). Put simply, my book breaks with the established convention of 'believing victims' in order to examine the kinds of violence that narratives of victimhood license in the context of the Partition.

In launching a hermeneutics of suspicion, I am not proposing a universal counter-doctrine. Nor do I endorse the reactionary anti-feminist, victim-blaming positions taken by many in response to the recent #MeToo campaign. In fact, I fully acknowledge contexts – current and historical – where believing victims and amplifying their voices helps speak truth to power. This includes sexual assault and harassment, the history of slavery, lynching and segregation (and now police brutality) in the United States, the politics of Truth and Reconciliation Commissions and the Holocaust, to name a few.

In all of these contexts, believing victims and amplifying their voices speaks truth to power because the erasure of survivor narratives involves a continuation of the violence of the past. But what of contexts where historical narratives of victimhood feed the retributive violence of fascist enterprises? What of contexts where the powers that be remember the violence of distant pasts in order to license persecution in the present?

By breaking with the convention of believing victims, I intend to recognise the narrative agency of my informants. Anindya Raychaudhuri (2019) has argued that Partition Studies' focus on trauma, pain and displacement has resulted in the tendency to see all those who are remembered as 'victims'. Raychaudhuri finds this problematic and argues that 'while the author of a Partition narrative may indeed be a victim, he or she most certainly does not have to be one' (10). Disabusing of this assumption entails recognising the agency survivors have as the authors of their narratives, recognising their ability to 'negotiate societal systems' and to make meanings for themselves. The latter is especially important for a book that aims to examine how Partition survivors rationalise their experiences of death and suffering.

Furthermore, the Partition's retributive violence and lingering ethnonational divide – that has been cemented in the enmity of the nuclear-armed Indian and Pakistani states – renders it difficult to make an easy distinction between victims and perpetrators. For example, while Hindus and Sikhs were victims of genocidal violence in Pakistan, they were also perpetrators of violence against Muslims in India during the same period. Many historians and anthropologists such as G. Pandey (2001), Zamindar (2007), Kaur (2007), Ramachandra Guha (2018), Talbot and Singh (2009), Rotem Geva (2014), Khan (2017a) and the memoirs of Anis Kidwai (2011) have also noted the participation of Hindu and Sikh refugees in retributive violence against Muslims in India, particularly in Delhi.

At issue is the problematisation of a certain model of trauma that is derived from the Holocaust and the Vietnam War. Tracing the genealogy of trauma, Didier Fassin and Richard Rechtman have argued that by giving the words of victims a clinical authority, the concept of trauma is itself based on certain moral premises. In treating even violent perpetrators as patients who suffer from invisible psychological wounds, the trauma concept attempts to humanise the 'inhumane'. The fact that remorseless perpetrators too can be said to suffer from the 'wounds' of the violence in their past attributes to them a sense of humanity that their past actions may be said to have lacked (Fassin and Rechtman 2009). It is the issue of suffering that most concerns trauma.

Although the genealogy of trauma begins as a medical category that sought to avoid any moral differentiation between victim, perpetrator and witness – by focusing merely on the invisible psychological mark left by the traumatic event – trauma has now become a category of moral judgement that accords validity to victimhood (283). Trauma provides the words of victims a 'clinical authority based on moral premises' (28) and has emerged as a 'universal language of a new politics of the intolerable' (99). The trauma concept demands that we abandon all suspicion of its traumatised victims, treating them as the innocent patients of an invisible, indescribable affliction. After all, the politics of victimhood comprises an 'anti-politics machine' (Jeffery 2006). As a part of everyday language, trauma 'has descriptive value, but more importantly prescriptive value, calling for action (clinical, economic and symbolic) and reparation' (Fassin and Rechtman 2009: 153).

By breaking with the convention of believing victims, I am also interrupting the generalised and uncritical use of the word 'trauma' to describe my informants and their experience. To clarify, I am neither disabusing the concept of 'trauma' nor arguing that the Partition was somehow not traumatic. Rather, in checking my use of the word, I am building on the work of Veena Das (2007: 103), who has similarly stated that 'the model of trauma and witnessing that has been bequeathed to us from Holocaust studies cannot be simply transported to other contexts in which violence is embedded into different patterns of sociality'.

One only has to look at the honour killing of women during the Partition to see the value of Das' argument. As stated previously, Butalia (2000) and Menon and Bhasin (1998) have shown that women's experience of the Partition sometimes entailed murder at the hands of male relatives for the sake of community 'honour'. We might problematise 'trauma' and 'victimhood' here by speaking of the men who coerced and even actively murdered the women of their own families and collectivities. How might we understand the 'trauma' and 'victimhood' of men in this context? The very men who may be seen as victims of this or that religious community might also have been perpetrators of gendered violence within their own collectivity, a violence that is certainly continued in memory by even those who were too young to have directly perpetrated violent acts.

To speak of trauma in a generalised sense – along with the moral claim to victimhood that that implies – only serves as a continuation of this violence and even of its erasure as violence (Misri 2014). Similarly, amplifying memories of Hindu and Sikh survivors who present the Partition as the unprovoked and singular violence of Muslims feeds into contemporary Hindu fascist rhetoric – thus legitimising Islamophobic violence and Hindu fascism in general in the present.

After all, as Yasmin Khan (2017b) notes, silence stalks these oral history archives, a silence of guilt and denial. This does not mean that I suspect all my informants to be killers or that I am intensely suspicious of their biographies. However, it does mean that on occasion, within reason, I do marshal historiographical and ethnographic evidence, and theory in opposition to some of the claims of my informants. This is visible in Chapters 2 and 3, for example, where I argue that my informants' stories of hard work are in fact fables that provide a *karmic* justification of caste and class privilege by understating the state's role in the rehabilitation of refugees. In Chapter 7 I tell the story of Dipankar, a Partition survivor who, by his own admission, received arms training from the Rashtriya Swayamsevak Sangh (RSS) before the Partition. Yet, he also stresses that he was never part of any 'real' violence. His story forces one to consider how far we would be willing to trust the words of someone who spent their youth training for genocide.

Therefore, in this book, instead of studying suffering to determine trauma, I am interested in understanding the interpretative frameworks Partition survivors use to rationalise their experiences with death and suffering. The foremost of these, for my informants, was Hindu nationalism. Focusing on the Partition's complex and vitriolic afterlife, this book wonders how remembrance in this context might be said to lead to healing. Is 'healing' even possible in the face of cataclysmic ruptures like the Partition? And, finally what does it mean to remember the Partition in the time of fascism?

Hindu Nationalism as Theodicy

My interpretation of Hindu nationalism as a form of theodicy needs careful explanation. To characterise the interventions of nationalism in memory as a form of theodicy that rationalises suffering builds on the postmodern understanding of memory. Drawing on Paul Connerton's (1989) and Maurice Halbwachs' (1992) works, in this book, I treat memory – including individual memory – as a social construction. Halbwachs describes memory as the end of the process of remembrance. Halbwachs describes the act of remembering as the process of arranging vignettes of the past into a meaningful discourse that is presented in reference to the present. Expanding on the social or 'collective' aspect of memory, Halbwachs demonstrated that individuals localise, contextualise, acquire and experience memory through their participation in social groups, whether based on kinship, social or cultural identity or any other kind of real or imagined community (see also Connerton 1989: 36–38). Therefore, as Connerton writes, Halbwachs 'demonstrates that the idea of an individual memory, absolutely separate from social memory is an abstraction almost devoid of meaning' (37).

The social constructionist understanding of memory also acknowledges the intertwining of the past and present in our experience of everyday life. Connerton details this link when he writes that because of the way we see our present as causally connected to the past, our experience of the present relies on a particular knowledge of the past. Additionally, while our experience of the present is shaped by the pasts to which we connect the present, the present too influences, shapes and distorts our understanding of the past (Connerton 1989). This entanglement of the past and present brings to mind Walter Benjamin's (2006) *angelus novus* – the angle of history – that faces backwards even as it lives forwards.

It is this recognition of memory as a malleable social construction that characterises my engagement with the memories of my informants. In this book, I have turned this quality of memory into the object of my study. My exploration of the memory of the Partition does not hope for a positivistic extraction of a 'pure' or 'authentic' retelling of the event. Rather, in recognising that memory animates the body of the past with the spirit of the present, I pay attention to the interventions of contemporary majoritarian mobilisations in the memories of my informants.

The central question that structures my book is this: what does it mean to remember the Partition in the time of fascism? It is this stark, singular question that drives my analysis of my informants' belief in Hindu nationalism as a form of theodicy. This question expresses a recognition of the intertwining of the past and the present in the memories of my informants, as the past is used to justify the current regime and the nationalism of the current regime is used to make sense of the past. Therefore, in posing this question, I recognise Connerton's insight that 'images of the past commonly legitimate a present social order' (Connerton 1989: 3). As I show in this book, my informants draw on the 'knowledge' of Hindu nationalism to not only sanctify 'useless' suffering as martyrdom and sacrifice but also draw on its historically conceived victimhood to demand a Hindu fascist state (and retributive genocide) as 'justice' or reparations for the suffering of the Partition.

My discussion of Hindu nationalism as a form of theodicy builds on Michael Herzfeld's (1992) description of nationalism as a form of secular theodicy. Herzfeld draws attention to the ways in which European nationalism resembles religion. The heart of this resemblance lies in the idea of transcendence, a term I have discussed previously. In religion, the problem of theodicy is resolved through a moral principle (*karma*) or deity (god[s]) that *transcends* space and time, attempting to reconcile belief in the existence of the supernatural with the imperfection of the world. This allows one to use, for example, the unknowable will of God or a divine test of one's character or faith to serve as explanations for the existence of evil and suffering in God's own world. Humanity's deliverance from sin and suffering – through either the grace of God or one's own 'good deeds' – takes the form of salvation in some religious systems (Herzfeld 1992).

As Herzfeld writes, 'The secular equivalent of salvation is the idea of a patriotic and democratic community, one that tolerates neither graft nor oppression' (6). It is against the latter injustices that nationalisms claim transcendent status, stabilising a national order that promises to guard against past injustices and present anxieties. Herzfeld explains:

> Nationalisms all claim transcendence, however, in two important senses. First, internally they claim to transcend individual and local differences, uniting all citizens in a single, unitary identity. Second, the forms of most European (and many other) nationalisms transcend even their own national concerns, in that the principle of national identity is considered to underlie and infuse the particulars of nation and country. (6)

Nationalisms claim transcendence through their description of a single, totalising national identity that is held to be static over millennia. This is comparable to Etienne Balibar's (2002: 86) critique of nationalist history-writing as a 'retrospective illusion'. Balibar argues that the history of nations presents the nation's establishment as the inevitable result of history. Invoking the nation state as destiny, such a history retrospectively binds successive generations of individuals that have inhabited a rough area of land into a national community, presenting their development and struggles as a compounded realisation of the national struggle. In a similar vein, Peter van der Veer (1994) has also identified nationalism's impulse to present the nation as an eternal, historical fact.

Where van der Veer and Balibar identify the retrospective, discursive construction of the nation through a particular form of history-writing, Herzfeld elucidates the theodicical function of this imagination. Herzfeld describes how nationalism, through national identity, transcends local differences and infuses the quotidian life of the nation. This addresses the heart of how nations imagine their national community,[10] the theodicy of nationalism attempting to stabilise the *nomos* that is the rule of law and freedom: the very idea of the nation and national character. At its core, this essentialism that imagines a stable kinship of the national community amidst the chaos and flux of history relies on the conflation of biological and cultural essentialism (Herzfeld 1992).

Although Herzfeld specifically discusses European nationalism, this discussion is especially apt for Hindu nationalism. The Hindu nation is held together through the millennia by a perceived sense of historical victimhood. This historical victimhood is the result of a nationalist history-writing that seeks to establish the Hindu nation as eternal fact, while simultaneously delineating an ethnically pure Hindu nation within a multicultural milieu. The Hindu nationalist perception of Indian history as a series of foreign invasions does not see modern India (and its diversity) as a product of historical political and economic processes, of cultural admixture produced by migration, trade, pilgrimage and invasions. Rather, it describes (Hindu) India as an 'abused', 'raped' and 'colonised' land. It reduces the specificities of Indian history to one of a passive victimhood to the allegedly nefarious colonising designs of Muslims and the British.

Paola Bacchetta (2000) writes that Hindu nationalism's 'foreign invaders' discourse is also a distinctly gendered discourse that memorialises the Hindu male failure to protect the *mother*-land from invasion, occupation and conversion. This is particularly visible in Hindu nationalist discourse on the Babri Masjid in Ayodhya, a piece of sacred Hindu soil (the Ram Janmabhoomi, or birthplace of Ram) that is literally seen to have been 'captured' and 'converted' by Islam. The feeling of emasculation here is deepened by Lord Ram's scriptural status as the 'ideal man'.

The Hindus as a nation take shape in the victimised shadow of this aforementioned narrative of 'sectarian aggression'. It is this sense of historical victimhood that is seen to hold the Hindu nation – the land and the people – through the millennia, a national community that is made to seem self-evident through the fact of a common victimhood. Through this narrative of a 'perennial struggle with barbaric outsiders', the Hindu nation transcends time itself (van der Veer 1994: 144).

Consequently, the image of a prosperous and advanced ancient India – a glorious past preceding ruination by Muslims – is romanticised. This narrative draws on an orientalist, colonial historiography that sought to legitimise British rule in South Asia by conjuring the image of an ancient India that stood despoiled by centuries of ruinous Muslim rule (van der Veer 1994: 144; Cohn 2000; Thapar 2009) – thus delegitimising the ruling class it sought to replace. The general tone of this discourse can be grasped from the thoroughly unironic title of Arthur Llewellyn Basham's (1954) book *The Wonder That Was India: A Survey of the Culture of the Indian Sub-continent before the Coming of the Muslims*. Hindu nationalism reproduces this discourse through *ersatz* nostalgia – nostalgia without lived experience (Appadurai 1996), and restorative nostalgia – nostalgia that seeks to rebuild or return to the imagined past (Boym 2001: 41).

On the whole, this narrative establishes the *foreignness* of Muslims and Christians in relation to an innately Hindu India (van der Veer 1994). Consequently, the presence of these minorities as seemingly influential electoral communities – through the myth that Muslims vote as a block for 'anti-Hindu' parties – feeds the perception that the liberation of India is far from complete. Assertions of Islamic identity in Pakistan, Bangladesh and Afghanistan also mirror and fuel the perception of a Hindu India besieged, both internally and externally, by a hostile 'Muslim horde'. Peter van der Veer succinctly summarises this formulation as follows:

> When in power, they [Muslims] oppressed Hindus; now, out of power they continue to withhold fundamental rights from the Hindus via the democratic system, as well as to act as the agents of pan-Islamism on Indian soil. (10)

In this way, liberal democracy itself is seen as the enemy, and its dismantling takes on the guise of urgent national reform. Meanwhile, this common historical experience is seen as the affirmation of the self-evidently 'peaceful', 'tolerant' and 'weak' national character of the Hindu citizen. 'Tolerance' is inaccurately construed from a style of oriental discourse that omits attention to power in its description of the alleged 'syncretism' and infinite, universalist assimilatory tradition of Hindu spirituality (67–68). At its worst, the famed 'tolerance' of Hindus is presented as historical fact through a discourse that constructs the innate moral superiority of Hindus in the fact of their victimhood, establishing Hindus as both victims and 'tolerant' hosts. One might ask why a collective historical memory of 'invasion', along with a politics for its redressal, even exists if the Hindu-fold is the 'tolerant', assimilatory sponge that this narrative claims. The lie of 'tolerance' can also be glimpsed from the VHP's stance, whose doctrine of 'tolerance' applies only to 'Indian religions' and not to 'foreign' religions. The Hindu nationalist organisation aspires to convert Muslims and Christians (67–68).

This myth of the Hindu national character as peaceful, tolerant and weak is seen to infuse the quotidian life of the nation to the point of creating the 'Muslim question' that occupies centre-stage in Hindu nationalist politics. Consequently, the 'meekness' of the Hindu is framed as something to be overcome through the militant aggression of Hindu nationalism.

Additionally, in the context of the Partition, Hindu nationalism provides transcendence in a third way. Hindu nationalism helps survivors of the Partition *transcend* the 'uselessness' of their suffering by recourse to the redemptive, sacrificial rhetoric of nationalism. Using the language of nationalism, my informants rationalise their suffering as a 'sacrifice' to the (Hindu) nation, branding the deaths of their kith and kin as 'martyrdom'. Invoking their membership of the Hindu nation allows the transformation of ambiguous suffering – of the death, pain and displacement endured *on the way* to the nation – into death and suffering *in pursuit of*, or, *for* the nation. Here, theodicy transforms 'useless', ambiguous death into hallowed martyrdom in service of the Hindu nation.

Modernity and Hindu Nationalism

Let us now return to my original question: what does it mean to remember the Partition in the time of fascism? This question concerns both the deployment of Hindu nationalism as a form of theodicy and the role that the Partition's memory plays in the Hindu fascist enterprise.

The Partition and its memory lie at the heart of India's 'Muslim question'. As a relatively recent trauma, the Partition is seen by many as proof of Hindu nationalism's claims on history and of the alleged 'untrustworthiness' of Muslims (van der Veer 1994; G. Pandey 2001; Das 2007). As stated previously, van der Veer (1994) has drawn attention to the way that Hindu nationalism perceives liberal democracy – and the state itself – to have been captured by Muslims and their 'secular apologists' (or 'sickulars' as they are now called by Hindu nationalist trolls).

However, what is new about this moment is the rise of the Sangh Parivar's Hindu nationalism to the status of a hegemonic ideology within Indian politics. Prime Minister Narendra Modi and his Hindu nationalist party, the BJP, are currently enjoying their second term in office with little foreseeable threat to their electoral supremacy. Their rise adds renewed salience to an examination of the Partition's memory, since the rhetoric of Hindu nationalism is no longer just rhetoric.

For Hindu nationalists, the Partition is a historical trauma and a lesson for the future. The BJP and the Sangh have consistently used Muslims to stoke demographic anxieties about the fertility of Muslims (allegedly due to polygamy) – akin to the European far-right's 'great replacement' conspiracy theory (van der Veer 1994). This is also often linked to fears of a 'second Partition'. In September 2018, Union Minister Giriraj Singh warned of an imminent 'second Partition' of India in 2047. He argued that since the population of India has grown from 400 million to 1.3 billion, the population of 'divisive figures' (a dog-whistle for Muslims and 'leftists') has also grown to alarming levels (Times Now 2018). In a BJP rally held in Delhi in July 2019, members of various Hindu nationalist organisations called for a new 'population control' law, while others present at the rally alleged a 'Muslim conspiracy' to hijack India's democracy through overpopulation.

Deporting Muslims en masse from the country and curtailing their human rights were some of the dystopian solutions that were fearlessly proposed at this rally (*The Print* 2019). With the passing of the Citizenship (Amendment) Act, 2019 (CAA) – which excludes Muslims – and the proposed National Register of Citizens (NRC) – a nationwide citizenship verification exercise – it is not difficult to see how this might be achieved.

What these discourses also articulate is a 'fatigue' of (Appadurai 2017) or *ressentiment* for liberal democracy. Weber (1965: 110) understood *ressentiment* as a form of 'theodicy of the disprivileged', as an attempt by ordinary people to accept their place within social hierarchies. As Jeffrey Olick (2007: 157) writes, 'Disprivilege, then, is compensated by righteous indignation at oppressors, though tempered by confidence in redemption of suffering'. *Ressentiment* is hatred and jealousy imbued with a moral content (Horwitz 2018).

In Neitzsche, Weber and Scheler's work, *ressentiment* is the result of the failure of theodicy (Simko 2012: 884). As a form of theodicy that meditates on a centuries-long victimhood, Hindu nationalism not only fails to deliver on its promise of *real* salvation but, by meditating on a historical narrative of disprivilege, actively engenders *ressentiment*. In this book, I draw attention to the *ressentiment* that occupies the narratives of my informants and the politics of Hindu nationalism in general.

What I have described as Hindu nationalism's *ressentiment* – a self-righteous rage that is directed at minorities and the liberal democracy seen to serve them – has been described by Arjun Appadurai (2017) as 'democracy fatigue'. Appadurai (2019, 2021) identifies India as the leader and innovator of a global wave of authoritarianism, a wave whose impulses he locates in a crisis of national sovereignty. According to Appadurai (2017), it is due to the modern nation state's lack of sovereignty over its national economy in a diffuse and globalised world economy that states have turned towards cultural sovereignty. Cultural sovereignty in this context includes ethnonationalism, cultural majoritarianism and the politics of belonging and citizenship. It is these that the modern nation state now seeks to control as fiercely as it once aspired to control and protect its national economy (Appadurai 2017). In the process, democracy comes to be seen as an institutional hurdle to the realisation of cultural sovereignty, a kind of demographic siege from within.

This shift towards cultural sovereignty marks the rise of statism over nationalism (Appadurai 2021). Statism is defined as the centralised and strict bureaucratic regulation of one's documented status as citizen. The result is the birth of the 'statizen': a new class of citizen who belongs by virtue of a state-certified document that functions as the well-spring of their rights. While the statizen as a form of citizenship finds historical precedent in the idea of colonial censuses, birth certificates and passports, statism takes this a step further, making documented citizenship the sole criterion for one's right to exist in society. Through exercises such as the NRC – a proposed nation-wide citizenship verification exercise – and CAA, India is attempting to create a population of statizens who are the 'counted, documented, loyal and certified supporters of the state' (308). In this endeavour, extreme nationalism functions as the alibi for or enabler of extreme statism. Thus, India has emerged as the global leader and innovator of a shift that constitutes a defining moment in the contemporary history of modernity and late-stage capitalism.

There is a tendency – both in India and abroad – to view religious nationalism and the violence of the Partition as an anti-modern reaction to modernity, as the resurgence or revival of 'backward', 'regressive' and 'tribal' passions. At issue here is a particular Western discourse of modernity, one that constructs the traditional as its antithesis (van der Veer 1994). In this understanding of modernity, nationalism and nationalist expression are seen as products of modernity, while religion is associated with that which modernity is posited to replace: tradition.

In the larger discourse of European modernity, secularism functions as a 'metaphor for modern society' (van der Veer 2014: 11). This perspective also informed colonial policy. The British colonial administration positioned itself as the 'neutral', 'secular' arbiter of incessant, cyclical and irrational 'communal' conflict[11] (van der Veer 1994). Contrasting themselves from the 'absurd' and 'endless' ritualism of Hindus and the 'backward', 'bigoted' and overly 'revolutionary' Muslims, the British presented their 'secular' and 'rational' regime as a modernising force that would hold the fort until Indian intellectuals had developed the capacity to rule themselves (21). This is internalised to a degree by some Indian secularists such as Nehru, who believed that 'communalism' would disappear with the modernisation of society (18).

In India, religious nationalism is called 'communalism'. In common usage, the word 'communalism' denotes the opposite of 'secularism' and means 'a condition of suspicion, fear and hostility between members of different religious communities' (G. Pandey 1990: 6). Gyanendra Pandey argues that the term 'communalism' is a form of colonial knowledge that merely conveys orientalist conceptions of the 'otherness' of Indian politics. After all, 'communalism' is never used in the same manner to describe facets of European politics. The description of religious nationalism as 'communalism' was a concerted colonial attempt to deny these movements their nationalist character in the age of nationalism. Religious nationalism, therefore, was not seen as a nationalist struggle, but instead dubbed the 'communal' machinations of self-interested religious and ethnic groups.

Ironically, Indian secular nationalists have continued the colonial usage of 'communalism' to deride religious nationalism, or ethnonationalism, as 'antinational' (G. Pandey 1990; van der Veer 1994). Consequently, the postcolonial state appears to have inherited the colonial administration's position – at least in theory – as the 'neutral' arbiter of 'communal' violence. This is visible in the continued description of pogroms and ethnic cleansing as 'communal riots'. In this, the Indian usage of the word differs from the way that the word is used across the world to describe a violent clash between the citizens and the state. The use of the word 'riot' involves hidden political connotations about the nature of the violence being described, implying that 'communal' violence is always equal and reciprocal[12] (I. Ahmad 2020).

The routine use of words such as 'communalism' to describe religious nationalism, and 'riots' to describe its violence mobilise an implicit diagnosis of religious nationalism and its relation to the state. The result is an account of violence that decontextualises sectarian violence by obscuring power, the participation of the state and hard distinctions between victim and perpetrator under the guise of 'balance' and 'nuance'. The result is an account that evades engagement with the specificities of violence. A number of pogroms in India's recent past – such as the 1984 anti-Sikh pogroms, the 2002 anti-Muslim pogroms in Gujarat and the 2020 anti-Muslim pogroms in Delhi, to name a few – have been effectively erased through the invocation of the word 'riot' (I. Ahmad 2020; Das 2007; Ghassem-Fachandi 2010). In the case of the aforementioned pogroms, this is complicated by the state's own participation in the violence.

How then do we define Hindu nationalism? Hindu nationalism imagines all Hindus – wherever they be – to constitute a natural nation based on an ancient Aryan-Vedic civilisation[13] that dates back to approximately 1500 BCE. The ultimate ambition is the creation of a Hindu Rashtra (state). The Hindu Rashtra promises to liberate Hindus from a long history of oppression and to secure their supremacy and the 'eternal glory' of Hinduism through the 'permanent' institutions of the state. The latter impulse is also borne out in Hindu nationalism's quintessentially 'modern' urge to prove the 'facts' of its belief as embodied in scripture, be they references to 'historical' events or 'scientific' practices and innovations (van der Veer 1994). What is observable in the process is the entrenchment of modernity, visible in the co-optation of the sciences of modernity – archaeology, history and philology (138) – to serve 'the most powerful ideology of modernity (nationalism)' (Hamilakis 2007: 15). In this way, while Hindu nationalism constitutes the revival of a 'native' identity – one based on religious community and discourse – the idioms of its articulation are familiar to those of European nationalism: one nation, one people.

However, Hindu nationalism does not represent the invasion of tradition by modernity (van der Veer 1994). Rather, Hindu nationalism – and religious nationalism in India – has emerged out of religious discourse and practice, and as a direct consequence of colonial policies such as religious and caste-based censuses and political representation based on religious community (van der Veer 1994; Cohn 2010). As opposed to a colonial imposition – a symptom of 'false consciousness' – Hindu nationalism must be seen as a product of Asian modernity (van der Veer 2014). Doing so, both acknowledges the distinctly indigenous – or 'alternative' – forms that modernity takes in postcolonial settings (Gaonkar 2001) and recognises the aspiration for autonomy and liberation located at the core of nationalist movements (Chatterjee 1993).

Hindu nationalism is often seen as an ideology that has cannibalised the 'inherently tolerant' belief system of Hinduism in service of the 'global nation-state system' (Nandy 1997: 157). For example, Ashis Nandy (1991) regards the ideology of Hindu nationalism as an upper-caste, lower-middle-class attack on 'pure' Hinduism. Nandy (1990) sees Hinduism as a faith that is based on an infinitely 'tolerant' way of life. Against this inherent 'syncretism', he sees this ideology as an outside intervention that radicalises a section of the faithful.

I disagree with Nandy's argument. I believe that the Hinduism versus Hindu nationalism debate is moot since Hindu nationalism has now become the hegemonic political and cultural mode by which a critical mass of Hindus expresses their religious and national identity. Nandy's argument is flawed since it hinges on a separation of politics from culture and religion from nationalism. In effect, Nandy's opinions comprise a back-handed voicing of the doctrine of 'Hindu tolerance' that has its genealogy in the early Hindu nationalist discourses of Swami Vivekananda (van der veer 1994).

But, is Hindu nationalism a distraction or a distortion from the 'real issues' of the day? Van der Veer argues that Hindu nationalism and other religious nationalisms should not be seen as 'ideological smoke screens that hide the real clash of material interests and social classes' (ix). Rather, Hindu nationalism must be seen as an expression for the aspiration for caste and class mobility. The latter is evident in the BJP's economic nationalism, in Modi's and the so-called Gujarat Model's promise of neoliberalism *done right*. Ann Kingsolver and Annapurna Pandey (2019) have observed how Modi's 'Make in India' campaign invokes the symbolism of the colonial struggle – Gandhi's Swadeshi movement – while simultaneously offering India's marginalised workforce to global capital for the production of domestically manufactured and nationalistically branded goods. Through the discourse of 'development', Hindu nationalist organisations (including the BJP, RSS and VHP) have sought to attract diasporic investment (Mathur 2014) while also echoing the desire for 'development' and mobility among domestic audiences.

Yet this has also gone beside a militant nationalist campaign. Chandana Mathur (17) has noted the VHP's success in redirecting funds raised in the United States – including community and corporate donations – to RSS-affiliated Hindu nationalist organisations in India. In the 1980s and 1990s money raised abroad directly contributed to a Hindu nationalist 'reconversion' drive directed at Adivasi communities; the program also involved violence against Christian Adivasi communities and Muslims. The complementarity of 'development' and violence in these discourses echoes the experience of Gujarat, where the 2002 pogrom and the increased ghettoisation of Muslims went beside rampant neoliberalism.

This seeming contradiction is compounded by Hindu nationalism's propensity for violence against Dalits, Adivasis and Scheduled Castes. The use of beating, lynching and sexual violence against lower-caste Hindus as a disciplining tool is a well-documented reality, one that has only intensified under the current regime.[14] Yet upper-caste violence against lower-caste Hindus has gone beside a noticeable Hindu nationalist outreach towards Dalit, Scheduled Caste, OBC[15] and Adivasi voters, since the 1980s (Ghassem-Fachandi 2010). The VHP, RSS and BJP – at least on paper – claim commitment to the eradication of untouchability (van der Veer 1994). This outreach, through 'cultural awakening programmes' and recruitment into Hindu nationalist organisations, has yielded both votes and boots on the ground. The participation of some members of Dalit, Scheduled Caste and Adivasi communities in pogroms against minorities has also been observed in recent times, especially in the pogroms of 1984 (Das 2007) and 2002 (Ghassem-Fachandi 2010). In the case of the 2002 anti-Muslim pogrom in Gujarat, the participation of some members of Dalit, Adivasi and Scheduled Caste communities involved a spatial division of the labour of violence between castes, as well as a test and performance of their loyalty to the Hindu-fold (Ghassem-Fachandi 2010).

How might we then reconcile the violence of Hindu nationalism with its aspirational imaginaries in a way that does not reduce its violent nationalism to an ideological smokescreen? After all, Hindu nationalism's success in attracting subaltern Hindus and Adivasis to the Hindu-fold is an astonishing development considering endemic upper-caste violence against these groups. Moreover, the Sangh Parivar's Hindu nationalism is built on the bedrock of a Brahmanical morality that hinges on cow protectionism, vegetarianism and the popularisation of Sanskrit and certain scripture such as Valmiki's version of the Ramayana (van der Veer 1994).

One explanation may be found through a creative deployment of M. N. Srinivas' (1966) idea of Sanskritisation. Srinivas defined Sanskritisation as 'the process by which a "low" Hindu caste, or tribal or other group, changes its customs, ritual, ideology, and way of life in the direction of a high, and frequently, "twice-born" caste' (6). Although not specifically posited in relation to Hindu nationalism, Sanskritisation locates an aspirational imaginary at the heart of the subaltern adoption of upper-caste Hindu (nationalist) culture. Aspiration and not false-consciousness is located as the driver of social change. We might think of Sanskritisation as a tactical acceptance of assimilation in pursuit of the aspiration for mobility.

Sanskritisation can be seen at work in the Sangh Parivar's success in recruiting some lower-caste Hindus to the Hindu-fold. Sanskritisation is now visible in those who hold the highest constitutional offices of the land: Prime Minister Narendra Modi, former President Ram Nath Kovind and President Droupadi Murmu. Long-time RSS members, Modi – a celibate, vegetarian and OBC; and Kovind – a vegetarian Dalit, embody the Sangh's Sanskritisation project. President Murmu, on the other hand, is a woman Adivasi leader and a long-time member of the BJP. Although subalterns themselves, they actively practice a Hindu nationalist politics that turns Brahmanical morality into state policy while integrating lower castes within the Hindu-fold. For subaltern Hindus and Adivasis, integration into the Hindu-fold is a sign of mobility while simultaneously consolidating the numerical might of the Hindu-fold. By actively recruiting Dalits, Scheduled Castes and Adivasis, Hindutva's Sanskritisation creates the illusion of the 'annihilation of caste' (to appropriate the title of B. R. Ambedkar's [2014] seminal book) while in fact consolidating Brahmanical hegemony under the homogenising banner of the Hindu-fold.

Violence occupies a central position in this aspirational imaginary due to what Appadurai (2019, 2021) has identified as the 'syndrome of aspirational hatred.' Appadurai diagnoses the violence of the Hindu Right, India's rampant sexual violence and looming fascism – as embodied in laws such as the CAA and a proposed national-NRC – as 'aspirational hatred'. While the word 'aspiration' is normally used in the context of social mobility, Appadurai uses it in this context to emphasise how the ruling party has normalised hatred and violence in mainstream society to the extent that violence has become a vehicle of social mobility. According to Appadurai (2021: 309), 'When we are ruled by thieves, killers and rapists, who enjoy and distribute immunity generously, it is no surprise that many begin to believe that hate, anger and the degradation of those who are even weaker than yourself can take you nowhere but up'.

Partition, Violence and Modernity

Thus far, I have located Hindu nationalism within modernity and identified it as the leader and innovator of a global wave of authoritarianism. In concluding this Introduction, I want to locate the Partition within modernity and offer a definition of violence.

While the Partition of India is squarely located within the horrors of the twentieth century, its violence is often construed as the product of ancient hatreds, as somehow cyclical and endemic. However, the impulse to partition and transfer populations emerged in the early twentieth century out of an aspiration to create perfectly homogenous, modern nation states (Özsu 2014). Gellner (1983) has argued that modern, industrial societies – in contradistinction to agrarian societies – desire cultural, linguistic and thereby national homogeneity for the purposes of efficiency.

Faisal Devji (2013) has shown that the period leading up to and following the First World War witnessed intense global intellectual discussion – including in India – on the idea of the 'nation' as an alternative to empire. It was in this context that the problem of the 'minority' emerged as an issue critical to the imagination of nations (Gilmartin 2015a). The first recorded population transfer occurred between Bulgaria and the Ottoman Empire in 1913, at the end of the Second Balkan War. In the Balkans, numerous such exchanges of populations sought to reverse a history of ethnic mixing that was seen as problematic to national unity (Özsu 2014) and thereby detrimental to 'efficiency' (Gellner 1983).

The 'minority' problem emerged as the central problem of the world order in the peace conferences that followed the First World War (Devji 2013). In 1923, as part of the Treaty of Lausanne, the political and ethnic borders of the defeated Ottoman Empire were redrawn under the influence of Britain and France. The treaty stipulated a 'compulsory' transfer of ethnic minorities between Greece and Turkey (Özsu 2014). The Greek–Turkish experiment with demographic engineering was cited by the Peel Commission of 1937 as a 'good precedent' while proposing the Partition of Palestine into a Jewish and Arab state. The Peel Commission was also noteworthy for its use of overtly medicalised, biopolitical discourse in support of a population transfer (Drew 2017).

In India, concomitant with these global developments, the 'minority' question gradually assumed centre-stage in national politics, becoming an enduring quandary of the anti-colonial struggle. An early example of this were 13 articles that Lala Lajpat Rai wrote in *The Tribune* between November and December of 1924, proposing the division of Punjab along religious lines to 'make majority rule effective' (N. Nair 2011: 77). Aamir Mufti (2007) links the emergence of Muslim 'minority' politics in India to the history of the Jewish minority question in Europe (also see Gilmartin 2015). Thus, Partition, the 'minority question' and the idea of Pakistan evolved consonant with global developments in modernity and biopolitics (Devji 2013).

The idea of *surgically displacing* an unwanted minority with the aim of promoting a well-ordered homogeneity captures the quintessentially modern, biopolitical impulses that underlie the logic used to justify partitions and population transfers (Bauman 1989, 2002). Elsewhere, Marilyn Strathern (1992) has written extensively about how the Euro-American concept of 'society' is imagined as internally homogenous and self-same such that national societies are like the 'individual' person. Partitions and population transfers merely attempt to establish this imagined homogeneity as 'facts on the ground'.

Anindya Raychaudhuri (2009) argues that the liberal use of the medical metaphor is one way in which Partition historiography has been co-opted to justify the project of nationhood. The medical metaphor recurs frequently in historiography and the discourses of political elites. Gandhi famously described the 'vivisection of India' as the 'vivisection of my own body'. Jinnah compared the Partition to 'a surgical operation'. Nehru described the Partition as a painful but necessary amputation, hoping that 'by cutting off the head we will get rid of the headache'. Ashis Nandy analogises the violence of the Partition to the bloody 'birth pangs' of new nations (470).

Joya Chatterji (1999) offers multiple interpretations of this metaphor. She argues that the recurrence of the medical metaphor partly reflects the British colonial regime's clinical detachment (also see Raychaudhuri 2009). Chatterji views this as complementary to the 'anthropomorphic conception of the nation-as-mother discourse'. Additionally, the Partition-as-surgery analogy helps the two nations represent each other 'as a diseased limb that had to be sacrificed for the health of the national body-politic' (168). The Partition is thus presented as a tragedy or sacrifice that was necessary for the greater good: independence (Chatterji 1999; Raychaudhuri 2009). However, as Yasmin Khan (2017a) reminds us, the nationalisation of history – of which the medical metaphor is a part – has obscured the reality that the Partition of South Asia was a long, chaotic and far from clinical process.

By delineating the quintessentially modern, biopolitical character of India's Partition, I wish to locate the Partition and its transfer of population within modernity as a technology of governance that sought to produce 'modern' homogenous nation states. It is in this sense that the Partition – with an implied and poorly estimated population transfer (Khan 2017a) – as a solution to ethnic conflict *made sense*, especially to the colonial regime. Locating the Partition is not an issue of contemporaneity – of an event that happened alongside others – but of identifying a larger political and historical landscape of which the Partition and its violence were and are a part. The horrific violence of the Partition was not the result of an innate 'tribal-ness' of South Asia but was coterminous with a larger history of the mutual exchange and 'unmixing' of populations in pursuit of national unity.

Having located the impulse to Partition within modernity, I now want to turn my gaze to violence. What is violence, and how might we understand memories of violence? Deepti Misri (2014: 9) argues that 'every writing (or representation) of violence is also a "reading" (or interpretation) of violence'. Misri's *Beyond Partition* focuses on representations and narrativisations of the violence of the nation state as found in literature, public performance and art. Misri's work is guided by the idea that 'violence "on the streets", as it were, is of a piece with the shifting ways in which something called "violence" is conceptualized and represented within culture' (9).

Misri argues that the murder of female relatives for 'honour' – during the Partition – was sanctioned and glorified by existing cultural notions about 'honour' and 'sacrifice', such as the tradition of *sati*: the ritual practice of burning alive a widow on her husband's funeral pyre. While a narrative of 'sacrifice' and 'honour' presents these 'deaths' as altruistic suicide, the concerted interruption of this narrative by feminist scholars has led to the recognition of violence in this context. Thus, Misri argues that representations of violence simultaneously involve an interpretation of violence. For Misri, violence is 'a historically and socially specific process that moves in the realm of discourse and helps construct it' (9).

In seeing representation as constitutive of violence, Misri treats violence as performative. Here, she follows Anupama Roy's advice against a 'purely instrumental' or 'utilitarian' definition of violence. Roy makes this argument in relation to her research on caste-based atrocities against Dalits. Roy argues that 'violence continues regardless of efficacy because it is also pedagogical instruction in a symbolic order obscured by modern state forms and discourses' (Anupama Roy 2009: 240).

Misri's (2014) idea of the performativity of violence also builds on Allen Feldman's view of violence as 'second representation'. Examining the aesthetics of terror, Feldman argues that 'the act of violence can be a visualizing apparatus, a lens, and a narrativizing frame all at once' (Feldman 1997: 36). Due to the fact that violence is already a narrativising frame – one that embodies an aesthetic of terror that draws on culture – violence is easily absorbed into collective memory. Although Feldman specifically speaks of Northern Ireland, he expresses an insight that has universal applicability:

> The wrack and ruin of dead, wounded, maimed bodies and buildings is already a representational configuration, a created or artificed scene that is prepared in advance for an ex post facto second representation by the media and various apologetics or condemnations. Typification and mimesis allow violence to function as collective memory because violence is grounded on the moral aesthetics of reenactment in Northern Ireland. The meaning and memory of any political act is

prepared in advance by an accumulation of mimetic moments and reenactments that weave together fate and fatality. (36–37)

Marxist historian Tanika Sarkar (2002: 2872) similarly describes Hindu nationalist violence as a form of 'carnivalesque' violence performed to serve real and imagined audiences. Writing in response to the anti-Muslim pogroms of Gujarat in 2002, Sarkar details a 'semiotics of terror' within the violence of the Hindu Right. According to Sarkar, the discourses of Hindu nationalism reveal 'a dark sexual obsession about allegedly ultra-virile Muslim male bodies and over-fertile Muslim female ones' (2874). She connects this violence to a history of gendered victimhood, a history that demands that its revenge be similarly sexed. Previously, Paola Bacchetta (2000) too has noted the gendered nature of Hindu nationalism's conception of history, a history of 'Muslim domination' that is perceived as a failure of Hindu masculinity.

Arjun Appadurai (1998: 919) establishes a link between this kind of proximate, bodily violence and globalisation. He describes such vivisectionist violence as a form of bodily examination that responds to the 'uncertainty' of globalisation. He argues that globalisation through its intensity, speed and scale of the movement of people, material and culture breeds uncertainty. These range from demographic anxieties to uncertainties around establishing the identity of one's proximate ethnic enemies. Through censuses and other population management tools of the state, globalisation obscures individuals within the labels of large-scale identities 'that have effects but no locations' (919). Appadurai sees vivisectionist violence as a macabre manner of establishing 'certainty' of the victim or other's identity amid this landscape of uncertainty.[16]

Such demographic anxieties are especially visible in Hindu nationalist discourses. These range from the fear of being 'replaced' by over-fertile Muslims to the fear of having their members recruited to the task of this demographic replacement through conversion and marriage ('Love Jihad'). The result is a Hindu nationalism that feels besieged from within and outside, surrounded by the hidden presence of lower-caste 'Others', communists, proximate enemy religions and their nation states. Amid this landscape of uncertainty, violence creates 'a macabre form of certainty', even intimacy, through a search for an otherness situated in the body (909). Yet, this violence also functions as a means of 'satisfying one's sense of one's categorical self' within the abstraction of identity (922).

Therefore, vivisectionist violence can also be seen as the performance of the unity of the Hindu-fold. Shakuntala Banaji (2018) expresses something of this through her idea of 'vigilante publics'. Banaji uses the term to describe the co-optation of large numbers of Dalits and Jains towards the cause of Hindu nationalism. She theorises the Hindu Right's propensity for spectacular, gory and public acts of violence as a form of communication, serving as a call to mobilisation for some and a warning to others. She also notes the widespread use of modern information communication technologies in the dissemination of videos of violence as well as propaganda messages.

Through his aforementioned idea of 'aspirational hatred', Appadurai (2019, 2021) draws attention to how the BJP's Hindu nationalism has fast bridged the gap between the 'fascism of law' and the 'fascism of the streets'. While the latter has historically marked its enemies for public execution, the former has now emerged onto the scene to provide absolute immunity to routinised mob violence. Under Modi, Muslims (and to a similar extent Dalits) have been 'open game' for quite some time. Appadurai (2021: 306) sees this as a form of 'cellular, metastatic fascism', in contrast to the centralised, 'vertebrate' fascism of Nazi Germany. Relatedly, Sudha Pai and Sajjan Kumar (2018) have the term 'institutionalized everyday communalism'. The spate of cow lynchings over the last nine years proves that we are witnessing the return of 'The Mob'.

Now when I use that word to describe this violence, I am specifically connecting it to memories of the Partition where the Mob is something of an enigma. In the grammar of Partition narratives, the Mob almost functions like a proper noun. It needs no introduction or explanation: 'The Mob came to our house', 'Or we heard the Mob'. To its survivors, those are both descriptions and explanations of violence.

The Mob is seen popularly as a headless mass of violent hooligans that will destroy everything in their path. But the Mob is anything but. The Partition presents myriad examples of the 'tactical' or agential (de Certeau 1984) use of ethnonationalist violence for personal retribution and aspirations. For example, Urvashi Butalia (2000) documents stories of mobs that abducted elderly widows and then forced them to adopt sons of the other community so that these men could inherit their property.

The coordination of the Mob was also visible in the rape and murder of 8-year-old Asifa in April 2018 by five Hindu nationalists in Kathua, Jammu. Asifa was kidnapped, sedated and raped repeatedly over the course of several days in a temple and then killed (Fareed 2018). After the incident came to light, the Jammu Bar Association tried to obstruct the filing of a chargesheet, alleging that it was biased against Hindu Dogras (M. Ahmad 2018). Furthermore, two BJP ministers in the then Jammu and Kashmir government led a flag march in support of the rapists. Asifa came from the nomadic Bakkarwal community and later investigations revealed that she was raped and murdered in an attempt to scare the Bakkarwal community away from Kathua (Fareed 2018). They succeeded. The intersection of sexual and sectarian violence here seems like something that would have happened during the Partition.

And so, when one really gets down to it, one finds that the Mob is rational to a fault. Its violence has a clear set of objectives – whether that's to inherit the property of widows, to drive Muslims off the land or, more recently, to terrorise university students into silence. The Mob then is a precipitated force that establishes a new rule of law through the generous use of violence. The Mob has a clear conception of history, a laundry list of historical injustices to avenge. The Mob has a clear set of political objectives in mind: the realisation of a Hindu nation. It isn't the breakdown of law and order but the imposition of a new sectarian order. There is a creative impulse at its core.

In this book I draw on these understandings of violence in myriad ways. For example, in Chapter 7, I examine how violence constitutes the formation of national community (G. Pandey 2001). Violence as a 'narrativizing frame' – both in the act and its representation after the fact (Feldman 1997) – visualises community (G. Pandey 2001). Violence happens and is only *seen to have happened* at the borders of community. That is, violence – the act – is not only a performance of community, but violence – in representation – creates and maintains those boundaries. Pandey argues that violence can happen only at the borders of the community; it is located outside it (188). It polices those borders by being remembered in collective memory as having happened to or outside the community, never within. Meanwhile, the violence that occurs within communities – such as the murder of women for the sake of 'honour' – is memorialised not as 'violence' but as 'sacrifice' or 'martyrdom', as death in service of the collectivity (G. Pandey 2001; Misri 2014). Violence as a 'narrativising frame' creates and maintains the boundaries of national community. At its core, the destruction of violence is a creative process that seeks to create order, to give physical form to an imagined homogeneity.

Overview of Chapters

As stated previously, this book argues that to the survivors of the Partition, Hindu nationalism functions as a form of theodicy that rationalises their experience of violence, suffering and displacement. This book is composed of three main parts whose content represents a chronological progression from the immediacy of remembering the suffering of the Partition, to the years of patient hard work and recovery that followed, to the *ressentiment* that has been left in the wake of this experience.

In Chapter 1, I begin my ethnography of the memory of the Partition. Guided by Svetlana Boym (2001), Michel de Certeau (1984) and Paul Connerton's (1989) insights on memory, this chapter introduces readers to the Partition's afterlife. It introduces readers to the site of my fieldwork: Delhi. Drastically transformed by the Partition's refugee crisis, this is a city that has been appropriated by Punjabi refugees. Assembling a mosaic of ethnographic vignettes, this chapter shows how encounters with the cityscape of Delhi are also encounters with the Partition's afterlife.

In Part II, titled 'Sacrifice and Suffering: The *Purusharth* of Refugees', I begin my discussion of Hindu nationalism as a form of theodicy that rationalises the suffering of the Partition. This substantial section, comprising Chapters 2–5, focuses on a discourse that was popularly articulated by my informants – that their hard work (or *purusharth*) following the Partition constituted a 'sacrifice' to the nation.

In Chapter 2, I retell my informants' stories of hard work in the years that immediately followed the Partition. In these didactic, fable-like stories, hard work is constructed as tough, physical and 'menial' labour. My informants also sanctified their hard work by referring to it as *purusharth*. Yet, where the canonical meaning of *purusharth* refers to the ultimate goal of one's life (Charis 1994), my informants used the term to sanctify their physical labour and acts of entrepreneurial cleverness, describing themselves as *purusharthi* (hard-workers) rather than as *sharanarthis* (refugees). Using Weber's (1965, 2013) insights on theodicy and karma, I argue that my informants' stories of hard work comprise a karmic justification of their current privilege.

In Chapter 3, I connect this discourse to Hindu nationalism. Valourising the hard work of the individual while minimising the role of the state, stories of *purusharth* make an important political statement on the national past. I connect this discourse to neoliberalism, the politics of *karni-bharni* ('reap as you sow') and Modi's image as a *brahmachari* who values 'hard work' over 'Harvard' (*The Hindu* 2017a). This discussion demonstrates how this narrative of the *purusharthi* Punjabi refugee is rooted in a specific upper-caste Hindu cultural and religious strain.

In Chapter 4, I analyse the way in which the discourse of sacrifice comprises a specific, organic grammar of mourning. Sifting through ethnographic evidence that ranges from the celebration of Hindu patriarchal masculinity to the description of the honour killings of women relatives as sacrifice, to interrogations of the meaning and price of freedom, I detail the theodicical impulses at work in this discourse. I argue that by remembering hard work and suffering as sacrifice, by remembering the victims of retributive ethnonational violence as 'martyrs', by erasing the memory of the honour killing of women, this discourse constitutes an articulation of the Hindu nation.

In Chapter 5 – the final chapter of Part II – I argue that this masculine discourse of sacrifice eulogises the lives of women and renders them in the image of the suffering nation while erasing their *actual* lives. I do so by documenting the quotidian lives of women, using the humble sewing machine as a key symbol of South Asian domesticity. The stories of women embody a 'subordinate discourse' (Messick 1987). Shunning the didactic, moralising tone of the stories of men, the stories of women often use humour and sarcasm to voice an organic critique of masculinity and the patriarchy. These stories show that although women value hard work, the terms of the discourse disallow the description of their labour as *purusharth*. Just as Veena Das (2007) observed how women incorporated their experience of the violence of the Partition into the 'ordinary' experience of being a woman in a patriarchal society, I observe how the hard work of women is absorbed and disappeared within normative understandings of the gendered division of labour.

The chapters that make up Part III, 'Remembrance and Healing: Reflections on the Post-Partition Context', collectively confront the question of what it means to remember the Partition in the time of fascism. In Chapter 6, I juxtapose the violence in India's present with the musealisation of the Partition's memory. I ask whether it is healing to remember the Partition in the current atmosphere. Examining the idea of 'speaking out' as 'healing', this chapter analyses the meaning of silence, trauma and narrative agency in this context.

In Chapter 7, I explore how violence – the act as well as its remembrance – functions as a narrativising lens (Feldman 1997) that constitutes the formation and performance of national community (G. Pandey 2001). This is visible in the memory of the Partition not only in the way that the honour killings of women are remembered as 'sacrifice' and 'martyrdom' – as not-violence (Misri 2014) – but also in the way that my informants attribute the worst excesses of the Partition to Sikhs and Muslims. When they do discuss the violence of their own community, they present it as an act of 'self-defence', as not-violence. Employing a hermeneutics of suspicion (Ricoeur 1970) in relation to the narratives of my informants, I critique the various ways in which my informants seek to other the violence of the Partition. Using a combination of ethnographic and historiographical evidence, I deliberately interrupt their imagination of a homogenous Hindu-fold.

In Chapter 8, I present the stories of two of my key informants: Gangaram and Pooran Chand. Their stories raise difficult questions about nostalgia and reconciliation in the post-Partition context. Both Gangaram and Pooran Chand had revisited Pakistan following the Partition and still had a number of friends there. Yet, even as they questioned the futility of the Partition, they expressed their staunch support for Modi and his violent Hindu nationalist politics.

In Chapter 9, I address the theme of victimhood. Building on my discussion in the preceding chapters, I discuss how my informants' perceived victimhood imbues their Islamophobia with the moralistic aura of justice. I explore this feeling of *ressentiment* – a feeling of self-righteous and toxic jealousy – that lies at the heart of their perceived victimhood. The realisation that one's sense of victimhood imbues one's hatred with putative righteousness allows us to understand how, to its followers, Hindu nationalism bears the guise of a political revolution. In this chapter, I wonder whether it is really 'healing' to remember the Partition when everyone, from the survivors themselves to the political leaders they idolise, seems to support a fresh cycle of violence in retribution for the past, to finish the unfinished work of the Partition, as it were.

Finally, in 'Conclusion: Field Notes on Global Authoritarianism', I build on my discussion of *ressentiment* to theorise the ongoing wave of global authoritarianism. With an obstinate 'democracy fatigue' taking hold in healthy and vibrant democracies the world over (Appadurai 2017), are we witnessing the end of liberal democracy? Or is democracy animated only by the basest of private emotions, driven by feelings of victimhood, *ressentiment* and envy such that we remember the tyrannies of others only to justify those of our own? Do the politics of hate have any limits? Is there a way out of the post-truth politics and its persistent crises of meaning? These are some of the urgent questions this chapter explores as it examines India's CAA and what it says about the crisis of meaning in the post-truth era.

Notes

1 As a mark of respect, I bequeathed his name, as a pseudonym, to an informant who was like a grandfather to me during my fieldwork.

2 In Hinduism, the fourth day – *chautha* – following a person's death is the main funerary event.

3 My use of these terms deliberately invokes Nadia Seremetakis' (1991) ethnographic work on mourning rituals in Inner Mani, Greece. Seremetakis describes a 'good' death as one that involves a public and vocal display of mourning. By contrast, a 'bad' death is an 'asocial' death, one signified by the absence of mourners and mourning. In Chapter 4, I use this idea of a 'bad' death in relation to the Partition of India.

4   Ranajit Guha's (2002a, 2002b) critique can be connected to the work of Eric Hobsbawm (2000), Etienne Balibar (2002) and Yannis Hamilakis (2007), who similarly identify the role history and archaeology play in nationalist projects as well as in reifying the hegemony of the state.

5   A genre of Urdu poetry that is often written in a rhyming verse.

6   *Heer* is the tragic tale of the star-crossed lovers Heer and Ranjha.

7   Urs are South Asian festivals that mark the death anniversaries of Sufi saints. Waris Shah was a Sufi poet of the Chisti order.

8   Sanjeev Jain and Alok Sarin (2018) list Manto's description of the emotional impact of the Partition in "Toba Tek Singh" as one of the inspirations behind the compilation of their edited volume, *The Psychological Impact of the Partition of India*.

9   Readers interested in a further exploration of the artistic, cinematic and literary representations of the Partition may refer to the work of Anindya Raychaudhuri (2009, 2019).

10   Through my phrasing, I deliberately seek to invoke Benedict Anderson's *Imagined Communities* (1983) here. However, I have refrained from an overreliance on Anderson's ideas due to my agreement with Herzfeld's (1992, 2005) and van der Veer's (1994) thoughtful critiques of Anderson. Both Herzfeld and van der Veer argue that while the nation is certainly imagined, there is far more specificity to the imagination of a particular nation. Shunning Anderson's top-down formulation, both Herzfeld and van der Veer seek to pay attention to not only how nations are imagined but also how these imaginations come to be accepted by the very people who are homogenised in this manner. Herzfeld and van der Veer pay attention to the internal contestations within these imagined national communities and, in doing so, produce a description of culture through the prism of power.

11   Jonathan Swift's (2003) classic novella *Gulliver's Travels* satirises precisely this colonial attitude; the comically large and 'rational' Gulliver literally looming over the 'irrational' squabbles of the midget Lilliputians.

12   I. Ahmad's (2020: 2–3) 'ditto theory' sheds more light on this. The 'ditto theory' describes a pervasive tendency within Indian society to present the violence of the majority and the minority as equal and indistinguishable halves of the same whole; as dittos of each other.

13 The term Aryan-Vedic civilisation refers to the (auto-)orientalist belief that Hinduism was brought to India by ancient European settlers called the Aryans (Goodrick-Clarke 2000; Thapar 1996, 2015; van der Veer 1994). This myth of the 'true' racial and ethnic origins of Hinduism is also known as the Aryan race theory. Nineteenth-century orientalist thinkers such as Max Mueller believed that the Aryans invaded South Asia and in doing so established an advanced ancient civilisation there (Thapar 1996). Mueller credited the Aryans with developing the Vedic Sanskrit language and also used the Aryan invasion theory to explain India's caste system. According to him, the caste system originated as a system of racial segregation such that modern-day upper castes and Brahmans were said to be descendants of the victorious Aryans, while the lower castes and Dalits were said to be descendants of the vanquished non-Aryan *dasas*.

Orientalist reconstructions of Aryan history sought to establish ancient India's connection to early European history to unearth common origins, 'untouched by the intervention of the Semitic peoples and languages' (6). Running parallel to the aforementioned British colonialist discourses of John Stuart Mill, this orientalist myth of the European and Asian split of a single united Aryan ancestor race provided colonised upper-caste Indians with 'status' and 'self-esteem' whilst also simultaneously acknowledging the inherent racial and cultural superiority of Europe (7). Between the 1920s and 1940s, common belief in Aryan race theory meant that German Nazis found a natural ally in (upper-caste) Hindu nationalists (Goodrick-Clarke 2000).

However, while European thinkers believed that the Aryans colonised India, the RSS believes that the Aryans were neither invaders nor colonisers, but were instead the 'original Hindus' (9). Romila Thapar details the RSS stance on the Aryans as follows:

[T]he original Hindus were the Aryans, a distinctive people indigenous to India. Caste Hindus or Hindu Aryas are their descendants. There was no Aryan invasion since the Aryans were indigenous to India and therefore no confrontation among the people of India. The Aryans spoke Sanskrit and were responsible for the spread of Aryan civilisation from India to the west. Confrontations came with the arrival of foreigners such as the Muslims, the Christians and more recently, the communists. (9)

In this way, the RSS frames the Aryan-Vedic people as the 'original Hindus' who have since been harassed by waves of 'foreign invaders'. This discourse establishes Muslims and Christians as un-Indian. However, there is some ambiguity in this discourse regarding caste-Hindus and Aryans. Specifically, regarding *only* caste-Hindus as the 'true' descendants of the Aryans also excludes lower-castes and Dalits from being considered as *real* Hindus. But, conversely for upper-caste Hindus and Brahmans claiming descent via the Aryans is pivotal to the legitimisation of their caste privilege as historical (and biological) fact. Yet, the pragmatic quotidian concerns of the RSS demand that the definition of 'Aryan descent' be expanded to include *all* Hindus, thus including the lower-castes and Dalits (Thapar 1996). Doing so would bolster the numerical superiority of those considered 'Hindu', and thereby better consolidate the Hindu-fold.

14   According to government statistics, reported crimes against Dalits went up by 6 per cent between 2009 and 2018, while in the last five years, 20.40 per cent of all reported cases of caste-based violence concerned sexual violence against Scheduled Caste women (*The Hindu* 2018). This, however, is merely a statistical breakdown of the cases that were reported, and in which caste was legally acknowledged as a factor contributing to the crime.

15   OBC is a legally designated term that signifies some lower castes as other backward castes for the purposes of their inclusion in affirmative action policies.

16   Appadurai's discussion of the hidden, secretive and treacherous presence of the other within one's society draws on Zygmunt Bauman's (1997) discussion of 'The Stranger'.

1

Listening to Ancestors

Ethnography in a Milieu of Memory

Stories about places are makeshift things. They are composed with the world's debris.

—Michel de Certeau (1984: 107)

Displacement and Memory

In *The Practice of Everyday Life*, Michel de Certeau (1984) analogises memory to a bird that lays its eggs in another's nest. He writes, 'Like those birds that lay their eggs only in other species' nests, memory produces in a place that does not belong to it' (de Certeau 1984: 87). De Certeau's analogy is profoundly relevant in the context of the Partition because it identifies the experience of displacement as crucial to the process of remembrance. De Certeau also emphasises the effect this has on the shape and form of memory. He continues, 'It [memory] receives its form and its implantation from external circumstances, even if it furnishes the con-tent (the missing detail)' (87). De Certeau sees displacement (whether in space or time) as a fundamental trigger to the production of memory. In this way, de Certeau too defines memory as a social construction whose narrative form is shaped by the present within which it is recalled (Halbwachs 1992; Connerton 1989; Boym 2001).

Frankish and Bradbury (2012: 305) note that the process of remembrance involves assembling one's memories into a narrative that gives a sense of 'who we were, who we are and who we could possibly be'. In a sentiment similar to de Certeau's idea of memory receiving its form from 'external circumstances', Michael Roth (2012: 85) notes that memory 'transforms the past as a condition of retaining it'. Halbwachs (1992) identifies this as the intervention of 'collective' frames of remembrance. Memory comes to be shaped by the 'collective' social frames within which it is (re-)constructed.

Nostalgia – the bittersweet longing for one's past – shares this quality of memory (Boym 2001). As Svetlana Boym writes, 'The nostalgic rendezvous with oneself is not always a private affair' (50). Boym describes nostalgia as 'a sentiment of loss and displacement, but ... also a romance with one's own fantasy' (xiii). Nostalgia is the process of creating 'perfect memories of imperfect worlds' (Finlay 2004: 150). However, nostalgia contains within it a 'utopian dimension'. Yet, nostalgia's poetic desire for utopia is not directed at the future. Nostalgia is at times directed at the past but at other times yearns to escape the linear progression of time. As Boym observes, 'The nostalgic feels stifled within the conventional confines of time and space' (Boym 2001: xiii). In this way the longing for utopia at the heart of nostalgia articulates the desire to rebel against temporality, or to recuperate it against itself.

The memory of the Partition is fundamentally a memory of displacement. At its most obvious level, confronting this memory involves a rendezvous with memories of abandoned homes, a memory of loss and suffering. After all, my informants' memories of Pakistan took shape in India, a land in which all things Pakistani are seen to not belong. But there is a deeper, more personal level at which the theme of displacement resonates with my interest in the Partition.

Looking back, I find that it was my migration to Ireland in August 2014 that made these familial memories of the Partition relevant to my identity. In those initial months as a postgraduate student in Ireland, I found myself struggling to grasp my newfound racial identity. I had simply never thought of myself as a brown man until I *became* a brown man in Ireland. Yet as I grappled with this identity crisis, it was my Pakistani neighbours Adeen and Mahvish who despite *not being of home* reminded me most of home. And just like that, my connection to the Partition, my Pakistani heritage, became relevant. Studying race and nationalism in the classroom made questions of belonging more relevant closer to home. These experiences led to my first engagement with Partition oral history, my MPhil thesis (Kohli 2015), a project that was driven by my (*ersatz*) nostalgia for the pre-Partition period even as it deconstructed my informants' nostalgia. That pilot project subsequently led to my doctoral dissertation and this book's manuscript. The 'egg' of memory had hatched in a foreign nest.

But, even as my nostalgia for this mythical pre-Partition period of interfaith harmony evaporated in the stark light of the day, there were other stories and themes that grabbed my attention. For example, having taken pride in the self-exoticisation of a certain South Asian work ethic – a migrant ethos so to speak – I became interested in my informants' stories of hard-working Punjabi refugees. Similarly, my yearning for a break from the hatred festering openly in Modi's India drew me closer to my informants Gangaram and Pooran Chand (see Chapter 8), whose stories seemed to deviate from the vitriolic norm. And although these hopes and dreams remained unfulfilled, these shared experiences of migration and displacement served as points of relation. Strangers I met in the field became grandparents in the process of long-winded discussions on their lives and the Partition. And it was in becoming kin-like relations that they became key informants. Consequently, I began to treat my grandparent-like informants like 'sites of memory'.

In critical memory studies, the term 'sites of memory' is considered controversial due to Pierre Nora's (1992) work on memory and history. Nora argued that modernisation and the modern turn to historicisation have obliterated *milieux de mémoire*, or social settings in which 'memory is a real part of everyday experience' (1). Nora interpreted the proliferation of archives, commemorations and museums as the death of spontaneous memory. For Nora such commemorations of history are necessitated by the degeneration of memory, because 'such things no longer happen as a matter of course' (7).

Nora's (1989, 1992) work assumes that a universal 'acceleration of history' is responsible for the annihilation of 'real' or 'true memory' as embodied in *milieux de mémoire* (Schäuble 2014). Implicit here is the juxtaposition of memory and history such that the presence of history annihilates memory, while the presence of memory signifies the absence of a historical consciousness. However, as Michaela Schäuble writes,

'Contrary to Nora's much criticised argument, however, the prevalence of "memory" over "history" … by no means excludes a local historiographical consciousness' (155).

In my fieldwork, I found that historical and political discourses informed the memories of my informants such that I was ultimately documenting a memory of history alongside a history of memory. In this setting, where memory was informed by a local historiographical consciousness while understandings of history were themselves derived from memory, it was impossible (and futile) to draw a neat distinction between history and memory.

Unlike Pierre Nora, who understands sites of memory as isolated islands besieged by the onslaught of an unstoppable tide of history, I use the term much like Ruth Behar (1996) does when she identifies her grandfather as a site of memory. While studying peasant traditions through the eyes of her grandfather and familial strangers in the Spanish village of Santa Maria del Monte, Behar found that in subjecting her grandfather to her anthropological gaze, in seeing him as a 'site of memory', she was drawn closer to others like him in the village. Following his death, Behar found discussing his death and the societal transformations that the death of this generation signified for the history of the village, cathartic as well as ethnographically productive. Meanwhile, the process of studying a shared past meant that she and her informants were beginning to see themselves as 'historically conceived', but by a history received from one's elders (62). For my work and Behar's, such points of relation are fundamental to the task of ethnography. We share not just a history but the debris of worlds lost to us both. And it is that shared sense of loss, as much as a shared culture, that makes us kin.

Good ethnography is not about 'studying' distant, exotic others under the microscope of social research. Rather, good ethnography is defined by listening. The relational nature of ethnographic research entails that more often than not, the people we listen to are our kin and kin-like relations. In the case of my research, this meant listening to my ancestors. Thus, my research follows a rich anthropological tradition that participates in the generational exchange of knowledge.[1] Ours is a tradition that listens to our ancestors.

Ethnography is a relational practice. Ethnographers learn about social relations by being part of and reproducing them. Ethnography is not just a research methodology but a unique style of representation and analysis. To some extent it is a research methodology in that it is a way of doing research. But ethnography is much more. Participant observation does not produce ethnography by default. Ethnography is a style of thinking moulded to specific contexts. It is a particular manner of observing and critiquing data, a way of presenting evidence – of thick description – that often draws on fieldwork to take one's readers back to the scene. Ethnography is both a research methodology and a unique style of representation. It is theoretical/conceptual and empirical all at once. The term 'ethnography' encompasses both the concept work and the fieldwork.

Ethnographic practice is shaped by the relationality between the space of observation, the field – and the domain of analysis, the desk.[2] Immersed in the space of observation, the ethnographer is always pulled in (at least) two directions: towards their own theoretically informed research objectives and towards the preoccupations of the people they work with in the field (Strathern 1999). In the field, the concerns and struggles of our informants tend to overshadow the theoretical preoccupations of the research proposal. Returning to the desk reverses this equation.

In this chapter, I want to introduce the reader to the site of my fieldwork: Delhi. Contemporary Delhi is a cityscape which Partition survivors have built for themselves. Created as a result of the Partition-era refugee exodus, this is a city that has been appropriated by Punjabi refugees. This chapter tells this history. A substantial portion of this chapter focuses on my ethnographic fieldwork in Faridabad: a satellite town of Delhi.

Modern-day Faridabad took shape when the Government of India decided to use the town to re-settle 50,000 refugees from the North-West Frontier Province (NWFP). The New Industrial Township (NIT) area of Faridabad struck me as a milieu of memory, a place where memory forms a 'real' and meaningful part of everyday life. NIT Faridabad includes its very own memorial to the 'martyrs' of the Partition, as well as a couple of place names that memorialise its people's connection to the legendary NWFP freedom fighter Khan Abdul Ghaffar Khan. Routinely socialising with a group of Partition survivors I befriended in Faridabad's Rose Garden, I was able to observe the afterlife of this memory.

Delhi and the Partition

As stated previously, the Partition of India remains the largest episode of retributive genocide and mass displacement in history (Aiyar 1995), with millions dead and an estimated 10–17 million people displaced in a haphazard transfer of population (Brass 2003b; Khwaja, Bharadwaj and Mian 2009). Delhi received the lion's share of refugees from West Pakistan. By 21 August 1947, 120,000 refugees had entered Delhi, adding to the city's existing population of 917,939 residents (as per the 1941 Census) (Kumari 2013: 62). Between 1947 and 1951, 329,000 Muslim refugees left Delhi, while 495,000 Hindu and Sikh refugees arrived in the city (Krafft 1993: 95). However, the 1951 census of Delhi calculated the city's population at 1,744,072, of which refugees comprised 28.4 per cent of the population (V. Datta 1986: 443; Kumari 2013: 62). In the decade following the Partition, a significant number of refugees (including some of my informants) sold the agricultural landholdings they had been allotted and migrated to Delhi. In the post-Partition years, Delhi emerged as an attractive destination due to its flourishing markets and the availability of government jobs. Thus, after the Partition, refugees came to comprise a major portion of Delhi's population.

In recent times, a significant body of literature has emerged documenting how the Partition has shaped the demography and architecture of South Asian cities. This literature documents the religious homogenisation that followed the Partition (Hill et al. 2008) as well as the way in which the Partition and its afterlife changed Amritsar's identity from an industrial centre to one associated with its sixteenth-century avatar as the holiest Sikh shrine (P. Sahni 2003). Bharadwaj and Mirza (2019) observe that from 1957 to 2009, districts with a greater refugee presence saw average wheat yields rise by 9.4 per cent, in comparison to others. Similarly, I. A. Chattha's (2009) comparative research on Sialkot and Gujranwala examines the impact of the Hindu and Sikh mercantile classes' outmigration, and the role of refugees and local craftsmen in economic reconstruction following the Partition.

V. N. Datta's (1986) analysis of the impact of Punjabi refugees on Delhi-NCR's transformation into modern India's principal urban hub follows a similar discursive arc.[3] Datta examines how the influx of refugees into Delhi necessitated the building of neighbourhoods, markets and factories to rehome and provide employment to refugees. Datta's work also briefly touches on Delhi's Camp College. Camp College, which operated in Kingsway Camp, Delhi, was affiliated with Punjab University and provided Partition refugees free access to higher education. My maternal grandfather, his younger brother (my granduncle, Om Prakash) and numerous other informants completed their higher education there. My own status today owes a massive debt of gratitude to institutions such as this that rehabilitated Partition refugees in their hour of need.

The refugee crisis of the Partition was unique in that, here, the refugees were seen to belong to the nation state in which they sought refuge (Riggs and Jat 2016). In fact, the crisis was a product of the very fact that they were seen to *not* belong in their ancestral towns and villages. However, the homogeneity manufactured by the violence of the Partition was as alien to the land as some Partition refugees were to Delhi. And the Delhi that came about as a result of the Partition was a far cry from the city's pre-Partition avatar.

Pre-Partition Delhi is often remembered as 'a city of the Muslims'. Medieval Delhi was famed for its astonishing beauty, prosperity and gaiety. This culture was itself in decline due to an extended tryst with colonial capitalism (G. Pandey 2001: 135). Nevertheless, the Delhi of the 1930s and 1940s remained the hub of a decaying feudal high culture. Pre-Partition Delhi was the world's Urdu capital with a material culture that subtly invoked its former glory as the Mughal Imperial capital (Dalrymple 1993). Written in the year 1940, Ahmed Ali's (2007) novel *Twilight in Delhi* provides a rare glimpse into the daily lives of pre-Partition Delhiwalas. The novel portrays a quasi-feudal society in decline as a result of colonialism and with it an advancing modernity symbolised by the ideas of individualism and nationalism (G. Pandey 2001).

Partition tore this world asunder. Contemporaneous accounts of Delhi's Partition violence state that the city descended into genocidal violence between 4 and 6 September. What began as sporadic incidents of violence intensified into a systematic pogrom, as fighting spread from Karol Bagh to the rest of the city (G. Pandey 2001). It was believed that Hindu and Sikh refugees arriving from Pakistan were responsible for the violence, setting in motion an escalating cycle of retributive violence (Zamindar 2007). It is estimated that as many as 20,000 Muslims were killed, while 'the dead lay rotting in the streets, because there was no one to collect and bury them' (21). In the days and months that followed, refugee camps housing Hindus and Sikhs from West Pakistan emerged as fertile recruitment spaces for the Rashtriya Swayamsevak Sangh (RSS) (G. Pandey 2001).

This memory of Karol Bagh as the epicentre of violence in Delhi is preserved by a seemingly innocuous place name. One of my informants, Gajendra Pal, remembered that Karol Bagh's famous Joshi Road and its Dr N. C. Joshi Memorial Hospital are named after Dr N. C. Joshi, a famous surgeon. Gajendra Pal and his family were living on Joshi Road at the time and witnessed the situation deteriorating first-hand. Gajendra Pal remembered that Joshi Road is the street where Dr Joshi was assassinated by Muslim assailants in September 1947. Gajendra Pal's story is repeated on the Delhi Government's official webpage for the Dr N. C. Joshi Memorial Hospital (Government of National Capital Territory of Delhi 2020).

However, in Gajendra Pal's retelling, it was the assassination that sparked the violence. Gajendra Pal's narrative presents the anti-Muslim violence as the 'reaction' to an 'action'. This is unlikely to be true since Dr Joshi was assassinated on 8 September 1947 (Government of National Capital Territory of Delhi 2020), while the violence in Delhi is said to have begun sometime between 4 and 6 September (G. Pandey 2001).

In this, Gajendra Pal's story differs sharply from the historical record which attributes the violence to the arrival of a large population of Hindu and Sikh refugees that sought revenge for what had happened to them in Pakistan (G. Pandey 2001; Zamindar 2007). As I write in Chapter 7, such narratives reflect a denial of the violence of one's own community, presenting the violence of their co-religionists purely as acts of self-defence or retaliation.

Due to the violence and the migration of refugees into Delhi, the city came to be straddled with twin refugee crises. On the one hand were the Muslims who had been made refugees in their own city, while on the other hand were the Hindu and Sikh refugees who had migrated from across the border (G. Pandey 2001). Located at the intersection of competing ethnonationalist claims, these twin refugee populations were embroiled in a scramble for contested urban geography such that the rehabilitation of one appeared to justify and necessitate the other's displacement (Zamindar 2007).

India's evacuee property legislation stipulated that property evacuated by Muslims fleeing for Pakistan and then subsequently occupied by Hindu and Sikh refugees – irrespective of whether the Muslim owner had *actually* relocated to Pakistan – could not be dispossessed off the refugees (Zamindar 2007). Rotem Geva (2014) argues that this along with physical violence directly led to the ghettoisation of Delhi's Muslims.

Gyanendra Pandey (2001) writes that the twin refugee populations scattered across the cityscape raised important questions about national belonging and community. Initially, the Indian government focused its resources on the refugee camps of Hindus and Sikhs, leaving the refugee camps of Muslims to fend for themselves. This disparity is corroborated by various social workers who observed a stark difference in the living conditions of the refugee camps of Hindus and Sikhs, in comparison to Muslims. In fact, it was only after a large Muslim refugee population emerged that the government even established an official refugee camp for them (G. Pandey 2001).

This approach to the management of Delhi's refugee crisis produced a governmental response that followed the biopolitical doctrine of 'make live, let die' (Zamindar 2007). In the worst weeks of the refugee crisis, while the Indian government had distributed thousands of blankets and quilts in the Hindu and Sikh refugee camps, the Muslim refugee camps received nothing (G. Pandey 2001). The blankets themselves were only symbolic markers of a larger shift in the borders of community within the new nation. The police too became openly partisan (Geva 2014; Zamindar 2007), a dark fact of Delhi's history that was repeated in the anti-Sikh pogroms of 1984 (Das 2007) and the anti-Muslim pogroms of February 2020 (I. Ahmad 2020). Thomas Blom

Hansen (2021) places such mob violence at the very heart of Indian democracy.

Delhi's Muslim residents became de facto foreigners in their own homes as the Indian government abrogated its humanitarian responsibility towards them, treating them as Pakistani citizens in waiting. This collapse of law and order, the chance to occupy 'abandoned' property and the implicit involvement of the local police meant that the newly arrived refugees from Pakistan had an incentive to target Delhi's Muslims (G. Pandey 2001; Zamindar 2007).

This situation persisted until Mahatma Gandhi moved to Delhi, in mid-September 1947. Through a number of public addresses, Gandhi persuaded the Indian government to treat Delhi's Muslim refugees as their own citizens and appealed to the citizens for inter-faith harmony (G. Pandey 2001). Although Gandhi's public addresses restored some semblance of calm, Delhi continued to simmer for months afterwards. In January 1948, it descended into chaos again, prompting Gandhi to start another fast unto death (his last) and address prayer gatherings (Ramachandra Guha 2018). Standard accounts emphasise that peace returned to the city immediately after Gandhi's assassination on 30 January 1948, as the city appeared to recoil from its own violence in disgust (Geva 2014). However, low-intensity violence continued in Delhi until the end of 1950, while some judicial cases concerning evacuee property remained unresolved for decades afterwards (Geva 2014; Zamindar 2007).

The Delhi that emerged after the Partition was a changed city. The violence had redrawn the borders of national belonging. Neither Delhi nor India would ever be the same again. Delhi's large Hindu and Sikh refugee population brought far-reaching changes to the cityscape. The city's refugee camps and rehabilitation colonies emerged as its new residential and commercial hubs (Kaur 2007). Delhi's culture too underwent a radical transformation. The city that was once considered the world's Urdu capital came to adopt Hindi as its *lingua franca*.

Interestingly, my informants' memories of those initial days and weeks in Delhi (and surrounding parts of north India) also reveal a memory of un-belonging. Coming from the rural hinterlands of Punjab and the NWFP, the overwhelming majority of my informants did not speak Hindi at the time. They could not read the script either. They spoke between them Urdu, regional dialects of Saraiki, Punjabi, Pashto and some English and Persian. To the Hindu locals of Delhi and north India, their material culture resembled that of Muslims. In fact, in their *salwar kameez*, my informants were considered so similar to Muslims that some were advised by their Sikh friends to wear a *kara*[4] to mark them out as 'allies' to Hindu and Sikh mobs. Such anecdotes also provide a glimpse into the kind of mob violence Delhi witnessed during this period.

Thakar Daas, a Partition survivor from Dera Ismail Khan (NWFP) recalled that the Hindu families living in Kurukshetra – the site of his refugee camp – treated the Frontier refugees with disdain. 'They thought we were Pakistanis. Muslims. *Habshi*-type,' Thakar Das remembered. The word *habshi* translates to barbarian or savage. In common usage it is often used to denigrate meat-eating or, more moderately, the consumption of uncommon or exotic animals. Thakar Das said that it was only when they witnessed the (Hindu) religiosity of the refugees that the ethnic tensions began to ease. But even then, they were often taunted for being 'Pakistani'. Meanwhile, my informants in Dehradun said that an unspoken divide between 'Pakistani' Punjabis and 'Indian' Punjabis persists till this day in their chapter of the Arya Samaj.

A 'New' Delhi

The history of the Partition is writ large over the neighbourhoods of Delhi. Even today, certain neighbourhoods of Delhi are associated with Partition refugees. Kirti Nagar, Derawal Nagar, Kingsway Camp, Malviya Nagar and Lajpat Nagar, to name a few, are known as neighbourhoods that were created to resettle Partition refugees. Plots and houses in these neighbourhoods were specifically allotted to refugees from Punjab in compensation for the property they had abandoned in Pakistan. Satellite towns around Delhi and other cities in Punjab, Haryana and Uttar Pradesh were also chosen for the resettlement of refugees.

During the resettlement process, the Indian government made a concerted effort to preserve the 'regional affinity' of refugees (Jain 1998: 104). As my informant Pooran Chand told me, 'Those who came from Jhang [Pakistan] were allotted Rohtak.... And those who came from

Dera Ghazi Khan, they got Palwal, Gurgaon district…. Us, Frontier-people got NIT Faridabad.' L. C. Jain, a former bureaucrat and recipient of the Magsaysay Award in 1989, played a pivotal role in the development of the Faridabad Township through his services in the Indian Cooperative Union and the Faridabad Development Board. Jain (1998) writes that in Faridabad the 'regional affinity' of refugees from the Frontier was preserved right down to the village level. In Faridabad, 5,000 housing sites were earmarked and further divided into five neighbourhoods with 1,000 sites each. Families were first listed according to their regions and then allotted contiguous sites based on the villages they were from (104). My informants in Faridabad credited their community's sense of kinship and unity to this system of allotment. This is a theme that recurs frequently in the narratives of my Faridabad informants.

While Faridabad was deliberately built to preserve a sense of 'regional affinity', in other neighbourhoods, Partition refugees pursued this on their own terms. Despite not having been specifically built to resettle Partition refugees, Rajouri Garden (in Delhi) is considered a 'Punjabi area' due to its high concentration of Punjabi families. Many of these are Partition survivors (and their descendants) who bought residential plots and shops there, in the 1950s and 1960s, using the money and property they had received from the government following the settlement of their claims for compensation. As my grandaunt Anjali and numerous other informants in Rajouri Garden, Kirti Nagar, Jangapura and Derawal Nagar told me, following their displacement from Pakistan, friends and families tried their best to stick together by purchasing plots close to each other, whenever possible. This instinct to stick together – an instinct produced by an implicit feeling of *foreignness* – is eventually what gave Rajouri Garden its distinctly Punjabi character.

Staying in Rajouri Garden with my grandaunt Anjali, I was able to experience the Punjabi-ness of this area for myself. There are two experiences from my time in Rajouri Garden that stand out. One evening on our way back from the grocery store we came across a Multani woman practising the unique Karva Chauth[5] ritual associated with the Saraiki belt of Punjab, a ritual performed on the night of Guru Nanak Dev Ji Gurpurab. Gurpurabs mark the birth anniversaries of the Sikh gurus. This particular Gurpurab was the anniversary of the first

Sikh guru, Guru Nanak, marked by the first full moon of the Indian lunar month Kartik.

Before we had even spotted the woman herself, my grandaunt had deduced her presence through the wheat *diyas*[6] that had been placed along the side of the street leading up to their house. My grandaunt pointed these out to me and explained their significance. While I was photographing the *diyas*, a woman emerged from her house and looked at the moon through a hole in a *roti*. After she had completed the ritual, my grandaunt approached her and struck up a conversation that ended with us discussing our shared Pakistani heritage and my research. While our family had migrated from Dera Ghazi Khan, hers had come from Multan. Like my grandaunt's parents, her parents too had been living in Rajouri Garden since the 1960s. And just like that, a chance encounter on a full moon night had uncovered the strata of history on which this city rests uneasily.

Explaining the ritual to me later, my grandaunt said that the traditional Karva Chauth full moon (which happens to be the full moon just before Guru Nanak Dev Ji Gurpurab) is thought to have been cursed by the Hindu deity Lord Ganesh. This is the reason it is seen through a sieve rather than with the naked eye. Since this Gurpurab moon is considered auspicious, one does not need to shield one's eyes from it. Sikhs consider this Gurpurab the most auspicious day of the year.

On another evening walk through the lively markets of Rajouri Garden, my grandaunt showed me the many tandoors that grace the streets around dinnertime. These are run by *dhabas* (roadside restaurants) and confectioners. One can bring semi-prepared *rotis* from home and pay the cook to finish them in the tandoor or buy *naans* and *rotis* from the *dhaba*. On chilly winter evenings it is a treat to stand beside a burning tandoor.

In decades past, Rajouri Garden was awash with communal tandoors that were run by groups of residents on a not-for-profit basis, charging people just enough money to provide fuel for the tandoor. Communal tandoors and stoves were also a common feature of refugee camps. As I write in Chapter 5, women Partition survivors have very fond memories of the bonds and friendships that were forged around the communal tandoors in those uncertain days. Yet, the tandoor's influence on the character of Rajouri Garden's streets is waning. While the *dhaba*-run tandoors stoically hold their own, the community-run tandoors have all but vanished. Rajouri Garden's transition from a Punjabi refugee enclave to a flourishing neoliberal market has eroded its sense of community, and with it consigned the communal tandoor to a quiet, lonesome death.

But Rajouri Garden is not the only place where one might unexpectedly encounter a layer of the city's history. Sometimes even a serendipitous encounter with a particular street is enough to provoke a memory. This happened in February 2018 when I was driving to Shakti Nagar (north Delhi) with my key informant Bhanwarilal. We were on our way to meet Gangaram, a Partition survivor and close friend of Bhanwarilal's who had revisited Pakistan 22 times since the Partition. However, we ended up losing our way a short distance away from Gangaram's house. The constantly expanding Metro-works and under-construction flyovers had made the cityscape unrecognisable to Bhanwarilal's eyes.

Turning to Google Maps for help, we ended up being re-routed through Chaudhary Gulab Singh Marg. As we turned onto that street, Bhanwarilal excitedly remarked that once upon a time, this street used to be called Thandi Sadak (cold street). Bhanwarilal told me that his elder brother used to live beside the Ghanta Ghar Chowk (clock tower roundabout) not far from here. That house is still in their family and his nephew lives there now.

Bhanwarilal's spontaneous turn to remembrance is itself an evocation of de Certeau's (1984: 117) theorisation of space as 'practiced' or embodied place. Bhanwarilal remembered that back when he was in school – in the 1940s – his parents would bring him here every summer. Bhanwarilal explained that Thandi Sadak was a semantically transparent place name that remembered the way the street used to feel. He said:

> The name Thandi Sadak caught on because earlier there were trees upon trees on both sides of this road. There were so many trees that when we used to come on this street, a cool breeze would be constantly blowing through it – just like an AC. Because of that it was called Thandi Sadak.[7]

Other times the mere mention of the name of a particular neighbourhood to a Partition survivor is enough to trigger a memory. This is something I realised in a conversation with Falguni, an informant who was a distant relative and my late maternal grandparents' neighbour in Faridabad's newer residential 'sectors'. Falguni's family used to live in the village of Karor Lal Esan, in district Layyah, in Punjab, Pakistan. She was 13 years old at the time of the Partition.

The city of Faridabad is laid out such that the newer and older sectors are separated by National Highway 19 (known locally as Mathura Road), which runs right across the middle of the city. The sectors that lie west of the highway are the older parts of town, while the ones that lie on the east are newer, having been built in the 1970s and 1980s. Newer gated communities and bungalows have now come up on the easternmost edge of the city, on the east bank of the Agra canal. The Agra canal runs parallel to NH19 on what would have been considered the city's eastern border in the 1980s.

Once, while I was visiting Falguni, I got a call from Nani Masi. Nani Masi lived in Sector 3 of Faridabad's NIT, one of the neighbourhoods built specifically to resettle Partition refugees. For Falguni, the mere mention of NIT triggered a recall of the neighbourhood's history. She immediately said, 'That whole area has been built by our people.' She launched into a spontaneous narration of NIT Faridabad's history, remembering that it was nothing but a 'fly-infested jungle' before the arrival of Partition refugees. She also described the houses there as tiny and poorly constructed, the latter a direct reference to the fact that these neighbourhoods had quite literally been built by the very refugees whom they were intended to rehabilitate.

In a metropolis as old as Delhi, the land is a book that can be read by those who speak the languages of memory and history. Nowhere is the coalescence of memory more apparent than in NIT Faridabad. I became interested in the story of Faridabad due to my grandparent-like relationship with my key informant Pooran Chand. Pooran Chand was someone I happened to meet by chance. He was a friend of my Nani Masi's acquaintance. The two would often greet each other on evening walks in NIT Faridabad's Rose Garden. I was given an introduction and time enough for an hour-long interview, and the rest as they say is history. Pooran Chand very quickly became one of my key informants and I, in turn, became his occasional evening walk partner. Many a times, I would just drop by Rose Garden to spend the evening with him. Despite having started out as complete strangers, our rapport came to be quite familial. Our conversations ranged from the Partition, to politics, to even Indian cinema and the writings of Tagore. My conversations with Pooran Chand are peppered all through this book, especially Chapter 8.

Pooran Chand was part of a group of elderly male Frontier refugees who would gather in the park in the evenings. Some of them would join us later in the evening after attending a *satsang*.[8] The *satsang* setting provided some of them with a rare opportunity to converse in their mother tongue Pashto. Spending time with Pooran Chand allowed me to become friends with them, and I interviewed all of them, in turn. The result was a comprehensive insight into the life and history of this relatively close-knit community of Partition survivors.

Displacement, Rehabilitation and Remembrance: The Story of Faridabad

NIT Faridabad was allotted for the resettlement of roughly 50,000 refugees from the Frontier in 1949 (Jain 1998). Yet the story of how the Frontier refugees were allotted Faridabad is not a simple one. As numerous informants told me, refugees from the Frontier were initially housed in a massive refugee camp in Kurukshetra, Haryana. The government first offered them Alwar (Rajasthan) as a potential site of resettlement. Pooran Chand remembered that a small delegation of their community's elders had gone to inspect Alwar but had returned unsatisfied. 'People there [in Alwar] would do agriculture. And our people did not know this, generally,' Pooran Chand explained. As a community of traders, businessmen and zamindars, the Frontier refugees felt that Alwar's agrarian economy would be unsuitable to their way of life.

So, they refused and requested an alternative site. A year passed and nothing changed. The Frontier refugees were not allotted another town or district and continued to live in the slum-like conditions of their tented refugee camps. Meanwhile, other refugee communities around them had either been resettled or were awaiting official sanction to move to their allotted districts.

In the year 1949, the spontaneous outpouring of anger and resentment at this situation coalesced into a non-violent protest. Every day, all of the adult men in the Kurukshetra camp would take the train to Delhi and walk 15 kilometres from the railway station to the prime minister's residence at Teen Murti Bhavan (Figure 1.1) to stage a peaceful demonstration outside its gates. At night, they would take the train back to Kurukshetra, and return to the prime minister's residence the following morning. Pooran Chand described this as the first mass movement of independent India. He emotionally recalled making the same trek himself, at mid-day (along with other children) to give his father lunch, at the site of the demonstration. 'All the men-folk would sit outside Nehru-*kothi* and there would be a lot of sloganeering also,' Pooran Chand told me, his voice wavering and cracking with emotion.

Figure 1.1 Teen Murti Bhavan. Prime Minister Jawaharlal Nehru's former official residence.

Source: Photograph by author.

Pooran Chand always called Teen Murti Bhavan – Nehru's official residence – 'Nehru-*kothi*'. *Kothi* is the Hindi word for mansion or bungalow and has rustic connotations. Today, Teen Murti Bhavan houses a museum, a planetarium and one of Delhi's most well-stocked research libraries. During my fieldwork, I spent a considerable amount of my time studying in the library. There was something surreal about driving through the very gates outside which Pooran Chand and his community had protested, all those years ago.

The demonstration outside Nehru's residence continued for several days. Pooran Chand remembered how they would see officials helping Nehru enter and exit the premises through a side-gate in order to avoid dealing with the protestors. Eventually, Nehru gave in to the demonstration and agreed to a meeting. There they made their grievances with Alwar known to the prime minister. In turn they were suggested three options in and around Delhi: Kalkaji Mandir, Bahadurgarh and Faridabad. After surveying all three places, the community's leaders picked Faridabad. Pooran Chand said that they found the other two places rocky and barren. Kalkaji Mandir, or Nehru Place as it is known today, is now a booming financial district; a significant improvement on the rocky landscape that the Frontier refugees surveyed. Remembering the reason they picked Faridabad, Pooran Chand said:

> So then they finally came to Faridabad, after a lot of wandering. So, in Faridabad [there were] mango trees, this bus stop is there *na* [*indicates with his hand*], here the trees were thick like a roof of trees, or a bridge. Meaning trees, and in our area trees were scanty, so they [elders/ leaders] said [*voice wavers with emotion*] this place is very nice. The thinking was different at that time.

This story of how the Frontier refugees were allotted Faridabad was on the lips of everyone in Pooran Chand's group of friends. But time has a strange sense of irony. Faridabad's landscape today is an entirely different story. Large-scale deforestation in and around the city has turned it into a hot, dusty, desert-like town. I wonder what the ancestors would make of contemporary Faridabad....

What unfolded in Faridabad was nothing short of an exciting experiment in community-based urban development. Prime Minister Nehru and President Dr Rajendra Prasad were both active members of the Faridabad Development Board. This New Industrial Township of Faridabad was developed with a spirit of cooperative federalism and included the consent of the local community leaders in almost all decisions (Jain 1998). As Pooran Chand told me numerous times, and as Jain too notes, the leaders of the Frontier refugees were principled men who were quick to block any decision that might pose a detriment to their people. They took an active part in decisions on the crucial subjects of housing and employment. Initially, due to a lack of employment opportunities in Faridabad, refugees were engaged as construction labourers. Some of the aforementioned neighbourhoods built in Delhi to resettle Partition refugees were built by refugees from the Frontier. Thus, Partition refugees were engaged in the work of their own resettlement and, through it, found a sense of solidarity as they came to be involved in each other's rehabilitation.

Pooran Chand remembered those days of hard labour often. He also remembered how Nehru's friendship with Khan Abdul Ghaffar Khan had translated into an affection for the Frontier refugees. This was reflected in Nehru's decision to pay the refugees bonus wages for their labour:

> So for this [employment] what the government did was, all the colonies that were built in Delhi, Lajpat Nagar, Malviya Nagar, Sarojini Nagar, all of these houses were built by our people. They would take us from here in trucks, for free, to work. They would take us free. So they would bring us back for free also and for that we would get Rs 1.5, Re 1 we would get as a bonus from the government.

With an eye on their long-term rehabilitation, the Faridabad Development Board instituted a monthly instalment plan that would allow the refugees to own the houses they were building in Faridabad. The housing plots were 235 square yards each and were priced at INR 1,800, which was collected in the form of monthly instalments of INR 6 over the course of 25 years (Jain 1998). Today, INR 1,800 is worth roughly USD 22.

Frontier refugees were initially paid INR 2.5 for a day's work. Eventually, after some time the INR 1 bonus was withdrawn. This led to the beginning of another agitation, as people stated their inability to pay the INR 6 monthly instalment (Jain 1998). Remembering their destitution at the time, Pooran Chand said, 'We could not pay that amount also.' Some families stopped paying their instalments altogether, effectively becoming squatters on their own property. Matters escalated to the point where a police officer sent to execute the court's eviction order was lynched by a mob of refugees.

> There was a big agitation and the courts also intervened, sent an inspector…. To forcefully evict people. So the policeman and a crowd clashed against each other. People took the policeman's pistol and then hit him…. This happened in 1959, 60. The Inspector died and 2–3 of our people died also. This is an old incident…. In those days we had a lot of unity. If anything was happening to anyone, a crowd would gather instantly.

Explaining the reason for their unity, Pooran Chand said that because the Frontier refugees would only marry among themselves, they were not just neighbours, they were also kin. With intricate kinship networks running all through these residential blocks, it did not take long for the entire community to unite when their interests were threatened.

These memories of their confrontations with the state reveal a memory of un-belonging, a reminder of their displacement and *foreignness*. Additionally, these memories comprise a narrative that invests the collective identity of their community with a moral content. It is in these moments of confrontation with the state – in protesting outside the prime minister's residence and squatting while defaulting on monthly instalments – that the Frontier refugees ascribe moral attributes to their community. This community is described not in terms of common interests but through the more enthralling discourse of a shared kinship. The use of the metaphor of family imbues a compelling moral content to their politics (Chatterjee 2004; Herzfeld 1992).

Partha Chatterjee (2004: 57) writes that this process is a key principle of the 'politics of the governed'. He argues that it is important to pay attention to the way political society[9] is positioned in relation to the 'legal-political forms of the modern state'. Therefore, he notes that 'to effectively make its claim in political society, a population group produced by governmentality must be invested with the moral content of community' (74). Significantly, the Partition survivors of Faridabad saw these protests as a continuation of the legacy of Khan Abdul Ghaffar Khan and his Khudai Khidmatgars. In Faridabad, the air was thick with fond memories of Khan Abdul Ghaffar Khan, a kindly spectre that overshadowed every conversation.

The Memory of Badshah Khan: Fieldwork in the Shadow of B. K. Hospital

Rose Garden, the place where I would meet Pooran Chand and his friends, was located just around the corner from B. K. General Hospital, Faridabad's civil district hospital. B. K. Hospital and its adjoining B. K. Chowk (traffic square or roundabout) mark the area's Partition-era connection to the Frontier. B. K. is an acronym for Badshah Khan, which along with Bacha Khan and Frontier Gandhi are some of the nicknames that Khan Abdul Ghaffar Khan accumulated over a half-century long engagement with civil disobedience. Born in Peshawar, Khan Abdul Ghaffar Khan was a Congress leader and Gandhian freedom fighter. Khan was an important part of the struggle against British colonialism. Defying the racial stereotype of the Pathans as irrational, violent and volatile people, Khan organised the Pathans of NWFP into a disciplined, non-violent anti-colonial movement (Banerjee 2003). His organisations, the Khudai Khidmatgars (servants of god) or *red shirts*, drew their inspiration from Mahatma Gandhi's politics of non-violent resistance, a collaboration that ultimately earned him the title Frontier Gandhi. Khan and his followers refused to accept the Frontier's integration into Pakistan and continued to campaign for an independent Pathanistan (a nation for Pathans) even after Independence (Banerjee 2003).

As I discovered during my time in Faridabad, B. K. Hospital's semantically transparent place name was the portal to a sea of memories. As Pooran Chand told me:

The meaning of Badshah Khan is that he was the King of Khans. Khans would call him Badshah Khan, because all the Pathans there [Frontier] were called Khan. So because of that B. K. Hospital they named Badshah Khan. They have kept a photo there, with Nehru, they inaugurated it on 5 June 1951. I was standing there.

Pooran Chand's memory of the date was so accurate that it helped me find a newspaper report of the hospital's inauguration, in *The Hindu's* newspaper archives. B. K. Hospital was inaugurated by Khan Abdul Ghaffar Khan and Prime Minister Nehru on 5 June 1951. Khan was in India at the time for medical reasons, having been released on bail by Pakistan (*The Hindu* 1951).

When I later told Pooran Chand that I had found this newspaper report, he said that he could still remember that day vividly. He had been a part of the large crowd that had gathered to welcome Badshah Khan. Pooran Chand's eyes filled with tears as he remembered seeing Badshah Khan in the flesh. In over a year of hanging out with him, I never once heard him take Badshah Khan's name without a crack in his voice and a lump in his throat.

Badshah Khan's memory continues to touch a raw nerve with this generation of people. In December 2017, Pooran Chand told me that there had been a massive controversy here when, a few months back, the municipality had tried to drop the 'B. K.' from the hospital's name. This had been opposed by the elders in large numbers, some of whom even wrote to the municipality in protest. Pooran Chand said that the authorities had dropped the 'B. K.' from the name because none of them had any idea what it stood for. Instead, they were puzzled that unlike other government hospitals in Haryana which are simply called District Civil Hospital, this one was called 'B. K.' The name change was their attempt at the imposition of bureaucratic uniformity. However, it was overturned after vociferous protests from the elders of the community.

In NIT Faridabad, people still remember and revere Badshah Khan. In fact, it was impossible to ever have a private conversation about him in Rose Garden. The very mention of Badshah Khan would pique the interest of anyone within earshot, making them enthusiastically join the conversation. People remembered having seen the Khudai Khidmatgars marching down the streets of Bannu and Dera Ismail Khan – in their famous red shirts – in the run-up to Independence. There was immense respect here, yes, but also a distinct feeling of surprise at the Pathan turning to non-violent resistance. This can be observed in the conversation here.

Interviewer [PK]: But he was very famous, and he had an immense amount of influence.

Pooran Chand [PC]: That is because [*voice cracks with emotion*] he went to jail a lot, and one time, in our area there is a Haripur [town], in Hazara. Hazara is a district, it [Haripur] is a tehsil of that. There he [Badshah Khan] had organised a session of the Congress. All the leaders of the Congress, this Nehru and all of them had come there. In Haripur, Frontier.

AA [a friend of PC sitting beside us spontaneously joins the conversation]: Haripur Hazara [*nods*].

PC: Yes.

AA: It is a mountainous region.

PC: Organising a session there is not an easy thing. All the Pathans. One, he showed them [the Congress] that all the Pathans are my followers. No one made any trouble. And this is not a very old incident, I am unable to remember the year, must be 1938–39 only.

This surprise at the Pathan turning to non-violent resistance comes across quite strongly in the Congress' dealings with Badshah Khan and the Khudai Khidmatgars, especially in Nehru and Gandhi's private deliberations on the success of the Khudai Khidmatgars. What also comes across is a distrust of the durability of this turn to non-violent resistance. Both are a product of orientalist stereotypes of the Pathans as a 'dim-witted' and violent community (Banerjee 2003). Yet, this distrust is completely absent in the memories of Frontier refugees. The people of Pooran Chand's generation proudly remember Badshah Khan's commitment to non-violence and his desire for Pathanistan: a sovereign nation state of Pathans, unaffiliated with the ethnonationalist Partition of South Asia.

Pooran Chand remembers how a referendum was conducted in the Frontier Province to give people the chance to decide whether they wanted the Frontier to be a part of India or Pakistan, after the Partition. Badshah Khan as well as the then Congress-led provincial government of the Frontier Province (with Badshah Khan's brother as chief minister) called for a boycott of the referendum, deeming it an unfair proposition. The boycott, along with aggressive campaigning by the Muslim League in favour of Pakistan, led to the Frontier voting in favour of Pakistan (Banerjee 2003; Jain 1998). The result was a series of communal flare-ups in the province, followed by the eventual exodus of Hindus and Sikhs.

Remembering the boycott, Pooran Chand lamented that Badshah Khan had not raised the demand for Pathanistan louder. All of Pooran Chand's friends remembered the rigging of the referendum. The dream of Pathanistan resonates with this generation even today, perhaps fuelled by the bitter memories of what happened instead. As Pooran Chand recalls:

> I do not know what would have happened. But I mean to say that we could have stayed there safely, because Muslims – Britishers had a habit of practicing divide and rule…. And all of us Hindu people, were taken forcefully to vote for that [Pakistan], they did not have proper voting anywhere. Partition, a line was drawn.

These memories question the conditions under which the Frontier was lumped with Pakistan for geopolitical convenience. Mukulika Banerjee notes that according to conventional logic, the Frontier, with its 96 per cent Muslim population, would be the last place where one would hope to find contestations against belonging in Pakistan. But in the run-up to the Partition, Badshah Khan and the Khudai Khidmatgars emphasised their ideological identification with the Congress, making light of their geographical contiguity with Pakistan (Banerjee 2003). Till as late as the 1990s, Khudai Khidmatgars continued to argue that if East and West Pakistan could be separated by the breadth of India, then the Frontier too could be a part of India while being geographically separated from it (31). The formulation of such claims also reveals the Frontier's position on the peripheries of the ethnonationalist divide. As

Banerjee writes, 'A frontier cannot be easily Partitioned because its very nature as a region of exchange does not allow it' (33).

Following the Partition, Badshah Khan continued his campaign for an independent Pathanistan. Badshah Khan and the Khudai Khidmatgars were branded traitors by the Pakistani government and spent more years in jail after Independence than they did under the British (Banerjee 2003). The Khudai Khidmatgar movement eventually petered out, leaving behind only a mirage of what might have been.

A Shrine to Martyrdom: The Story of the Gurdwara Shahidane Gujrat Train

Just as the B. K. Hospital and Chowk brought to the fore the bittersweet memories of Badshah Khan, a more sombre memory was evoked by the nearby Gurdwara Shahidane Gujrat Train. This *gurdwara* (Sikh place of worship) was built in NIT Faridabad in the 1950s to memorialise the 'martyrdom' of those who died in the Gujrat train massacre. The *gurdwara*'s name literally translates to 'gurdwara of the Gujrat train martyrs'. The Gujrat train massacre gets its name from the Gujrat Railway Station in Pakistan. This is not to be confused with the state of Gujarat in India. In January 1948, a train full of Frontier refugees bound for India was massacred at this station. The killing was accompanied by the abduction of Hindu and Sikh women.

According to Jain (1998: 78), the train left Bannu on 10 January and was attacked two days later, on the 12th, while waiting for a signal at Gujrat Railway Station in Pakistan. The massacre of this train was even noted in a diplomatic cable from Nehru to the Pakistani Prime Minister Liaquat Ali Khan. Dated 15 January 1948, the diplomatic cable reads as follows:

In the attack in Gujrat on the train carrying Hindu and Sikh refugees by tribesmen and Muslim refugees, sixty-one Indian soldiers fought gallantly until they ran out of ammunition and a large number of Hindu and Sikhs were killed. Of 2400 people in the train only 700 have arrived in Gujranwala [Pakistan] of whom a high proportion have been seriously injured. It is significant that these do not include any women who are reported to have been abducted *en masse*. I am informed that of the 1700, of whom there is no trace yet, the bulk have been killed, wounded or kidnapped. (Diplomatic cable[10] from Jawaharlal Nehru to Liaquat Ali Khan, quoted in Jain [1998: 14])

The memory of this event is as visceral as that of Badshah Khan. Everyone from Pooran Chand's generation was aware of the tragic event memorialised by the *gurdwara*'s semantically transparent name. During one of the many evenings I spent in Rose Garden, I was introduced by Pooran Chand to Mohan Lal. Mohan Lal was of Pooran Chand's age and hailed from the town of Bannu. Mohan Lal had many fond memories of Bannu and considered it the 'Switzerland' of this region, a crown jewel of sorts. Mohan Lal also had a personal link to the history of the Gujrat train, as not only had the train originated from Bannu, but his paternal uncle was travelling by that train and witnessed the massacre.

Mohan Lal: A very sad incident had taken place during that time. Gujrat train of 10 Number is what we call it. That, approximately 80 per cent people had been killed by Muslims. 'Get down!', they got down … the people; people hid under the corpses. My *chachaji* [father's brother] had told me this, he was in that train. And the cream of our city was in that train. The people who were quite rich. We were not that rich but in that the city's rich people were mostly there, the rich people of our city had come by it.

Interviewer [PK]: All of them were in that train?

ML: They were all killed, 80 per cent people. After that the few who survived came to Faridabad, their memorial is in Faridabad even today. [A] Gurdwara in 5 number [sector] is there by the name of Gujrat Train Gurdwara.

PK: It's been named Gujrat Train Gurdwara only?

ML: Yes, that train was of number 10, it was a train of 10 number. It's called the 10 number train.

Chetan [seated beside us, joins the conversation]: It was of the date 10 [January 1948]. That means the date of the train was 10, so….

Figures 1.2a and 1.2b   The Gurdwara Shahidane Gujrat Train in Sector 5, NIT, Faridabad.

Source: Photographs by author.

This *gurdwara* (Figures 1.2a and 1.2b) not only memorialises the victims of the Gujrat train massacre but in a larger sense also serves as a memorial to all those who died during the Partition. I emphasise the latter due to the fact that until the inauguration of the Partition Museum in Amritsar in August 2017, India did not have a single official museum, monument or memorial dedicated to the memory of the victims of the Partition (Butalia 2000). In the absence of state memorials, sites of memory such as the Gurdwara Shahidane Gujrat Train have long filled this vacuum.

It is in this context that the use of the word *shahidane* in the *gurdwara's* name becomes interesting. The word *shahidane* translates to 'martyrs of'. This memorialisation of the victims of Partition violence as 'martyrs' of the nation is evocative of a larger discourse of sacrifice. As I argue in Chapter 4, this turn to the discourse of sacrifice is a form of theodicy that seeks to rationalise the 'uselessness' out of their suffering. Through the turn to the discourse of martyrdom, their suffering is presented as a heroic act of sacrifice performed in service of the Hindu nation. What makes this theodicical discourse of sacrifice doubly interesting in the case of this *gurdwara* is its status as an active place of worship: the performance of a literal theodicy. In Chapter 9 I connect this discourse of sacrifice and heroic martyrdom to victimhood and the thirst for vengeance.

Conclusion

I began this chapter by reflecting on ethnography as a relational practice that is predicated on listening to one's ancestors. The time I spent conducting fieldwork in Faridabad, I learnt, was itself folded within traditional practices of remembrance. One evening, while talking to my informant Chetan, I learnt that so much of the knowledge I was absorbing from these elders had been passed down to them by their elders. Chetan, for example, was just 3 years old at the time of the Partition. He did not have any substantial memories of the Partition and whatever he knew now had been learnt from talking to his elders, our shared ancestors. One evening, while we were sitting together on a bench in Rose Garden and discussing the progress of my fieldwork, he smiled and said, 'We too would listen to our elders like this, at the age of 12 years, 15 years, we would sit with them at night.' You and I are similar, he meant to say. And for a moment, I pictured Chetan as a teenager sitting cross-legged beside his elders, listening to their stories about the Partition and the Frontier. This was a moment that seemed to place my ethnographic practice within our community's history. That is, by listening to these memories I was participating in a larger culture of memory.

While Pierre Nora (1992) perceived the death of memory in the construction of sites of memory, my fieldwork in Faridabad suggested that the opposite was true. That is, Faridabad as a *millieux* of memory served not to diminish the memory of the Partition but to amplify it. In Faridabad, as in Delhi as a whole, the land itself remembers. Meeting my informants just a few hundred metres away from Badshah Khan Hospital made it impossible to ignore the resonance of Khan Abdul Ghaffar Khan's memory among this community. Similarly, the Gurdwara

Shahidane Gujarat Train was both a product of and a contributor to the discourse of sacrifice I observed in the narratives of my informants (see Chapter 4). These places were evocative of established grammars of remembrance. In fact, it is precisely because buildings and places evoke individual and collective practices of remembrance that they earn the distinction of 'intimate enemies' (although 'proximate' is more apt) in times of ethnic conflict (Bevan 2006).

In recent times, the Bharatiya Janata Party (BJP) has led a nationwide campaign to build grand statues to Hindu cultural icons such as Lord Ram, Emperor Shivaji, Prithviraj Chauhan, Maharana Pratap and Sardar Patel. The BJP has also sought to convert several (often 'Muslim-sounding') place names to those derived from Hindu mythology and 'pre-Islamic' history. Thus, Gurgaon has become Gurugram (*India Today* 2016); Allahabad, Prayagraj (V. Pandey 2018); Faizabad district, Ayodhya (R. Ahmad 2018); and the Mughalsarai Junction Railway Station, Deen Dayal Upadhyay Junction (R. Ahmad 2018; V. Pandey 2018). In the case of Delhi's famous Qutub Minar mosque, this has involved a literal conversion of the monument through the performance of a *yajna*, a Hindu purification ritual (Rajagopalan 2011). Meanwhile, a 'Grand Temple' to the Hindu deity Lord Ram is currently under construction, with the assent of the Indian Supreme Court – a meek surrender to majoritarianism (Ayyub 2019a) – at the site of the Mughal-era Babri Masjid (mosque) that the Hindu Right demolished on 6 December 1992 (van der Veer 1994).

Here, the aspiration for 'development' is expressed not through real material work or social justice but rather through the 'invention of tradition' (Hobsbawm 2000) – expressing continuity with an imagined past; and 'restorative nostalgia' (Boym 2001) – a desire to rebuild or return to a romanticised past. These place names and statues seek to 'restore' the Indian landscape to an imagined 'Hindu golden age', creating the Hindu Rashtra as 'facts on the ground'.

But the politics of Hindu nationalism aside, in my fieldwork, I encountered numerous such scattered places and place names that evoked the memory of the Partition. For example, my fieldwork also took me to Palwal, a town 30 kilometres south of Faridabad, on the road to Agra. In the years following the Partition, a number of refugees from the rural areas of district Dera Ghazi Khan (including my maternal grandmother's family) were resettled in Palwal. Even today, Palwal's main market is called 'Camp Market', a quiet reminder of its history as a Partition-era refugee camp.

On the other side of the border, Lahore's Sir Ganga Ram Hospital (built in 1921) is a famous example of the same. The hospital is named after its benefactor Sir Ganga Ram Aggarwal, who was the executive engineer and town planner of Lahore for the British government, before the Partition (Tikekar 2005). Following the near complete eviction of Hindus from the Pakistani half of Punjab, places like Lahore's Sir Ganga Ram Hospital memorialise a kind of syncretism which seems inconceivable in South Asia today.

Notes

1   This is embodied by the work of Ruth Behar (1996); Keith Basso (1970, 1988, 1996); and Charles Briggs (1986), to name but a few.

2   Although, the two can almost never be cleanly separated in this manner, which is beside the point for now.

3   Frykenberg's (1986) volume *Delhi Through the Ages* – of which Datta's chapter is a part – compiles the history of Delhi through the centuries.

4   A steel or cast-iron bracelet worn by most Sikhs. It is a sacred symbol and a sign of one's initiation into the *khalsa*.

5   Karva Chauth is a Hindu ritual observed by married women where they observe a fast from sunrise to sunset to pray for their husband's long and prosperous life. The fast is broken only after the woman observing the fast has seen the rising moon through a sieve, followed by her husband's face. In the Derawali (or more broadly, Saraiki) variation of this ritual, a hollowed-out *roti* (flat-bread) is used instead of a sieve.

6   Small oil lamp.

7   Any quotation not accompanied by a formal citation is taken from interviews conducted by the author.

8   A small religious (or spiritual) congregation that sings devotional songs and discusses scripture.

9   Partha Chatterjee (2004) draws a distinction between 'civil society' and 'political society'. According to him, 'civil society' – while not of the state – is led by elites and is organised. He writes, 'Civil society then,

restricted to a small section of culturally equipped citizens, represents in countries like India the high ground of modernity' (41). By contrast, 'political society' lacks this organised and formalised character and is thereby more difficult for the state to manage. Although the members of political society are notionally citizens of the state, the relationship they share with the state may not be one envisaged by the constitution (38). Inhabiting the margins of society – often even in the realms of 'illegality' (as the Frontier refugees, in the above instance) – the members of political society are not considered members of civil society by the institutions of the state, nor treated as such. Yet, the state is unable to ignore them. For Chatterjee, this distinction between civil and political society was necessitated by the reality of stark socio-economic inequalities in countries like India. As he observed, 'Most of the inhabitants of India are only tenuously, and even then ambiguously and contextually, rights-bearing citizens in the sense imagined by the constitution' (38). His idea of political society then attempts to observe the specificities of the political actions of the disprivileged and how they are in turn managed by the state.

10 With its precise round numbers, this diplomatic cable is a prime example of what Gyanendra Pandey (2001) describes as the imprint of rumour. See Chapter 6.

Part II

Sacrifice and Suffering
The *Purusharth* of Refugees

2

Stories of *Purusharth*

Hard work is a very big thing. We have worked hard, quite a lot…. We have worked quite hard for our earning. We are getting the benefit of it even today, even today we are reaping it.

—Mahendar

Hard Work, Karma and Theodicy

'Whatever you write, you should focus on the achievements, that what all have been the achievements of our community. If you write about suffering, then your [book] might not be cleared. That might rub someone the wrong way,' Jaideep advised me. On that chilly February morning, Jaideep, Bhanwarilal and I had found ourselves serendipitously congregating in Bhanwarilal's bungalow in Mianwali Nagar, Delhi. Cups of tea and a plate of biscuits in hand, we had decided to sit on the terrace to bask in the weak wintry sunshine.

Bhanwarilal, one of my key informants, had just recovered from a severe bout of ill health. Jaideep and I had both happened to drop by at the same time, to check in on him. This was the first time I was meeting Jaideep. He was a neighbour and a distant relative of Bhanwarilal's. At roughly 60 years of age, Jaideep, like my parents, was part of the second generation of Partition survivors. His parents had witnessed the Partition first-hand and had moved to Delhi from Mianwali in 1947.

Thus, Jaideep took a natural interest in my work. His advice to me, to focus on the 'achievements' of Partition survivors, came out of an interest in the narrative frame of my research. I tried to deflect his insistence by telling him simply ignoring suffering does not mean that it did not happen. 'Not that.… Suffering, in reality, now no one wants to read about it. You focus on the achievements – that what all they have built after Partition,' Jaideep replied, doubling down on his insistence.

Jaideep's presence was an interesting addition to my conversation with Bhanwarilal. Jaideep had begun our conversation about the Partition by asking me what I thought was the reason for the Partition. When I clarified that my project is ethnographic and not a historiographical analysis meant to apportion blame, Jaideep began to give us his own answer. Using the analogy of a family, Jaideep explained that the most common reason for the division of families are brothers (or sibling rivalries). Jaideep then went on to state a popular Hindu nationalist conspiracy theory that alleges that Jawaharlal Nehru, Mohammed Ali Jinnah and Sheikh Abdullah were all sons of Motilal Nehru and were thereby half-brothers. This conspiracy theory alleges that Motilal Nehru made a pact with the British to split British India into three portions, to be inherited in turn by each son: India for Jawaharlal Nehru, Pakistan for Jinnah and Jammu and Kashmir for Sheikh Abdullah. This is a very popular conspiracy theory among middle-class Hindu nationalists in Delhi and one I encountered numerous times in my fieldwork. Ultimately, this conspiracy theory seeks to portray the Nehru–Gandhi family (and the Congress party by extension) as power-hungry dynasts who divided the country for personal gain. As Gangaram – whom we meet in Chapter 8 – said, the Partition was simply a case of 'gaddi ki bhook' (the hunger for high-office). This conspiracy theory also implicitly articulates the RSS view that Gandhi's non-violent anti-colonial movement was little more than a grandly staged 'drama'.

Before Jaideep could finish retelling this alternative history, he was interrupted first by me and then by Bhanwarilal. While I highlighted the obvious flaw that Motilal Nehru and Jinnah were only 14 years apart and were therefore extremely unlikely to be father and son (in addition to their respective family trees being remarkably well-documented by historians), Bhanwarilal used sarcasm and the authority of firsthand experience to denounce Jaideep's argument.

Beginning by reminding Jaideep of Sheikh Abdullah's negligible role in the Independence movement and Partition, Bhanwarilal launched into a spectacular rant about the 'sacrifices' of Punjabi refugees. He began by speaking in an angry and fast Mianwali-*boli* that later mellowed into Hindi. 'Partition te sirf jede Punjab da hoya' (only our Punjab was partitioned), Bhanwarilal practically spat out the words. In a direct jibe at Jaideep – one that I had also heard him use for contemporary Indian politicians on occasion – Bhanwarilal said that the people here, in India today, do not know anything about the Partition. They never suffered because of it. He then continued:

> Only Punjabis know what we have undergone and what all *sacrifices* we have made. Murders took place, women jumped into wells to commit suicide, we cut off the heads of our daughters ourselves. But, on the other hand we also feel we came at a good time. There we would have stayed among Muslims as a minority. Although we were a minority, we would *dominate* them. All the financial power was ours. And what did we get here? What *compensation* did we get here? Land in place of land! We had 68 acres of our own there and here the whole Mianwali Nagar has been settled on 52 acres. Even in compensation they [government] said if you have [assets worth more than] Rs 10,000 then you will get 10,000. Ours was not worth 10,000 so we got nothing for that. We got nothing in compensation. We got agricultural land in Ambala, what would we do with that? There [in Pakistan] we had Muslims, they would work the crops and give them to us. Here [Ambala] we had kept someone but he would instead give us a bill and no profit at all. We sold it [land] for a pittance.

Here, Bhanwarilal begins by talking about sacrifice and suffering but also lays emphasis on 'compensation' or reparations. This exchange between Jaideep, Bhanwarilal and myself encapsulates the broad contours of the theme that I focus on in this chapter and in Part II as a whole: sacrifice and stories of hard work. In the above exchange, while Jaideep describes the hard work of Punjabi refugees as their 'achievements', Bhanwarilal reframes this discourse as one of 'sacrifice'. For Bhanwarilal, the suffering endured by his people during the Partition constitutes a sacrifice to the nation. Bhanwarilal's understanding of the suffering entailed by the Partition includes the years of hardship that followed their displacement. Where Jaideep celebrates the latter as an 'achievement', imploring me to write about 'what all they have built after the Partition', Bhanwarilal sanctifies this story of hard work as a form of sacrifice. According to him, this sacrifice also merits compensation. What they both agree on is the need to be remembered as heroes and martyrs.

Bhanwarilal's use of the word 'sacrifice' captures an important nuance. The Punjabi refugee, in his narratives, was someone who not only laboured honestly and virtuously to overcome the poverty thrust upon *him* by the Partition but whose hardship constituted a sacrifice to the nation. As is evident in the brief quote above, the wealth that the Punjabi migrant had left behind in Pakistan, the relatives who had been killed along the way, the women relatives whose 'honour' and 'dignity' *he* had 'protected' by killing them with *his* own hands were all part of an immense sacrifice *he* had made for the nation. The Punjabi refugee in this construction is not just a hard-worker whose displacement has forced *him* into poverty but someone who has actively sacrificed *his* wealth and privilege for the nation's freedom. *He* is an unacknowledged martyr. Here, I deliberately use the word 'martyr' to draw on its archaic meaning of a person forced into suffering because of their religious beliefs. And, within this feeling of the lack of acknowledgement of one's sacrifice is the desire for adequate compensation; a perceived neglect which is related to a bubbling *ressentiment*.

At its core, this discourse rationalises the 'uselessness' out of their suffering and functions as a form of theodicy. As I have stated previously in the Introduction, theodicy attempts to render asymmetrical experiences with death, suffering and misfortune meaningful within a perceived social order: a *nomos* (Das 1997; Herzfeld 1992; Weber 1965, 2013). In describing my informants' discourse of sacrifice as a form of theodicy, I use the word in a metaphorical and secular sense, as an interpretive frame that attempts to address the enduring question of the meaning of death and suffering.

Emmanuel Levinas (1988) writes that the task of theodicy has been rendered more urgent by the bloody history of the twentieth century. Levinas argues that the twentieth century's history of horrific war and genocidal violence can only be described as one of 'useless suffering'. He states:

> This is the century that in thirty years has known two World wars, the totalitarianisms of the right and left, Hitlerism and Stalinism,

Hiroshima, the Gulag, and the genocides of Auschwitz and Cambodia. This is the century which is drawing to a close in the haunting memory of the return of everything signified by these barbaric names: suffering and evil are deliberately imposed, yet no reason sets limits to the exasperation of a reason become political and detached from all ethics. (Levinas 1988: 161–162)

As the single largest event of forced migration and retributive genocide in recorded history (Brass 2003b), the Partition of India sits squarely within the twentieth century's list of horrors. The senselessness and savagery of the violence unleashed during this period evades all attempts at stable rationalisation. And, it is an attempt to reach such a discourse, to rationalise the uselessness out of their suffering that many of my informants turn to the discourses of Hindu nationalism. Describing their suffering as 'sacrifice', branding the futility of death 'martyrdom', they sanctify their blood, tears and sweat by offering them upon the altar of Hindu nationalism. Embodying a particular pedagogy of pain, Partition survivors express the invisible scars of their displacement in a myriad ways to underline their belonging within the Hindu nation. They are not refugees petitioning the state for support but hard-workers of the Hindu nation. Their blood and sweat is the fact of their belonging; their hard work, a performative document of fortitude.

Therefore, it is important to define hard work and to locate it within Hindu philosophy. *Purusharth* (also spelt as *puruṣārtha*) is the Hindi or Sanskrit word my informants used to describe their hard work, stressing that they are not *sharanarthi*s (refugees) but *purusharthi*s (hard-workers). *Purusharth* occupies a central space within Hinduism and is intimately linked to the Brahmanical order of *varnashramadharma* (B. Singh 2020). The *varnashramadharma* connects a Hindu person's caste (*varna*) to the work and duties (*shrama* and *dharma*) they must perform in life (B. Singh 2020). In this way, *purusharth* is the semiotic sum of the fourfold values of Hinduism: *artha* (meaning/essence), *kama* (desire), *dharma* (duty or the right way of living) and *moksa* (enlightenment/emancipation) (B. Singh 2020; Devi 2009). In his work on the theology of Vaishnavism (a Hindu sect), Charis (1994) defines *purusharth* as the ultimate goal of one's life. On the other hand, while providing a cultural frame for understanding organisational behaviour in India, Jai Sinha (2002: 159) defines *purusharth* as 'constant efforts'. Concurrently, the Centre for South Asian Studies' (CEIAS) understanding of *puruṣārtha* as 'what concerns man' – which the CEIAS interprets as 'an Indian way of naming the field of social sciences' – has served as the inspiration for its long-running Puruṣārtha Collection: a series of multidisciplinary texts on Indian society.

The philosophy of *purusharth* is closely related to *karma*. By constructing persistent and sincere hard work (or 'struggle') as a virtue, *purusharth* reifies the karmic philosophy that 'one reaps that which one sows'. Weber's (2013) sociology of religion defined *karma* as a form of theodicy that provides a justification for good and bad fortune. After all, while theodicies attempt to render violence and suffering meaningful, they also provide explanations for good fortune (Mavelli 2016). Where the rationalisation of suffering is an attempt to answer the quintessentially human question of 'what did I do to deserve this?' justifications of good fortune are aimed at presenting it as 'legitimate fortune' (Mavelli 2016). In the words of Max Weber (2013: 271):

> The fortunate is seldom satisfied with the fact of being fortunate. Beyond this, he needs to know that he has a right to his good fortune. He wants to be convinced that he 'deserves' it, and above all, that he deserves it in comparison with others. He wishes to be allowed the belief that the less fortunate also merely experience his due. Good fortune thus wants to be 'legitimate' fortune.

Thus, my informants' stories of *purusharth* serve as karmic justifications for good fortune. Rich in moral instruction, these stories resemble modern-day fables. They express moral truths about the virtues of hard work. However, in the way that my informants deploy the term, acts of street-smartness are also routinely presented as *purusharth*. The conflation of these two seemingly contradictory terms serves a legitimising function, presenting the street-smartness of Partition survivors as 'virtuous hard work'. It reconstructs their desperate struggle for survival in the morally instructive discourse of a fable. The conflation of these two seemingly contradictory terms is an important part of the stories we encounter in this chapter.

Stories of *purusharth* are part of how Partition survivors (especially those from Punjab) express and identify with their status as middle-class Hindu citizens of India. These narratives are rich in comments that disavow their status as refugees, as 'passive victims' dependent on the 'charity' of the state. Instead, by emphasising how hard they worked to rebuild their lives, they not only express agency but also position themselves as citizens deserving of their place within the state. In doing so, this discourse presents their recovery from poverty as a story of social mobility. These stories help explain their own unusually 'good fortune' in the context of India's stark economic inequality. Implicit within this discourse is a memory of unbelonging within India, during the months and years immediately following the Partition. In a climate where they were seen as outsiders, as 'refugees' availing the 'charity' of the Indian state, the insistence on being seen as a hard-worker rather than a refugee, was a way of asserting their belonging within the new nation.

This dichotomy between hard-workers and refugees is illustrated in the following conversation I had with Bhanwarilal on 18 August 2017. Here, Bhanwarilal explains the meaning of the words *sharanarthi* (refugee) and *purusharthi* to me.

Interviewer [PK]: Ok, so I want to ask you one more thing. Going back to the Partition, you were saying *sharan*…. Did the people of Haryana [Haryanvi] call you *sharaniya*…?

B: *Sharanarthi.*

PK: [*Repeating it*] *Sharanarthi.*

B: Haryanvi did not say that. When we first came, everyone used to say they are *sharanarthi*. So after being called *sharanarthi,* in many places people started protesting [figuratively]. We started saying that we are not *sharanarthi*, we are *purusharthi*.

PK: What does *purusharthi* mean?

B: We are earning through our *purusharth*. We are earning through our hard work ['mehnat']. We are hard-working people. *Sharanarthi* is if we came to seek refuge ['sharan'] then *sharanarthi* [refugee]; [*speaking forcefully*] we are not that. We are recovering through our *purusharth,* we are recovering through our hard work. What refuge did they give us? Did they give us their houses? Or did they give us employment? We sat on the streets and sold rice, we sat on the streets and sold blankets, we sat on the streets and worked, and it is through that, that we have recovered. So we have done our *purusharth*, we have worked hard ourselves. There is a lot of difference between *sharanarthi* and *purusharthi*.

PK: So they are opposites of a sort?

B: Yes, that is why, if you actually see, the people who came, so they had been labelled *sharanarthi* but they were not *sharanarthi*, they were *purusharthi*. Using their *purusharth* they learnt to stand on their feet on their own. Today, if you consider we had a house there, 4 houses or 10 houses, whatever, we had to abandon them. So after coming here, we rebuilt them through our own hard work. We did not ask them for anything. Did not ask anything from the government. We used our hard work to build our house. Established ourselves again through our hard work. Because ours was not a case of dependence like others who came in the beginning and got a room somewhere or two room flats were allotted to refugees as and when refugees came, they got and then later they [government] said alright lets regularise them, just deposit a little money. These were regularised at a cheap rate and they got. 90 per cent or 80 per cent people that are there, they stood on their own *purusharth*. 10–20 per cent were there [for] whom government did, but which government could help everyone? The whole of the *pranth* [region] had got up from there and come here. And they went and settled in all of Hindustan [India], it was not like they settled only in Delhi so they could turn Delhi into a colony and give it to them. They went and spread in the whole of Hindustan. Wherever whoever got work they took it. And there they supported themselves, made a name for themselves, that look we did our hard work and made an identity for ourselves. We had 4 houses, 10 houses, adding 2–2 we rebuilt it.... How much did Government do? Nothing. The people who came, brought their luck with them, government did nothing special for them. This is definitely there that when Partition happened, it happened on our corpses. Happened on our property. We lost it all and came. The people who were here, what did they lose? They lost nothing. They have not lost anything.... This is why the people who came here they stood back up on their own feet, through their hard work, stood up through their honesty. Stood up through *purusharth*.

Bhanwarilal begins by juxtaposing refugees and hard-workers. While he consistently harps on the hard-working nature of Partition survivors, he also questions what India did for his people. When framed against rhetorical questions such as 'What refuge did they give us?' the narrative of hard work also becomes one of *ressentiment*. This is especially palpable towards the end when he asserts that the Partition 'happened on our corpses'. He contrasts this intimate suffering with that of the rest of the country, angrily observing that 'the people who were here, what did they lose? They lost nothing.'

In the way that Bhanwarilal recounts his suffering in order to establish the justness of his demand for compensation – a common feature of this and his other remarks in this chapter – his discourse is evocative of another aspect of Weberian theodicy. Weber (2013: 353) notes that the demand for 'just compensation' is a consequence of theodicy. While theodicy rationalises 'unjust suffering' and presents the cosmos as well-ordered and 'meaningful', the meaningfulness of the cosmos posits that 'unjust suffering' be rectified by 'just compensation', or justice (Weber 2013). This demand is a consequence of the belief that one inhabits a meaningful world overseen by a benevolent deity, one where unjust suffering is compensated appropriately.

This theodicy inevitably fails. This failure of theodicy leads to the feelings of hatred, envy and revenge – a self-righteous, moral outrage – known as *ressentiment* (Olick 2007; Simko 2012). Weber (1965: 110) understood *ressentiment* as a form of 'theodicy of the disprivileged', as an attempt by ordinary people to rationalise their (lack of) status in life (also see Olick 2007: 157). Disprivilege and suffering in the present is rationalised through the hope for 'future compensation' and/or the 'desire for vengeance' (Weber 1965: 110). Weber writes:

In this theodicy of the disprivileged, [*ressentiment*] the moralistic quest serves as a device for compensating a conscious or unconscious desire for vengeance. This is connected in its origin with the faith in compensation, since once a religious conception of compensation has arisen, suffering may take on the quality of the religiously meritorious, in view of the belief that it brings in its wake great hopes of future compensation. (110–111)

However, Weber goes on to claim that due to the individuated understanding of suffering in Hinduism and Buddhism, *ressentiment* is not found in the believers of these religions. I disagree. While Weber's view that Hinduism understands one's suffering as corrective punishment for the individual's 'sins' is correct, in the narratives of my informants, the Partition is seen as a singularly exceptional period of *collective* suffering. That is, the suffering of the Partition is seen as *collective*, arbitrary and incomparable. Consequently, its survivors are unable to justify this cataclysmic episode of *collective* suffering – the misfortunes of their and others' experience – by reference to their own past sins.

This failure of traditional Hindu theodicy results in the turn towards Hindu nationalism as a form of theodicy. As I show in Chapter 9, Hindu nationalism as a form of theodicy is substantially motivated by the desire for vengeance, a desire that is itself legitimised by a visceral narrative of victimhood. This narrative of a historically disprivileged Hindu nation finds its companion in the *ressentiment* of Partition survivors. A bubbling self-righteous outrage, their *ressentiment* is directed against not only those whom they hold responsible for their suffering – Muslims, the British (or Christians) and the leaders of the Congress party – but also all those who are seen to have *not-suffered*: the *unfairly* and *undeservingly* fortunate.

Folded within this refusal to be remembered as 'refugees' is also a resentment of the welfare state and welfarism in all its manifestations: a *ressentiment* of those who are seen to have been rewarded without suffering. Additionally, Partition survivors direct their *ressentiment* at even those generations born in India following the Partition. The latter are seen as the undeserving beneficiaries of the fruits accrued from the *purusharth* and sacrifices of Partition survivors. Bhanwarilal's remarks earlier in this chapter and in Chapter 4 and Mahendar's comments in the following section are good examples of the *ressentiment* that my informants feel against those who have not endured the Partition's suffering.

However, in the stories of *purusharth* I tell later in this chapter, readers will observe an inherent essentialism. These stories of hard work construct the Punjabi community as inherently different, as innately hard-working. This emphasis on *purusharth* is comparable to the self-stereotyping discourse of national character. In fact, *purusharth* is seen as the singular defining quality of the Punjabi refugee.

Herzfeld (1992) analogises conceptions of national character to the religious discourse of predestination.[1] Predestination is the Christian belief that all happenings on Earth follow the will of God and that this will is foreshadowed in the individual's soul or character. Similarly, the discourse of national character comprises a self-justifying, tautologous rhetoric wherein the 'character' of the nation is embodied in the blood of its citizens, evident in a history that is presented specifically in justification of the 'truth' of its national character (7–9). One observes the same impulse at work in these stories, as the Punjabi refugee is presented as innately hard-working, even as the Partition's hardship is seen to have made them hard-working. Their *purusharth* is paradoxically presented as both an innate quality and a product of recent experience.

Ultimately, these stories of sacrifice and *purusharth* comprise a masculine discourse (Anjali Roy 2019). Here, it is important for me to briefly clarify my use of masculine pronouns in some of the paragraphs in this section. My use of masculine pronouns is a conscious, political decision. It stems from the observation that these are stories told using masculine pronouns and that the main actors in these stories of *purusharth* are also always men. This is somewhat unsurprising considering that the *varnashramadharma* system to which the philosophy of *purusharth* is linked also provides a justification for (Brahman) patriarchal supremacy (B. Singh 2020).

Thus, stories of *purusharth* are essentially stories of men at work, or man-work. This idea of *purusharth* as 'man-work' is my own bilingual spin on the word's literal meaning. Although the word *purusharth* comes from Sanskrit, in Hindi the word *purush* means masculine or male. While the idea of *purusharth* is embedded in Hindu scripture, my characterisation of *purusharth* as man-work is both a bilingual pun and recognition of the masculine nature of this discourse. Ultimately, these stories of hard-working Punjabi men are stories of patriarchs who did all they could to take care of their families, including the sacrifice of women relatives.

The Man-Workers of Punjab

'What work did you do?' I asked Mahendar. At 81 years of age, Mahendar was one of the oldest members of the Arya Samaj in Dehradun. His friends Naagesh and Dilip, who were also 81 years of age, were with us in the room at the time, along with my grandaunt Anjali and Dilip's friend, Ashok. Aged 68, Ashok was not a Partition survivor. However, when Dilip had casually mentioned my research and the purpose of my brief trip to Dehradun, he had decided to tag along. Dilip had invited us all to congregate in his office in the Arya Samaj branch there. As a result, what I had initially foreseen as a series of back-to-back one-on-one conversations had effectively turned into a focus group discussion.

While Dilip, Mahendar and Naagesh respected each other's turns, preferring to be silent while another was telling their story, Ashok loved to chip in with his insights as and when he saw relevant. As someone who had grown up in the shadow of the Partition, these stories of hard work resonated with him deeply. When I posed my question to Mahendar, Dilip had just finished telling us about his family's journey and his memories of the Partition.

'Try to guess, what will a 12–13-year-old boy do?' Mahendar leaned in towards me, a mischievous glint in his eyes as he built up the suspense.

'Uncle [Dilip] was just telling us that he used to sell toffees in trains. Right?' I nodded my head slightly in Dilip's direction and received an affirming nod from him in return. During their initial days in India, Dilip had started selling toffees in the trains passing through the Ambala refugee camp. He had been 11–12 years old at the time and had had nothing else to do. This had seemed like a viable way of supplementing his family's income. His story was reflective of the abject poverty that their wealthy, land-owning family had been reduced to and of the near-mythical determination of Punjabi refugees to take on any kind of work available.

'You won't imagine!' Here Mahendar paused dramatically and launched into an Urdu couplet: 'Daana agar kuch martaba chaahe, mitta de apni asthi ko, mitta de apni asthi ko agar kuch martaba chaahe ke dana khwaab main milta hai gul o-gulzarta hai.' Mahendar then began to explain its meaning:

> A seed that you put in the soil will only blossom into a tree when it has buried itself in the soil; it will have to destroy itself. So we people have destroyed ourselves and started from zero. There is a thing that after many zeroes you get a one. We, Punjabi people who came, had a lot of self-confidence. Loads, even today. I am 80-plus. Even today I have the confidence that if you throw me out of the house, by evening I would have put together five to seven rupees.

Ashok agreed with Mahendar and offered his own interpretation of this phenomenon of Punjabi self-confidence.

> This is a very strong feature that their self-confidence and their determination power, that was really commendable. This, the area they were from there [in Pakistan], they would have toiled hard there before coming here. So this is a common feature there that when they came here, then in these people the ambition to become bold, determined.... See, what we call *sankalp shakti*, what we call determination power, that feature was extremely prominent in this community. And because of that, you see that refugees, the people who were called refugees, in those people you will see that how much ever they were suppressed, they rebounded that much higher.

Nodding enthusiastically in agreement with Ashok's Newtonian analogy, Mahendar said:

> In fact I will say that when people came from there [Pakistan], a kind of.... What do I say...? Maybe if we had remained in Pakistan then there would have been people to nurture us, family would have supported us, so maybe people would not have been able to do so much. Today there are so many children who are nurtured well in the home, and studies are also progressing, TV is also there, but they are

unable to do anything. They end up becoming useless. And us people, we came from there, no one was there to host us. Starting from zero, that is something else.

For Punjabi refugees, stories of *purusharth* are not merely stories of the hard work they did in the immediate aftermath of the Partition but stories that in their retellings have become part of the very essence of what it means to be Punjabi. This essentialism comprises a self-orientalising discourse. Often, as in the case of Ashok's dialogue above, the innately hard-working character of Punjabis is connected to the harshness of an agrarian life.

However, this conception of the Punjabi national character is also a tautologous construction. On the one hand, Punjabi refugees insist that Punjabis owe their innate self-confidence and determination to the harshness of their homeland. Yet, they present the Punjabi turn to *purusharth* as one necessitated by the experience of the Partition, of having been reduced to 'zero'. In support of the second, Mahendar furnishes the analogy of the seed. He analogises the Punjabi refugee to a seed such that it is *his* destiny to destroy himself – through *purusharth* – in order to reap the fruits of *his* labour.

Together, these examples show how the idea of national character functions as something of a predestination. National character – *purusharth* – is simultaneously the Punjabi's innate quality – his destiny – and a value learned in the face of adversity. Through an after-the-fact rationalisation that draws on a tautologous logic, the idea of national character functions as both a prophecy and an explanation for what transpired (Herzfeld 1992). This articulation of the *purusharthi* character of the Punjabi as both explanation and prophecy consistently recurs in the stories of my informants.

Mahendar's acknowledgement of his past privilege alongside his criticism of today's youth as 'useless' demonstrates how stories of hard work serve as a karmic rationalisation of inequality. His stories present him as a hard-working citizen worthy of the wealth he enjoys (and used to enjoy) in a starkly unequal society. He contrasts the worthiness of this wealth and privilege with that of today's youth by juxtaposing the 'uselessness' of this generation with the resourcefulness of his generation. By emphasising the self-made nature of his current survival and success, his stories serve to legitimise his past and current privilege.

When Mahendar remarks that today's youth is unable to achieve anything despite access to television (or technology, in general), education and a stable household, one detects a hint of *ressentiment*. His juxtaposition of the hardship of his own childhood with the luxuries available to the modern child betrays the *ressentiment* he feels towards those who have not had to suffer the hardship of the Partition. Here, the lack of suffering endured by the post-Partition generations is seen to have weakened them and also appears to disqualify them from the enjoyment of the comforts of modern life. That his own hard work is seen to exacerbate this inequality of suffering rankles him further.

Additionally, these stories possess a fable-like quality. The karmic justification of their privilege is a part of this. Rich in moral instruction about the virtues of *purusharth*, these stories represent attempts to overcome the chaotic, 'useless suffering' of the Partition through the construction of a *nomos* where good deeds accrue good fortune.

Mahendar's family migrated to India from Khushab, Pakistan, in 1947, at the height of Partition violence. They were forced to leave their home in the middle of the night, when news reached them of an arson attack on the town's Hindu burial ground. The people who worked and slept there, along with the priest in charge, were burnt alive. Standing on the roof of their house that night, Mahendar and his family saw the smoke from that fire. That night, they packed their belongings and left. They made their way from Khushab to the refugee camp in Sargodha with some difficulty. From there they boarded a goods train, which took five–seven days to cross the border into India and dropped them at Attari. From there, they went to a refugee camp in Kaithal, a small town in modern-day Haryana. Starting almost entirely from scratch in Kaithal, Mahendar's father did not let them eat the food being served in the refugee camps.

> Let me tell you one thing, that in all the [refugee] camps the government would serve free food, but our father – we stayed so many months in the camps – he did not let us eat there. Did not let us eat free food in the camp. I remember even today. During the day we would go to Gurgaon to get vegetables to sell there [Kaithal], we

would earn a full 2 rupees, and there we would put three bricks together, keep a pan on it and *rotis* would get cooked. So our father tried a !ot that we would not have to eat free food…. So during the day we have to earn, father said this. I will not let you eat for free. Whether you earn one rupee, or two rupees, you should earn during the day.

Shunning the charity of the state, Mahendar's father instead taught him the value of work. The first time Mahendar brought money home was through his father's help. His father purchased a crate of oranges from the wholesale market, set it beside a well-frequented road and told Mahendar to sell the whole crate. 'But how will I do this?' Mahendar asked him. 'Just sell it,' his father replied cryptically and left the scene. A man then approached Mahendar, asking to buy an orange. Mahendar instead offered to sell them only by the dozen. Ultimately, charmed by young Mahendar, the man bought two dozen oranges from him. And like that, Mahendar sold the whole crate of oranges.

Some days later, while they were still living in Kaithal, a family friend offered Mahendar a loan of INR 12 and a business opportunity: wholesale vegetable trading. Under this man's instruction, Mahendar began to make regular trips to the nearby town of Kurukshetra. Mahendar would get the last train to Kurukshetra and spend the night sleeping on the railway station there. Early in the morning he would visit the wholesale vegetable market (in order to get the best pick of vegetables) and spend the full INR 12 there, collecting a variety of fruits and vegetables. Transporting the sacks of vegetables either by rickshaw or a horse-carriage, Mahendar would then catch the 7 a.m. bus out of Kurukshetra and return to Kaithal by 8 a.m. There he would aggressively sell his stock in Kaithal's vegetable market and try to earn at least INR 14 from his sale. All this just for a profit of INR 2.

Mahendar chose work over school and plied his trade for a couple of years, while their family lived in Kaithal. Later, when his father's compensation claim came through, they were allotted land in Ambala. In Ambala, Mahendar resumed his schooling. However, his family was still far from financially secure and could not even afford to pay his school fees. Remembering their poverty, Mahendar said:

Every year my name was removed from school, every year I was scolded two-three times [for late payment of fees] and every year my fees was paid by a man from Uttar Pradesh. He gave me support. His name was Dr Bin Bihari Lal.

Dr Bin Bihari Lal was a dentist who lived in the neighbourhood. Mahendar had struck up an unlikely friendship with him on the streets and would greet him with a 'Ram, Ram' every morning, on his way to school. Dr Lal was passionate about education and supported Mahendar's schooling for a couple of years. However, things took an unlikely turn when the headmaster of Mahendar's school invited scholarship applications from the school's underprivileged students. The headmaster rejected Mahendar's application in the interview, citing Mahendar's neatly turned-out uniform. *Someone so neatly dressed could not possibly be poor*, the headmaster insinuated. However, for Mahendar, the shame of poverty had made it all the more necessary to be neatly turned out, a performative disavowal of his current status.

My dressing style has been tip top from the beginning. Even though we had been ruined, I had only one pair of clothes, I would wear the t-shirt, wash my shorts and iron it in the evening. We did not have an iron at home. My uncle's son had a dry-cleaning shop. So I had told him that before you close the iron for the night, at 10 or 9, give it to me. So I would go at 10, 9 and iron my clothes. Now when I would leave in the morning, it would look as if I was the son of a rich man with a nice pant-shirt.

With his scholarship application denied and no money at home to pay it with, Mahendar felt too ashamed to ask Dr Lal for the INR 2.5 he needed to pay his fees. It was then that a classmate advised him to start riding a cycle rickshaw at night. His initial reaction to this suggestion was one of shame. 'Will I not feel ashamed in riding this, I live inside the city after all?' Mahendar had asked his friend. 'If you feel ashamed then how will you study?' came the reply.

Swallowing his pride, Mahendar once again chose the path of *purusharth*. Mahendar's classmate put him in touch with a man who offered cycle rickshaws on hire. Mahendar then began to ride the rickshaw from 9 p.m. to midnight, two nights a week. He would keep his books with him on the rickshaw and read them underneath the street lights, whenever he got a chance.

> You won't believe, I would return exhausted at 12 in the night. It was winter then. You might not have gone to Ambala. In Ambala if you go to Ambala Cantonment, then beside Central Jail there is an incline, a climb. I have ridden up that with two people sitting in the rickshaw. I would not take one person alone…. I remember, even today, I had begun to sweat in winter. And even in the end of December I would often remove my shirt; that's how much I sweat.

At night, Mahendar would wait outside the Ambala Railway Station for rides. As middle-aged men who saw Mahendar as a son, the other rickshaw riders adored him and gave him first preference whenever someone approached them for a lift. One night, Mahendar's headmaster and his wife approached them for a lift and were re-directed to Mahendar.

> They came out of there from the gate, so they sat them on my rickshaw. My whole face was covered, only my eyes were visible. It was winter. So they asked me how much, [and] in a low voice I said 2 rupees. So they thought that they have to tell me the address, tell me where to go. But I thought I have seen their house so I started for their house. They both sat, husband wife, and I started moving. They thought now I'll ask for the house, now I'll ask for the house, but I took them to their street and stopped the rickshaw outside their house. And without saying anything, asking any questions. So he said, 'You did not ask me the address. You brought me straight to my house. How do you know this is my house?' I started crying, and I said, 'I recognise you, but you do not recognise me.' He asked, 'Who are you,' so I said, 'Mahendar.'

> [*Voice chokes and starts crying. Tries to speak while sobbing.*]

> His wife started crying and hugged me and asked which class do you study in, I said 9th. 'You study in 9th?' I started crying and she took me inside the house and said you are not going anywhere. They

switched on the lights and we sat down. They were returning from a wedding so they gave me some sweets.... Anyway, they gave me sweets and 2 rupees. She said now you will not go anywhere, go straight back home. Then the next day headmaster-*saab* called me. I said when I wanted [the scholarship] you did not give it to me [*starts crying*], now I do not want it. I have left the home [figuratively] so I earn 1 rupee every day. I do not want this at all, forgive me. Maybe some other poor person.... So he insisted a lot but I did not let him. I would work two days in a week so I would make 2.5 rupees. Then I never again asked for a fee waiver. And he respected this.

Later, news of this incident reached Dr Bin Bihari Lal. Dr Lal had a long chat with Mahendar and made him understand that if he kept working like this, he would be unable to study. Dr Lal finally got through to Mahendar and convinced him to give up the rickshaw. Dr Lal then spoke to Mahendar's headmaster and had his fees waived for the remainder of his schooling. However, in retelling this story, Mahendar emphasised the respect he had earned through his *purusharth*. He said that Dr Lal had told him that he respected what Mahendar had done, but he could not let him continue doing this for his own good. Dr Lal also gave Mahendar a new goal to aim for: a rank position. Mahendar not only achieved that but also went on to complete his BA. Bringing his story to a close, Mahendar remarked:

Everything came to us with great difficulty. But I am proud of that. If we had stayed in Pakistan, whether our parents had taken care of us, or if we were independent, then we would not have done so much [work].... So the people from Pakistan did not come so easily. The people from Pakistan remember their stories even today. Even today we remember those stories.

Ashok provided the closing comments to Mahendar's story by adding:

Three things come out very clearly from your words. Self-esteem. Confidence. And *purusharth*, the desire to achieve something. These 3–4 factors emerge from your story and they were common. The people of that time, if you will find something common in them, it is these 3–4 factors.

Mahendar's stories follow the broad discursive contours of the stories of *purusharth* I encountered during my fieldwork. This idea of hard work as a redemptive sacrifice was a common thread running through these stories. Talk of the Partition commonly inspired the retelling of such redemptive stories of *purusharth*, whether those of their own experience or that of others. In Mahendar's stories, we observe a clear attempt at the karmic justification of wealth and privilege. His stories assert the moral and political claim that 'one sows that which one reaps' but also that 'one must *only* reap that which one has sown'. The latter is emphasised by him right at the beginning, when he remembers his father's refusal to accept the free rations being distributed at their refugee camp. The moral of this anecdote is reinforced in all of his stories, especially the tale of his serendipitous midnight encounter with his school's headmaster. Thus, these stories are also fables or morality tales.

Additionally, Ashok's implicit description of *purusharth* as 'the desire to achieve something' adds a layer of complexity to our discussion of *purusharth*. Deviating slightly from the didactic, orthodox definition of 'hard work as virtue', Ashok's phrasing adds ambition to this mix. As I found in my fieldwork, my informants often implicitly described other values such as ambition, cleverness and entrepreneurial instincts as *purusharth*. Clubbing these together, we can understand this mix of values as 'street-smartness'.

As with Mahendar's stories of hard work, the stories of some of my informants also emphasised the street-smartness of the Punjabi refugee, literally recounting how *he* had managed to turn even dust into gold. Rajaram, a 91-year-old Partition survivor I met in Gurgaon, told me the story of a Punjabi refugee who made a profit by selling sugar at cost price. This appears to be a well-known Punjabi legend. In *Since 1947*, Ravinder Kaur (2007: 21–22) too makes a note of this legend. Like Mahendar, Rajaram too begins the sugar-seller's tale by distancing the Punjabi community from the refugee label.

Interviewer [PK]: Do you still consider yourself a refugee?

R: No. We did not believe that earlier and neither do we believe that now.

PK: When did this change?

R: So we, our Punjabis did not accept that we are refugees, we are *purusharthi*. This Partition happened, because of that we had to come. We do not depend on them [local Indian people]. Let me tell you one more story, make sure you write it. The Punjabi never spread his hands in front of anyone that help me. [*Spreads his hands in front of me to mimic a begging gesture.*] No Punjabi did. [*Swipes the air with his index finger in a decisive 'no'.*]

PK: So they ate whatever they ate from their own hard work.

R: Yes, whatever they ate, stayed hungry also. Did not drink milk, did not drink buttermilk ['lassi']. But have not asked from anyone, from these Baniyas or the Jats here. This has been a quality of Punjabis. They [Baniyas and Jats] have succeeded by copying us. There is a strange tale of a man in Merut. That had not even occurred to anyone here. What he would do? There was a shop there of a Muslim in Merut; he captured it. Who would refuse? They allotted it to his name. But the shop was not doing well. What did he do? He wrote, *bhai*, rate for rate sugar available. Do you understand rate for rate?

PK: Yes, he was selling it at the rate at which he had purchased it.

R: What we have purchased in wholesale that he was selling at that rate. The first day he sold one sack. The second day, two. His 40-40, 30-30 sacks would sell like that. There his competitors were astonished that *bhai* how is he eating on this? Someone asked him, Lala, what do you eat? The cost at which you buy, that cost…. He replied, I sell at the cost at which I buy. And then when I dust out the sack, I get some sugar from that. I sell that. The sack that is left, I sell that. When I sell 10 sacks, that's my *roti* done.

… So he would get the worth of the sacks in his earnings. Now *bhenchod*[2] when he has sold 20-20 sacks, yes, yes? So how much money has he saved? Why?

PK: He saved a little but his survival is met.

R: He became very rich. People would come from all places, *bhenchod*, they would imitate him, he was selling so much. So Punjabis found ways to earn. Otherwise these people were committing daylight robbery.... So alongside hard work, Punjabis developed schemes so that we would be self-supported.

Here again, Rajaram invokes hard work and 'self-sufficiency' as the innate national character of Punjabi refugees. The idea that Punjabis never begged for money, or asked for support of any kind, was something Rajaram referred to often in his stories. In another conversation I had with him, he re-emphasised the hard-working nature of Punjabis and went on to add that he and his father had also worked as daily wage construction labourers, during their initials days in Gurgaon.

R: Punjabis did not do any kind of begging. You must write this.

Interviewer [PK]: They ate off their own labour.

R: Yes, they ate off their own labour. Stayed hungry. This is the main point. I told you *na* how he [the sugar-seller] did it. And the reply that he gave, '*bhenchod*, at least the sack will sell'. You did not understand?

[*He assumes I did not understand and recounts the sugar-seller's tale again.*]

R: Like this people rode rickshaws. This New Colony [Gurgaon] here, you've seen it right? New Colony. Here, we did *mazdoori* [construction labour]. Even my father did *mazdoori*. I also did *mazdoori*. We carried all those bricks. But I never did dishonesty.

Rajaram once again returns to the story of the sugar-seller. Recapping it and sharing the story of his own physical labour, he emphasises the virtuous and honest nature of the work that Punjabis did. His repeated emphasis on how Punjabis never begged is similar to Mahendar's comment about how his father never let their family eat the free food in refugee camps. In addition to justifying wealth and privilege (through *karma* and the predestination of national character), such stories assert their pride and agency. They present the Punjabi refugee as an exceptionally hard-working and resilient worker.

Another theme that emerges strongly from these stories is the implicit definition of *purusharth* as backbreaking, physical man-work. Stories of *purusharth* seldom concern middle-class office jobs; this despite the fact that most of my informants including Bhanwarilal, Rajaram, Mahendar and Dilip worked in regular desk-based office jobs for most of their lives. Stories of street-smartness add to the dramatic character of these stories of *purusharth*.

The following story told by Bhanwarilal of the success of a button-seller combines all of these elements. Here, Bhanwarilal was telling me about the kind of *purusharth* he witnessed Punjabi refugees performing, just after the Partition. While Bhanwarilal was in Mianwali at the time that the Partition riots broke out, his brother and mother were in Delhi. His brother was a civil servant and in 1942 had purchased an apartment in the vicinity of the historic Roshanara Garden of Old Delhi. It was to this house that Bhanwarilal somehow returned in November 1947, after having spent numerous harrowing months on the refugee trail.

When we came from there, so they [people] would bring a bundle of rice and sit downstairs in the vegetable market close to where we stayed. All day they would sell rice. They would make just one rupee extra. That one rupee was their earning. Household expenses would come from that, however they came.... These people who are established today have established themselves on that and today they have even built their own houses. These people have worked so hard after coming here. Sat on the streets to sell. I have a friend, he sat on the street and sold buttons, in Sadar Bazar [Delhi]. These buttons for different button holes in coats. Today he has four-four houses. He says when he came from Pakistan, he would sit on the street with a box of buttons; every morning he would sit with buttons on the streets of Sadar Bazar.

Continuing with this story Bhanwarilal said that one day, his friend, Hansraj, was approached by a man who owned a button-making factory in Delhi. This man offered him a loan to set up a proper shop and offered to supply him regularly with buttons. Hansraj balked at the thought of paying off a hefty loan and refused initially. But the man waived off his concerns and insisted that he only had to pay him as and when he could spare some money from his earnings. Hansraj initially set up a shop in partnership with his brother-in-law. However, the two had a falling out. In disgust, Hansraj walked out of his own shop and returned to selling buttons on the streets. The same man found Hansraj again, and this time gave him a bigger loan to set up shop again. Hansraj accepted the loan and opened a new shop directly opposite his brother-in-law's. Over time Hansraj's shop emerged the more successful one of the two and he built back his wealth, little by little. 'Today he has 4 houses, 3 in Mianwali Nagar alone,' Bhanwarilal commented, concluding Hansraj's story.

Ultimately, these stories of *purusharth* provide karmic justifications for the current and former wealth and privilege of my informants. Disavowing the role of state supports in their recovery, these stories re-assert their agency while restoring a sense of pride. We get a glimpse of this in both Mahendar and Rajaram's stories where they repeatedly say that Punjabis only ate from what they earned and went hungry when they could not earn. Framed against the helplessness of displacement, the idea that Punjabis would go hungry rather than suffer the indignity of begging, expresses agency in their suffering. By emphasising the pride inherent in the Punjabi refugee, these stories reassure the listener that despite everything that happened to them, Punjabis never lost their sense of honour and dignity.

Whether it is Dilip's story of selling toffees, or Mahendar's story of riding a rickshaw, or Rajaram's story of *mazdoori*, or Bhanwarilal's story of the button-seller, all of these stories comprise dramatic tales of harsh, physical labour. Yet, they are all stories of men who did whatever it took to support their families. Suffering the indignity of selling whatever they could on the street, these men are valourised for having saved their families (and by extension the Punjabi community) from the dishonour of begging. Also implicit in these stories is the valourisation of street-smartness as *purusharth*. Rather than have 'their women' suffer indignity, rather than beg or steal, rather than have their physical and social bodies polluted by the 'other', Punjabis chose 'sacrifice' and suffering over dishonour.

Yet, this discourse hides as much as it reveals. After all, the wealth and real estate of my informants (and the friends they cite as examples) cannot be accounted for by manual labour or the sale of buttons or leftover gunny sacks. In its dramatic, redemptive retelling of the success of 'man-work', these stories obscure the role of the state in the resettlement of Partition refugees. In the following chapter, I examine the political and moral statement this obscuration constitutes. I also explore the ways in which the discourse of *purusharth* is part of the politics of Hindu nationalism.

Notes

1   Here Herzfeld's (1992) work builds on Max Weber's (2005 [1930]) work on *The Protestant Ethic and the Spirit of Capitalism*.
2   Although *bhenchod* literally translates to 'sister-fucker', it is also sometimes used as a crude expression of exclamation.

3

A Story Half Told

The Moral and Political Claims of Purusharth

On the one hand are those [critics of demonetisation] who talk of
what people at Harvard say, and on the other is a poor man's son, who
through his hard work, is trying to improve the economy.... In fact,
hard work is much more powerful than Harvard.

—Narendra Modi (*The Hindu* 2017a)

In the previous chapter, I drew attention to how stories of *purusharth*
comprise dramatic tales of physical labour. Stories of *purusharth* did not
include stories of everyday office work or any other kind of stable, long-
term employment. In contrast to the former, stories of the latter were
devoid of any details. Ravinder Kaur (2007: 141) observes this contrast
in the stories of Partition refugees and writes that such stories 'were
presumed too ordinary to mention, as it had little to do with the general
theme of struggle successfully waged by the refugees'.

I am drawing attention to this here to argue that due to this recurring
trope of the helpless refugee waging a dramatic struggle in pursuit of
success, stories of *purusharth* place the individual at the centre of their
narrative. In doing so, the framing of this narrative obscures the state's
active role in the rehabilitation of refugees. Yet a closer reading of these
stories reveals the state lurking in the background.

For example, in the previous chapter, Mahendar mentions that his
family was allotted a house in Ambala in compensation for the property
they had lost in Pakistan. While the compensation may have been paltry
compared to their former wealth, it nevertheless meant that despite

riding a rickshaw for a living, Mahendar's family was never at the same socio-economic level as those workers who could *only* ride a rickshaw for a living.

Similarly, while Bhanwarilal extols the 'sacrifices' of Punjabi refugees and alleges the lack of adequate reparations, his stories are also laced with occasional descriptions of the compensation their family received. For example, in his passionate exposition on the sacrifices of Punjabi refugees at the beginning of this chapter, Bhanwarilal acknowledges that his family received agricultural land worth INR 10,000. While this was significantly less than their former wealth, it nevertheless provided the family with an important source of capital. Moreover, while reminiscing about the idyllic 'Thandi Sadak' boulevard (in Chapter 1) and while talking about Punjabi refugees selling vegetables in Delhi's Ghanta Ghar, Sabzi Mandi area (in Chapter 2), Bhanwarilal mentions a house his brother owned in Delhi at the time. Bhanwarilal's brother was a civil servant and had purchased a flat in Delhi, near Roshanara Garden, in 1942. In 1947, following the Partition, this was the flat to which the rest of their family moved. Thus, while Bhanwarilal experienced chronic hunger and thirst during the four months he spent on the refugee trail, he and his family were never reduced to the abject poverty of daily-wage labourers. There is even an implicit recognition of this in his stories. After all, he rarely speaks about his own *purusharth*. Rather, he recounts the *purusharth* and hardship of others, allegorising their experiences to that of the entire community.

In his stories of the establishment of Faridabad's NIT, Pooran Chand also alluded to some of the special concessions that the government made for the refugees. As stated previously in Chapter 1, Pooran Chand remembered Prime Minister Nehru's decision to give the Frontier refugees INR 1 bonus on top of their daily wages. Pooran Chand also remembered that the government started a subsidised monthly instalment scheme towards housing refugees. In this way, 5,000 housing plots of 235 square yards each were given to the Frontier refugees in lieu of monthly instalments of INR 6 paid over 25 years (Jain 1998). Priced at INR 1,800 in the 1950s, these houses are estimated to be worth somewhere between INR 8 and 12 million today.

However, in restating these facts and figures, I do not mean to imply that Partition refugees did not face hardship in the effort to rebuild their lives. Rather, my argument is that middle-class and caste-Hindu refugees such as my informants did not face quite as dramatic and hopeless a path towards rehabilitation as their stories of *purusharth* imply. In her examination of the rehabilitation claims filed by Punjabi refugees, Kaur (2007) found that by creating a compensation system that awarded land (up to INR 10,000) on the basis of previously owned land, the Indian government created two classes of refugees: the landed and the landless. According to Kaur, 'This pre-requisite straightaway barred the homeless and poor migrants from staking any claim in the new scheme of nation-building. They could continue to live on the margins just as before, while new territories were being carved out for the middle class refugees' (101).

In doing so, the compensation system reproduced past social hierarchies. All of my informants, without exception, were middle-class upper-caste zamindars. As a result, even though the compensation system did not restore their former wealth, it nevertheless preserved their status as a propertied class. Moreover, all of my informants had the privilege of education, having completed a basic level of education prior to their migration. As stated previously in Chapter 1, following the Partition, many could access higher education through government-run Camp Colleges (V. Datta 1986). In the short term, their education helped them navigate convoluted bureaucratic procedures in pursuit of their compensation claims, while, in the long-term, their education helped secure relatively stable employment. This was by no means a simple or easy process, but middle-class, upper-caste refugees were helped along by their social and culture capital (Bourdieu 1986) and the state's welfare initiatives.

In the compensation system's recreation of past hierarchies, Kaur (2007) locates a typically colonial impulse. As stated in the Introduction, the Indian state inherited the colonial regime's position as the 'moral protector' of an 'ancient' civilisation (94), assuming the role of a neutral arbiter of 'communal conflict' (I. Ahmad 2020; G. Pandey 1990). The former influenced the state's policy to actively salvage and preserve pre-Partition hierarchies through the rehabilitation process (Kaur 2007). An example of this was the caste-based segregation of refugee camps. Similarly, the establishment of resettlement colonies along ethnic lines was also intended at preserving these social orders (94–139).

The Indian state's inheritance of a colonial positionality is also visible in its representation of Partition violence. *The Story of Rehabilitation* – a 1967 document published by the Publications Division of the Government of India – presents the violence of the Partition as an unimaginable, one-off event where religion 'warped' the minds of 'men' such that 'they forgot their humanity and turned upon one another with the ferocity of jungle beasts' (87). Positioning itself as a 'benevolent parent' that hopes to restore the 'lost dignity' of refugees, the state effectively absolves itself of any responsibility for its inability to control or pre-empt the violence of the Partition (89).

Yet, state–refugee relations on the ground were characterised by confrontation and suspicion (95–96). In order to receive their compensation, refugees were forced to confront the unwieldy bureaucratic apparatus of the state. Administrators, in turn, were supposed to carefully scrutinise compensation claims and treat them impartially. To the refugees, this conveyed the state's mistrust of their suffering. The state's mistrust of the refugees was mirrored by the refugees' mistrust of the state; they felt the state did not treat their claims seriously. This in turn gave the refugees incentive to exaggerate the story of their losses (95).

Kaur argues that in the confrontations around the compensation system, both the refugees and the state were attempting to create 'the universe of moral obligation' (123). That is, by establishing a system of compensation, the state expressed the moral obligation it felt towards refugees due to their suffering, while, by confronting the state with claims based on accounts of suffering, refugees felt the state was morally obliged towards them. This element of moral obligation is visible in my informants' quotes where they cite their suffering as a sacrifice that necessitates just compensation. There is, in this discourse, the articulation of compensation as a moral obligation.

What Kaur describes as a 'universe of moral obligation' can also be understood as an attempt at the restoration of a fractured *nomos*: of a social order that would compensate suffering with justice. Recognising this impulse helps understand refugee–state contestations around compensation in terms of Weberian theodicy. I draw attention to these dynamics for the way in which they combine to establish the discursive structure of the stories of *purusharth*.

Emphasising their loss and suffering (even exaggerating it at times), Partition survivors confront their listeners with their burning desire for justice, a justice that they feel is morally owed. Posing destitute and helpless before the state in pursuit of compensation is experienced by them as a communal shame. They recover their pride and agency through the retelling of these dramatic stories of *purusharth*, retrospectively constructing themselves as hard-workers. In the way that these stories frame the individual at the centre of a tough struggle for rehabilitation, these stories require the obfuscation of the role of the state. This discourse allows no space for the acknowledgement of any sort of reparations or compensation. After all, to accept, or rather to admit to having accepted compensation would undermine their status as hard-workers.

Visible in this obfuscation is also a refusal to acknowledge one's caste and class privilege. After all, Kaur (2007) has also observed that Dalit and Scheduled Caste refugees acknowledged and appreciated the state's rehabilitation measures far more than caste-Hindu and Sikh refugees. This despite the state having spent significantly fewer resources on the former (Kaur 2007; Sen 2012). In contrast to these subaltern Hindu refugees, my informants valourise their *purusharth* to provide a karmic justification of their present and former privilege. Edging the state into the background, they present themselves as the heroes of their own rehabilitation.

However, this karmic justification of wealth and privilege as the fruit of one's *purusharth* reifies a meritocratic view of society. As stated previously, the legitimation of one's own wealth and good fortune is also simultaneously a moralising discourse that blames the poverty and misfortune of others on their present and past conduct (Weber 1965, 2013). Simultaneously, one's wealth is also seen as a mark of one's moral goodness (Weber 2005 [1930]). As a philosophy of the ruling class, this has much in common with the idea of the American Dream. It uses the moralising labels of 'hard work' or its absence as generalising and simplistic explanations of inequality.

In this way, my informants' denunciation of refugees and the 'charity' of the welfare state are demonstrative of a trenchant neoliberalism. Denouncing the state's responsibility towards 'dependent' populations (such as refugees and minorities), they assert the individual's responsibility in the making of one's own 'success'. Although this assertion is watered down by their demand for compensation from the state, this is seen by them not as dependence or weakness but as a moral obligation. The state owes them compensation not because they believe in the welfare state but because they see themselves as inhabiting a meaningful cosmos where suffering warrants reparations. That the state is seen to have failed in this is taken as evidence that the state has in fact been captured by minorities and self-serving liberal elites. We can see here how stories of *purusharth* breed *ressentiment* and thereby feed into a pervasive 'democracy fatigue' (Appadurai 2017). This is an idea I return to in Chapter 9.

The Politics of Hard Work: Karma, Neoliberalism and the Meritocracy

In *Lessons from Hell*, Christopher Pinney (2018) examines the culture of *karni bharni* imagery in India. The term *karni bharni* is derived from the words *karam* (action) and *bharan* (payment or reward). These images comprise the karmic cultural belief that the universe repays one's actions with proportionate reward or punishment: that one reaps what one sows. These images are often called *karam ke phal*, or 'the fruits of one's deeds' (16).

Mass-printed since the 1880s, these images contain graphic depictions of the punishments that await sinners in hell. The punishments they depict are often an iconic replication of the misdeeds they condemn. For example, the person who commits the allegedly sinful work of butchery is hacked to death by demons or the person who kills a bird is condemned to a divine-ordained pecking by a flock of his former victims (20). More often, the images feature sinners tied to a pole while being inventively tortured by demons as punishment for their alleged sins. In identifying a number of 'sins' and their ordained punishment, this culture of imagery details a comprehensive moral philosophy of 'right' and 'wrong'. Consequently, Dalit rights activists such as Jyotirao Phule, B. R. Ambedkar and Kancha Ilaiah have critiqued the upper-caste morality that these images reify (Pinney 2018).

The larger philosophy of *karni bharni* imagery provides a karmic justification for suffering and misfortune: a form of theodicy. Where the philosophy of *purusharth* conjures a meaningful order where virtuous hard work is rewarded with success, *karni bharni* provides its complementary opposite, promising divine retribution to those who sin. Where *purusharth* presents one's good fortune as legitimate fortune, *karni bharni* images provide an explanation for misfortune and suffering. Under the philosophy of *karni bharni*, only those who have sinned suffer, and if a sinner does not suffer in this world, then they are condemned to punishment in hell.

Pinney notes the prevalence of the tropes of *karni bharni* within contemporary Indian politics, especially the politics of Anna Hazare and Narendra Modi. Pinney notes that Anna Hazare's 2011 anti-corruption Jan Lokpal (Public Ombudsman) campaign articulated the imagery of *karni bharni*. Hazare's discourses on corruption in India – of shady deals being struck in 'smoky black rooms' – mobilised some of the tropes found in *karni bharni* images on *rishvat lene ka phal* (the fruits of accepting a bribe) (Pinney 2018: 128). Hazare has also frequently iterated his support for 'hanging corrupt politicians' and '"cutting off the hands" of thieves' (129).

Hazare's endorsement of a kind of justice that, like *karni bharni* imagery, awards a punishment that is the iconic replication of the crime is a consistent pattern within his politics. As a self-proclaimed 'Gandhian activist', Hazare's history of 'social reform' in Ralegan Siddhi – his natal village – comprises a similar pattern of graphically retributive 'justice'. Hazare celebrates as his 'achievement' the imposition of prohibition in his village. Shopkeepers in the village also claim to have not sold tobacco products in the last 13 years.

However, the 'success' of Hazare's campaign was largely predicated on 'the public thrashing of alcoholics by Hazare himself (they are tied to a pole and he thrashes them with his army belt)' (Pinney 2018: 129). The image of a sinner tied to a pole while being punished for their sin(s) is eerily reminiscent of *karni bharni* imagery. The similarity is heightened by Hazare's treatment of the consumption of alcohol and tobacco as 'sins', thus making his programme of 'social reform' the bland imposition of Brahmanical morality.

Pinney notes that while Hazare disappeared from Indian politics soon after 2011, his legacy has endured. Hazare succeeded in reviving the *karni bharni* critique of corruption. Hazare created an unusual political space that fused a traditional upper-caste Hindu cosmology with the politics of the modern nation state. By 2014, this space had been inherited by Narendra Modi, who like Hazare was seen to be un-corrupt, celibate and an austere vegetarian (Pinney 2018). While Modi comes from an OBC caste, through his celibacy and austere vegetarianism he embodies the lifestyle of an upper-caste Hindu: a prime example of Sanksritisation (Srinivas 1966; see Introduction) within the Hindu-fold. Through careful management of the media, Modi has also been presented as a devoted son. Meanwhile, his abandonment of his wife at a young age, to join the RSS, is celebrated as evidence of his selfless nationalism. Therefore, Modi is seen as an elderly *brahmachari*: a celibate ascetic (Pinney 2018).

Interestingly, there were many similarities in the way that my informants described themselves as hard-workers and the way in which they would praise Modi's qualities. Modi was seen by my informants as a selfless, hard-working politician who only has the interests of the nation at heart. During my fieldwork, I regularly encountered people who expressed their awe at Modi's hard-working nature. Widely publicised claims that Modi only sleeps four hours a night and never takes vacations were cited as evidence of his dedication.

Another theme that emerged in this discourse of Modi as an honest *purusharthi* was the allusion to his lack of family ties. Modi's image as an elderly bachelor was contrasted with the nepotism and corruption of the Nehru–Gandhi family. Modi has himself furthered this contrast by positioning himself as a *kamdar* (working man, or hard-worker) against the *namdar* (dynast) Rahul Gandhi (S. Singh 2018). Here, Modi is helped by the Nehru–Gandhi family's visibly dynastic hold over the Congress party.[1] In a larger sense, Modi's discourses such as his famous comment that 'hard work is much more powerful than Harvard' (*The Hindu* 2017a) comprise a denunciation of privilege while also reinscribing the centrality of the United States to global concepts of prestige. Thus, Modi as a former tea-seller is largely considered a self-made hard-working leader of the masses.

There is an interesting observation to be made here regarding kinship. Readers will recall my argument that not only were my informants' stories of *purusharth* justifications of wealth but also distinctly familial or communitarian in their values. After all, my informants saw their hard work as a service to their families (and through it the larger collectivity). Similarly, Modi's *purusharth* is seen to serve the family that is the Hindu nation.

During my stay in Dehradun, my informant Naagesh and I had a conversation that crystallised this perspective. We were evaluating Modi's public image when Naagesh praised Modi as a nationalist leader who is selflessly devoted to the service of the nation. I countered that with a tongue-in-cheek remark at Modi's failed marriage. I said, 'A man who could not be faithful to his own wife, how could he ever serve his country?' Through this, I hoped to draw attention to Modi's hypocritical failure to live up to the traditional Hindu family values his politics claims to defend. But Naagesh's reply reframed Modi's life as the *purusharth* of a *brahmachari*. Naagesh replied, 'He left his wife *for* his country.' Naagesh's reply implicitly frames Modi as an unacknowledged father of the nation,[2] as a man who left his own family to serve the family that is the Hindu nation.

The way in which 'real' kinship is seen to be in conflict with national service reveals something about nationalism. Herzfeld (1992) observes that nationalism relies on the symbolism of kinship in its imagination of a united nation. Kinship forms 'the bridge between body and polity, the locus of that spectacular conversion which all successful nationalisms effect between "blood" and "culture"' (76). The implicit imagination of the nation as family allows the hard work of my informants to serve as a contribution to both their *real* family and the nation-as-family. In the case of Modi, his abandonment of his 'real' family is seen as a denunciation of nepotism and corruption. After all, as Herzfeld explains, corruption and nepotism – the use of political power for personal and familial ends – scandalise the notions of bureaucratic rationality and rule of law that are seen to be enshrined in the state. A violation of these principles constitutes a violation of the *nomos* that is the nation state. However, Herzfeld also reminds us that the discourse of corruption is not an absolute discourse but is dependent on the observer's positionality.

Specifically, in the context of Hindu nationalism, Modi's celibate *purusharth* reaffirms the RSS philosophy. Leading RSS ideologues such as Golwalkar and Hegdewar imagined the Hindu citizen-body in purely masculine terms as 'the men born in the land of *Bharat* [India]' and 'sons of the soil' (Bacchetta 2019: 382). In this way, the nation is imagined solely as a 'fraternity of men' (McClintock 1995). For the RSS, homosexuality is a threat due to its alleged disruption of homosocial male comradery. The operative binary here is not between hetero- and homo-sexuality but between a-sexuality and sexuality (383). For the RSS, the ideal Hindu man is a *brahmachari* – an asexual ascetic that severs all familial bonds in order to serve the Hindu nation and society. As an exclusively male brotherhood sustained by firm homosocial bonding, celibacy is a necessary mark of one's dedication to the nation (383–385).

The hallowed status of ascetic celibacy also draws on aspects of Hindu religious discourse. The tension between ascetic celibacy and domesticity is visible in Hindu mythology and is even embodied by the high-gods Shiva and Vishnu, and the former's avatars Ram and Krishna (van der Veer 1994). In Vaishnavism, celibacy and physical strength (*bal*) combine to produce the Hindu idea of power (*shakti*) (72). The retention of semen within the body is said to imbue supernatural power, such as in the legendary strength of the *brahmachari* ape-god Hanuman (72, 96–98).

Historically, ascetic celibacy also formed a major feature of the moderate Hindu nationalism of Mahatma Gandhi. Gandhi took a vow of celibacy at the age of 36 and believed that his political power (*shakti*) was derived from disciplining his body (96). For Gandhi, it was his asceticism and celibacy that fed into the political power of his *ahimsa* (non-violence) (96–97). Gandhi's infamous practice of testing his celibacy by sleeping beside young naked women was linked to this idea of the retention of semen as the source of power (97–98). Following an increase in Hindu–Muslim violence in 1946, Gandhi suspected that his *ahimsa's* power was being choked by something. Building his *shakti* through a test of celibacy, Gandhi sought to enhance the political power of his *ahimsa* (97). This draws on a specifically gendered Tantrik tradition (97–98) that is beyond the scope of this book.

It is therefore no coincidence that Modi is also seen as a strong leader, both in his resolve and his ability to perform violence. As Appadurai (2021: 306) writes, 'He [Modi] is a Hindu *samraat* [emperor] full-blown, often wearing the turbaned head gear of royalty, who also picks up on the iconography of the militant sadhu and the celibate ascetic'. As a contemporary incarnation of a Hindu *samraat*, Modi is seen as the promised harbinger of the return to a Hindu Rashtra. As a *brahamachari* he is seen, by his followers, to be above personal temptation and thereby 'corruption'. Furthermore, as a 'tea-seller' and common man who has risen to high office from the lowest rungs of the RSS and BJP, he is seen as a self-made man, someone who reminds my informants of their own past struggles. Yet, this affective identification with Modi is not merely symbolic. Modi's neoliberal market economics too find resonance within my informants' discourses on hard work and self-reliance. The retreat of the state – whether through the privatisation of public services or in the proposed downscaling of welfare and affirmative action policies – is largely seen as a step in the right direction. Here, the support for neoliberalism intersects with casteism. For most urban middle-class Indians – including my informants – what is ultimately hoped for is a downscaling of the state's caste-based reservations.[3] The abolition of reservations that is hoped for represents the liberation of the state from undeserving minorities (predominantly Dalits and Adivasis) – and the liberal elites supportive of them – who are seen to be feeding off the fat of the land. Therefore, for my informants, *purusharthi brahmachari* Modi holds the promise of an unfettered Hindu state.

Notes

1   Some political commentators have pointed out that nepotism and political dynasties are a larger fact of Indian politics. For example, some recent newspaper reports have shown that 11 per cent of the BJP's current ministers of parliament (MPs) have dynastic linkages, while some of the BJP's current and former regional allies such as the Shiv Sena, the Shiromani Akali Dal (SAD) and the Lok Janshakti Dal (LJD) are family-run dynastic parties (Arnimesh and Pandey 2020). However,

the top political leadership of the BJP, unlike that of the Congress, is not controlled by a fifth-generation political dynasty. It is here that the Congress party's nepotism appears infinitely more pervasive than that of any other Indian political party.

2   In fact, meeting on the sidelines of the United Nations General Assembly in New York on September 24, 2019, US President Donald Trump went so far as to christen Modi the father of the Indian nation (*India Today* 2019). He said:

> I remember India before [before PM Modi rule], not intimately, but I remember India before, it was very torn, it was a lot fighting and he brought it all together. Like a father would bring it together. Maybe he is the father of India. We will call him the father of India. He brought things together, you don't hear that anymore. (Trump quoted in *India Today* [2019])

While Indian opposition leaders and Twitter users mocked Trump's ignorance by reminding him that India already had a 'father' of the nation – Mahatma Gandhi – Trump's remarks were vociferously defended by Modi's party (*The Hindu* 2019b). Some such as Union Minister Jitendra Singh went so far as to say, 'This is the first time that an American President has used this kind of words of praise not for an Indian Prime Minister but for any other world leader, and if someone is not proud of this, then maybe he does not consider himself an Indian' (*The Hindu* 2019b).

3   Positive discrimination or affirmative action policies in India.

4

Sacrifice and Hard Work

Martyrdom as Theodicy

We are not *sharanarthi* that we have come into your refuge [*sharan*].
Arre[1] we have sacrificed and come. You have not made any sacrifice.

—Bhanwarilal

'A lot of people call what happened to them during the Partition as "sacrifice" [*kurbaani*], that we have sacrificed this for the nation. What do you think about this?' I asked Lata and Kulbhushan. Lata and Kulbhushan were an elderly Partition survivor couple who lived with their eldest son in Pitampura, New Delhi. They had been married for more than 50 years. While Lata was 4 years old at the time of the Partition, Kulbhushan was 10. Although Lata was too young to remember the Partition, Kulbhushan vividly remembered the day his family was forced to flee their village in district Dera Ghazi Khan.

'So what else? If this is not sacrifice then what is it? So many lives were lost, what is this?' Kulbhushan asked rhetorically in reply. 'We brought nothing from Pakistan,' Lata added in a firm but gentle voice. Kulbhushan, reminding me of the stories he had shared with me during our last conversation, said:

We had absolutely nothing. Some people had brought a little money or something. We had nothing. We were in deep trouble. [My] Father had died there, we were all small-small. My [eldest] brother, I had told you, you know that he had been finished [killed] there and he was very healthy.

Kulbhushan's father and brother had been lynched by a mob of Muslims. The mob had begun by burning their shop. When his father and eldest brother fled the scene and hid in a nearby farm, the mob followed them there. Cornering both father and son in the fields, they savagely hacked both of them with swords. While his father died on the spot, his brother succumbed to his injuries later.

'I remember you told me, he had been killed with swords,' I acknowledged.

'Our homes, everything was divided, everything.... When he [brother] was in Dera Ghazi Khan hospital, who knows how many wounds were there on him, on his neck, his eye, over here, here.' Kulbhushan patted parts of his body to indicate the various places his brother had been wounded. 'He had a finger that was cut off, this.' Kulbhushan held up the index finger of his left hand. 'This was connected by just a small bit,' Kulbhushan said, as he paused to indicate that his brother's wrist had been cut so badly that it remained attached to the rest of his arm by only a sliver of skin and tendons. 'Even later it did not heal, he could not close his hand, it stayed like this,' Kulbhushan said, showing me his outstretched palm.

'He did not have full control of his hand...,' I said.

'Yes, yes. When the doctor put stitches on him, so even the doctors were left stunned. So strong that he would not even say, "Uff". They [doctors] kept saying we have not seen a man like this,' Kulbhushan continued, recounting his eldest brother's final moments in the hospital ward.

'But I found the word "sacrifice" a bit weird because would you consider this sacrifice? Sacrifice is a kind of voluntary thing. Like how someone might sacrifice a goat [in a ritual].' Realising my faux pas, I halted my somewhat opaque and potentially disrespectful analogy. Changing tack, I continued, 'You were not like that. What happened to you all was murder, crimes, riots, it was not sacrifice. It was not like you wanted to give this sacrifice for the nation.'

'Consider this in helplessness or whatever it is,' Kulbhushan responded, unconvinced.

'Yes so that is why I feel the word "sacrifice" is not right here,' I argued.

Unconvinced by my argument, Lata and Kulbhushan reflected in silence for a few moments. For my part, I was hesitant to press my disagreement any further for fear of seeming dismissive of their loss and suffering. Finally, Lata broke the silence by comparing the rioters in Pakistan to the terrorists of today. Kulbhushan disagreed and clarified that they were not terrorists but just Pathans and people of other ethnicities who stoked the flames of hatred. Silently reflecting on the meaning of 'sacrifice', I watched the conversation drift into irrelevance.

During my fieldwork, I encountered many informants, like Lata and Kulbhushan, who insisted that their suffering during the Partition constituted a 'sacrifice' to the nation. Like them many of my informants insisted that the deaths of their relatives (and co-religionists), the loss of their property and the sheer fact of their displacement could not be considered anything but sacrifice. Often voiced in this rhetorical structure of 'What is this if not sacrifice?', this idea of Partition suffering as a national sacrifice comprises a popularly held common-sense understanding of the Partition. Here I use the term 'common sense' not in its generally positive connotation of 'good sound practical sense' but in its Italian form of *senso commune* – as elaborated by Antonio Gramsci – as beliefs, ideas and opinions uncritically held by a group of people (Crehan 2011: 273–274).

This common-sense understanding of Partition suffering as sacrifice differs from my (and social scientific) understandings of the word 'sacrifice'. This was essentially the crux of my discussion with Lata and Kulbhushan. To me, sacrifice implies a voluntary act of renunciation. It has implications of choice and agency. To sacrifice something implies that they 'chose' to do so, that one had the power to commit the said sacrifice. Sacrifice implies an element of altruism, the giving up of something in pursuit of a greater good. It is in the context of the latter that nationalist discourses frame national sacrifice: a sacrifice to the nation (in material, bodily or symbolic terms) for its betterment and progress.

In this chapter, I focus on exactly this conflict of meanings, drawing attention to the contradiction between the apparent involuntariness of their suffering and its retrospective (re-)imagination by them as a sacrifice to the nation. It is precisely this process of rationalising the 'uselessness' out of their suffering by reference to the nationalist discourse of sacrifice that I refer to as a form of theodicy. By (re-) imagining their suffering as a sacrifice to the nation, my informants sanctify their suffering as an offering to the greater good; as their contribution to the nation. Through recourse to this theodicy, they make sense of death and suffering (as witnessed on a hitherto unparalleled scale), giving it meaning and significance. This is visible in Lata and Kulbhushan's words above, where when confronted with the idea that all that death and suffering might have been for nothing, they defensively ask, 'So what else? If this is not sacrifice then what is it? So many lives were lost, what is this?' There is, after all, no suffering more traumatic, more fundamentally threatening to one's sense of humanity, than one without meaning.

Remember Us as Martyrs, as Freedom Fighters

One of my informants for whom this idea of suffering as sacrifice resonated deeply was Bhanwarilal. Bhanwarilal – whom we have encountered previously in Chapter 2 – hailed from the town of Mianwali in Pakistan. Born in 1931, he was 16 years old at the time of the Partition. A highly opinionated, outspoken and well-read man, Bhanwarilal was someone I spent a lot of time with during my fieldwork. Through the time we spent together, Bhanwarilal came to address me as his student and grandson. Whenever I visited him, Bhanwarilal and his wife Bhavna would generously ply me with snacks and beverages and insist on making me stay for lunch. He would also often count on me for lifts to the nursing home and some of the meetings of the All-India District Mianwali Association. The latter became my way of immersing myself further in the life of this community.

Despite having worked in the Indian Railways all his life, Bhanwarilal was at his heart an academic. Over time, he had assembled a priceless collection of Urdu and Hindi books. These included anthologies of poetry, editions of magazines that had long gone out of print, newspapers and fiction and non-fiction books. Many of them referenced the Partition and/or the history of Punjab: his two foremost fascinations.

During our conversations, he would often recommend books to me, and sometimes he would even read out chosen passages from them, for the benefit of my Dictaphone. Although he was 87 years old when I first met him, he was still an active contributor to two monthly magazines. He served as the mentor and editor for an Urdu *Smarika* (magazine) and also contributed some writing to the All-India District Mianwali Association's monthly gazette.

An organic intellectual, Bhanwarilal was the first among my informants to describe his suffering as a sacrifice. This was an idea that resonated with him deeply, one that he confidently restated on numerous subsequent occasions. However, our first conversation on this subject occurred on 18 August 2017. The 71st anniversary of India's independence was celebrated on 15 August 2017, while 17 August 2017 marked the 71st anniversary of the official announcement of the Radcliffe Award. This was the day on which the borders of India and Pakistan were released to the public. What made 17 August 2017 particularly significant was that Captain Amarinder Singh (then chief minister of Punjab) had inaugurated India's first and only Partition Museum. This news had made it into most national dailies on 18 August. While we talked, I noticed a copy of the *Hindustan Times* on his bed. Open at page 9, the headline 'Capt. Amarinder and His Visit to Partition Museum Takes Him Down Memory Lane' caught my eye. This article sat somewhat revealingly beside an op-ed headlined 'India Today like Nazi Germany'.

I suspect that the historical significance of that week, along with the saturation of political commemorations and speeches, had affected Bhanwarilal deeply. That day, as we retreated into his study with cups of tea, Bhanwarilal began to talk about the hollowness he perceived in political discourses on the Partition. Beginning with a recent Independence Day celebration he had attended in the park close to his house, Bhanwarilal went on to talk about why he felt that Partition survivors were the 'real losers' of the Partition.

B: So they had a function on 15 August – the people who come to that park. Now in that park they were talking about all this, that we got freedom, freedom led to this, freedom led to that. So I was sitting there so they took my name. I said, all those who were speaking before me, they were talking about the Partition, they have not seen the Partition. They were born here. What actually happened, they are not witness to that.

Interviewer [PK]: They would have told the things they had heard.

B: They were saying things they had heard. I have seen with my own eyes, what the situation was. People showed a lot of curiosity. So then I told them how I saw things on the way and I came after this September or October. When August went by then 14 August was when Pakistan celebrated [Independence] and on 15 August India did. So I came near about October, in the end of October or November. So I came 4–5 months after that [Independence]. And the situation on the way, how they sent slaughtered trains, how they responded, the Indians, how we were stuck along the way we did not get food for two days, did not get water. They were astonished to hear. As they heard me many of them started tearing up. So I said it is alright whatever the Partition was, but after that at that time, we have stood up on our feet and they are enjoying the freedom. Whereas we are the losers. We lost everything and came here. Their parents must have lost and come here but they do not know this, the people who are speaking on stage at the moment. They do not know anything. That what actually … I am from that generation that has seen this with its own eyes. Those conditions I have told you before.

PK: So in a way, do you find Independence Day celebrations – the way we celebrate freedom – a little hollow? That this might not be a day of celebration for you?

B: I find them hollow because, son, the present generation or the present ruling [government] or the present persons who are happy or they remained ministers in UPA [previous coalition government] or in the NDA [current BJP-led ruling alliance], they have not seen the Partition. There is no strength in their sympathy. What all actually went on, that only our people who suffered in north Pakistan have suffered.

PK: Maximum [violence] happened in that Punjab belt.

B: The people who came from Punjab were the sufferers. Delhiites did not move. Delhiites are just sitting there.... Those ahead of Delhi are also sitting there. What have they seen, they have seen nothing.

PK: South India has not seen that much also.

B: Today this belt of Rohtak,[2] that we call Haryana, in which Jat[3] people live. They created trouble, look *bhai* the refugee have come. *Sharanarthi* have come. Actually we are not *sharanarthi*.... We are not *sharanarthi* that we have come into your refuge [*sharan*]. *Arre* we have sacrificed and come. You have not made any sacrifice.

PK: So does that mean you also do not like these words such as refugee or *sharanarthi*?

B: It is like this, I mean that all this that these people do, all of it seems hollow. They actually do not know about that suffering. Imagine if there was a father there, he saw that here the Muslims are attacking us. He has four daughters. He said where will I take these four daughters? On the way, these people will rape them. Using his own hands he took out a knife and cut the necks of those girls and threw them in a well. So that neither will they be with us, nor will they be raped. He cut them with his own hands and threw them. Look at their courage that the children they birthed, the children whom they nurtured and the children for whom they made offerings [to god], in the end what did those parents do? Rest of the life they are crying after their children. But their circumstances were like that. But in those circumstances they could not bring their children with them. The female children mainly, the male they brought however they came. And some reached here such that their parents had died there [in Pakistan]. When they came they would see where can we go, whom can we stay with, who will give us shelter?

PK: What they did, to kill their daughters with their own hands, that is a kind of honour killing, is it not?

B [*hysterically*]: What could we do? There was no alternative, there was no protection. If they migrated with them then would they have been protected? On the way there were such kind of things happening where they would grab the girls and marry them forcefully. A case came to me…. Now these people were from Bannu. Among them in Dera Ismail Khan, some people in Bannu, some in Dera Ghazi Khan, stayed behind out of selfishness. Some converted their religion. They became Muslims, so that 'we will stay here so whatever is our land, the agricultural land of our caste, we will get the rest also, and our houses will stay with us'. Now the thing there is that they [Muslims] are 500 people there, they [Hindus] are 5. Five hundred are the residents of that place, and 5 people are the ones who have converted. Or in those 5 people, 3 are converts, 1 person says I will stay a Hindu. So that, they are pinpointed, these are the 5 peoples, who have been left here after the Partition. They [Muslims] do not allow them into the mainstream. Every other day they attack them [Hindus/converts]. Every other day they dishonour[4] them. They are second or third-grade citizens. They are lying there. Tolerating it they are lying there. Now in that suppose if a Hindu was left behind. So that Hindu has no worth, neither does he have any means. He would have to bring and arrange stuff there, would have to buy their vegetables there, use them.

Bhanwarilal's narrative here is complex, and I unpack aspects of it sequentially. Responding to the deluge of discourses commemorating India's Independence and Partition suffering, Bhanwarilal begins by expressing his displeasure towards them. He perceives these discourses and commemorations as 'hollow', since to him these derive from people who 'do not know' about Partition suffering. However, the issue here is not that they *do not know* but that they *have not suffered*. The crux of Bhanwarilal's narrative here is his *ressentiment* for people who have not suffered the Partition's excesses. '*Arre* we have suffered and come,' he says at one point. 'You have not made any sacrifice.'

Bhanwarilal's *ressentiment* also extends to political elites and their perspectives on the Partition. For Bhanwarilal, the Partition and India's Independence are indelibly linked. To him, commemorations of India's Independence seem 'hollow' as they seem to come from a class of people who remained unaffected with what he sees as the 'cost' of that freedom: the suffering of the Partition. Through this formulation, he frames his suffering and that of his community as a 'price' that was paid for the fulfilment of freedom.

This juxtaposition of the suffering of the Partition, with the fulfilment of Independence, was articulated by many of my other informants. For example, Jogesh and Kishore, two of the informants I met in Gurgaon, recalled the suffering endured by people during the Partition and demanded that Partition survivors be recognised as freedom fighters.

> Kishore: We became nation-less, became homeless, came here. That is a different thing that we established ourselves.... But we sacrificed a lot for *azaadi* [freedom], *lakhs*[5] of people died. Our people, in front of parents, they saw daughters being raped. What did we get, what did they give us? ... Murders happened, fathers were killed. People ate poison and many died consuming poison, things like this they could not see there and they were buried alive there. What did we get? In fact we should get the status of freedom fighters.

> Jogesh: Did not get it. No asks about us, who does? Who has asked?

> Kishore: If they [people arrested during the freedom struggle] stayed in jail for 6 months so they are getting pension and those whose houses were destroyed, children were killed, and all their sources [of livelihood] finished, became homeless and had to come here, for *azaadi*, nothing for them. [We] should get the status of a freedom fighter.

> Jogesh: We should get the status. Pakistani, Pakistani, they would call us.

Like Bhanwarilal, Kishore remembers the suffering of the Partition and wonders, 'What did we get?' His discourse too is evocative of the *ressentiment* that Bhanwarilal expresses. By demanding the status of 'freedom fighters', they demand a form of symbolic compensation, the recognition of their suffering.

Other informants expressed this sentiment differently. Some, for example, took issue with the inherently undemocratic process of the Partition, pointing out that they were never once consulted about the borders that ultimately decided their future. Where the Partition constituted an act of supremely callous political high-handedness, political commemorations after the fact seem to add further insult to injury. Speaking about it in May 2015, during my MPhil fieldwork, my granduncle Om Prakash had said:

> Did you ask the population what is to be done, and what not? Democracy was not there at the time. We call it a democracy now. Now when something happens so then they ask, *bhai*, put it to the public. What do the people want? What was it then? Back then everyone was after their own seat [high-office]. Everyone only talks about the sacrifices of Pandit Nehru. *Arre* their sacrifices, are our sacrifices less that our entire property, our hard-earned ancestral property, that we left behind? And what did we get in compensation? Broken-broken houses. Where we had mansions.... So it made a big difference, *na*.

Contrasting the loss of his ancestral property and privilege as zamindars with the valourisation of the lives of the prominent politicians of the Independence movement, Om Prakash expresses a deep-seated *ressentiment* for what came to pass. His heartrending appeal for the recognition of the 'sacrifices' of Partition survivors is also a call for the recognition of the suffering engendered by the Partition. In the process, Partition suffering is also implicitly juxtaposed with the realisation of India's Independence. While Om Prakash does this by asking, 'What did we get in compensation?', Bhanwarilal does so by telling his audience that they have benefitted from and 'enjoyed' freedom whereas he and his people 'are the losers'. Implicit in this juxtaposition is the idea that their suffering constitutes a debt to the nation paid in blood, sweat and tears.

This is clearest in Jogesh and Kishore's demand that Partition survivors be honoured as freedom fighters, juxtaposing their suffering against the apparent lack of any kind of compensation or reparations. By branding themselves the victims and 'losers' of this experience, by demanding what, if anything, they got in return, one can see them struggling to rationalise the apparent uselessness of their suffering. 'Tell me what this was all for?' they seem to wonder. Amidst the bleak hopelessness of this realisation, 'sacrifice' becomes the discursive crutch to which they turn for support.

Martyrdom: An Organic Grammar of Mourning

On a deeper level, the juxtaposition of the Partition and the 'unfulfilled promise of freedom' – as it were – addresses a fundamental cleavage in Indian history. While Independence is celebrated, commemorated and memorialised *ad nauseam*, the suffering of the Partition has been largely consigned to the margins as an unfortunate by-product. Gyanendra Pandey (2001) and Mira Debs (2013) argue that the reason for this is located in the complexity of the Partition itself. As a period of reciprocal and retributive sectarian violence, the Partition does not lend itself easily to national commemorations and memorialisation (G. Pandey 2001; Debs 2013).

Pandey (2001: 6) has also observed a tendency within Indian historiography to treat the Partition and other episodes of 'communal' violence in India as 'someone else's history – or even, not history at all'. Locating the source of this tension in an earlier separation between the oral historical and archival branches of Partition Studies, Pandey remarks, 'Nationalism and nationalist historiography … have made an all too facile separation between "Partition" and "violence"' (6–7). Although the Partition is inseparably entangled with nationalist historiography, its violence has often been left unacknowledged and unaddressed.

This separation itself springs from the aforementioned common-sense understanding of 'communalism' (ethnonationalism) and its violence as not nationalism (G. Pandey 1990). Thus, to a certain 'secular' imagination, the Partition is not seen as an example of the violence of nationalism but is instead seen as aberrational to the 'secular' character of the Indian nation state. In this way, the violence of the Partition has been separated from nationalism and nationalist historiography. However, this neat separation between Partition violence and Independence (or nation state formation) is absent from the discourses of its survivors, with memories of the Partition flowing freely into the themes of violence, nationalism and national sacrifice.

Comparing and contrasting the Indian state's mourning and memorialisation of the assassination of Mahatma Gandhi with that of the Partition, Mira Debs (2013) writes that the former was a fundamentally easier event to publicly mourn and memorialise than the latter. This despite the fact that the Partition and the en masse displacement of Hindus and Sikhs from Pakistan were cited by Nathuram Godse (2015) as his motive for assassinating Gandhi. Unlike the Partition's entangled victimhood–perpetrator positions, Gandhi's assassination presented a clear distinction between the perpetrator and victim, a distinction that also allowed for an instant outpouring of grief. Moreover, as the assassination of a 'secular' freedom fighter by a Hindu nationalist terrorist in pursuit of a sectarian (and fascist) agenda, the assassination and its subsequent memorialisation became an opportunity for the Congress to preach its brand of 'secular nationalism' while denouncing the Hindu Right's 'communalism'.

Consequently, the Indian state has found itself memorialising and commemorating the Independence movement and Gandhi's assassination to the neglect of the Partition. As a result, while commentaries on the Independence movement and Gandhi's assassination follow a well-established grammar of sacrifice and martyrdom, faced with the sheer scale of 'useless suffering', commentaries on the Partition ultimately struggle with a mono-syllable expression of shock: 'Why?'

Commenting on the politics of mourning in relation to the Partition, Veena Das (2007) invokes Nadia Seremetakis' ethnographic work on mourning rituals in Inner Mani, Greece. A 'good death' is performed and embodied via the presence of mourners, with their screaming, vocal lamentations and the act of a community bearing witness to and actively participating in the mourning of the deceased (Seremetakis 1991). A 'bad death', in contrast, is an 'asocial' death, with the silence of the mourners signifying the absence of witnessing (Das 2007: 48; Seremetakis 1991).

The lack of state commemorations and memorialisation coupled with the violence of the Partition has condemned victims of the Partition to a 'silent', 'asocial' and by extension, 'bad death'. With the passing of time, this has further problematised the task of mourning. Urvashi Butalia (2000) drew attention to an aspect of this when she observed that while museums and memorials dedicated to freedom fighters and the Independence movement abound, there were none dedicated to the Partition. This changed on 17 August 2017 with the inauguration of the Partition Museum in Amritsar. Yet despite the curiosity this generated among my informants, especially after my visit to Amritsar in March 2018, this memorialisation of Partition suffering was undeniably too little too late.

Writing years before the Partition Museum became a reality, Anindya Raychaudhuri (2012: 185) poignantly stated that this absence of public memorialisation 'fits the displaced, scattered, grieving condition of so many survivors and their descendants so much better than an actual memorial ever could'. She also cautioned, 'An actual memorial, if one was to be erected, would inevitably appropriate the victims' grief in order to reinforce the hegemonic reading of the past' (185). As I show in Chapters 5 and 6, this warning was rather prescient.

The absence of the mourning of the physical death of the victims of the Partition has given way to other symbolic acts of mourning. In the absence of a grammar of commemoration unique to their suffering, Partition survivors have developed their own rituals, memorials and idioms for honouring and mourning their dead. Veena Das (2007: 49) mentions the use of ritualistic devices such as the breaking of a pot (symbolic of the deceased person whose corpse their kin cannot access) as a symbolic and private funerary practice.

Similarly, in Chapter 1, I have documented a memorial shrine that Faridabad's Partition survivors have built in honour of the dead. Faridabad's Gurdwara Shahidane Gujrat Train (whose name translates to '*Gurdwara* of the Gujrat Train Martyrs') pays homage to those who were killed in the massacre of a train full of refugees fleeing the Frontier, at the Gujrat railway station in Pakistan. Although a Sikh place of worship, this *gurdwara* functions as something of a non-denominational shrine – drawing both Hindus and Sikhs – to the memory of the Partition's 'martyrs'.

This *gurdwara* is especially interesting due to the fact that as an active place of worship, the discourse of sacrifice here invokes not only a form of secular theodicy but also religious theodicy. As such, the impulse to build shrines in memory of the martyrs of one's faith captures something of a universal impulse within most world religions. After all, religious discourse provides both a well-established form of theodicy and a grammar of mourning.

Relatedly, Levinas (1988) has argued that the experience of death and suffering makes faith necessary. In such times, faith not only provides comfort – a 'sacred canopy' (Berger 1967) – but also suffering due to religious persecution (whether the Holocaust or the Partition) makes it all the more necessary to believe in that which is seen to define us: our faith. Thus, Levinas concludes that the suffering of the Holocaust made it necessary for Jewish people to believe in their faith. In the face of persecution – especially genocide – faith emerges not only as a form of theodicical comfort but also becomes a revolutionary act of resistance[6] (Levinas 1988).

We can observe something similar at play in the religiosity and religious nationalism of Partition survivors. Perhaps it is the necessity to believe in the faith for which one has seen others die that makes Hindu nationalism such an effective form of theodicy to this generation of Partition survivors. Religious idioms and discourses were invoked by many of my informants in their remembrance of the Partition's suffering. Often, these went no further than reflexive invocations of god(s) and karma such as 'May God never show anyone such days' and 'God knows what we did to deserve this fate'. At other times, the collective nature of the suffering of the Partition was invoked as a comforting fact such that 'Partition did not happen to us alone. This has happened with everyone'. Yet, such invocations of God(s) and karma did not comprise sophisticated theodicical explanations for the suffering of the Partition.

However, there were a couple of occasions on which religious discourse and the supernatural seemed to delineate the hand of god within the godless suffering of the Partition. The first of these occurred during my MPhil fieldwork, on 1 June 2015. While remembering his suspenseful train journey from Muzzafarnagar to Lahore (and ultimately Attari, India), my informant Sunder Lal said that he believed that it was the presence of an idol of Lord Krishna in their train that ensured their safety. He said:

The train would move some twenty, thirty kilometres and then the Muslims would stop it. The Muslims were running the train, it did not belong to Hindus. Their driver, their staff, so thankfully no looting-killing happened in our train. But the ones that went before us, in them looting-killing happened, and in some they were cut [murdered] but in this nothing happened. One reason I believe is that Gopinath-*ji's* [Lord Krishna] idol was there, God's idol. There was a temple of Gopinath there [Dera Ghazi Khan, city]. That idol [of the temple] was in the last bogie [carriage] of our train. Just possible that because of the presence of his image, God ordained that, *bhai*, in this no looting-killing should happen. So we survived that.

Here, Sunder Lal attributes his safe passage to the presence of an idol of Krishna. He indulges the possibility that Krishna might have been watching over them due to the presence of his idol in that train. In doing so, he attributes his train's *collective* good fortune – the lack of violent suffering – to their *collective* faith in this deity.

In contrast to Sunder Lal, whose invocation of the supernatural was fairly explicit, Bhanwarilal's remembrance of the Partition often involved an implicit identification with religious discourse. For example, while recounting his experience of chronic thirst and starvation in a refugee camp somewhere near Attock (formerly Campbellpur) and Hasan Abdal, Bhanwarilal began to tell me a story of Guru Nanak's (the first Sikh Guru) experience with thirst.

So Hasan Abdal station that is there, Sikh travellers go there. Panja Sahib is there. Panja Sahib is a pilgrimage destination. Even today people go to the *gurdwara* there.... So when people go from here, the importance of Panja Sahib is that, once Guru Nanak Dev-*ji* was travelling through that area with his disciples [Bhai] Bala and [Bhai] Mardana, when they became thirsty. So when they got thirsty they noticed that above them was [the house] of a Muslim *fakir* [ascetic]. So they sent a messenger and said we are thirsty.... So they said, "Will we give water to a *kafir* [infidel]? Get lost!" So they said our Guru is with us and he is thirsty. But in reply, they threw a boulder at them from the top of the mountain, a big one; and he [Guru Nanak] stopped it with his hand. That boulder stopped there. And where his hand touched the boulder, there you can see the imprint of his hand. And from that imprint in the boulder, water is flowing. So that is why it is called Panja Sahib because the *panja* [hand] is imprinted on it and water flows from that; natural water.

Although Bhanwarilal began telling this story due to his refugee camp's proximity to the famous Sikh shrine of Panja Sahib, the story is implicitly made relevant due to his own experience of thirst and starvation during the Partition. Spending months in those very same mountains, suffering from chronic thirst and hunger as a result of being persecuted for his faith, there is an uncanny parallel between the themes of Guru Nanak's legend and Bhanwarilal's experience of the Partition. In the way that he recounts the legend of Panja Sahib, one can sense his inchoate identification with the thirsty Guru Nanak, whose suffering ultimately proved the superiority of his faith.

This was merely the first of many times that Bhanwarilal invoked the Sikh Gurus while remembering the Partition. Another time, while discussing the narrative framing of my ethnography, Bhanwarilal told me that the Partition will only make sense to my readers if I frame it against a larger history. When I asked him what this might be, he responded with a spontaneous and detailed exposition of the history of Punjab. Bhanwarilal stressed that I must start my book by giving a background of the history of Punjab. His conception of this history began in the fifteenth century with the life of Guru Nanak and later the arrival of the first Mughal Emperor Babur. He emphasised the egalitarian and spiritual teachings of Guru Nanak and then went on to detail the 'anti-Hindu' reign of Babur; the two men were contemporaries. He recounted the names of all of the Sikh Gurus and laid particular emphasis on the martyrdom of Guru Arjan Dev and Guru Tegh Bahadur. Guru Arjan Dev's execution was ordered by the Mughal Emperor Jahangir in 1606, while Guru Tegh Bahadur was publicly beheaded in Delhi's Chandni Chowk in 1675 on the orders of the Mughal Emperor Aurangzeb (K. Singh 2004).

Bhanwarilal then went on to recount the 'Muslim invasions' of India by Ahmad Shah Abdali, Mahmud of Ghazni (although he lived from 971–1030 CE) and Nadir Shah. He mentioned Abdali's desecration of the Golden Temple, the holiest Sikh shrine. He then gave a brief overview of the British colonisation of India, including the brutal suppression of the First War of Indian Independence in 1857. Following this, he detailed a common-sense understanding of the Independence movement and Partition high-politics. As he moved from speaking of the secessionism and atrocities of the Muslim League to his own experience of the Partition, he paused to remind me that the Sikhs, throughout history, have been heavily oppressed by Muslims.

Much of what Bhanwarilal says in relation to history would be familiar to my readers as a repetition of the Hindu nationalist conception of its historical victimhood. But Bhanwarilal also references religious discourse – laying particular emphasis on the martyrdom of the Sikh Gurus, Guru Arjan Dev and Guru Tegh Bahadur – to access a specifically Sikh discourse of sacrifice and martyrdom.

The discourse of sacrifice and martyrdom plays a key role in Sikh religious discourse (Dorn and Gucciardi 2011; Fenech 1997; McLeod 1992). In Sikhism, salvation, or *mukti*, is intimately tied to the performance of *seva*, or altruistic service (J. Singh 2019). The first Sikh Guru, Guru Nanak is said to have laid the foundation for this discourse by teaching his disciples that the path to salvation lay in the liberation of the individual from self-centredness and the fear of oppression, insecurity, injustice and want (Dhillon 2010: 36; Fenech 1997). However, the Sikh discourse of *seva* is gendered such that for men the ultimate form of *seva* is altruistic sacrifice or martyrdom, in defence of the faith (J. Singh 2019). By contrast, *seva* for women does not entail sacrifice but rather service of the Sikh patriarchy through the performance of specifically gendered tasks (such as cooking) in religious settings (607–609).

Sikh phenomenology differs from that of Hinduism in that the dominant strands of Hinduism believe the physical world to be an illusion (Dhillon 2010). The latter also feeds into the Hindu view of ascetic monasticism – the renunciation of the physical world and its material comforts – as one possible path to salvation (Wilson 2002: 115). For Hindus then, salvation is attained once one's soul has been released from the burden of reincarnation: the cycle of life and death (Albertson 2009).

In Sikhism, salvation is found through an activist-like practice of one's faith combined with a universalist love for all, especially the oppressed (Dhillon 2010). Within this larger Sikh phenomenology of sacrifice as the path to salvation, the martyrdom of Guru Arjan Dev and

Guru Tegh Bahadur functions as an important historical symbol (Dorn and Gucciardi 2011; van der Veer 1994). When considered along with the martyrdom of the last Sikh Guru, Guru Gobind Singh, one finds that 3 of the 10 Sikh Gurus feature as martyrs (Dorn and Gucciardi 2011). What emerges from this is a religious and cultural history of the Sikhs and Punjab whose essentialism frames sacrifice and martyrdom as the national character of its people (Fenech 1997; van der Veer 1994).

Bhanwarilal taps into this sub-nationalist strain to extend his understanding of Sikhism and Punjab's history of sacrifice and martyrdom to encompass his own experience of the Partition. I am detailing this connection to cultural history to show that my informants' turn to the discourse of sacrifice builds on specific cultural crosscurrents that include historical and religious discourses. Additionally, Bhanwarilal's affinity for Sikh religious discourse must not be seen as undermining his belief in Hindu nationalism. As I detail in Chapter 7, Bhanwarilal – in line with the discourses of the RSS – believes that Sikhs are the 'sons of Hindus' and that the Sikh Gurus were also Hindus. Bhanwarilal's reverence for the Sikh Gurus is not an example of syncretism but is instead characterised by a chauvinistic hierarchisation of Sikhism as little more than a strand of Hinduism.

However, my larger point regarding my informants' turn to cultural and religious idioms of sacrifice and theodicy is that the recent wave of Partition oral historical and ethnographic literature has not percolated down to the lives and discourses of everyday people. What has pervaded the everyday consciousness instead is a piercingly sectarian question: 'If the Muslims got their Pakistan, why can we not have our *Hindustan?*' This demand for a Hindu nation, voiced through the juxtaposition of 'secular India' with 'sectarian Pakistan', is merely the logical progression of a discourse that seeks to understand what the Partition achieved. 'What was the point of all this?' they wonder. In this way, the sheer 'uselessness' of suffering, the futility of 'bad', 'asocial' death on an unimaginable scale, provokes the search for a form of theodicy.

Using culturally derived idioms of 'sacrifice' and 'martyrdom', the victims are elevated from the ignominy of 'useless suffering' and 'bad death' to the exalted status of national heroes, as 'martyrs' and 'freedom fighters'. This theodicy – this rationalisation of loss through a specific performance of mourning – features prominently in Bhanwarilal's narrative. Bhanwarilal's idea of sacrifice includes a broad swath of events ranging from the loss of property to the death of co-religionists and the *purusharth* of refugees in the immediate aftermath of the Partition. Bhanwarilal also refers to Partition-era honour killings as 'sacrifice'. He extolls the 'courage' of fathers who slaughtered their own daughters, branding them heroes. He frames their violence as 'sacrifice' and the women as 'martyrs'. And, while I specifically refer to Bhanwarilal's words here, in the ethnographic evidence I have used so far in this chapter, we have observed the universality of these tropes.

Previously, in the Introduction, I have referred to Ritu Menon and Kamla Bhasin's (1998) work on the phenomenon of women who were murdered by their own family for honour. Menon and Bhasin (32–60) found that the male relatives of these women remembered their murder as a kind of 'voluntary sacrifice'. Remembering them as honourable and virtuous women who 'chose' to die rather than risk the 'taint' of rape or forced marriage to the 'other', the men disguised their murder as assisted suicide. Menon and Bhasin identify this phenomenon as a direct consequence of the 'shame–fear–dishonour syndrome', a toxic circumstance where the 'shame' of rape was seen to bring 'dishonour' to the victim's relatives and communities such that death seemed like the only 'honourable' option (59).

In identifying the 'shame–fear–dishonour syndrome', Menon and Bhasin show that this violence of 'sacrifice' was itself sanctioned by a pre-existing cultural understanding of sacrifice and martyrdom. This comprised ritual practices of honour-based 'suicide' such as *sati* (the ritual burning alive of a widow on her husband's funeral pyre) and *jauhar* (the medieval Hindu practice of collective suicide to avoid 'defilement') (Misri 2014).

In this context, culture not only sanctions violence but provides an interpretative framework for the description of violence as 'sacrifice', as not-violence (Misri 2014). Menon and Bhasin (1998) observed that the men remembered these traumatic memories by reference to political and historical narratives, thus framing the murder of women as a 'necessary' and 'unavoidable' action. The men accessed the 'protective shadow of a coherent narrative' in how they understood these events (55). Reference to discourses rooted in history, politics and the patriarchy allowed men the cushion of a comforting narrative to explain away suffering, death and even murder committed off their own hands.

In contrast to the men, women survivors of the Partition remembered the violence differently by retaining '"the memory of loot, rape and plunder" in their bodies' (55). Thus, women absorbed the experience of rape within existing impressions of how they visualised the relationship between their bodies and society, understanding their sexual assault as a continuing 'fact' of the gendered exploitation of their bodies (Das 2007). This grim understanding of their body as a literal and symbolic receptacle of pain and violence in a patriarchal society was one of the ways in which women incorporated the extraordinariness of Partition violence within the ordinary (54–55).

What Menon and Bhasin (1998: 55) document here as the 'protective shadow of a coherent narrative' has been described by Benedict Anderson (1983) as nationalism's capacity to turn the individual deaths of its citizens into a shared immortality. To Partition survivors, this articulation feels inherently empowering, even emancipatory. It lifts their death and suffering from the ambiguous stateless (and helpless) position of a death *on-the-way-to-the-nation* to a death *for-the-nation*. It comprises an act of redemption.

Anderson's argument has been criticised by Herzfeld (2005) as a top-down formulation that fails to adequately theorise how and why individual citizens respond to the appeal of nationalism in the way that they do. Herzfeld argues that while the shared immortality of the nation provides existential comfort to the citizen, it also raises the question of whether this symbolic immortality *actually* helps individuals transcend their own *real* deaths. Herzfeld wonders, 'Why should people be willing to die for a formal abstraction?' (5).

While Herzfeld raises important questions that warrant attention, his questions reflect an understanding of 'sacrifice' that is different from my informants' usage of the term. My informants do not profess the wish to die for the nation but instead hallow the suffering in their past within the redemptive shared immortality of the nationalist imaginary. The description of 'bad' death and suffering as a sacrifice to the nation is not meant to transcend death but rather to transcend the 'uselessness' of their own suffering.

The discourse of sacrifice here emerges from an existing cultural understanding of sacrifice and martyrdom. The shared immortality it alludes to feeds into and off of larger nationalist discourses, grounding national belonging in the fact of a shared victimhood. This idea of a shared immortality lies at the heart of the idea of a 'homogenous population that is unified and anchored in a common mythological past and identified with a particular place and territory to the present day' (Schäuble 2014: 159). The theodicy that is the discourse of sacrifice transcends not only the 'uselessness' of suffering but also individual and group differences, producing a wounded sectarian nation out of a collectively victimised population.

A 'War of Fathers': The Gendered Connotations of the Discourse of Sacrifice

However, this discourse of sacrifice is also a masculine discourse in the way that it inters the ashes of the dead within the decorative urn of nationalism. I am intentionally drawing out this funerary analogy in order to draw attention to the gendered aspect of mourning visible here. Veena Das observes that 'it is the task of men to ritually create a body for the dead person and to find a place in the cosmos for the dead' (2007: 48). In the case of the Partition, men have done so by recourse to the discourse of suffering as sacrifice, disguising even their own violence using the pall of martyrdom. Thus, Das remarks, 'Just as women drank the pain so that life could continue, so men longed for martyrdom by which they could invite the evil back upon themselves and humanize the enormous looming images of nation and sexuality' (56).

This process of 'inviting the evil back upon themselves' through the discourse of martyrdom can be observed in Bhanwarilal's narrative. Bhanwarilal's ascription of sacrifice and martyrdom to the act of fathers murdering their daughters normalises the violence by implicit appeals to safeguard the honour and purity of the family and, by extension, the nation. 'What could we do? There was no alternative, there was no protection,' he insists, presenting these fathers as 'helpless', lacking any agency. He contrasts the sacrifices of these 'heroes' with the 'selfish'

Hindus and Sikhs who chose to stay in Pakistan even after the Partition. Bhanwarilal describes their decision as an act of selfishness, born out of greed for wealth and ancestral property. He sees these people as hapless minorities surrounded by a hostile majoritarian Islam, innocent lambs awaiting the coming of the wolf. The latter also reflects local ambiguities of the word 'refugee' since in the context of the Partition, a 'refugee' did not designate an alien or stateless person but instead 'a member of a communal minority in need of a majoritarian sanctuary' (Naqvi 2012: 475).

On the other hand, in presenting the hard work necessitated by the Partition, as sacrifice, this discourse helps survivors of the Partition retrospectively reconstruct their agency. Through stories of blood, sweat and toil, my informants present themselves not as victims of history but as martyrs and hard-workers of the nation. They present themselves as a community of men who did everything they could – including murder – to save their families (and nation) from dishonour.

Kinship is an important metaphor here. Veena Das (2007: 34) argues that the systemic rape and abduction of women during the Partition is best understood as a 'war of fathers'. Discourses of the Indian and Pakistani governments around the 'recovery' of abducted women visualised justice as the act of reuniting abducted women with their families (24–25). These simplistic discourses did not anticipate societal complexities concerning the 'dishonour' and 'shame' of abduction and rape. Social workers on the ground were confronted with the paradox of abducted women who refused to cooperate with their repatriation for fear of being rejected by their kin (29). Menon and Bhasin (1998) also argue that in circumstances where abducted women had found some measure of stability in domestic life with their abductors, forcibly repatriating them was akin to re-displacing them.

Das (2007) notes that these actions and discourses were symptomatic of the state seeing abducted women as passive victims awaiting saving. By envisioning and enacting justice in this context solely as the act of 'recovery', the state attempted to recover its own 'fertile female bodies' even as it sought to restore 'correct' patriarchal authority. Thus, Das (34) writes, 'The state's commitment to the recovery of women is the acknowledgment of the authority of the father as the necessary foundation for the authority of the state.'

The Indian government's implicit framing of the 'recovery' effort as one of the restoration of patriarchal authority involves a conflation of nationalism with kinship. The symbolic discourse of kinship imbues a moral content to politics (Chatterjee 2004) and serves as the foundation for the imagination of the nation (Anderson 1983). Anderson argues that improvements in print technology which allowed for the spread of vernacular literature to the masses helped establish 'linguistic national imagined communities' (see also Yuval-Davis 2003: 15). Building on that, Anderson (1983: 143) argues that people view their membership within the nation as 'natural' and not chosen or happenstance. Simultaneously, it is this veneer of a 'natural membership' that draws on essential ties based on blood and kinship that 'the nation, like the family, can ask for sacrifices – including the ultimate sacrifice of killing and being killed' (Yuval-Davis 2003: 15). After all, as Katherine Verdery (1996: 233) observes, nationalism is primarily a discourse of imagined kinship 'that is organized around ideas of youth and age, male and female, shared substance, blood and bone, and exclusion'. Furthermore, 'gendered images of kin – images of "brotherhood", "forefathers", and "mother" or "fatherland" – are at the very heart of nationalist imagery' (233).

The symbolism of kinship is evident in the way that the female body functions as a representation and delineation of the national homeland (Schäuble 2014; Yuval-Davis 2003). Thus, while fathers (and men in general) are seen as protectors of the nation, mothers (and women in general) come to symbolise national suffering. Michaela Schäuble (2014: 184–185) elucidates this link:

> As literal and symbolic reproducers of the nation, mothers and motherhood have become interchangeable with national suffering in the sense that the personal suffering of mothers in times of war is portrayed as a (voluntary) sacrifice for the nation. The suffering mother thus signifies the suffering of the homeland and the maternal body serves as a marker and maker of the nation and national territory.

Through the well-established trope of the suffering woman as a symbol for the suffering motherland, women are remembered not as 'heroines of history' but as its hallowed victims: as martyrs. Studying the politics of commemoration in the nineteenth and twentieth centuries, John Gillis (1994: 12) observes that the contributions of women are 'represented largely in terms of sacrifice, a traditional female role that only reinforced gender stereotypes'.

In contrast to men who are remembered as heroic soldiers and hard-workers, women are remembered only as martyrs. They are remembered as mothers and daughters who had to be 'sacrificed' to preserve the (Hindu) nation's 'honour'. In this way, the bodies of women – remembered only in sacrificial terms – become the 'surfaces on which their text of the nation is written' (Das 2007: 46). Raping, killing, sacrificing and abandoning women for the sake of honour and purity – resting on the authority of self-sacrificing, *purusharthi* fathers – the discourse of sacrifice delineates the boundaries of the Hindu nation, a boundary that is literally drawn across the bodies of women.

Ultimately, remembering hard work and suffering as sacrifice, remembering the victims of retributive genocide as 'martyrs', this discourse is an articulation of the Hindu nation. An inherently redemptive discourse, it shifts the death and suffering of kin and co-religionists from one *on-the-way-to-the-nation* to a sacrifice *for-the-nation*. Elevating the 'silent', ignominious suffering of the Partition to the status of martyrdom, it transcends the 'uselessness' of their suffering.

Notes

1 A dramatic or forceful exclamation.

2 Rohtak is a major industrial city of the state of Haryana. During the Partition a number of Punjabi Partition refugees (including many from Mianwali) were resettled here.

3 A largely pastoralist north Indian ethnic group. In the context of the displacement of the Partition, they may be regarded as the 'indigenous' residents of the land.

4 This could be a reference to sexual violence; remains unclarified.

5 'Lakh' is a unit followed in the South Asian numbering system, where 1 lakh = 100,000.

6　This is observable even in contemporary geopolitical contexts such as Israel-Palestine. Palestinian author and activist Dr Ghada Karmi (2015) has observed something similar in her memoir of her return to the besieged Gaza Strip. Karmi noted how the Palestinian people appeared to have responded to the Israeli state's relentless siege and persecution through zealous assertions of an Islamic Palestinian identity. Here too the existential threat posed by systematic persecution appeared to have made the assertion of one's faith a revolutionary act of resistance.

5

The *Purusharth* of Women

But their women come here to collect scrap paper. Our women did
not do any work.

—Rajaram

'I just have one last question, and I'll leave after that,' I told Rajaram as
I prepared to wrap up our conversation. It was a warm August morning
and we had been talking for nearly two hours. I could tell that he was
getting tired. 'My last question is this, now keeping in mind some of the
other refugee communities, such as Bangladeshis, Sri Lankans, or Syrian
refugees, does your experience of displacement, of living in camps and
tents make you feel any sense of solidarity towards them: that they are
like you?' Rajaram had a lot to say in reply:

Look, I'll tell you, every man.... Every community has its own
philosophy. I do not know about theirs. But their women come here
to collect scrap paper. Our women did not do any work. I have got to
know there is a park here where they have 500 tents. From many years.
That community, their Muslim societies might be helping them. I do
not know. Why? That community, I understand, is still backward. They
are weak. Understood? They have 500 tents. They live in tents. We did
not stay in tents for 5 years. We took over whatever the Muslims left
behind. Yes? Or, those who were the biggest [most prosperous] whose
possessions had survived, they came and they started their businesses.
I do not know what their livelihood is. Our people never took this
long. Assamese Muslims are here. They do not even have experience
of farming. Our people had experience of running a business. So

everywhere they did business. Whatever they could. Just like the examples I told you, some people opened a barber's shop. We have done work, have not asked [begged].... They are here from 5 to 4 years, I have got to know. But they do not have any experience of business yet, I think. What do they do? I just see that they are poor.

At this point Rajaram paused and asked his shop assistant for a *saree*.

I do not remember theirs. They work hard, they do *mazdoori*, I have not seen them in business. I have not seen these Assamese doing any work besides this scrap paper. Now they have two wives, two children, two girls. You understand? I do not know what condition they are in. Why, because I have not seen much. But those who came from our Punjab they have neither asked [begged], nor did they stay in tents for too long, nor did we take too much free ration.

A *saree* in hand, Rajaram paused again and pointed at his shop assistant. Rajaram said that his assistant had told him about a Muslim woman who lives in one of these tents and works as a rag-picker. So, Rajaram had told him to procure some *sarees* for them and has been distributing them as a way of helping them out. '6 women have taken them so far,' he said with a smile. Setting the *saree* aside, he continued:

During the winter, some people had distributed jerseys in the refugee camps. The biggest people. And to those recovering in hospitals. So in the camps they did this because the prosperous people of this area, of Delhi, they got blankets from the factories in Panipat and distributed those in the camps. This has happened. But no one ever said, 'Sir, my child is dying, give me two rupees so I can buy milk.' The government gave our ration for 2 years. Alright? But we did not depend on the ration. Alongside that we did physical labour. Now I do not know about these Assamese. I do not know what they do. I had said, we should distribute clothes for those children. So a man showed up, 'Whatever day you come, tell us and we'll distribute for you.' That means they still need it *na*? For us it was not like this. After we came we hosted weddings also. Marriages also happened in the tents [refugee camps]. But, whatever we could do, or a relative gave something, or a maternal uncle gave something, a paternal uncle gave something, we accepted, but no one said like this that we have very little. Or no one said like, 'Sir you are a rich person....' Nothing. Even during our girls' weddings we did not ask for anything. What is their system, I do not know. I gave someone the responsibility to study them and if they are very poor, then please help them.

At this point, I pointed out that contrary to his assertion that 'our women' had not worked, women had played an integral role in the post-Partition recovery of Punjabi families. I gave him examples of working women from my own family and from some of my informants. Aside from their labour within the home, some women had held government jobs, while others supplemented the family income through needlework, by running informal boutiques from within their homes. This led to the following exchange:

R: Yes, but that work is not bad.

Interviewer [PK]: Stitching, that is what I am saying that even the women did work, it is not like that.

R: Our girls have also done that. This work is not bad [demeaning].

PK: No, no that is not what I am implying.

R: To work is not a bad thing. Asking is bad.

PK: I see, I was just responding to what you said about how 'our women' did not work.

R: No that is not what I said. They did not do work *like this* [rag-picking].

PK: I see, they did not do work like that and asking [begging] is bad, is that what you are trying to say?

R: And they did not even do work *like that* [emphasising those final words].

This exchange encapsulates the gendered and sectarian nuances of this discourse of suffering and *purusharth* as sacrifice. When asked about the solidarity he feels for other contemporary refugees – in light of his past experience as a refugee – Rajaram begins to talk about a slum settlement of Assamese Muslim migrants in the vicinity of Gurgaon. This implicit conflation of Bangladeshi refugees with Assamese and Bengali Indian migrants echoes the muddle of mainstream political discourse. In recent times, the BJP has often branded slum settlements of poor Assamese and Bengali Indian Muslims as 'Bangladeshi' and 'Rohingya' in order to whip up hysteria about the scale of 'mass-infiltration' (undocumented immigration) along India's eastern border. This has been a key argument for the BJP in its attempts to construct the CAA along with a nationwide NRC as exercises necessary to weed out the 'termites' and 'intruders' 'corrupting' India's body politic.[1]

Rajaram's speech lacks the BJP's vitriol but retains its implicit racialisation of Assamese and Bengali Muslims (especially the poor) as un-Indian. Rajaram begins by drawing attention to the fact that 'their women come here to collect scrap paper. Our women did not do any work.' Later, when pressed on his comments about women, he returns to his observation that he has seen Assamese women working as rag-pickers. He clarifies that he did not mean to imply that Punjabi women did not do any work at all but merely that, in contrast, Punjabi women *only* did work befitting their dignity, such as needlework. Framing it in the sense of 'Our women did not do any work, *like this*' transforms this into a classist and sectarian discourse of Hindu patriarchal pride.

Drawing attention to how women often carry the 'burden of representation', Nira Yuval-Davis writes that women are 'constructed as the symbolic bearers of the collectivity's identity and honour'. Building on this, Yuval-Davis observes that in the nationalist imaginary, men go to war (or work) for the sake of the 'womenandchildren [*sic*]'. Women are firmly associated with the familial, within the imaginary of the collective. Moreover, the 'womenandchildren' are seen as passive beneficiaries (dependents) of the actions of men (Yuval-Davis 2003: 45).

In Rajaram's narrative, the destitution of Assamese Muslim women symbolises the destitution of the entire community. Conversely, by drawing attention to the displacement of women from their familial (and domestic) realms, Rajaram implies a disruption of the 'natural order'. So, by questioning why 'their women' are reduced to such harsh and 'degrading' labour, Rajaram insinuates a fundamental deficiency within these communities. Remarking on how he has seen these women rag-picking, he moves on to an exposition on the 'weakness' and 'backwardness' of this community. He insists that unlike Punjabis, these people have overstayed their time in tents. Where Punjabi refugees are constructed as resourceful, determined and hard-working, Rajaram constructs Assamese and Bengali migrants as passive victims dependent on the support and charity of others.

It is revealing then that in the hard work of these Assamese Muslim women, Rajaram perceives not *purusharth* but destitution. That these women make a livelihood from rag-picking is not seen as an example of resilience but as evidence of the symbolic impotence of 'their men'. He reminds us that Punjabi men were *purusharthi* and clever. He also reaffirms the success of Punjabi men by reminding us that 'our women' were not reduced to performing 'this work' on the streets. Rajaram's differentiation of 'good' and 'bad' work is fundamentally casteist. In drawing attention to the 'bad' work that the women of this community have been reduced to, caste and gender hierarchies intersect to articulate a deeply problematic, othering discourse. Where the labour of Assamese and Bengali women is used to malign their communities, the labour of Punjabi women is obscured to assuage the pride of *purusharthi* Punjabi men, a discourse that is both classist and sexist.

In the stories of *purusharth*, as told by men, women are conspicuously absent from the scene. If they feature at all, they do so as beneficiaries of the man-work of refugees, as their dependants. This misogyny is reflected even in the Indian government's rehabilitation efforts. In the state's discourses, women were not seen as 'useful workers' but at best as secondary or tertiary earners for their households. Furthermore, the economic value of their domestic work was ignored altogether (A. Datta 2019).

This was far from the reality of the role women played during this period. However, in this game of smoke and mirrors that obscures, disguises and undermines the hard work of women, women were not just passive victims. The women I encountered in my fieldwork, often played an active part in reproducing this discourse of man-work, supporting and reifying the discourses of men. As my grandaunt Anjali explained, the fact that women did not want to highlight their contributions did not surprise her in the least as this is what was expected of them as 'good' wives and daughters. That is, by retelling and reifying the stories of *purusharth* of their closest male relatives, these women were merely performing their traditional gender roles as 'good women'.

In the obfuscation of the hard work – or *purusharth* – of women, we observe how women absorbed their experience of the Partition within the fabric of their everyday lives. Just as Veena Das (2007) found that women's experience of sexual violence was absorbed within the 'ordinary', so too I found that the memory of their hard work was absorbed within the ordinary rhythm of domestic life. The hard work of women – especially within the home – was seen as a given, a signifier of normality. On the other hand, the labour of men was seen as a product of the disruption and displacement caused by the Partition. By emphasising the harsh physical and 'menial' nature of the labour of men, stories of *purusharth* contrast the life of *zamindari* prosperity with the poverty that followed the Partition. Here, the labour performed by men is seen as unusual but necessary.

Thus, the domestic work of women was seen as a continuation of the natural order, assumed and invisible. All of the work that women did during this period – cooking in communal tandoors, sewing, domestic chores and providing care, including childcare – within the household remained largely unacknowledged. It was subsumed within images of domesticity since 'this is what women are *supposed* to do anyway'. Where women worked commercially, even seeking employment outside the household, their contribution was omitted for the sake of patriarchal pride.

The erasure of the hard work of women is a well-established narrative trope that is visible even in the state's musealisation. For example, this can be observed in the Partition Museum's (Amritsar, Punjab) memorialisation of the experience of women. In a sprawling hall whose props and exhibits seek to convey something of the Partition's denomising violence, the museum prominently displays a well. A banner detailing the statistics concerning 'abducted' and 'recovered' women hangs above it. The well itself is meant to memorialise the 'suicide' of Hindu and Sikh women in the village of Thoa Khalsa. Over the years, the *jauhar* (collective suicide of women) at Thoa Khalsa has become a symbol of the 'sacrifice' and 'martyrdom' of Hindu and Sikh women during the Partition (Butalia 2000; Menon and Bhasin 1998; G. Pandey 2001). This memory has also been used generously by the Hindu and Sikh far-right for Islamophobic propaganda (Butalia 2000; G. Pandey 2001).

At the very end of the museum's chronological memorialisation of the Partition lay a room that was dubbed the 'Gallery of Hope'. A plaque situated in this gallery – the last room in the museum – argued, 'What helps societies to overcome trauma is memory, and hope'. The gallery contained the biographies of some Partition survivors who went on to become spectacularly successful in their respective fields. The illustrious names listed here included Milkha Singh (Olympian athlete), Dharampal Gulati (the founder of MDH spices) and Brijmohan Lal Mujjar (founder of Hero Cycles and Hero MotorCorp). The gallery also included references to some of the impactful literature on the Partition. This included the works of Gulzar, Bapsi Sidhwa, Khushwant Singh, Bhisham Sahni, Krishna Sobti, Joginder Paul, Intizar Hussain, Qurratulain Haider, Rajinder Singh Bedi and Nanak Singh. With the exception of a passing reference to Krishna Sobti and Qurratulain Haider, all of the individuals mentioned in this gallery were men. The omission of Amrita Pritam was particularly glaring given her fame and literary acclaim. Similarly glaring were the omissions of Ahmed Ali, Saadat Hassan Manto and Faiz Ahmed Faiz. Intizar Hussain's inclusion – the only Pakistani individual in this gallery – appeared to be little more than a token gesture.

The latter were evidence that the 'Gallery of Hope' appeared to have paradoxically accepted the post-Partition borders of India, Pakistan and Bangladesh. Here, 'hope' was predicated on an uncritical acceptance of the Partition. 'Hope' in this gallery was to be found only in the 'achievements' of Hindu and Sikh Partition refugees and not among the biographies of those who went across the border. In its omission of women and of refugees who migrated to Pakistan and Bangladesh, the 'hope' museumised by this gallery was a fairly standard articulation of the narrative of *purusharth*.

The 'Gallery of Hope' in fact musealises the ethnic and gendered contours of the post-Partition nation. This museum implicitly imagines the nation as a 'fraternity of men' (McClintock 1995), memorialising the hard work and achievements of men, and the 'hope' these symbolise. Women are largely confined to sacrificial commemoration as 'martyrs', their wounds and suffering symbolising the suffering, wounded nation.

James E. Young (1988) observes that museums and memorials reflect particular kinds of political and cultural knowledge. Young (1993: 21) argues that 'the state-sponsored monuments' traditional function [is] as self-aggrandizing locus for national memory'. Thus, memorials remember the past as per the political needs of the present (Raychaudhuri 2012). This is especially visible in the Partition Museum's reproduction of the discourse of sacrifice and martyrdom.

In this chapter, I interrupt this discourse by documenting the *purusharth* of women. The turn to specifically focus on the stories of women comes from a recognition of the way in which the discourse of sacrifice eulogises women while obscuring their *actual lives*. This discourse draws on the gendered body of the nation to focus on the suffering of women as a symbol for the suffering nation. In the process, women are remembered in purely passive terms, as victims and martyrs. It is in this vein that John Gillis (1994: 10) observes that 'women and minorities often serve as symbols of a "lost" past, nostalgically perceived and romantically constructed, but their actual lives are most readily forgotten'. While Gillis makes this observation in the context of the West's politics of commemoration, he articulates an important observation about the discourse of sacrifice. That is, these nostalgic and romantic constructions of self-sacrificing women martyrs, overwrite the *actual lives* of women.

Of Sewing Machines and Needlework

I became aware of the nuances of this discourse only after I encountered the meanings invested in sewing machines. In relation to the hard work of women, sewing machines function as a root metaphor. According to Sherry Ortner (1973: 1341), root metaphors function as a 'source of categories for conceptualizing social phenomena'. Sewing machines were (and to a very large extent still remain) an integral part of most upper- and lower-middle-class households in South Asia. The women of my grandparents' and great-grandparents' generation learnt needlework (including stitching, sewing, embroidery, tailoring and knitting) at a very early age, with sewing often being introduced to them as a form of play. The women of this generation often received a sewing machine of their own – as part of their dowry – as a symbolic marker of their passage into womanhood. Equipped with a sewing machine of their own, Punjabi women, especially, would often sew their clothes themselves, in addition to household linen such as pillow covers, runners, throws and other such miscellaneous items. Women would also knit prolifically, making their own shawls, pullovers, jackets, caps, gloves, scarves and mufflers. In the era that preceded the mass-consumption of ready-made garments and linen, the needlework of women comprised a substantial economic output.

In the years that followed the Partition, sewing machines were used by the Indian government as part of its rehabilitation efforts. Ritu Menon and Kamla Bhasin (1998), for example, note that women living in institutions were provided with organised and self-employment through the setting up of tailoring centres and the distribution of sewing machines. Anjali Bhardwaj Datta (2019) observes that the kind of work and training that the government offered women refugees reflected clear biases and assumptions of the kinds of work considered appropriate for women. Thus, women were offered training and employment primarily in the fields of embroidery, stitching, tailoring, and weaving (1937).[2] This is yet another example of what Kaur (2007) has observed as the Indian government's resolve to leave the social order of refugee communities undisturbed.

During my fieldwork in Gurgaon, I found that a family friend of my grandaunt Anjali still had the sewing machine that their mother had received from the Indian government (Figure 5.1). She had received this Usha brand, Indian-made sewing machine in 1948, while she and her family were still living in a refugee camp in north India. While no one in their family had any memory of the specifics of this story, they had held on to this sewing machine as a symbol of her memory. However, despite its symbolic value, the machine was not seen as a relic of the past. As visible in the following picture, the machine was well-oiled, threaded and ready to use.

As other informants told me, a similar story had unfolded within the home, where women prohibited from seeking employment outside

Figure 5.1   The Usha-make sewing machine my grandaunt Anjali's family friends still possessed

Source: Photograph by author.

the home began to run de-facto boutiques from within their homes. In this way, women were not just passive recipients of the *purusharth* of men but were active workers in their own right. Their needlework constituted a substantial source of income while also contributing materially to their household in the form of home-made linen intended for domestic use.

Thus, deeply embedded within this cultural context, sewing machines are a potent root metaphor imbued with 'great conceptual elaborating power' (Ortner 1973: 1340). Sewing machines symbolise a process of production, economic recovery, gender relations and memory to women survivors of the Partition of India. Closely intertwined with the traditional gender roles of femininity, speaking of sewing machines also evoked contestations of the hegemonic masculine discourse of *purusharth* as sacrifice, but also organic, everyday critiques of patriarchy.

This tension constitutes an important part of the stories of women. On the one hand, sewing machines and needlework in general symbolise traditional gender norms. Women informants not only subscribed to these ideas but also played their part in reproducing discourses that devalued their own hard work. But, on the other hand, speaking of needlework also evoked organic critiques of such dominant ideologies. Thus, in the way that these subtle critiques coexist beside a dominant patriarchal ideology, they are best understood as 'subordinate discourses'.

Brinkley Messick (1987) defines subordinate discourses as discourses that while conversant in the grammar of the dominant ideology also comprise subtle subversions of the dominant discourse. They do not seek to overthrow but rather coexist while establishing a degree of autonomy. In this, subordinate discourses share something of Michel de Certeau's (1984: 29–40) idea of 'tactics'. Tactics, like subordinate discourses, comprise small acts of appropriation rather than a full-blown revolution. Tactics are the resistive techniques of everyday individuals when confronted with the panoptic power of institutions: 'strategies'. Tactics are survivalist and emanate from an impulse of 'making do' (de Certeau 1984: 29; Buchanan 2000: 108).

Subordinate discourses are different from alternative or competing ideologies, since the latter involve an 'oppositional conceptual order' (Messick 1987: 217). The subordinate status of such discourses is based on the social efficacy of the dominant ideology. The hegemony of dominant ideologies like the patriarchy is explained by the fact that 'women subscribe to them, at least in a public sense, for there is no other "world" to live in' (216). This is an important nuance since, even though the association of needlework with femininity represents the hegemony of patriarchy, needlework was not remembered by my informants as a site of oppression. Rather, some of my informants, such as Falguni, found a genuine measure of freedom in their lives through the commercial success of their needlework. The latter is consistent with Messick's observation:

In communicative worlds jammed with patriarchal cultural constructs, a distinctively female perspective is to be found not so much in what women say as in what they do, located in the structure of such women's spaces as menstrual huts, and in such specialized women's activities as weaving. (Messick 1987: 217)

Therefore, speaking of needlework with women informants helped create a discursive space where such subordinate discourses were remembered and articulated.

I became specifically interested in the hard work of women shortly after my trip to the Partition Museum in March 2018. The Partition Museum had on display a number of random artefacts such as a sewing machine, a comb, a dagger and other such simple everyday trinkets which were among the few personal possessions that refugees brought with them during the Partition. I had found these exhibits captivating since, inspired by Aanchal Malhotra's (2017) work on 'material memory', I had similarly been on the lookout for old personal artefacts that my informants might have still retained from their Partition journeys.

My visit to the museum had provoked a significant degree of curiosity in my grandaunt. She had originally planned to accompany me to Amritsar but had been unable to due to other personal commitments. The morning after I returned from Amritsar, we talked about the museum, and I told her about all the artefacts they had on display. When I mentioned the sewing machine, her eyes lit up and she said that she had an old sewing machine like that lying at home (Figure 5.2).

A few days later, she had the storeroom cleaned and together we dragged the machine out. Removing the dusty cloth that covered it, she pointed at the embossed panel on the machine. 'Tolaram Ramdass and Co., Post Box No. 130, Karachi', it said – the address of the seller I assumed (Figure 5.3). 'This machine was my mother's,' she said. 'This is from her dowry. She got married in 1942 and they brought it with them from Pakistan.' She beamed with pride as she said, 'Back then there were only three types of sewing machine: Usha, Singer or the German-made Pfaff. This is Pfaff. Pfaff was the best.' I ran my fingers over the panel in awe. This sewing machine had been sitting here all along, here, in the very house that I been staying in for a significant portion of my fieldwork.

Figure 5.2   My grandaunt's sewing machine

Source: Photograph by author.

Figure 5.3   The embossed panel on the machine that reads, 'Tolaram Ramdass &
Co., Post Box No. 130, Karachi'

Source: Photograph by author.

My grandaunt had no idea how this sewing machine had reached Delhi. She was born in India, in 1950, three years after the Partition. As a result, she neither had any first-hand memories of this event nor did anyone else in our family remember how this had come to pass. However, she suspected that her father had been transferred to Delhi a few months before the Partition, allowing them the luxury of migrating with most of their possessions.

For my grandaunt, this machine was not a symbol of the Partition or our family's displacement. In the hierarchy of meanings that my grandaunt associated with this machine, its connection to the memory of her mother stood foremost. 'I will not give it to anyone. This is a token of my mother,' my grandaunt declared. And then, almost as an afterthought, she added, 'I can no longer thread the needle...'

As my grandaunt remembered her mother, she drew my attention to some of the objects with whom my great-grandaunt's memory was attached. The little pink cover, on top of the machine (visible in Figure 5.2), had been stitched by her. A beautiful chequered throw that covered the table on which I kept my suitcase had been made by her care-worker in the terminal stages of her illness. The throw (which I now wish I had photographed) was made from discarded pillow covers. These had then been stitched together, front beside back, to form four red and white checks. 'In those days all women would stitch and we never let any cloth go to waste. If something got old we would just cut it up and make something new. Recycling,' my grandaunt added with a hearty laugh.

Having my attention drawn to the memories and cultural practices embedded in seemingly ordinary pieces of linen was eye-opening. Even though my great-grandaunt and her care-worker no longer inhabited this home, their essence – embodied by the remnants of their stitching – lingered. But in order to see it, one had to look closely. Like the cover and the throw, the stories of the hard work of women had hitherto inhabited the margins of my peripheral vision, subsumed within a normative idea of the 'ordinary'. To make them visible, I now needed to turn my attention towards these very images of domesticity.

As we continued this conversation over the course of the next week, my grandaunt gave me two potential leads. She told me that Dayaram's wife, Basanti, had done stitching on a big scale. Dayaram was my late grandfather's best friend, and I had interviewed him in December 2017 during my visit to Dehradun. 'Government jobs did not pay that much. She worked a lot,' my grandaunt revealed. According to her, Basanti had stitched, altered and sold clothes from within her home on a big scale. In this way, Basanti's hard work – domestic and commercial – had been instrumental in the rehabilitation of her family. This fact about Basanti stood in stark contrast to the way she had excused herself from our conversation, when we had visited them. Basanti had simply said that she was only 6 years old at the time of the Partition and as a result, did not have any significant memories of it. Happy to be left alone with Dayaram, I had not pressed any further.

When asked why neither Basanti, nor Dayaram had mentioned this, my grandaunt replied, 'In reality, women will never talk about this. They do not want to go against their husband. The thing is male ego can be very touchy, especially about money.' My grandaunt explained that while many of the women of that generation had worked and earned money, few would talk about it at length, even if their husbands had passed on. They feared that it might be seen as undermining their late husband's memory. My grandaunt's critique of the fragility of masculinity, however, was ambiguously positioned beside her awareness and performance of traditional gender roles. It constituted a subordinate discourse, one that strives for survival under the shadow of a dominant ideology.

Furthermore, my grandaunt's remark also reminded me of my own positionality within this discourse. As a male researcher, women were always unlikely to bring up 'feminine' topics such as needlework in conversation. So, the hard work of women had remained additionally hidden from me because women informants (my grandaunt included) had presumed my lack of interest.

The second lead that my grandaunt provided me was that of Falguni. While I could not visit Basanti and Dayaram again (due to the distance involved), Falguni lived in Faridabad and, incidentally, had been among one of my first informants. I had first been introduced to her in June 2015, while I was conducting fieldwork for my MPhil dissertation. Although I never used any of the material from that interview in my thesis, I had enjoyed listening to her stories.

When I returned to Delhi in July 2017, I had gotten back in touch with her. Since she lived a mere 10 minutes away from my maternal uncle

Shailendra's house (where I stayed for a major portion of my fieldwork), Falguni and I fell into a regular routine of tea-chats. Every few weeks, whenever I came to stay with my maternal uncle, I would meet Falguni for a cup of tea at her place. And yet, despite the frequency of our meetings, this was the first time that anyone (including Falguni herself) had ever mentioned sewing. My grandaunt told me that Falguni was an expert at sewing and knitting. Apparently, she had done sewing on a massive scale, substantially contributing to the household income. However, 82 years old now and bed-ridden since 2015, Falguni had not done any sewing in years. The only journeys she embarked on now were figurative in nature. She loved to tell stories and I was only too happy to listen.

Falguni's Story

Falguni was 12 years old at the time of the Partition. While her family originally hailed from Karor Lal Essan (a village mid-way between Layyah and Bhakkar), they had been living in Karachi at the time of the Partition. Her father had owned and run a massive departmental store in Karachi, the biggest in the city, according to Falguni. Her family migrated to India in September 1947. By then, Karachi had been engulfed by what seemed like endemic violence. Although, in her experience, the situation in Karachi had not been as bad as in other places, the non-Muslim minorities of Karachi no longer felt safe in the city. Travelling by train through Hyderabad and Mirpur (in Sindh, Pakistan), they reached Ambala. Later, their family moved to Delhi as they were allotted a house in the up and coming refugee colony of Lajpat Nagar.

Falguni began learning needlework at an early age. In fact, while living in Karor sewing was a form of play. One of her older cousins had a tailoring shop there and at the end of every day, he would send home a sack of waste cuttings. Falguni and her cousin would scavenge through the sack looking for the bigger cuttings and use them to make something new. 'In the evening, my father would come home, what did you do, today we made this,' she laughed heartily, reminiscing.

While they were staying in Ambala, Falguni received some formal instruction in sewing, at her school. In the fifth grade, Falguni remembered that her all-girls school had had a class dedicated to teaching them cooking and sewing. Falguni earned a name for herself on the very first day when she re-stitched a *salwar* that her teacher had cut up to test her. 'That *salwar* of mine was shown to the whole school. All the lines were straight, there were only straight lines.... So she started saying your work is very neat. I said I even stitch my own clothes at home,' Falguni remembered.

At the age of 15 – while they were living in Lajpat Nagar – Falguni took a course on sewing. One of their neighbours had started a sewing school for girls within her house. She sent word to other families in the neighbourhood, requesting them to enrol their daughters. The woman organising the course was a Partition refugee herself, and thus, supporting her family by teaching sewing to the children of other refugees. 'Back then the fees was just 3 rupees. Money had value then. So I went. I knew everything before that as it is,' Falguni said. Falguni was at such an advanced level that she ended up finishing that six-month course in just three months. Over the course of those three months, she also became friends with her instructor. 'She told me your work is very neat, you should start your own work [shop]. I said that comes later. I said after marriage who knows where my husband will go, won't go, will he support me, will they let me work.'

However, contrary to her doubts about the prospects for sewing commercially, events seemed to transpire in her favour. One day, a neighbour of hers requested the alteration of one of her blouses. Her neighbour had heard from someone that Falguni was extremely good at sewing. For her part Falguni quickly finished the work and had sent it back to her house. When she received it, she was overjoyed and came over to Falguni to tell her that this was the first time she had gotten her blouse sewn from a woman. This comment provoked a vociferous response from Falguni. Falguni retorted, 'I do not do the work of a woman, I do the work men do. The work I do is of a tailor. Not that of women.'

Falguni explained that the sewing of women is seen as a hobby, whereas a man doing the same is considered a *darzi* (professional tailor). 'The difference is that women do not get paid as much. "Yes, they'll just do it like that, they do not know." So even if men are not skilled, they are still men. So that is why,' Falguni said. I in turn cited the culinary industry as a similar example of an industry where men are handsomely rewarded for commercialising typically 'domestic' skills.[3] Falguni exasperatedly remarked, 'Yes! But ... that.... That is what men do,' making both of us laugh.

Subordinate discourse is visible in this example. This is so as Falguni perceives the ascription of femininity to her work as an affront that undermines its value. Instead, by equating her work to that of a man, she establishes a higher value. She appropriates the *darzi*'s hallowed masculine status to score a point for herself, while leaving the supremacy of masculinity itself unchallenged. She does not defend the tailoring of women as a whole, but instead distinguishes her work from that of other women.

At other times, the subordinate discourse at play was more subtle, observable in her memories of the impact her newfound financial independence had on her life. As word of Falguni's skills spread through her network of family and friends, she began to receive a steady stream of work. The money she earned brought her a degree of autonomy. Falguni remembered that through her sewing she was able to pay for her own wedding dresses. Even after marriage, Falguni kept her savings private. 'I would not give my money to anyone. I would save it for myself.... Now, whenever I would visit [family in] Delhi, then I would not ask him [husband]. All my Delhi expenses also I made from that,' Falguni said.

Over the years, Falguni's savings comprised a consistent and substantial contribution to the overall wealth of their household. When she and her late husband were constructing the house she currently lives in, she paid for all the doors. 'These doors that you see these were built by my money.... All of them. We would not have money. It would run out,' Falguni said, beaming with pride as she drew my attention to the doors in her home.

Her financial independence also gave her the power to assert her own stance unhindered by familial and patriarchal moral codes. For example, Falguni remembered the time she helped her visually impaired cousin elope with his girlfriend. Her cousin, known affectionately as Tej-*ji* (pseudonym), was a professor of philosophy with a Hindi Sahitya Ratan and a PhD in philosophy. He fell in love with a woman whom he would often meet at the bus stop, on his way to work. However, while the young couple were keen to get married, her family did not approve of Tej-*ji* due to his disability. Falguni intervened in favour of her cousin's marriage, standing up to both her own family and that of her sister-in-law's. Using her savings, Falguni helped the young couple elope and accompanied them to the registrar's office to register their marriage. Later Falguni also accompanied Tej-*ji* to his in-laws' home, so that they might try and soothe their anger. In this way, Falguni's financial freedom enabled such everyday acts of subversion.

An interesting aspect of Falguni's stories was that they did not comprise fable-like tales of *purusharth*. This is not to say that Falguni, and other women refugees, did not value hard work. However, the terms of the discourse did not allow for the celebration of their own work as *purusharth*. The exuberance and extraordinariness of the stories of *purusharth* told by men was contrasted by the sparseness of details in Falguni's descriptions of her work. This difference was also evocative of femininity's normative association with needlework. For Falguni, her performance of needlework was not a disruption of the 'natural order'. Needlework, like the domestic work of women, was considered work that women were *supposed* to do. This normativeness meant that there was nothing special or redemptive about her performance of it. By contrast the dramatic stories of blood, sweat and toil told by men were implicit admissions of how unnatural physical labour felt to them.

For Falguni, the only 'unusual' aspect of her needlework was the way in which its commercialisation granted her access to the market economy. It is for this reason that her subordinate discourse is closely linked to money. She places great emphasis (and pride) on the fact that she kept her savings private. She used her savings to tactically subvert her husband's influence on the things that were important to her: her visits to her parents, shopping and indulging her children and grandchildren. In this way, while her savings indirectly contributed to the household finances, she used them to establish her independence. Her money gave her the means to resist some of the influences of patriarchal authority on her everyday life. While the story of her cousin's elopement provides a particularly dramatic example of this, the quotidian impact of this was far more subtle.

Falguni did not always succeed in her subversion of patriarchal authority. One of her biggest regrets was that her family had not supported her ambition for a career outside the home. Falguni was highly educated and like her cousin Tej-*ji* held a Sahitya Ratan – the equivalent of an MA – in Hindi. Following that, she and a friend of hers, Manjeet, had completed a teacher training course together. However, Falguni's family – especially her brothers – refused to support her in pursuing this any further. Part of the reason for this was that her eldest brother relied on Falguni for his infant son's childcare. While her needlework (including its commercialisation) was seen as a natural extension of her domestic responsibilities, a career outside the home was considered a step too far. She recounted this incident with great regret.

F: There was a Manager [in Eastern Post] whom we knew. He was a relative. He came home, said your daughter has passed with excellent scores. Show me the mark-sheet. I showed the mark-sheet so he said, 'Come I'll see to it that you get a job.' So my brother started saying, 'No, among us, women do not do jobs. They will say can her brother not feed her?' Seriously if I had got that job, today I would have retired at such a good position. [*Pauses.*] He [husband] would always say, your family are completely *koop-mandook* [*laughs*].

Interviewer [PK]: What does *koop-mandook* mean?

F: A frog that lives in a well [*laughs*]. They are called *koop-mandook*.

PK: As in they can't see the world beyond their well [*smiling*].

F: Yes, they don't want to see. Anyway he said there are seats in English [for teachers] do you want them? I said I'll go home and tell you. I came home and there was a storm in my house. He [brother] is crying. Those two brothers, one after the other are pacing the room. [*Both laugh.*] They said, no need for this.... So then my teacher training went to waste. Feel very sad about it. That Manjeet got her placement, she did it. I said Manjeet you did well out of this, my whole boat only sank. [*Laughs, seems forced.*] After marriage men should offer support. Both these brothers could not do that. They could not take care of a small child. He [her nephew] must have been one and a half to two years.

Recounting this bitter argument, Falguni uses humour to criticise her brothers. Interestingly, Falguni recounted this conversation twice. In her first iteration of this story here, she remembers her husband being similarly critical of her brothers. In this version, it is her husband who mocks her brothers by calling them *koop-mandook* (frogs in a well). Her husband's sarcasm implies that he would have been supportive of Falguni's teaching job.

This, however, changed when she retold this story in June 2018. This time she remembered this conversation as relatively more vitriolic. She put all of the blame on her elder brother and his disinterest in parenting his own son. She remembered how her brother had influenced her father, arguing that letting Falguni work would 'dishonour' them all. 'What will people say? Now will we eat *rotis* earned by our sister?' her brother had declared. Far from her usual cheery, sarcastic tone, she seemed (understandably) bitter and remorseful as she recounted this.

In this retelling, she also implicitly connected her brother's misogyny to her husband. Speaking in a low voice, as if she was sharing a secret, Falguni said that her husband had also been quite traditional in his ways. She remembered that before they got married, he had liked her because she did not have a job. He wanted a housewife and had even said that 'I do not want to earn money. I want to establish a home.' Explaining this, Falguni said that this was unusual at the time as most Punjabi men and families preferred working women, since back in those days one person's salary was not enough to support a household. As someone who earned her money by working within the home, Falguni combined the best of both worlds. The invisibility of her earnings assuaged patriarchal pride while also satisfying urgent material needs. This was as close as Falguni ever came to critiquing her husband in my presence.

However, Falguni's critique of these traditional, patriarchal values was perplexingly followed by a somewhat chiding aside about her daughter-in-law's lack of domesticity. Falguni's daughter-in-law was a working professional and had been working even before her marriage. Rather than channel her own unfulfilled career ambitions into expressing solidarity for her daughter-in-law's career, Falguni lamented that she had had to manage the household of their joint family almost till the day she became bedridden. Falguni told me that despite always having had domestic help, she had been doing most of the cooking and overseeing all of the housework. When I tried to defend her daughter-in-law, Falguni disagreed saying, 'She did not have those feelings [domesticity] from the beginning.' The implication was one of neglect and indifference to her 'domestic responsibilities'.

With a great sense of irony, I observed how, in this scenario, one woman's right to work meant another's domestic prison (in addition to their paid domestic help). Her daughter-in-law had made her contribution to the processes that had kept Falguni anchored to her kitchen. Yet to see Falguni's words as resentful of her daughter-in-law would also be a disservice to their relationship. Despite all the talk, to the best of my knowledge – as gleamed even in conversations with common relatives – no one in that household, including Falguni, had ever stood in the way of her daughter-in-law's career. *The frogs were no longer trapped in their well.* Perhaps there was some unspoken solidarity there, after all.

One day when I went to visit Falguni, I found her sitting up in bed, reading her cousin Tej-*ji*'s autobiography. She showed it to me with pride and then said that she had not read it in a while and so felt like re-reading it. Later that day, with a tinge of sadness in her voice, she told me that she and Tej-*ji* had always had very similar interests, whether that was the Sahitya Ratan in Hindi or creative writing. Falguni told me that in her youth she had written a number of short stories but unlike her cousin, had never had the courage to publish them. 'My talent has been completely wasted,' she lamented.

Seeing my interest in the subject, Falguni briefly narrated one of her short stories from memory. The story was called 'Namaste-*ji*' and was based on a real-life incident where she and a friend of hers were once catcalled by a persistent group of young men. The men stalked them for a good distance, continuously calling out to them with cries of '*namaste-ji, namaste-ji*'. When she crossed the bridge that marked the halfway mark to her house, she turned around and very politely said, 'Since you have come till here, why don't you come home with us so we can welcome you properly.' Confronted by Falguni, the men apologised and crept away in silence. When I asked her why they ran away like that, Falguni explained that it was because by inviting them home, she had implied that she was going to get her family together and have them beaten up. Falguni said that she could have had them beaten up in the market itself, had she called for help. But she had chosen not to. At this point she looked into my eyes and in a firm and sincere voice said, 'I was not afraid of anyone then.' In that moment, as our eyes met, there was no doubt about the truth of what she spoke.

Like her mocking description of her family as *koop-mandook*, her short story too comprises a subordinate discourse. In the story, she deliberately interrupts the male gaze by turning around and challenging her stalkers. Additionally, her final comment to me about her lack of fear drives home her rejection of the notion of male saviours, a theme evident in many of the other stories from her youth. Yet, interestingly, when confronting her stalkers, Falguni falls back on the symbolic protection of her male relatives. This is not a full-blown critique of the patriarchy so much as an act of everyday resistance within it. It constitutes survival more than revolution, but a survival on her own terms nonetheless. This theme of an underlying subordinate discourse symbolises the role that sewing played in the lives of women. As much as sewing upheld a certain domestic order, the money it generated brought women like Falguni a measure of freedom.

Bhagwanti's Story

Discovering this side of Falguni – an informant I had known for a considerable period of time – made me return to other women informants with similar questions about needlework. It was in this way that I ended up talking to Bhagwanti about sewing. Like Falguni, Bhagwanti was someone I had first met during my MPhil fieldwork in May 2015. In fact, Bhagwanti's nostalgia for the Sundays she had spent frolicking in Dera Ghazi Khan's canal had featured prominently in my MPhil thesis (Kohli 2015).

Aged 19 years at the time of the Partition, Bhagwanti was one of my most elderly informants. She had a wealth of stories to tell about Pakistan (especially Dera Ghazi Khan and Karachi) and the Partition, as well as life in post-Independence Delhi. Having lived in Delhi since 1947, she had seen the city change and grow right before her eyes. Bhagwanti lived just a short drive from my grandaunt's house in Rajouri

Garden, and so, by default, she became someone I frequently visited during my fieldwork.

Yet, in all the time that I had known her she had never once mentioned sewing. Instead, she had spoken numerous times about her father and her late husband's occupations. Her father had run a transport business in Dera Ghazi Khan, owning a fleet of buses and trucks. Her husband had worked in a privately owned business corporation in Delhi. Overshadowed by their stories, she had never really spoken about her own hard work (or perhaps I had neither asked nor really listened). This was an interesting omission considering that the story of Bhagwanti's engagement with sewing was tied intimately to her experience of the Partition.

Bhagwanti had married her late husband in 1945 at the age of 17. She then moved to Karachi, from Dera Ghazi Khan, to live with her husband and in-laws. This meant that in 1947, when South Asia was partitioned, Bhagwanti was in Karachi with her in-laws. As the city descended into violence, her husband put her and her mother-in-law on a flight to Delhi. He reached Delhi several months later, after the Partition had made it impossible for him to stay on in Karachi. However, during those initial months that Bhagwanti and her mother-in-law spent in Delhi following the Partition, they were on their own. Through a family friend of her in-laws, they had found lodging in Tibbia College. In my MPhil thesis I had drawn attention to Tibbia College's murky history as the site of a massacre. I had written:

> Tibbia College was not a government designated refugee camp but was instead an Ayurvedic and Unani medical college that was forcibly occupied by incoming refugees (Sharma 2011). The college's property was ransacked and its boarding house was occupied (ibid.). (Kohli 2015: 41)

Bhagwanti remembered the rooms of Tibbia College being littered with dead bodies when she first visited the college. The college was then cleaned and its rooms were occupied de facto, with two–three families often sharing one large room. With their male relatives back in Pakistan and the violence of the Partition still raging across Delhi, Bhagwanti and her mother-in-law were completely on their own. They had neither savings to fall back on, nor any other source of financial support. It was then that they took to knitting as a way of supporting themselves. As Bhagwanti explained, she and her mother-in-law would receive wool from a nearby shop and get 5 *annas*[4] for stitching it into a sweater:

It was like this, when we came, we did not have money. He [husband] was there. So, we used to get wool from the shops. So for making a sweater they would give what, 5 *annas*. Back then they would use *annas*. Yes? They would give. Quickly we would bring that thick-thick wool, then there only, I would make sweaters. Sitting through the night till 12-12 o' clock, by the next day the sweater was finished.... It was a plain sweater. The wool was thick so we had to make it thick, it was not fine. If it is fine then it takes time. This wool was thick-thick, they would give thick-thick wool so that sweater is also made thick-thick. So it would not take time to make.

In this way, Bhagwanti and her mother-in-law spent most of their time in Tibbia College knitting sweaters so that they could make enough money to support themselves.

Tell me what am I doing in the morning? After breakfast, what do we do, daughter and mother-in-law? So then I would set myself to work. We would do that till 12 in the night, to finish it completely. In the morning my mother-in-law would go and give it to the shopkeeper. And bring more [wool]. That's it, I kept doing this work, yes, I kept doing the sweaters. Till the time he [husband] did not come, we managed, so you do manage somehow something or other happens or comes. So I would do this work.

In addition to knitting, Bhagwanti also did sewing and stitching. With the passage of weeks, they had succeeded in making contact with more relatives, as an increasing number of their family crossed the border and sought each other out. This allowed her access to the money her father had given her in-laws as part of her dowry, intended for a sewing machine. Again, working for orders and using the cloth and measurements supplied by the local shopkeeper, she now began to stitch underwear, *kurtas* and pyjamas.

Then they would give us that, underwear. To make underwear, for stitching, on the machine. I did not have a machine. They had given me money for a machine in my dowry. My father had given, that *bhai*, Singer machine is available for 500. Then my mother-in-law's brother, he found out that here machines are available, in Delhi, so it is for 500. There was a tailor somewhere he did not want it so they said take it. We bought the machine. Bought the machine, after that the shopkeeper would sometimes give us *kurtas* and sometimes pyjamas. Why, because I had learnt sewing from Dera Ghazi Khan only. I did not sit like that, I completed my education in the house, inside. When I did not go further in that I learnt sewing. After learning sewing I learnt everything. Then after that we would get clothes from there, some underwear, some pyjamas, for sewing. Sewed and returned. Sewed and then I gave it back to them. They would not give that much money but still we would manage to survive. It was a survival.... After that our food or whatever else this would go towards that, however.

Bhagwanti would earn about 4–5 *annas* per finished piece, whether that was a sweater, a pyjama or a *kurta*. While it took her longer to knit a sweater, she would do between 3 and 4 units of *kurtas*, pyjamas and underwear, in total. In this way, sewing and knitting between 5 and 6 pieces every day, Bhagwanti would earn a little over INR 1 for her labour, just enough for their survival.

Here, it is relevant to draw attention to Bhagwanti's closing comments, 'They would not give that much money but still we would manage to survive.' Although Bhagwanti invokes the word 'survival' here, she does not do so in the didactic, moralising terms of the men's stories of *purusharth*. While Bhagwanti and her mother-in-law did *whatever it took to survive*, their hard work is not remembered in the redemptive tones of man-work. As stated previously, the reason for this lies in the very nature of the work they did. Where the physical work performed by zamindar patriarchs implied a disruption of the 'natural order', the knitting and stitching done by women was seen as normative.

There is an additional layer of specificity here in that while needlework was normatively associated with femininity, its commercialisation under these circumstances was anything but normal. The fact that women had to also earn for their survival is experienced as a sign of hardship, of shame and suffering. In this context, the hard work of the women is not seen to be redeeming but is instead perceived as a failure of masculinity. As I have stated previously, the latter fuels the need for the omission of these stories.

Life in the refugee camps was especially difficult for women. Recreating the most basic domestic comforts in these cramped and austere settings rested solely on the constant hard work of women. Yet, in remembering those days, Bhagwanti implicitly absorbed this memory of hard work within the ordinary fabric of everyday life. To her, the domestic work she had to do in the camp (including caring for her mother-in-law) was merely a continuation of her normative responsibilities as a dutiful daughter-in-law.

However, what she was more inclined to remember were the bonds that developed between the women in the camp, as they pooled in their resources to ease the burden of domestic chores. As families (often complete strangers) living in cramped conditions, it made sense to share whatever they had. Through a strange twist of fate, Bhagwanti and her mother-in-law found themselves living beside my grandfather and their family, in Tibbia College. This was a nugget of personal history that we serendipitously discovered while talking about life in the refugee camps. Bhagwanti fondly remembered my great-grandfather Chaman Lal and his eldest daughter, my late grandaunt Pushpa.

Living and working in such close quarters, Bhagwanti and Pushpa become close friends. Out of all of my grandfather's siblings, Bhagwanti remembered only Pushpa clearly. 'Back then Pushpa was, meaning, she was elder to them. Among the sisters. This was the thing. She was older. Would talk some,' Bhagwanti remembered. At night, when the residents of Tibbia College would set up their mattresses on the roof, to sleep out in the open, Bhagwanti remembered always setting hers up beside Pushpa. It is in simple acts like these that one can sense the meaningfulness of the bond between them. Bhagwanti and Pushpa would also perform numerous chores together, including cooking at the communal tandoor and filling water at the communal tap. The conversations shared during these times created a strong bond between the two women, a bond whose memory has endured in Bhagwanti even though she lost contact with Pushpa after they moved out of Tibbia College.

These bonds were strengthened by the omnipresent threat of sexual violence. Without identifying the fear as such, Bhagwanti also spoke about how women in Tibbia College would take trips to the toilet together as it was some distance away from their rooms.

> Everything, together. The bathrooms and all were far away. So we went together, let's go, if we needed to in the morning, let's go, like that it was a good distance like this Bhawan [local landmark] is from here, it was that much. We were right in the back. So then like 2–4 together, as we came out [of the room], yes, let's go.

These group trips also offered more opportunities for conversation. As Bhagwanti remembered, 'It provided some company, then only meaning we would talk also or something.' In these recollections, it is particularly interesting to note that the bonding of women occurred while they were working. With the sheer quantum of work needed to be performed in order to maintain a functional household, women often only had time to talk while they were working. This makes the absence of the stories of women from the discourse of *purusharth* as sacrifice, even more glaring.

Bhagwanti and her mother-in-law stayed in Tibbia College for a couple of months. Once her husband reached the city, they occupied an 'abandoned' house while they waited for their claim for compensation to be approved. Bhagwanti kept sewing and knitting all through this period. However, once their claim had been processed and her husband had found himself a job, she gave it up. 'Then staying up late at night, for just one odd [rupee], what was the need. Had to manage the house also, that also fully. So then I gave it up,' Bhagwanti said. Staying up late nights and constantly balancing multiple jobs through the day had also taken a toll on her health. 'Then your health also becomes like that, if food is not right or something so then I had become like this, completely like this,' Bhagwanti said as she held up her slender index finger to indicate how weak she had become. 'Whenever my father met me after that he would say, she has come, our bangle-seller, the bangle-seller,' Bhagwanti smiled sadly before adding, 'That is how thin I had become. I looked like a poor bangle-seller.'

Where the sweat and toil of men was borne as a battle-scar – a redeeming wound – Bhagwanti's weight loss became an object of humour. While her father's joke is undoubtedly affectionate, it is revealing that he compares her to a 'bangle-seller'. The implication here is one of the lowering of her status. Her weight loss is considered unbecoming of her status as the daughter of a zamindar businessman. Ultimately, the effects of Bhagwanti's hard work on her body are not seen as redeeming; they are demeaning. Her father's joke implicitly articulates a sentiment similar to Rajaram's casteist and classist take on the work of women at the beginning of this chapter. And, it is because the hard work of women is seen as a symbolic failure of masculinity – as the lowering of the status of the family and the woman herself – that the masculine discourse of sacrifice demands its obfuscation.

Hard Work and Caregiving

In this chapter, I have sought to move past sacrificial tropes of martyrdom to document the hard work and lived experience of women. This is part of a larger discussion about the masculine nature of this discourse of *purusharth* as sacrifice. In this final section, I want to briefly highlight the stories of other such women – including some of my informants – whose hard work and care-work (the two are not mutually exclusive) has gone unacknowledged.

Here I am reminded of Kusum, my granduncle Om Prakash's wife. I do not remember Kusum because she succumbed to breast cancer when I was an infant. However, I grew up hearing stories about her. My mother was particularly fond of her. As a working woman with a successful career, Kusum was a feminist icon for my mother. One of her favourite stories about Kusum was of the time she included my mother and her daughter Poonam in a school-children's photo-op with the then prime minister Indira Gandhi (Figure 5.4).

Kusum worked as a producer in Doordarshan, India's national broadcaster. She rose high within Doordarshan's hierarchy, consistently outpacing her husband's salary as a deputy postmaster. Moreover, the government accommodation she was entitled to was far more comfortable than that guaranteed by her husband's post. As a result, they always lived in the accommodation provided by Doordarshan. Interestingly, while Om Prakash acknowledged all of this while talking

Figure 5.4   My mother's photograph with the then prime minister Indira Gandhi. My mother can be seen kneeling (wearing a polka dot shirt) in the left-most edge of the photograph. Her cousin Poonam, Kusum's daughter, is just behind her. For me, this photograph has come to symbolise the *purusharth* of a woman Partition survivor.

Source: Photo from author's family album, taken 50 years ago.

about his life after the Partition, he never framed his wife's employment as a story of *purusharth*. Her meteoric rise within Doordarshan's hierarchy was not given the redemptive gloss of the economic miracle of Punjabi refugees. Instead, she was remembered as a loving and dutiful wife.

Similarly, during my fieldwork, I met Aadarsh and Chandini. They had witnessed the Partition at the ages of 10 and 5 respectively and had been married for over 50 years. Like my grandaunt Kusum, Chandini had held a far better paying job than her husband. Chandini had worked in the Reserve Bank of India (RBI) for over three decades, until her retirement. Her husband, Aadarsh, on the other hand was a car mechanic. Despite the fact that their household had been run predominantly through Chandini's job and its supplementary benefits (including pension and healthcare), there was no recognition of

Chandini's labour as *purusharth* in Aadarsh's narrative. In fact, while sharing his memories of the Partition and their life immediately after it, Aadarsh had barely mentioned Chandini and her job. It was actually through my grandaunt Anjali that I learnt of Chandini's work within the RBI. The couple of times that we met, Chandini herself was hesitant to speak at length about her job and never really went beyond the bare detail of her employment. Unlike other male informants, she never extolled the virtues of her work as 'sacrifice'.

Another informant that I encountered in the field, Lakshmi, had spent her life working as a government school teacher. Lakshmi was a Shastri by qualification: a degree awarded to students after seven years of higher education in the Sanskrit language. Lakshmi was a scholar of both the Sanskrit language and the Vedas. As a school teacher, she had taught Hindi and Sanskrit to students of all ages. Even at the age of 85 (when I met her in 2017), Lakshmi was quite active within her local Arya Samaj circle. Lakshmi's stories about her work lacked the redemptive gloss of the stories of men. She was proud of herself and what she had achieved, but she never analogised her hard work to that of the Punjabi community.

In addition to the hard work of women there is another aspect of work that remains largely unacknowledged in this discourse: caregiving. Iain Wilkinson and Arthur Kleinman write, 'Social suffering requires a response of care and caregiving practices' (2016: 15–16). While an ethnography of caregiving in the context of the Partition is beyond my scope (and perhaps even the scope of temporality), I nevertheless want to draw attention to its implicit presence in the stories of women in this chapter. Besides holding down a job and fulfilling their domestic responsibilities as 'good women', women refugees also provided an unquantifiable amount of care within the household. This is implicit in Falguni's story, where despite being denied the opportunity to pursue a career in teaching, she continued to play the role of a 'good' sister and helped raise her nephew.

Another example of caregiving is visible in Bhagwanti's story. During the time that Bhagwanti and her mother-in-law lived in Tibbia College, they had had no news of her husband. Meanwhile, Bhagwanti's own family had crossed the border with great difficulty. Bhagwanti's mother had contracted cholera somewhere along the refugee trail.

She was also breastfeeding her 1-year-old son at the time. She continued breastfeeding him all through the difficult journey, even after she came down with cholera. Caring for her son despite her illness and in the absence of proper food, water and medicines ultimately took an insurmountable toll on her health. She died a week after their family reached Rohtak, Haryana. Her death was so sudden, and their family so scattered, that Bhagwanti's father never made it to his wife's funeral. While Bhagwanti did attend the funeral, she was forced to hurry back to Tibbia College to care for her mother-in-law. Meanwhile, the complete radio silence from her husband had adversely affected her mother-in-law's mental health. Bhagwanti recalled,

> My mother-in-law would keep saying, my child is also gone in Pakistan and my money is also gone. Yes? Home, what did she say, I don't know she used to use a particular word. So I would say why do you say that? They will come. After all everyone is coming, it is not a big thing. Then my father, meaning, he had someone coming from Pakistan to meet him so then he passed on the message through them that *bhai*, you try to send my son-in-law quickly, somehow put him on a train.

Consoling her mother-in-law while she worked herself ragged and mourned the death of her own mother, signifies the unquantifiable psychological burden that Bhagwanti shouldered during the Partition. Similarly, the other women whom I have written about in this book all provided care within their own families, work that remains largely unacknowledged.

Conclusion

In the chapters of Part II, I have deconstructed the discourse of sacrifice. I have argued that the description of Partition suffering and the hard work that followed, as a 'sacrifice', by my informants, is a retrospective imposition that aims to rationalise the 'uselessness' out of their suffering. That is, this narrative is a form of theodicy that attempts to make sense of death and suffering, while elevating the 'bad', 'asocial' death of their coreligionists, kith and kin to the glorious and redemptive status of martyrdom. Within this larger theodicy, my informants' stories of hard work or *purusharth* serve a central role. These stories serve as karmic justifications of wealth and privilege (in their past and present) – as a rationalisation of the inequality of suffering and hardship – presenting 'good fortune' as 'legitimate fortune' (Weber 2013).

In Chapters 2–4, I have shown that this discourse of sacrifice is a specifically masculine discourse. As stories told by men about the back-breaking physical work performed by men, these are essentially stories of man-work. These stories remember male refugees (especially fathers) as hard-workers who upheld the pride of their collectivity by *doing whatever it took to survive*. As we are reminded constantly by my informants, these men are not refugees but hard-workers: self-reliant and productive workers of the (Hindu) nation. By contrast, women are remembered in the purely passive, sacrificial terms of martyrs. They are eulogised for their 'sacrifices' even as their actual lives are forgotten (Gillis 1994). Within nationalist discourses, the image of the suffering, sacrificing woman comes to symbolise the suffering nation (Schäuble 2014).

In this chapter I have interrupted this discourse by documenting the quotidian life and hard work of women, using the humble sewing machine as a key symbol of South Asian domesticity. These stories show that although women value hard work, the terms of the discourse disallow the description of their own hard work as *purusharth*. Just as Veena Das (2007) observed how women incorporated their violent experiences of the Partition within the 'ordinary' experience of being a woman in a patriarchal society, I have observed how the hard work of women was absorbed and disappeared within the ordinariness of domestic life.

In concluding this chapter, I want to connect this discourse of sacrifice to victimhood, the principle theme of Part III. Interestingly, the trope of Partition migration as sacrifice is extremely pervasive in how the Partition is remembered across the border (Naqvi 2012). In Pakistan, Partition refugees are known as 'muhajirs' (Naqvi 2012; Zamindar 2007). Canonically, the term originates from Prophet Muhammad's migration from Mecca to Medina in 622 CE (Naqvi 2012).

The classification of Partition refugees as 'muhajirs' imputes religiosity to their (forced) migration, reimagining displacement as pilgrimage (478). In doing so, the construction of Pakistani citizenship deliberately draws on the cultural meanings of migration within a wider Islamic tradition. As Tahir Naqvi (478) elaborates, 'Within the Islamic tradition, migration is viewed as a form of religious and political action whose goal is to separate the believer in both moral and physical terms from sources of evil and ignorance'. Naqvi traces the genealogy of this trope of sacrifice to Mohammad Ali Jinnah (479). In a speech to the general assembly of the All-India Muslim League in July 1947, Jinnah acknowledged the 'unparalled sacrifices' made by Muslims in Hindu-majority states in support of the Pakistan Movement. This not only prefigures displacement as pilgrimage but also establishes a relationship between sacrifice and citizenship (Zamindar 2007). In doing so, it articulates the contours of a nation through reference to a common sacrifice.

While the genealogy of the imagination of 'sacrifice' follows a different contour, in the Indian context, it has the same effects. Here, a certain discourse of sacrifice is folded within Hindu and Sikh religious discourse and history. At times it reaches into history to make inchoate identifications with the sacrifices of the Sikh Gurus and, Punjab, in general. This discourse sanctifies ambiguous, ignominious suffering and even the murder of female relatives, through the redemptive discourse of sacrifice. Transcending time as well as individual and group difference, this theodicy articulates the contours of a sectarian nation by reference to a shared victimhood. This victimhood binds the Hindus of the Hindu nation together.

In Part III, as I analyse the idea of healing though remembrance, we find an unresolved sense of victimhood underlying remembrance of the Partition. This victimhood, and the *ressentiment* it produces, leads to fresh insights on the politics of Hindu nationalism, as well as the global rise of authoritarianism.

Notes

1   In this pathologisation of immigrants as a disease, readers may be reminded of Susan Sontag's (1978) brilliant work on the use of illness as a metaphor.

2   In addition to needlework, government-run work centres provided training to women in pickle-making, basketry, block- and fabric-painting, and calico-printing. These skills and objects strongly evoke attributes of domesticity and femininity (A. Datta 2019: 1937).

3   My remark was inspired by Ortner's (1972: 20) observation that 'when a culture (eg., France or China) develops a tradition of haute cuisine – "real" cooking as opposed to trivial ordinary domestic cooking – the high chefs are almost always men'.

4   *Annas* are a now demonetised unit of currency. 16 *annas* made INR 1. 8 *annas* or 1 *athanni* was INR 0.5.

Part III

Remembrance and Healing
Reflections on the Post-Partition Context

6

The Fractured *Nomos*

Silencing the Present, Remembering the Past

On 22 June 2017, Junaid Khan, a 16-year-old resident of Ballabgarh district was lynched aboard a local train (NDTV 2017a). That day, Junaid along with his brother and some friends had gone to Delhi to buy clothes for the upcoming Eid festivities. While returning on a Mathura-bound train, the boys became embroiled in a dispute over seats (Lakhani 2017; NDTV 2017a). In their testimony, Junaid's brother and friends alleged that the dispute took a communal turn and escalated quickly. Soon, a violent mob of Hindu men gathered to face them. The men taunted them by calling them 'beef eaters' and 'anti nationals' (Lakhani 2017; Razdan 2017). They also pulled their beards and flung the boys' skullcaps to the ground (S. Nair 2017; Razdan 2017). The altercation turned violent as the men pulled out knives and tried to pin the boys down. At some point during this scuffle, one of the men stabbed Junaid multiple times as others held him in place. None of the onlookers in that crowded train compartment intervened. The men then threw Junaid, his brother and his friends out of the train and onto the Asaoti Railway Station where Junaid bled to death in his brother's arms (S. Nair 2017; NDTV 2017a).

Junaid's lynching caused nationwide outrage. It dominated the news headlines at the time and led to the '#NotInMyName' protests, which were attended by thousands of people across the country (S. Nair 2017; Wilkes and Srivastava 2017). Although Junaid had been lynched in broad daylight, in a crowded train compartment, within the geographical limits of India's National Capital Region, no eyewitnesses came forward in the days that immediately followed (NDTV 2017b).

While public outrage ensured that arrests were made, the police investigation sought to deliberately water down the Islamophobic nature of the crime. In its statement to the media, the police presented Junaid's lynching as an aggravated dispute over seats (Ahsan 2018). The police insisted that while 'caste abuses' had been used, it claimed that its interrogation of Naresh Kumar – the self-confessed killer – had revealed no 'communal angle' (*The Hindu* 2017b).

This disappointingly tepid police investigation is itself part of a larger pattern whereby such beef-related lynchings have been normalised in Modi's India. The search for justice for these victims has been characterised by glacial investigations, unending judicial proceedings and threats to their families, often with the counter-charge of cow slaughter. The lack of strong condemnation from political leaders and large sections of civil society has further consigned the victims to the forgotten margins of society (Apoorvanand 2018).

Meanwhile, the BJP has routinely mobilised in defence of the perpetrators. In July 2018, BJP leader and then union minister of state for civil aviation Jayant Sinha honoured and garlanded eight men convicted for the lynching of Alimuddin Ansari in Ramgarh in June 2017, in an act of alleged cow vigilantism. These men had been found guilty of this crime by a fast-track court and sentenced to life imprisonment in March 2018. They were out on bail when they were hosted at Jayant Sinha's residence, with the minister greeting them with sweets and garlands (*Times of India* 2018b). It later emerged that Jayant Sinha along with other members of the BJP had also paid the legal fees of six of the convicts (News18 2019).

This was not an isolated incident. In February 2018, members of the BJP marched alongside the right-wing Hindu Ekta Manch (Hindu Unity Platform) in a protest march in Jammu's Kathua district. The protest was held to demand the release of Deepak Khajuria – a special police officer (SPO) who had been arrested for his involvement in the rape and murder of Asifa (M. Ahmad 2018). Asifa was an 8-year-old Muslim Bakkarwal girl who was kidnapped, drugged and then raped repeatedly in a Hindu temple in Kathua with the specific intention of teaching the local Bakkarwals 'a lesson' (Fareed 2018; *Scroll* 2019). The protest rally marched under the Indian flag and was attended by several prominent BJP members, including the then BJP state secretary Vijay

Sharma. BJP members and spokespersons at the time had alleged a conspiracy to defame Hindus (M. Ahmad 2018). Deepak Khajuria and five others were ultimately found guilty of the crime (Ohri 2019; *Scroll* 2019).

More recently, on 15 August 2022, hours after Prime Minister Modi's annual Independence Day address to the nation, 11 men convicted of raping Bilkis Bano were granted early release after 15 years in jail (NDTV 2022). During the 2002 pogroms in Gujarat, Bilkis Bano was gang-raped by a Hindu mob that also murdered 14 members of her family, including her 3-year-old daughter. Bilkis Bano was 21 years old and five months pregnant at the time (*The Wire* 2022). The early release of these murderers and rapists was defended by the Gujarat MLA and BJP leader C. K. Raulji (representing Godhra). Raulji said, 'I don't know whether they committed any crime or not. But there has to be intention of committing crime.... They were Brahmins and Brahmins are known to have good *sanskaar* [manners/upbringing/habitus]. It might have been someone's ill intention to corner and punish them'. Raulji was part of the Gujarat government panel that unanimously approved the convicts' early release (NDTV 2022). Additionally, during the hearing for their release, Supreme Court Justice Ajay Rastogi made a similarly shocking remark: 'Merely because the act was horrific, is that sufficient to say remission is wrong?' (*The Wire* 2022).

Junaid's lynching was simply one among a series of beef-related lynchings that have come to define Modi's 'New India'. Lynchings by themselves are not new to India. In the past, lynchings have played a key role in disciplining lower castes and indigenous communities. However, since the BJP's rise to power in 2014, cow vigilantism fuelled by a Hindu religious revivalism has gained traction. Between 2010 and 2017, 63 attacks involving cow-related violence were recorded in India (S. Nair 2017). Almost all of these 63 attacks occurred after Modi came to power, in 2014 (Wilkes and Srivastava 2017). The lynchings themselves are often video-taped by perpetrators and shared widely in the WhatsApp groups run by the Hindu Right ecosystem (S. Nair 2017; Banaji 2018). Apporvanand (2018) dubs the lynchings a veritable epidemic and an unmistakable symbol of Modi's 'New India'. Thus, the spectacle of lynching Muslims and Dalits has emerged as a distinctly modern way of imposing upper-caste Hindu supremacy.

Mukul Kesavan (2019) has observed that the most terrifying aspect of this 'New India' is the normalisation of this violence in law as well as by those in high office. From Kathua to Unnao to Hathras, the BJP has used the party machinery (including its famed IT Cell), institutions of the state (especially the police) and the media to openly and tacitly defend the rapists and murderers involved (R. Kumar 2020). In this way, not only have criminals become lawmakers, but those in government draw their power from criminality (Appadurai 2019). From the 2019 Citizenship (Amendment) Act to the way the investigation into the 2020 Delhi pogroms has been used to clamp down on dissent, 'New India' has emerged as a Hindu fascist state where violence and criminality are enshrined in law and high office. Sudha Pai and Sajjan Kumar (2018) describe this as 'institutionalized everyday communalism'. Its defining features are the 'shift of riots from earlier classic/endemic sites to new ones, recruitment of local BJP–RSS cadres/leaders who carry out sustained, everyday grassroots mobilization using local, mundane issues and imaginary threats, and spread of communalism and riots into villages' (Pai and Kumar 2018: 1). This alongside the active incorporation of lower-caste Hindus serves to consolidate a united Hindu-fold with the 'Muslim' as its antithesis. Relatedly, Appadurai (2021: 309) uses the term 'aspirational hatred' to describe a violent culture of impunity where hatred functions as a legitimate mode of upward mobility.

Junaid's lynching was a dystopian introduction to my field site. While I had not been in Delhi at the time of his murder, Junaid's death did not feel like a distant event. I began my fieldwork in the first week of July that year, all too aware of my proximity to the time and site of the lynching. Junaid's family lived in a village in Ballabgarh district, a mere 10 kilometres from my uncle's home in Faridabad. Later on in my fieldwork, I even made a few trips to Ballabgarh to interview Partition survivors.

My perceived proximity to Junaid's lynching affected the way I approached the memories of the Partition. I found myself increasingly disinterested in the sense of Hindu victimhood that my informants sought to convey. The Hindu is 'peaceful', 'tolerant' and 'timid', they insisted. Yet, all around me, I saw a resurgent, militant Hindu nationalism at work.

Supriya Nair locates the violence of cow vigilantes (known locally as Gau Rakshaks, or cow protectors) within a perceived history of victimhood. Nair writes that Hindu nationalism's revisionist view of Indian history presents the historically and culturally significant 300-year rule of the Mughals as 'a form of Muslim settler-colonialism that oppressed Hindus'. Against this narrative, the continuance of cow slaughter is presented as an enduring symbol of Hindu enslavement. During his 2014 Prime Ministerial campaign, Narendra Modi alleged that under Manmohan Singh's Congress government, Indian cows and livestock had been slaughtered with wild abandon and even been stolen and smuggled to Bangladesh. This fear-mongering was based on a convenient distortion of the fact that under Manmohan Singh, India had seen a rise in its meat (especially beef) exports. What followed was a gradual rise in beef-related lynchings across India as 'cow security squads', or Gau Raksha Dals, emerged across India and began operating with impunity (S. Nair 2017).

Observing and living through this period of *de facto* state-sanctioned lynching made me question the relevance of my own work. Why was I, living in this India, recording the victimhood of a people who were no longer oppressed? What relevance did these memories have at a time when violent Hindu mobs were openly lynching Muslims?

It was in September 2017 that I first began to articulate this inchoate tension between the present I was living and the past I was recording. This tension was brought to the fore during my visit to an exhibition organised by the 1947 Partition Archive (Figure 6.1). The exhibition had been organised to commemorate the Partition's 70th anniversary. The exhibition featured a small collection of personal artefacts (that Partition survivors had migrated with), snippets of oral history interviews, archived news reports, photographs and documents.

There were two things in this exhibition that caught my attention. In a corner, the organisers had installed a TV which played a montage of oral history interviews on loop (Figure 6.2). Among this montage was an interview of Sarah Kirby, a citizen historian of the 1947 Partition Archive. While reflecting on her experience of interviewing Partition survivors, Kirby remarked that she felt that the process of remembering the Partition is part of the 'process of healing'.

Figure 6.1 The 1947 Partition Archive's exhibition in Delhi's Kamladevi Complex, September 2017

Source: Photograph by author.

Figure 6.2 Members of the public watch a montage of interview snippets, at the exhibition

Source: Photograph by author.

Elsewhere in the exhibition, I encountered a snippet of an oral history interview. In it Promod Mehra, a Partition survivor 'remembered' life in Lahore during the Partition (Figure 6.3). Mehra's story caught my eye because of the way it told the story of the riots by juxtaposing the

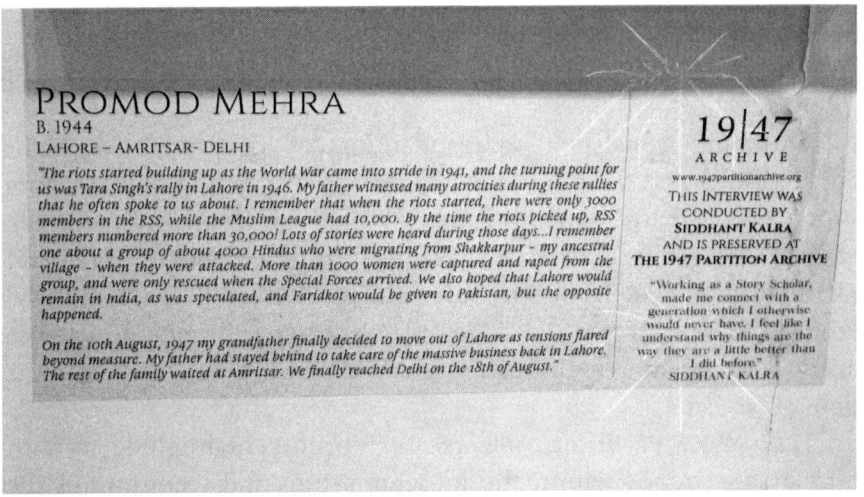

PROMOD MEHRA
B. 1944
LAHORE – AMRITSAR– DELHI

"The riots started building up as the World War came into stride in 1941, and the turning point for us was Tara Singh's rally in Lahore in 1946. My father witnessed many atrocities during these rallies that he often spoke to us about. I remember that when the riots started, there were only 3000 members in the RSS, while the Muslim League had 10,000. By the time the riots picked up, RSS members numbered more than 30,000! Lots of stories were heard during those days...I remember one about a group of about 4000 Hindus who were migrating from Shakkarpur – my ancestral village – when they were attacked. More than 1000 women were captured and raped from the group, and were only rescued when the Special Forces arrived. We also hoped that Lahore would remain in India, as was speculated, and Faridkot would be given to Pakistan, but the opposite happened.

On the 10th August, 1947 my grandfather finally decided to move out of Lahore as tensions flared beyond measure. My father had stayed behind to take care of the massive business back in Lahore. The rest of the family waited at Amritsar. We finally reached Delhi on the 18th of August."

19|47
ARCHIVE

www.1947partitionarchive.org

THIS INTERVIEW WAS
CONDUCTED BY
SIDDHANT KALRA
AND IS PRESERVED AT
THE 1947 PARTITION ARCHIVE

"Working as a Story Scholar, made me connect with a generation which I otherwise would never have. I feel like I understand why things are the way they are a little better than I did before."
SIDDHANT KALRA

Figure 6.3   An excerpt from Promod Mehra's oral testimony on display at the exhibition

Source: Photograph by author.

membership numbers of the RSS and the Muslim League. Mehra's reference to the RSS' swelled numbers, followed immediately by a story he had heard about the abduction and rape of 1,000 Hindu women, reminded me that for the RSS talking about the Partition references a golden era of service. For the RSS, the Partition represents a time when they protected Hindus in the streets and fed the refugees coming into India; a time when they beat back the Muslim 'other' in service of the Hindu nation. After all, as I have stated previously, the Hindu-fold is not innate but is rather performed through such acts of violence and solidarity.

As I perused the snippets of oral history interviews in the exhibition, I wondered for whom these memories might be considered healing. In the months that had followed Modi's ascension to the Prime Minister's Office, the RSS' *shakha*s (branches) and ranks had expanded visibly. Furthermore, with their spokespersons being invited to most prime time news debates, the RSS had shifted dramatically from a fringe organisation to a visibly hegemonic force within Indian politics. The so-called fringe-elements of the Hindu Right could no longer be considered fringe. By 2018, Mohan Bhagwat (the leader of the RSS) could be seen publicly boasting about his ability to prepare an army in three days, for the 'defence' of the nation (*Times of India* 2018a). Against whom, one might wonder....

With the consistent mainstreaming of fringe Hindu Right organisations and their violence, the display of Promod Mehra's story struck me as particularly tone-deaf. Would these memories of the enthusiastic recruitment of the RSS bring healing to the family of Junaid Khan, I wondered. It was in this juxtaposition of Sarah Kirby and Promod Mehra's words that I began to articulate the question at the heart of this book. What does it mean to remember the Partition in the time of fascism?

The 1947 Partition Archive's exhibition highlighted certain problematic trends within the museumisation and recording of the Partition's memory. Chief among these is its reification of rumours. This is clearly visible in Promod Mehra's story. According to the Archive's plaque, Mehra was born in 1944. Yet despite having been a mere 3 years old at the time of the Partition, Mehra claims to 'remember' the events of Lahore. He also claims to 'remember' having heard of the abduction of 1,000 Hindu women, at the time. One wonders how a 3-year-old child could vividly 'remember' such specific details.

Far from a first-hand testimony, Promod Mehra's story relies on hearsay and dubious secondary sources. More importantly, the precise round-numbered statistics that Mehra quotes bears – what Gyanendra Pandey (2001: 91) has labelled – 'the stamp of rumour'. Pandey writes that 'rounded-off figures are one indication of the persistence of rumour, precise and yet extravagant – suggestive of so much more than the numbers themselves' (70). Observing the use of such precise, round-numbered statistics in primary, secondary and tertiary sources, Pandey argues that in their usage, these numbers are akin to figures of speech. They are not precise death tolls based on verifiable research but instead hope to convey to their audience the scale of the violence. In Mehra's story precise, round-numbered statistics of 4,000 people, 1,000 women, 10,000 Muslim Leaguers and 30,000 RSS workers are used to convey the scale of violence and victimhood. By using concrete numbers to convey abstract emotions, Pandey argues, these numbers are 'even more overpowering than a verifiable statistic; for it shares the power contained in rumour, which worked to produce the new beliefs and emotions of the day, with all their deadly consequences' (73).

Observing the self-referential quality of rumours and rumoured statistics, Pandey argues that most Partition related statistics can be traced back to dubious oral reports such as FIRs, memoirs and the testimonies of bureaucrats and social workers. Extending his scepticism to the larger field of scholarship, Pandey wonders whether 'the most "likely", "consensual", "estimates" are thus accepted as true and recycled – because they have been heard, or heard repeatedly, in various forms and contexts' (91).

Pandey (2001: 89) observes how the figures of 200,000–2 million, cited by Urvashi Butalia (2000), vary considerably from the figures of 500,000–1 million used by Menon and Bhasin (1998). Others whose works touch on the Partition seem to quote similarly varying figures such as Mohammed Waseem (who chooses 'about half a million'), Stanley Wolpert ('approximately one million'), Phillip Ziegler ('a million dead'), Chandulal Trivedi (225,000), Penderel Moon (200,000), Ian Stephens ('about 500,000') and Richard Symonds (half a million dead and 12 million homeless as the 'lowest estimate'). There are similar discrepancies in the estimates of 'abducted women' with some speculating the number to be about 75,000 while others insist that it might well be as high as 200,000 (G. Pandey 2001: 89–90). Elsewhere in this book, I have used Paul Brass' (2003b) estimate of between 200,000 and 2 million dead with 10–17 million people displaced and Khwaja, Bharadwaj and Mian's (2009) estimate that 3.4 million migrants went missing.

Questioning the evidence for some of these estimates, Pandey (2001: 90) concludes that 'nothing in the surviving records, in the calculations made at the time, or in the contentious debates that have gone on since then, gives us anything like a persuasive basis for such an inference'. Instead, Pandey observes that despite the uncertain nature of these statistics, the figure of 500,000 dead seems to function as a sort of 'median'. He asks whether this figure has stuck because it 'allows one to emphasise the enormity of Partition and point to our surviving humanity at the same time? Or is it a figure that has gained credibility in academic circles simply by repetition?' Pandey goes on to ask whether most of the general discourse on the Partition continues to function as 'something like a gigantic rumour, albeit a rumour commonly presented as "testimony" (or "history")?' (91).

My objective in questioning the validity of Promod Mehra's testimony is not to insist on some kind of positivistic, retrospective distinction between 'truth' and 'rumour', but to draw attention to the 1947 Partition Archive's problematic use of oral historical narratives. It is the Archive's lack of attention to the complexity of rumour, memory and history that is particularly concerning. In presenting snippets of oral history narratives as part of an 'archive' of memory, the Archive implicitly presents memory as an absolute fact, as a 'truth' whose validity is reified by the moral force of lived experience.

Yet, as I have stated previously in the Introduction, memory is a social construction (Connerton 1989; Halbwachs 1992). The process of remembering, of narrating events from the past, is also fundamentally a process of making sense of the past (Tuncel 2014). Memory is neither an absolute truth nor a faithful reconstruction of lived experience. Memory is the body of the past reanimated with the spirit of the present. The staccato process of remembering needs to be kept in mind when dealing with memories of genocidal violence. This is because memories of violence are marked by their silences and fragmentariness. As Pandey (2001: 67) writes, '… they move, in fits and starts, through jerks and breaks and silences – incoherent, stuttering, even incomprehensible – between the poles of testimony and rumour'.

The object of my critique is not to insist on a sifting of fact from fiction (although this is necessary to some degree), but rather to show that the 1947 Partition Archive seems oblivious of these academic discourses. By using the narratives of survivors as a 'document' of the past and by not acknowledging the socially constructed nature of memory, the Archive seems to readily absorb, amplify and thereby reify rumour and hearsay.

The 1947 Partition Archive also appears to edit out the hate speech of Partition survivors. My attention was drawn to this at the exhibition when I serendipitously came across a snippet of an interview that was attributed to one of my informants (Figure 6.4).

I had met Thakar Daas through Pooran Chand. Thakar Daas was one of his oldest friends. The two of them would meet in Rose Garden almost every day. After I spotted this plaque at the Archive's exhibition,

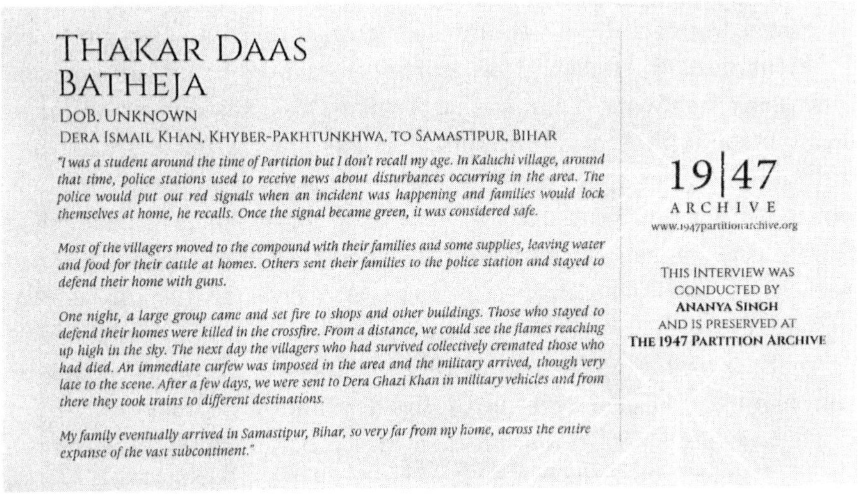

THAKAR DAAS
BATHEJA
DOB. UNKNOWN
DERA ISMAIL KHAN, KHYBER-PAKHTUNKHWA, TO SAMASTIPUR, BIHAR

'I was a student around the time of Partition but I don't recall my age. In Kaluchi village, around that time, police stations used to receive news about disturbances occurring in the area. The police would put out red signals when an incident was happening and families would lock themselves at home, he recalls. Once the signal became green, it was considered safe.

Most of the villagers moved to the compound with their families and some supplies, leaving water and food for their cattle at homes. Others sent their families to the police station and stayed to defend their home with guns.

One night, a large group came and set fire to shops and other buildings. Those who stayed to defend their homes were killed in the crossfire. From a distance, we could see the flames reaching up high in the sky. The next day the villagers who had survived collectively cremated those who had died. An immediate curfew was imposed in the area and the military arrived, though very late to the scene. After a few days, we were sent to Dera Ghazi Khan in military vehicles and from there they took trains to different destinations.

My family eventually arrived in Samastipur, Bihar, so very far from my home, across the entire expanse of the vast subcontinent.'

19|47
A R C H I V E
www.1947partitionarchive.org

THIS INTERVIEW WAS
CONDUCTED BY
ANANYA SINGH
AND IS PRESERVED AT
THE 1947 PARTITION ARCHIVE

Figure 6.4   An excerpt from Thakar Daas Batheja's oral testimony at the 1947 Partition Archive's exhibition

Source: Photograph by author.

I went back to Thakar Daas to confirm whether that really was him. Thakar Daas told me that some time back, a researcher from the Archive had approached him for an interview. But until that day, he had no idea what they did with his interview. I showed Thakar Daas the picture of his interview excerpt and translated it for him.

The excerpt of Thakar Daas' interview brings up several issues. Firstly, the plaque states that his date of birth is 'unknown'. This is untrue. Pooran Chand went to school with Thakar Daas in Faridabad and insisted that Thakar Daas was just 6 months older than him. Both Pooran Chand and Thakar Daas were between 13 and 14 years of age at the time of the Partition (thus born around 1933–1934). The failure to accurately state Thakar Daas' date of birth to me exposes the superficiality of this attempt at oral history. It also shows that the Archive's single-minded obsession with 'memory' translates into a lack of engagement with the community that Partition survivors inhabit, as well as the context in which these memories are remembered. What is neglected is the way memories are evoked, localised, experienced, interpreted and retold in reference to one's community and the present.

More importantly, I found it astonishing that the Archive's representation of Thakar Daas' story glosses over his Islamophobia. During my fieldwork, I found that Thakar Daas was one of my most vocally Islamophobic informants. For example, Thakar Daas (like Jaideep in Chapter 2) believed that Nehru and Jinnah were half-brothers and that the Congress party was a 'Muslim' party. When I challenged him on this, he insisted that because he had read it on Facebook, it *had* to be true. In other conversations, he also revealed his disdain for Mahatma Gandhi, especially what he perceived to be Gandhi's role in allegedly exacerbating Partition violence. Thakar Daas believed that by campaigning for peace in north India, Gandhi had advocated for Muslims while 'our Hindu brothers' were being killed in Pakistan. Thakar Daas extolled the example of Sardar Patel, praising his decision to allegedly order the slaughter of two trains of Muslims in response to every train of dead Hindus and Sikhs that came from across the border.

However, Thakar Daas' Islamophobia was not restricted to his views on the Partition alone. I realised this when one time, while hanging out with Thakar Daas in Faridabad's Rose Garden, he introduced me to some of his friends. His friends belonged to the generation that was born immediately after Independence. Thakar Daas' conversations with his friends were Islamophobic on a level I have rarely ever witnessed first-hand. We entered the conversation at a point when one of his friends was arguing that communal riots only occur in those districts where the population of Muslims is over 10 per cent. 'Even at 15–20% these people [Muslims] do riots, they don't have any other work,' he said. All of the others in that little circle nodded their agreement while another man chimed in that the Muslims of Faridabad seemed poised to organise riots. He urged the others to procure a skullcap as camouflage.

They then moved on to alleging that mosques and madrasas were brainwashing Muslims into terrorism. 'The Quran-*sharif* is not *sharif* [noble/innocent], it is *badmaash* [crooked],' quipped Thakar Daas to the raucous laughter of his friends. Emboldened, one of his friends began to mimic the words of the *namaz* and asked the others why it sounded like that. When he did not get the answer he was looking for, he said, 'Gas [flatulence]'. He then bent forward in his chair and began mimicking someone doing the *namaz* while making fart noises. 'This is how they release gas,' he said, as all of them broke out in laughter. Unrelated, someone quipped, 'Who are these Congress [leaders] anyway? They are all descendants of Muslims.'

This marked a change in the conversation as they now began to talk about how Islam is antithetical to nationalism and national progress. Someone raised the issue of how some mosques glorify the Mughals while another built on this to remind the others how a number of Delhi's streets are still named after Mughal rulers such as Akbar, Humayun and Aurangzeb. Predictably, the mention of Aurangzeb evoked even more anger.

'Tell me one thing what will you do? Five times in a day you read the *namaz*, when will you work for your country or family or home? Where will you get your *roti* from, tell me?' another quipped rhetorically. One of Thakar Daas' friends now told the others how the government building Shastri Bhawan had been planned in a way that would avoid demolishing the mosque beside it. Other such examples of roads and architecture literally 'making way' for mosques followed. These examples of the alleged reorganisation of urban architecture around mosques and shrines seemed to confirm the 'fact' of the Indian state's literal and symbolic appeasement of its proximate enemy.

The conversation shifted to politics when someone mentioned that Muslims cannot take a joke and would kill anyone who dares to insult their god. Speaking of the supposed tribalism of Muslims brought up the ongoing protests in Kashmir. They alleged a grand conspiracy by Kashmir's Muslim political leaders (with the Jammu and Kashmir National Conference leader Farooq Abdullah chief among them) to foment separatism and encourage stone-pelters. Repeating the popular Hindu Right claim at the time, they alleged that stone-pelters could be purchased for 50–200 rupees.

There was nothing particularly new or shocking about this conversation. I had heard variations of these discourses in different contexts before. But what did surprise me was the way in which Thakar Daas and his friends felt emboldened enough to air these views in public, at the top of their lungs. This was no shy sharing of extremist views. Rather, their demeanour suggested not only their unflinching faith in these discourses but also the awareness that their views were now part of the mainstream.

In addition to this, Thakar Daas struck me as an incredibly orthodox man (even by the standards of his own peers). Once when talking about Bangalore, he told me that he had visited the city in the 1980s while on holiday with his wife. While exploring the city, the couple had somehow accidentally found their way into a 'Muslim' restaurant. Thakar Daas said that as soon as he realised that this was a 'Muslim' establishment, he apologised to the staff and asked them to guide him to the nearest 'Hindu hotel'. His refusal to eat in a 'Muslim' restaurant was a continuation of the age-old Hindu upper-caste practice of untouchability against Muslims (Kohli 2015; Talbot 2006).

In general, Thakar Daas showed a high propensity for bigotry, rumour and conspiracy theory. My point in highlighting this side of Thakar Daas is to show that his Islamophobia was inherently linked to his memory of the Partition. That is, not only did his sense of historical victimhood fuel his Islamophobia, but that Thakar Daas' Islamophobia was so deeply embedded that it was also the lens through which he remembered the Partition.

The contrast between mine and the 1947 Partition Archive's treatment of Thakar Daas' memories reveals a deeper methodological problematic. Contrary to the rapport-building intimacy of long-term ethnographic fieldwork, the Archive relies on one-off interviews conducted by amateur volunteers – often strangers to the Partition survivors they interview – armed with stock questionnaires (Dandekar 2019). Deepra Dandekar argues that 'this interview process with a virtual stranger therefore objectifies Partition narratives as exhibits of national memorialization within the public domain, musealizing nation-making events and moments'. Contrary to its nature as a social construction, this process implicitly understands memory as an indexical narrative, a figurative object to be extracted for exhibition. Dandekar describes Partition memorialization as 'a personal endeavour mixed with political practices rooted in the present (394). These memory-narratives involve a process of temporalization that imposes the frame of 'Partition' – pre-configuring beginnings and endings – to narratives that are in fact free-flowing meditations on one's past (Kabir 2013). Dandekar (2019: 394–395) cautions that such 'objectified and musealized individual oral narratives are in danger of being co-opted and deployed within Indian and Pakistani nationalist agendas'.

The latter is a significant critique considering that Partition Studies' turn to oral history was motivated by the urge to subvert the silences mired within patriarchal and nationalist structures (Dandekar 2019; Das 2007). Pandey (2001) has written eloquently about the ways in which oral historical narratives of the Partition challenged nationalist historiography's silences on 'communal' violence and suffering. Ashis Nandy (2007: 104) once described the pall of silence that hung over survivors' memories of migrating in violence-hit caravan-trains as 'not the silence of unconscious memories', but rather 'the silence of a secret self'. In this period, it was these social, political and gendered silences that oral historians and ethnographers sought to pierce by documenting the micro-histories of Partition survivors.

Urvashi Butalia's (2000) seminal foray into oral history sought to bring memories of the Partition into mainstream public and academic discourse. Omitting the hate speech and bigotry of the survivors she interviewed, she provided them with the space to remember, mourn and vent about the suffering they had endured. By recording these memories, Butalia wanted to contribute to their unsilencing, to access *the other side of silence.*

However, Deepra Dandekar (2019) argues that the narrative silence that one finds in this space today is agential despite the disempowering quality of the experience itself. Narrating the events of the Partition more than 70 years after the fact, narrators furnish narratives that convey their current conception of an evolving sense of self, often discarding events that do not fit this narrative script. This agential, self-making quality of memory – that ascribes the values of the present to understanding the past – is especially evident in the stories of *purusharth* we have encountered in Part II.

While some of the scholarship on Partition Studies shows an awareness of this, this seems absent from many of the public memorialisations and oral history projects. Here, the continuing simplistic urge to unsilence memories of the Partition often produces fresh omissions. For example, Aanchal Malhotra's (2017) foray into the Partition's 'material memory' is driven by the urge to unsilence the memories contained in the personal artefacts and family heirlooms that have survived the Partition's displacement. Tracing the migrations and family histories of Partition survivors, Malhotra focuses exclusively on their feelings of nostalgia and displacement. Her stories of Partition survivors who revisited their homelands are especially poignant. Malhotra indulges in a careful omission of the hate speech and bigotry of her informants, steering clear of 'communal' rants and competing ethnonational claims. Fleeting references to violence are as far as she allows herself to wander off this script. Instead, Malhotra focuses on her informants' nostalgia for the 'good old' pre-Partition days, for their ancestral homes, their yearning for simpler times.

Malhotra (2017) implicitly packages this nostalgia as a trenchant belief in secularism, as somehow evidence that those who remember the Partition do not believe in the excesses of the time. This positions the violent perpetrators and their bigotry outside society. Malhotra also neglects a critical examination of the demography of her informants. The personal artefacts whose stories Malhotra records include the pearls of Azra Haq (a gift from the Maharaja of Bikaner) and a massive stone plaque from Mian Faiz Rabbani's pre-Partition mansion. These stories speak volumes of the wealth and privilege that these people lived in, conditions that were far removed from those of the majority of the people at the time. The wealth and privilege of informants forms an important part of their experience of the Partition, determining, for example, whether the individuals in question crossed the border on foot in crowded caravans or in the relative safety and comfort of trains and flights.

Although beautifully written, Malhotra's book is ultimately a compilation of stories that memorialise the wealth of upper-caste, upper-class individuals. Such wealth and privilege also problematises nostalgia in this context, as nostalgia for the pre-Partition days also constitutes nostalgia for one's former wealth and status.

Mara Ahmed's documentary on the Partition, *A Thin Wall* (2015), relies on a similar narrative. The film focuses purely on Partition survivors' nostalgia for pre-Partition South Asia. In a narrative trope similar to Malhotra's, *A Thin Wall* romanticises the alleged peace and harmony of the pre-Partition past in an effort to express a hope for a peaceful future. Both the film and Malhotra's (2017) book remember the Partition through such well-intentioned informants, implying that if there had been more such individuals around, then the Partition might never have happened.

Kavita Puri's rich body of work attempts a similar unsilencing of the Partition's memories in the UK. Puri's book *Partition Voices: Untold British Stories* (2019) and three-part BBC Radio 4 series (2017) observes the Partition's visceral afterlife in British society. Remembering the Partition through the voices of British Asians and colonial British citizens who witnessed the Partition, Puri's work problematises the British Empire's legacy. These narratives also reposition the UK's current diversity within a larger history of colonialism and globalisation.

Yet, nostalgia, like memory, is a social construction. Nostalgia involves an idealisation of the past, a process whereby individuals make 'perfect memories of imperfect worlds' (Finlay 2004: 150; Damousi 2001). Not only do these works naively believe the nostalgic recollections of their informants, but they also mistake this nostalgia for lack of bigotry.

In my fieldwork, I found that all the Partition survivors I spoke to were prone to Islamophobic discourses; an Islamophobia that was explicitly derived from a trenchant belief in Hindu nationalism. Sweet nostalgic recollections of the perfect homes they had left behind in Pakistan were often followed by Islamophobic rants. They might remember Muslim friends and neighbours from their childhood quite fondly, but they would also brand all Muslims as inherently treacherous and untrustworthy. They would recall their lives being saved by Muslim strangers, but they would also simultaneously blame the Partition on Muslims and stress that Muslims had 'committed more violence' than the Hindus and Sikhs. This apparent tension between nostalgia and Islamophobia needs careful attention.

The larger point here is that the afterlife of the Partition is diverse and polyphonous. It lives on in multiple spaces and, in being invoked in diverse ways in the public domain, is latched on to different bandwagons. In my discussion, I have consciously tried to focus on some of the more 'popular' accounts to engage with the Partition's public afterlife. The Partition Museum (whose problematics I have discussed in the previous chapter), the 1947 Partition Archive, and

Aanchal Malhotra's and Kavita Puri's work enjoy a wide audience and are thus influential through their wide reach.

But do these public acts of remembrance provoke reflection on the lessons to be learnt from history? Or do they instead cement a memory of Hindu victimhood, thus justifying violence in the present? What does it mean to remember the Partition in the time of fascism?

Academic literature on the Partition has consistently drawn attention to the Hindu nationalist abuse of memories of the Partition (Butalia 2000; G. Pandey 2001; Das 2007). The memoirs of social activists such as Anis Kidwai (2011) complement this body of academic literature by providing a contemporaneous account of the violence and bigotry that drove the Partition's retributive genocidal violence. Neeti Nair's (2011) work goes a step further to examine some of the ways in which Partition survivors grapple with the nostalgia, trauma and bigotry left in the wake of the Partition.

Yet, despite this rich engagement with the Partition's violence and trauma, Partition Studies appears to have been unable to resist the Hindu Right's ability to wrap the complexity of the Partition within the body-bag of Hindu victimhood. Nair (2011: 252) notes, 'In the last two decades, scholars have begun detailed analyses of the trauma and pain that accompanied Partition. But trauma and pain know few boundaries and have become, in the hands of untrained practitioners, breeding grounds for narratives of bigotry.' She adds that the triumph of Hindu nationalism in India has dressed these memories in 'a sheet of unreflective prejudice' (255).

To a sizeable section of Indian society – especially those who identify with Hindu nationalism – the Partition continues to function as an effective dog whistle for demographic anxieties (see Introduction) and the allegedly ever-present threat posed by the proximate presence of the 'Muslim other'. It serves as a dark portent of the future of a 'weak', 'democratic', 'secular' society and thereby as a justification for Hindu para-militarisation, not to mention the militarisation of the Indian state. Why then are we spurred to continue remembering the Partition? Does the reflexive and continuous unsilencing of these memories provide healing? How might we treat the narrative silences and trauma located at the heart of the Partition's afterlife?

Silence, Trauma and Healing

I want to briefly return to the question posed by Gyanendra Pandey. Pandey (2001: 90) had asked whether the figure of 500,000 dead is 'the "median" that allows one to emphasise the enormity of Partition and point to our surviving humanity at the same time?' This question about how the Partition's death and suffering – as embodied in the weight of a number – endangers our sense of humanity, is a deeply anthropological one. The 'sense of humanity' that Pandey refers to comprises a veritable *nomos*. This *nomos* is fractured by the violence of the Partition. This history, where enormous numbers of people organised themselves to enslave, rape, murder and loot millions of others (A. Hansen 2022), threatens to destroy one's faith in god and its secular equivalents (Indian society and humanity). It is in this context that a death toll – as a statistical expression of suffering – becomes morally troubling.

My interest in this discussion stems from how oral historical and ethnographic work on the Partition – by documenting the fact of human suffering on an unimaginable scale – carries a fundamentally denomising quality. It is because hearing/reading stories of the Partition fractures our *nomos* – making us question our faith in India, humanity and/or god – that faith in the therapeutic qualities of remembrance itself becomes necessary. It is because stories of the Partition fracture our *nomos* that belief in memory's ability to heal becomes necessary.

In *Charred Lullabies*, Valentine Daniel (1996) writes about anthroposemiosis. Semiosis describes the activity of dabbling in signs. Anthroposemiosis is semiosis that involves 'human beings' knowledge or awareness of the relation of signification'. What sets anthroposemiosis apart from other semiotic exchanges in nature is that humans are conscious of these semiotic processes while participating in them (121). As Zygmunt Bauman (1992: 12) writes, 'Unlike other animals, we not only know, we know that we know'. Daniel writes that anthroposemiosis defines what it means to be human. Conversely, silence, especially silence that disrupts or resists this process, is seen as threatening to our sense of humanity (Daniel 1996). It is in this vein that the stunned silence of victims of violence seems particularly disconcerting. Similarly, the silence of the authorities or a general lack of public outrage on perceived injustices provokes introspection into whether we have lost our sense of humanity. On the other hand, the ability to render a potentially traumatic lived experience and the myriad emotions associated with it into words seems to restore a sense of normality. This is an idea that is quite prominent in the philosophy of counselling. A counsellor or therapist encourages you to dwell on your experience and helps you process it by extracting meaning from it. This conscious turn to the meaning-making processes of narrative memory through the resuscitation of anthroposemiosis is seen as 'healing'. It is in this way that speaking about one's trauma is seen as 'healing' (Fassin and Rechtman 2009).

This idea of the therapeutic qualities of remembrance are implicit in oral history. Oral historians often mention the 'healing' their work brings to these troubled histories. They present the act of remembering the Partition as a healing experience for its survivors. Meanwhile, the use of phrases such as 'reckoning with history' and 'confronting the past' express a similar hope for healing in the larger context of the past that is remembered. Here, remembrance is constructed as somehow healing for the society that enables it, thus interrupting society's 'traumatised silence'.

Oral historian Alessandro Portelli (1998) described oral history as a unique methodology that amplifies the voices of those who have been historically silenced. Similarly, while reflecting on oral history's relationship with violent and traumatic histories, Sucheta Mahajan (2011: 291) wrote:

> Much oral history is about giving voice to the voiceless, the silenced, especially those rendered so in situations of terrible violence. The very recording of testimonies is believed to have a cathartic and healing effect for victims of trauma, as in the case of survivors of the Jewish Holocaust.

Sometimes, as in the case of the 1947 Partition Archive, these discourses seem almost self-congratulatory. The Archive sees itself as a community of 'concerned global citizens' and describes the impact of its work using the following words:

Turning the tide on public acceptance: The sharing of lived memories over social media, millions of times has helped create a 'critical mass' acknowledgement of the human suffering that resulted from Partition. As a result, we are watching a change in tide of public consciousness. We are watching as memories of Partition are becoming accepted in the mainstream and drawing attention from popular film makers, media makers, news organizations and educators. An honest look at our past, with scrutiny will help us move toward a more just future. (1947 Partition Archive 2011; emphasis in original)

The 1947 Partition Archive, and other oral history projects like it, often valorise the act of remembrance as a therapeutic action. The recording of memories is framed as an act of healing, one that helps the individual as well as their society somehow transcend the past through the mere act of remembering it.

This idea of remembrance as healing derives from the antimimetic theory of trauma. In her genealogy of approaches to trauma, Ruth Leys (2000) identifies a binary classification for academic approaches to the study of trauma: mimetic and antimimetic theory. According to Leys, although the act of 'imitation' is central to both theories, they both understand imitation differently. The mimetic theory holds that due to being unable to recall the traumatic incident, the traumatised subject is doomed to act out its content or imitate it in other ways (hypnotically). Leys writes, 'The idea is that the traumatic experience in its sheer extremity, its affront to common norms and expectations, shatters or disables the victim's cognitive and perceptual capacities so that the experience never becomes part of the ordinary memory system'. Due to the fact that the traumatic incident is assumed to have never become part of the victim's memory, the mimetic theory disputes the authenticity of the victim's testimony (298).

The antimimetic theory, on the other hand, holds that the victim can represent the traumatic event to others and themselves but fundamentally remains aloof from it (298). As Leys explains:

The antimimetic theory is compatible with, and often gives way to, the idea that trauma is a purely external event that befalls a fully constituted subject; whatever the damage to the latter's psychical autonomy and integrity, there is in principle no problem of eventually remembering or otherwise recovering the event, though in practice the process of bringing this about may be long and tortuous. (299)

Furthermore, the antimimetic theory of trauma rejects the mimetic theory's claim that the victim experiences an inchoate identification with their aggressor, an identification represented in the impulse towards 'hypnotic imitation' of the traumatic episode. The antimimetic theory understands violence as an external action on the victim and rejects the mimetic theory's impulse to consider the victim as somehow complicitous in the act of violence directed at them (298–299). Because the antimimetic theory considers the victim aloof from their trauma and yet simultaneously capable of recalling it, it advocates the 'speaking cure'. The conscious turn to narrative memory in this context is meant to 'heal' the alienation of this experience in the victim's memory system.

The objective of my critique here is to show that the common sense understanding of remembrance as healing is predicated on a number of problematic assumptions, chief among them the pathologisation of silence and the erasure of the distinction between victim, perpetrator and witness. This is due to the fact that in contemporary discourse, trauma has emerged as 'the universal language of a new politics of the intolerable' (Fassin and Rechtman 2009: 93).

Didier Fassin and Richard Rechtman note that the trauma concept began as a medical category that sought to avoid any moral prescription between victim or perpetrator or witness. By medically establishing the idea of a psychological wound – akin to a bodily injury – the idea of trauma focused solely on 'the mark left by the event'. However, this has evolved over time such that 'rather than a clinical reality, trauma today is a moral judgement'. The validity accorded to the trauma of the victims of a genocide (such as the Holocaust or the Partition) 'is not the validity of a clinical category but rather of a judgement – the judgement of history'. As a category of moral judgement that defines legitimate victims and the reparations they are due, the concept of trauma articulates a larger philosophy of what it means to be human (284).

I am emphasising this aspect of the trauma concept in order to connect it back to my starting point: anthroposemiosis. In the public act of remembering the Partition, silence is implicitly and explicitly framed as something to be overcome, as something to be fixed or 'healed'. Silence, in this context, is visualised as an abrupt event horizon that allegedly delineates the boundary between semiosis (speech) and its absence (silence). Implicit here is the conflation of silence (as the 'interruption' of anthroposemiosis) with trauma – an illness to be overcome.

Imagining oral history as a therapeutic project that seeks to heal victims by provoking them to speech, informants become patients. Focusing its gaze onto these victims of history, the oral historian as therapist provokes them to speech, moving their narratives from the obscurity of forgetting to the public consciousness-raising act of remembrance. In this act of 'excavation', it restores semiosis, beginning the healing of historical ruptures. This transition from darkness to light, from silence to speech, from forgetting to remembrance is framed within the very title of Urvashi Butalia's (2000) pioneering ethnographic oral history. Thus, to remember the Partition is to access *The Other Side of Silence.*

What emerges in the process is a pathologisation of silence that relies heavily on the assumption that silence exists only in dialogical opposition to the act of speech. This interpretation of silence neglects the myriad ways in which silence is folded within semiosis. For example, anthropologist Keith Basso (1970) observes the various meanings that silence holds for the Western Apache. Basso documents a number of situations where the Western Apache choose to keep silent. These include situations where one is spending time with someone who is either sad or angry, where one is courting a new lover and when meeting someone new. Basso argues that 'status ambiguity' signifies the common denominator in all of these instances. Basso defines 'status ambiguity' as a situation when 'participants perceive their relationships vis-à-vis one another to be ambiguous and/or unpredictable' (225). Therefore, the Western Apache use silence as a response to uncertainty and unpredictability in their social relations. While the specific situations that constitute 'status ambiguity' are culturally specific to the Western Apache, Basso's work reminds us that contrary to unreflective truisms, silence – like speech – is a mode of communication. He shows how silence is folded within semiotic practices and constitutes a deeply meaningful response in the way that individuals navigate social relations.

A second assumption that follows from the assumption that silence signifies the absence of semiosis is that silence in the narratives of Partition survivors is somehow subordinate to the act of speech, or remembrance. By characterising silence as subordinate to speech, the silence of survivors of violence is often understood as a sign of their oppression or as the repression of trauma. This oppression-repression binary fails to recognise that there is agency in silence (Greenwood 2019).

Anindya Raychaudhuri (2019) notes that agency and coercion are assumed to exist in a binary such that if one is seen to be a victim, then one cannot be said to have agency and vice versa. Raychaudhuri writes that Partition Studies' overwhelming focus on trauma, pain, displacement and loss suggests that the voices of its marginalised survivors can only participate in this discourse as victims. She finds this suggestion problematic and instead argues for the recognition of the narrative agency of Partition survivors. She draws on Helen M. Buss' definition of agency as 'the ability of individuals to negotiate societal systems to make meanings for themselves' (quoted in Raychaudhuri 2019: 10). Thus, Raychaudhuri reasserts survivors' authorship over their narratives and the meanings they make – including their silence. Ultimately, Raychaudhuri reminds us that 'while the author of a Partition narrative may indeed be a victim, he or she most certainly does not have to be one' (10).

In a similar vein, Fassin and Rechtman (2009) argue that it is necessary to recognise the agential dimension of trauma (and silence). This includes the way that individuals might themselves mobilise the concept of trauma in practice of the politics of reparation, the politics of testimony and/or the politics of proof. Fassin and Rechtman clarify that the recognition of this is not cynical but rather a pressing ethical imperative. They write that 'in asserting the tactical dimension of trauma we are recognising the social intelligence of the actors involved' (11).

How then do we remember the Partition without reducing its survivors to passive victimhood? How might we write about the enduring silence of those who choose not to share their memories? In *Charred Lullabies*, Valentine Daniel (1996: 150) reflects on a 'drone of silence' that persists over his conversations with victims of violence, a silence that 'does not settle for the anthropologist'. During my fieldwork, I too observed this silence that 'does not settle for the anthropologist'. This feeling was most palpable while interviewing Ambunath.

Ambunath was an 82-year-old Partition survivor who was originally from Choti and now lived in Gurgaon. Out of all the people I interviewed, Ambunath had had perhaps the most intimate experience of death and violence. Most of Ambunath's family had perished during the Partition. In August 1947, when the violence first began in that region, four of Ambunath's uncles were murdered. As the violence escalated and showed no signs of abating, their family moved to the city of Dera Ghazi Khan for safety. After spending four months in a makeshift refugee camp in Dera Ghazi Khan, the military evacuated them to Multan from where they boarded a train to Lahore. At the Lahore railway station, as their train awaited clearance from the signalman, they were attacked by a mob of Muslims. As the mob swarmed their compartment, Ambunath and his mother hid under a bleeding corpse. Ambunath remembered:

> After reaching Lahore around 3 o'clock, they attacked us, Muslims. My mother was with me. You know how inside the train they have these planks [berths], there someone was already lying [dead], and he was bleeding. My mother had kept me hidden. She put a *dupatta*[1] over me. That blood was dripping over me, was flowing. So they [the mob] came, saw, thought we were dead and moved on. That they are dead, bleeding, so they left me thinking I was dead. But they kept killing as they went ahead. A lot of damage happened. After that at 5 o'clock the train started moving and then Attari [India].

Such vivid descriptions were relatively rare for Ambunath. He was, for the most part, a quiet and reserved man. Where other informants would barely need a prompt to narrate their life histories, Ambunath spoke predominantly in one-word answers. The conversations that I had with him were generously punctuated by silence. He disavowed any interest in politics and political discussions. The couple of times that I tried to steer our conversations towards politics, he precluded my attempts with dismissive (but polite) comments emphasising his quotidian material concerns over lofty discussions of high-politics. He claimed he had no hatred for Muslims despite the suffering in his past.

Even among his community he was known for his quietness. Jogesh, his neighbour and also a Partition survivor, remarked that while

Ambunath came out to the park every evening, he never spoke to or sat beside anyone, preferring instead to sit by himself in the comfort of his own silence. Jogesh's son Mrinal confided in me that Ambunath's wife had died relatively early while his son had also died young. His son, Mrinal told me, had died of the 'fruit of his own deeds' (*karmon ka phal*). When I responded to that comment with a confused expression, Mrinal lowered his voice to a conspiratorial whisper and told me he had died of AIDS. The moralisation of his death[2] and the sheer lack of grief in its remembrance stayed with me for long after that conversation.

My awareness of the death and suffering in Ambunath's life had the paradoxical effect of pushing our subsequent conversations further into silence. Even though I visited him with the objective of recording his memories, I often felt hesitant to disturb the silence. What was the point of remembering relatives who had died long ago, I wondered. What might be gained by talking about his son, a death the local community had clearly moralised. Nothing I might have said or written had the power to heal these ruptures. My attempts at speech for the sake of ethnography felt like a deliberate scratching of barely concealed wounds.

In the face of this suffering that he clearly wanted to keep private, ethnography felt a deeply invasive and disrespectful task. Thus, in Ambunath's presence, the task of ethnography became meaningful through silence. To some degree, I had come to understand his silence. Rather than unearth his wounds in pursuit of speech for the sake of speech – of some simplistic notion of healing – I instead chose to respect the agency of his silence. In this way, the silence that we shared became one of solidarity. For me, these moments of silence became an opportunity for reflection on the problem of theodicy, something I grappled with extensively in my everyday thoughts during this final phase of my fieldwork. I do not know whether he had similar thoughts. But I do know that the silence we shared was companionable and somewhat cathartic.

To many, the idea of a silence that is ethnographically meaningful might scrape against the very nature of the task. Words are after all the anthropologist's most valuable currency. The fact that silence might be valuable to ethnography appears *prima facie* to run counter to this idea. But perhaps that is what is at issue here: a troubling urge to produce speech for the sake of words. Although I do not claim to propose an alternative, I return to the difficulty of remembering the Partition in Chapter 9.

Notes

1   A shawl-like cotton scarf that is traditionally worn by women in South Asia.
2   Mary Douglas (1994: 92) provides an insightful account of the moralisation of diseases and the discrimination that ensues from this, through the idea of 'libel'. Douglas (92–93) writes:

> The simple food libel (foreigners eat disgusting foods), and the sex libel (the demeaned category is promiscuous, effeminate, incestuous), escalate to violence and perversion, and if the determination to exclude is fixed, it resorts to the blood libel (the enemy is murderous, and even murders children). The culminating infamy that incites ethnic persecution combines blood, sex, food, and religion.... Imputing filth to the victims enables them to be rejected without a qualm.

7

Remembering Violence

Where Are the Perpetrators?

Yasmin Khan (2017b) notes that despite the recent surge in oral historical work on the Partition, it ultimately remains 'a history layered with absence and silences'. Khan observes that while most Punjabi families can tell a Partition-era story of loss and displacement, either of their own or of someone they know, 'far fewer are willing to discuss the role of their own locality in contributing to the violence'). As a result, while oral histories of 'victims' abound, 'guilt and silences stalk the archive' (Khan 2017b).

This total absence of perpetrator testimonies characterises my work too. During my fieldwork, I did not encounter a single informant who admitted either their own or their locality's role in violence. The closest I ever came to a perpetrator testimony was when one of my informants[1] admitted to having been trained for 'self-defence'. Aged 16 and living in Dera Ghazi Khan at the time of the Partition, Dipankar became an RSS *swayamsevak* (volunteer) at a young age. He subsequently rose through the ranks to become a *naik* and then a *gatanaik* (group leader).

In 1947, as ethnonational tensions simmered, his RSS *shakha* (branch) organised its members into teams to carry out training exercises. Donning the typical RSS attire of a white shirt, khaki shorts and a *lathi*,[2] they would set off early in the morning to patrol 'their' (Hindu) neighbourhoods. Since the RSS was a banned organisation at the time, most of their activities took place in secret. Dipankar admitted that sometimes senior members of the *shakha* would also organise elaborate drills to test their alertness and combat readiness.

So what we did, no one would get to know. Suppose 50-something men have come to the *shakha*. So there the *shakha* would be set up beside a *gaushala* [cow shelter], early in the morning. So then suddenly they would say, *bhai*, Muslims are coming from there, they are 10–12, we have to beat them up, we have to catch them, and they are coming to attack us. They have knives in their hands, they have daggers in their hands, and a *lathi*. So you 2-2, 3-3 men go do them. But afterwards when they [Muslims] would come we would use a *lathi* – now we knew how to fight with a *lathi*, we knew how to do *gatka*,[3] we had also learnt to use swords. So we would run after them. Later we would learn that these are Hindus. They are people from our *shakha* who are just conducting an exercise – *bhai*, if the need ever arises.

Dipankar was always very careful about packaging his riot drills and weapons training as an exercise in self-defence. He admitted that his *gatanaik* at the time – a 20-something young man who was the son of a local mid-ranking police officer – would organise regular arms training for them.

So there were brick kilns there, he would call us there at 4, alright? There he would teach us everything. And we would hide from the government. Now, when we would return from there, like we are wearing our [*khaki*] shorts, we would wear a *tehmat* over it, a *dhoti*. So that no one would know this is a man from the [RSS] *shakha*.

Though their training had included firearms too, Dipankar said he was unable to learn to use a gun properly. Dipankar also denied any involvement in riots or any *actual* attack on Muslims or their property. Although, listening to his stories made me wonder how far I was willing to trust his words. Could I seriously believe that someone who had trained for violence all through their youth had never actually participated in a pogrom or attack of some sort?

Dipankar's story sheds some light on the more shadowy aspects of Partition history. It is evocative of Yasmin Khan's (2017a) observation that even today India and Pakistan remain in denial about the nature of Partition violence. This question of 'who were the killers?' has been described by Khan as the 'mystery at the dark heart' of the Partition and by Joya Chatterji (2014: 311) as the 'gaping void at the heart of the subject'. Within the larger field of South Asian Partition Studies, this is not so much an actual mystery as it is the weasel-worded invocation of 'complexity' towards the denial of an obvious reality. At other times, this question has been avoided through the articulation of the dubious claim that the violence of the Partition was an uncontrollable, spontaneous aberration.

Yasmin Khan (2017a, 2017b) boldly identifies the killers as the young men of organised militias such as the RSS and the Muslim League. The crux of Khan's argument is that far from a chaotic spectacle of blood-letting, there was a fundamentally organised character to the violence of the Partition. The violent mobs that survivors refer to in their stories were made up of real people who came from specific backgrounds and were often very skilled in the violence that they perpetrated (Khan 2017a). Others such as Anders B. Hansen (2002), Ian Talbot (2006), Talbot and Singh (2009), Gyanendra Pandey (2001) and Vazira Zamindar (2007) have similarly revealed the role of partisan policemen, political parties, pseudo-military gangs and even Partition refugees in the violence that unfolded across north India. Hansen in particular provides an exhaustive account of how Punjab descended into retributive genocidal violence as a combination of political miscalculations, colonial apathy, the militarisation of the countryside, the complicity of local policemen and civil servants, and a number of other intersecting local issues. Moreover, there were numerous politicians who actively instigated communal violence in pursuit of other political objectives (Hansen 2002).

These analyses of the organised character of Partition violence have gone beside broader historiographical examinations of the phenomenon of 'communal violence' in India. Paul Brass (2003a: 32) argues that Gandhi's emphasis on a nonviolent mass movement directly sprung from his knowledge of Indian society and politics 'from his own understanding of the violent mechanisms that could so easily be brought into play under the cover of the vast mass movements that he launched, which would undercut their purposes and direct local political energies to other targets'.

Following the death of Nehru, these violent mechanisms have solidified into what Brass dubs 'Institutionalized Riot Systems' (32). These networks create communal tensions and 'riots' at regular intervals, making them endemic in various parts of the country. Brass has shown that this system of deliberate polarisation with the objective of consolidating Hindu communal sentiment has paid huge electoral dividends for the BJP and other Hindu nationalist parties. Sudha Pai and Sajjan Kumar (2018) have subsequently built on Brass' work to argue that these Institutionalized Riot Systems have evolved into institutionalised everyday communalism.

Following on from my discussion of the narrative agency of Partition survivors in the previous chapter, in this chapter I use memories of the Partition to problematise abstractions such as the 'Hindu-fold' and 'communal' violence. This chapter shows how violence and its memory functions as a narrativising lens (Feldman 1997) that (re-)shapes the boundaries of community (G. Pandey 2001). This chapter explores the interconnections between the memories of 1947 and 1984 and shows how these memories are integral to the imagination of a Hindu-fold in this context. It also discusses the tactical use of violence and local memories of interpersonal conflict in an attempt to pay attention to the experience, memory and performance of violence on the ground.

My discussion in this chapter is guided by Herzfeld's (2005) critique of Anderson's (1983) work on nations as 'imagined communities'. Herzfeld critiques Anderson's argument as a top-down formulation that fails to adequately theorise how and why individual citizens respond to the appeal of nationalism in the way that they do. Herzfeld (2005: 5) wonders, 'Why should people be willing to die for a formal abstraction?' This question is one that is central to the discipline of anthropology whose main concern is interpretive; that is, 'why do people do (or believe in) the things they do?'

Therefore, in line with its ethnographic and interpretive geist – evident also in my focus on theodicy – a substantial theme within this chapter's discussion of violence is the tactical use of violence. Put another way, this is the question of why people want to participate in and kill/die for the abstraction that is 'communal' violence. Additionally, building on Gyanendra Pandey's (1990) work on 'communalism' as a colonial form of knowledge, I check my use of the word – substituting it for religious nationalism, ethnonationalism and ethnic or sectarian violence as appropriate – and actively reflect on violence as a narrativising lens.

Violence and Community

In accounts of the Partition, violence is routinely described as having occurred 'outside', having been perpetrated by 'outsiders' or as an act of 'self-defence'. Such descriptions of violence are not unique to the Partition. The Hindu Right's description of the 2002 anti-Muslim pogroms in Gujarat as an act of 'self-defence' is a particularly stark example of how deliberate mass-murder can be justified and obfuscated in this manner (Brass 2003a; Ghassem-Fachandi 2010; Sarkar 2002). Gyanendra Pandey (2001) identifies this discourse as something intrinsic to nationalism and the re-constitution of community in the aftermath of violent ruptures. The ruptured community that Pandey refers to might be seen as the rupturing of a *nomos*, a certain idea of a syncretic, secular India, a conception of 'us' – of modernity itself. However, this rupture is also a constitutive force.

Previously, I have cited Pandey's critique of Indian historiography's tendency to treat Partition violence and other episodes of communal/ sectarian violence as 'someone else's history' (6). Pandey attributes this tendency to the intolerance that is fundamentally built into nationalism: a call to conformity that is the unnoticed common political denominator of nations. Pandey argues that nations deal with violence in their past and present by drawing a boundary around themselves, presenting the violence as either caused by the other or necessitated due to the other's actions (the narrative of 'self-defence'). In this act of boundary-marking through the categorisation of violence as 'out there', Pandey observes the constitution of community. Pandey writes:

> Violence happens – and can only happen – at the boundaries of community. It marks those boundaries. It is the denial of any violence 'in our midst', the attribution of harmony within and the consignment of violence to the outside, that establishes 'community'. (188)

Pandey's observations spring from his own ethnographic fieldwork on the Partition in the Sikh village of Dhamot. Various informants told Pandey about an incident where 40–50 Muslim women were brought to the village, following a 'raid' on a neighbouring village. The women were kept in the village *gurdwara* for a night and then killed in the temple compound the following day. In his interviews, Pandey noted that his informants were always careful to point out that the murders had occurred 'outside' the village. Pandey writes:

> The location of the site of violence 'outside' the village – even the precincts of the gurdwara, which appears to have been the shared property of several villages, might technically be considered 'outside' – seems to be a matter of some importance to the informants. (181)

Pandey's informants insisted that not a single Muslim had been harmed 'inside' their village, although they admitted to having forced their Muslim neighbours to eat pork 'for their own safety' (181). Pandey connects these statements to the othering of Partition violence, observing that by establishing the site of this violence as 'outside' the geographical bounds of their village, his informants sought to figuratively distance themselves from it.

In this way, the violence of the Partition involved the constitution of a national community, a collectivity whose boundaries had to be sketched in blood. The community is shaped as much by the actual physical use of violence – the ethnic cleansing of those who do not belong – as much as its representation after the fact. For example, Pandey's informants construct their community as a metaphorical island around which the rivers of blood flowed. Where, in actuality, the metaphorical island is constructed by violence – the coagulated mass of severed limbs, guts, blood and gore – in its remembrance after the fact, the island is essentialised as eternal fact. In this retelling, violence does not happen within the community so much as it happens *to* or *around*, or, better yet, 'outside' the community (G. Pandey 2001).

Yet, these seemingly natural boundaries are also inherently fluid and unstable. This fact is evident in Pandey's fieldwork in the way that his informants find it necessary to continuously and obsessively establish the location of violence as 'outside' their village. This reflexive narrative urge betrays an anxiety around these boundaries, an urge that demands constant maintenance of the boundary in narrative. Pandey notes, 'Face-to-face local communities have to live with disturbing memories of this kind more uncertainly, and continuously, than nations and states' (177). In everyday life, these boundaries are reinforced through the performance of identities, by acting like a Hindu. Everyday acts of structural violence, of discrimination and casual misdemeanour, not only uphold the physical fact of these boundaries but are also reflective of the nature of violence as a 'narrativizing frame' (Feldman 1997). Here, violence performs the seemingly self-evident character of these boundaries.

We may connect Pandey's discussion of violence as a performative delineation of the boundaries of community to Herzfeld's (1992) idea of nationalism as a form of theodicy that transcends local differences and also, to Marilyn Strathern's (1992) idea that the Euro-American concept of 'society' (or 'group' or 'nation' or 'collectivity') is imagined as homogenous and internally undifferentiated, as analogous to the 'individual' person. The larger argument this related body of work articulates is that the community or collectivity (or nation) is fundamentally based on the imagination of homogeneity and absolute conformity. As Strathern writes, 'Generalisation implies that collectivities are made up of units which can be enumerated. Society can thus be imagined as a plurality of particulars, as "a society of individuals"' (26).

Key to this imagination is the performance of homogeneity through violence. Here, it is relevant to remember Allen Feldman's theorisation of violence as 'second representation', that is, of the act of violence itself as a lens or 'narrativizing frame'. Violence then perceives, constructs, imagines, narrativises and performs the homogeneity that characterises conceptions of (national) community (Feldman 1997: 36). In this way, violence both performs and imagines community. Furthermore, as Deepti Misri (2014) argues, representations of violence are also interpretations of violence. Thus, the violence of the Partition – both in its performance at the time and in its representation after the fact – comprises one long process of the delineation of national community (G. Pandey 2001).

In this chapter, I explore this idea by paying attention to two themes within the narratives of the violence of the Partition. First, in the following section I use some of my own ethnographic evidence to discuss my informants' othering of the violence of the Partition. This representation of violence, I argue, is evidence of the continuous process of the construction and reconstitution of the Hindu-fold. Second, in the section following, I draw attention to the local and intimate histories of conflict that can be glimpsed within my informants' stories of the Partition. I argue that these local and intimate acts of violence prove the lie of the imagination of homogeneity on which the idea of national community rests. That is, not all violence during the Partition was motivated by religious and ethnic identity. Some of it was motivated by a personal desire to settle scores, a desire that in actuality had very little to do with the Partition.

Memories of 'Violent' Sikhs: Imagining and Re-imagining the Hindu-Fold Through Time

During my fieldwork, I observed that the othering of violence (not just of the Partition) always conformed to the shifting boundaries of the Hindu-fold. One of the ways in which my informants othered the violence of the Partition was by attributing it to Sikhs. This was an imprint of the events of the 1980s, of the way in which the violent contestations between the Indian state and the Sikh nationalist movement for an independent Khalistan problematised the position of Sikhs within the Hindu-fold. In this book, I have alluded numerous times to the fact that the Hindu-fold is an imagined community that loosely pulls together a variety of antagonistic castes and distinct religions (specifically Sikhs and Jains). But, as van der Veer (1994) and others have shown, the Hindu-fold is little more than an illusion whose boundaries are fluid through time.

The ghost of 1984 – along with its problematisation of the Hindu-fold – is far from extinct. I found this performance of community active in the way that the events of 1947 and 1984 were remembered. More often than not, whenever I confronted my informants with questions that asked them to reflect on the violence perpetrated by Hindus (often in response to their Islamophobic descriptions of violence), my informants responded by attributing the worst of the violence against

Muslims to Sikhs. My granduncle Om Prakash, for example, described the September 1947 violence in Delhi as the work of organised mobs of Sikhs, not Hindus. 'The Sikhs did a lot [of violence]' and 'The Sikhs had a greater conflict [with Muslims]' were refrains I commonly encountered. In this way, the aberrational character of the violence of 1947 was attributed to the so-called innately violent nature of Sikh masculinity. My informants routinely described Sikh men as aggressive, violent and fanatical. My granduncle even admitted to being 'afraid' of Sikhs, even today. 'One can never trust when they [Sikhs] might start killing,' he said while talking about the Partition as a living memory. These stereotypes were contrasted with the inherently 'peaceful' and 'tolerant' character of Hindus. 'The Hindu still stays low[4] [or subjugated]' was a common refrain in this regard.

These stereotypes were not restricted to descriptions of communal violence alone. In July 2018, when my grandaunt Anjali began to look for new tenants for her other Rajouri Garden flat, her eldest brother told her to steer clear of Sikh tenants. The fear was that if a Sikh tenant decided to 'capture' their property, then there would be no way to evict them, especially not in the Sikh-Punjabi-dominated Rajouri Garden. To them, the Sikhs represented a singularly aggressive, homogenous mass of people. Muslim tenants were so far out of the question that they did not even warrant a discussion.

These discourses mirrored and reflected the discourses of Sikh militant leaders from the 1980s. Veena Das (2007) has observed that between 1981 and 1984, Sikh leaders began to articulate new images of the Sikh self in relation to the Hindu self. The Sikh 'self' was constructed as pure and righteous while the Hindu 'other' was seen as 'weak', 'effeminate' and 'cunning'. The weakness of the Hindus was emphasised by reference to a history where they were seen to have depended on the Sikhs for protection (112). This was also related to a larger historical narrative of Sikh sacrifice and martyrdom that I have mentioned previously in Chapter 4. In this way, a new Sikh national identity took shape, one that was juxtaposed against the Hindu other.

Metaphors of male relatedness were an important part of this racialisation. Religious ties between Sikhism and Hinduism were disavowed as a Hindu 'insult' to the Sikhs. Sikh leaders saw their community as the 'true sons' of Guru Gobind Singh (the last Sikh Guru and the founder of the Khalsa tradition), rather than the 'sons' of 'weak', 'effeminate', Hindu men. Sikh masculinity was presented as one based on strength, virility and dignity. This understanding of Sikh masculinity was itself an internalisation of the British colonial (orientalist) categorisation of the Sikhs as a 'martial race' (112).

The claim to 'pure ancestry' – voiced through anxieties around one's 'true father' – are also demonstrative of the fact that the Sikh and Hindu nations thus imagined, are quintessentially masculine nations. Belonging – within both nations – is conditional on 'correct' patrilineal genealogy. For the Sikhs, acceptance of the Hindu nation construed a symbolic betrayal of their 'true father'. While, for Hindus, Sikhs could not belong within the Hindu nation until they acknowledged Hinduism as the 'parent' religion, a symbolic acceptance of Hindu hegemony (112).

These racial boundaries were reinforced through the re-imagination of violence in the past. Just as my caste-Hindu informants attributed Partition violence to the Sikhs, Sikh separatist leaders of the 1980s re-imagined the history of communal conflict as a specifically 'Hindu history' (112). Notably, the 'Sikh memory' of communal violence in Punjab in the 1920s and in 1947 reframed 'communal' violence as a purely Hindu–Muslim contestation. This narrative connected medieval violence and 'communal' violence in Punjab's recent past (in the 1920s and 1947) to the violence of the 1980s. In the process, the 'Hindu majority community' was presented as the source of all violence, while the (Hindu) Indian state and its institutions were presented as an imposition on the Sikh people (115–116).

Recording Partition oral history in the 1980s and 90s, Butalia (2000) noted how the anti-Sikh pogroms of 1984 and the demolition of the Babri Masjid in 1992 had reopened the wounds of the Partition. Butalia noted, '"We didn't think it would happen to us in our own country" was a feeling expressed by Sikhs and Muslims in 1984 and 1992'. For the Sikh community, the events of 1984 were doubly traumatising for they were seen to be a betrayal of the Partition (276). This was mirrored on the other side in the 'Hindu' view that Sikh separatism similarly constituted a grave and treasonous betrayal of the state, as well as what they saw to be a shared religious heritage. After all, Sikhs had, for the most part, been an intimate part of the Hindu-fold, with shared places of worship and familial ties. This is not to say that Sikhs and Hindus represented a homogenous Hindu-fold, but that the imagination of the Hindu-fold assumed the assimilation of Sikhs.

But the events of the 1980s came to necessitate a careful maintenance of these boundaries. As a result, there were strong similarities in the way that my informants racialised Sikhs and Muslims. This is evident in the following conversation I had with Bhanwarilal and his friend, Gangaram. This discussion began when Bhanwarilal shared that day's major news story with Gangaram. That morning (27 February 2018), the newspapers had broken the story that in secret talks with the Indian government, Sikh separatist groups had made an offer for reconciliation (Laskar 2018). They had offered to give up the demand for Khalistan in return for (*a*) an apology from the Prime Minister in an international forum for the Indian Army's 1984 desecration of the Golden Temple, (*b*) special status for the Golden Temple akin to that of the Vatican City and (*c*) unconditionally open talks on justice for extrajudicial killings of Sikhs and the 1984 anti-Sikh pogroms (Laskar 2018). Our discussion went as follows:

Bhanwarilal: If you [Indian government] do all this, then we have a compromise. Meaning, those are the discussions that are on. But, one cannot trust them [Sikhs]. There is no trusting them that way.

Gangaram [*in agreement*]: No, no.

Interviewer [PK]: So uncle, you do not trust them? You do not trust these Sikh organisations? As in you do not believe they will honour their end of this bargain?

B: They can still demand Khalistan.

G: They are still demanding this. These Sikhs, they are very sectarian. Very sectarian.

B: They are like Muslims. Just like how Muslims talk to you and then betray you.

G: They always say, 'Sikh first'. Just like how Muslims say, 'Islam first'. Sikhs-Muslims. After that anyone else. These Sikhs also, they do not go to Hindu temples. Hindus go to *gurdwaras*, in 100, 80 men are

Hindu. 20 are Sikh. But in temples 95 out of that 100 men are Hindu, 5 will be Sikh. [To Banwarilal] What do you say, isn't it right?

B: Yes.

G: Hindus go to *gurdwara*s, Sikhs don't go to temples.

B: We go to *gurdwara*s and pray with complete faith, but those people [Sikhs] will not come here, will not come to temples.

G: Sikhs do not come. They will never come.

B: And they, they especially have this feeling. Today Sikhism is only 550 years old. Meaning …

G: No no, in reality it is only 300 years.

[Some back and forth over whether Sikhism began in the fifteenth century, with the preaching of Guru Nanak, or more recently, after the establishment of the Khalsa by the last Sikh Guru, Guru Gobind Singh.]

G: [On the subject of Sikh Gurus] *They were all Hindus.*

[Argument over age of Sikhism continues.]

B: It has been 300 years. Now in 300 years they say we are a separate community. We have no connection to Hindus.

G: They have a lot of hatred.

B: They are not relatives of Hindus. *Meaning, they do not even believe that they are sons of Hindus.* So that is why you cannot trust them, because, they have come from the main [Hindu-fold] and separated. We are still walking with them, still believe in them: the Gurus. The faith those people [Sikhs] have in them [Gurus] is less than what all of our people do. They [Sikhs] may become whatever they want but they only do bad things [in the name of the Gurus].

In the exchange above, Bhanwarilal and Gangaram, both racialise Sikhs and Muslims as inherently fanatical, sectarian and untrustworthy. Bhanwarilal also goes a step further and remarks – exemplifying Veena Das' observations regarding the anxieties of 'true' patrilineal descent – that Sikhs neither acknowledge their connections to the Hindu-fold, nor that they are 'sons of Hindus'. Their insistence on the similarity of Hindus and Sikhs seems paradoxical considering their recognition of the deep differences that allegedly divide the two.

At this point in the conversation, I decided to play the devil's advocate. Repeating Butalia's (2000) observations about the Sikh feeling of anomie and betrayal, I wondered aloud whether the entrenched separatism they allegedly observed was a response to the events of 1984. Bhanwarilal responded rather angrily:

> Bhanwarilal: That 1984 is another event. Look the event of '84 is what they did to the Prime Minister, her guardians who were Sardars [Sikhs]. People had said remove them, Indira Gandhi said no, no they are alright. And they only killed her.
>
> Interviewer [PK]: But that was also said to have a reason, that the army was sent into the Akal Takth [Golden Temple].
>
> B [*shouting*]: Arre, it is a humanly reaction son. There will be a human reaction. That if you do one thing for one minute – a wrong thing – so that will have some or the other reaction *na*? She is the Prime Minister of the country. And that Prime Minister who had been given the status of Durga [Hindu demon-slaying warrior goddess]. When Bangladesh was attacked, they conquered Bangladesh, won, cut it off from Pakistan, so then they ['people'] had said that she is Durga to us, she is an avatar of Durga.
>
> Gangaram: They had given that [title] to her.
>
> B: So see that is the difference. So what if those '84 riots happened? Why, are they now not even part of their own country? This has happened to them [Sikhs] because what happened that was a reaction to a reaction. That happens everywhere.

Seeing Bhanwarilal get worked up, I deescalated the conversation by clarifying that I was merely thinking out loud as a philosophical exercise. In reply, Bhanwarilal sardonically quipped that my subject was the Partition and not 1984 and that I would do well to focus on that. To him, 1947 and 1984 were unrelated events.

Bhanwarilal's comments in these exchanges demonstrate many of the patterns of thinking about violence that I have discussed previously in this chapter. He describes the anti-Sikh pogroms of 1984 as 'a reaction to a reaction', thereby justifying the violence of the 'peaceful' and 'tolerant' Hindu as an act of self-defence. As a reaction to an action, the pogroms are rationalised as an act necessary for the disciplining of an allegedly errant Sikh community.

This justification of pogroms as a disciplining tool extends the parental metaphor to the much darker realm of the management of entire populations. Although the parental metaphor implicitly identifies common ancestry – an extension of the discourse of nationalism as kinship – the act of disciplining by definition is an act of boundary-marking. It delineates the parent from the child, the ruler from its subjects, the hegemonic majority from its minority. It demarcates ethnic boundaries whilst establishing power and hierarchy.

The 1984 pogroms also marked the boundary between the Sikhs and the Hindu-fold at the lowest levels as some Hindu Chamars (an 'untouchable' and oppressed caste) participated in the violence against Sikhs. Das' work (2007) maps the violence in north-west Delhi (Sultanpuri and Prem Nagar) down to the street and block level and documents how local politicians and police officers were complicit in the pogroms. Her work explains why some streets and blocks saw more violence than others. Specifically, Das focuses on the horrific violence that unfolded between blocks A2 and A4 of Sultanpuri.

This example is relevant to our current discussion given that it shows not only the remaking of the boundaries of national community, but also that this ethnocidal violence was itself foregrounded by a prior history of antagonisms. Das reminds us that the Sikhs were not a homogenous group but instead differed considerably on the basis of 'caste, sectarian allegiance, and place of origin' (144). This diversity could be observed in the spatial organisation of the blocks that made up these neighbourhoods. Block A4 was inhabited by the Sikh Siglikar community while A2 belonged to the Hindu Chamar caste. Since 1982, the two groups had violently clashed over local issues concerning the use of shared land. Additionally, the Pradhan (leader) of the Chamar community saw the region as his fiefdom. There was also a growing economic inequality between the Siglikars and the Chamars as some

Siglikar men had succeeded in finding employment in the Middle East. Their aspirational status was resented by their poorer Chamar neighbours.

On 31 October 1984, the assassination of Indira Gandhi became the flashpoint of a verbal exchange that quickly spiralled out of control. The Pradhan of the Chamars shouted at the Siglikars that the Sikhs must apologise for the assassination of 'their mother' (154). But the Pradhan of A4 responded to this with casteist slurs. The confrontation escalated quickly and a few hours later the Pradhan of A2 returned with the local station house officer (SHO) and some police constables at the head of a violent mob. The mob pulled the Siglikar Pradhan out of his house and, after torturing him and his sons, burnt them alive. The mob then proceeded to systematically pull all of the Sikh men of A4 out of their homes and burnt them alive. The Siglikar homes were then looted and the 'foreign-made' clothes of Siglikar women acquired a trophy-like status for the Chamar families.

Das focuses her analysis on the insults traded between the Pradhans of A2 and A4, in particular a comment by the Pradhan of A2 where he requested an apology from the Sikhs because they had killed 'our mother'. By referring to Indira Gandhi as their 'mother' and whose death had to be avenged, Das notes that the Chamars had constructed themselves as 'the true sons of the nation'. In this way, the Chamars, despite being one of the poorest and most oppressed castes within the (Hindu) nation, expressed solidarity with the most privileged echelons of society. Das understands this as a moment of 'brokered subjectivity' (Das 2007: 159). Identifying Indira Gandhi as their 'mother', the Hindu Chamars of A2 expressed their belonging within the Hindu-fold, in opposition to the 'Sikh other'. This verbal confrontation and the ethnocidal violence that followed served as a final event of the delineation of the new boundaries of the national community.

Das' observation of the participation of this oppressed Hindu caste in the violence against the Sikhs – a violence meant to discipline an 'unruly' minority – is part of a larger phenomenon in Indian politics. While the participation of some Hindu Chamars in the violence of 1984 was a moment of 'brokered subjectivity' – of a violence in solidarity with and on behalf of upper-caste Hindu ruling elites – in recent times, the participation of lower-caste Hindus in pogroms and communal violence is part of a larger, deliberate consolidation of the Hindu-fold.

Parvis Ghassem-Fachandi (2010) has observed a similar consolidation of the Hindu-fold in Gujarat's 2002 anti-Muslim pogroms. The violence in Gujarat was unusual for the way in which it involved the participation of lower- and upper-caste Hindus, and Adivasis in the ethnic cleansing of Muslims. Ghassem-Fachandi (164) writes:

> In opposing the Muslim minority, there was a complementary division of labour at work between upper castes (*savarna*) and classes, and lower classes, including many members of scheduled castes and Adivasi (tribal), the *avarna* and *bekwad* (backward) groups. According to some scholars, the larger participation by subaltern and other marginal groups distinguishes the 2002 violence from previous rounds. In a spatial division of work, looting and burning shops was accomplished on the west side of the city, while beyond the Sabarmati River, and outside of the historical city, looting and burning was accompanied by massacres.

As I have detailed previously in the Introduction of this book, the consolidation of the Hindu-fold through the assimilation of Adivasis and Jains (Banaji 2018) is a deliberate strategy pursued by the various Hindu nationalist organisations that make up the Sangh Parivar. Its success has been driven by effective grassroots mobilisation and 'cultural awakening' (Ghassem-Fachandi 2010), as well as by Sanskritisation (Srinivas 1966) and aspirational hatred (Appadurai 2021). In this way spectacular acts of street violence play a pivotal role in the performance and imagination of the Hindu-fold.

Violence – as a narrativising lens (Feldman 1997) – delineates the boundaries of community, both in the act itself and its representation and interpretation (Misri 2014). The 'dead certainty' established through violence provides the illusion of stability – by locating difference in the body of the 'other' – to what are in fact infinitely fluid ethnic imaginations (Appadurai 1998). As I have shown in this section, the events of the 1980s have come to retrospectively alter the memory of the Partition. Where the Sikh nationalist discourse re-imagines 'communal violence' as a purely Hindu–Muslim issue (Das 2007), the Hindu nationalist discourse has attributed the worst anti-Muslim violence to 'fanatical', 'aggressive' Sikh men. Here, narratives of violence delineate the boundaries of national community establishing the victimhood or innocence of the 'self' whilst blaming the 'other'. After all, as Gyanendra Pandey (2001) writes, violence can never happen 'inside' the community but instead happens *to* it or *outside* it.

Problematising Community: Local Histories of Violence

Thus far in this chapter, and this book, I have steadfastly rejected the idea that national communities are homogenous. In the previous section, this took the form of a discussion of violence as a narrativising lens that delineates the boundaries of national community. In this section, I continue this discussion by focusing on the local histories of violence. These stories of antagonisms that predate the Partition can be glimpsed through a closer reading of the literature on the Partition and the stories of my informants. My discussion here is inspired by Veena Das' (2007) aforementioned ethnographic work mapping the spatial distribution of the violence in Sultanpuri during the 1984 anti-Sikh pogroms. Just as her work reveals a history of conflict between Blocks A2 and A4 that predated the events of 1984, so too I hope to explore some of the specificities of Partition violence.

Here, I want to return to the claims of Pandey's (2001) informants – which I quoted in the previous section – that no violence was done to 'our' Muslim neighbours in 'our' village. This claim also evokes an enduring romanticised understanding of the violence of the Partition (especially in Punjab). I am referring here to the fantasy that even as Punjab descended into violence, that neighbour did not turn on neighbour. Rather, it was mobs of 'outsiders' who were responsible for the violence.

One encounters this fantasy routinely in survivor narratives as well as in literature. We find this expressed, for example, in J. Nanda's (1948) account of Partition violence. Nanda's *Punjab Uprooted* straddles the thin line between memoir and contemporaneous history as it documents Partition violence as it unfolded in Punjab, starting from the March riots of 1947. Struggling to reconcile the brutality of violence with the famed idea of *punjabiyat*,[5] Nanda writes:

Inevitably, old personal scores were paid off in a few cases, but as a rule, the raid on the minority of a village was not made by the majority community of the same village, but of a different village. This is a very important point: the communal riots did not suddenly destroy the bonds of neighbourliness between immediate neighbours who could never commit such bestialities on each other as were perpetrated by *outsiders*. It was not an individual Muslim warring against an individual Sikh, but an individual Muslim at war with the Sikh community. (18; emphasis added)

While Nanda admits that some of the Partition violence was motivated by local antagonisms that predate the event, he goes on to provide an elaborate model that blames 'outsiders' for the violence that unfolded on the ground (18). Despite its neatness and the alluring romanticism of a society where neighbour would not turn on neighbour even amid the collapse of a moral universe, Nanda's model remains nothing but a fantasy. Nanda provides no evidence in support of his claim and there is nothing in the historical record that indicates the truth of this claim. Furthermore, Nanda's idea of an individual 'Muslim' or 'Sikh' at war with the collectivity of the 'other' expresses an inchoate neoliberal understanding of the individual's place within society. Nanda conceives of individuals and their hatred as somehow located 'outside' of society.

Khushwant Singh's *Train to Pakistan* (2009) give us another version of this fantasy. In Singh's novel, it is a group of militant Hindu and Sikh men from a neighbouring village who fan the flames of communal tension in the fictional village of Mano Majra. It is these 'outsiders' who convince the Hindus and Sikhs of Mano Majra to attack the train on which their Muslim neighbours intend to flee to Pakistan. In doing so, Singh attributes the genocidal impulses of the villagers of Mano Majra to 'outsiders', implicitly othering the bloodlust that subsequently grips the village.

Versions of this fantasy routinely crowd the oral history archives as scores of survivors stress that their homes and neighbourhoods were burnt by violent mobs of 'outsiders'. In my fieldwork, I found that a number of my informants expressed similar views. When asked to describe the violent mobs they had witnessed during the Partition, my informants were often quick to specify that the mobs had come from 'outside'. Yet, such statements that sought to other the violence from their midst were often contradicted by statements that acknowledged some familiarity with the individuals that made up these mobs. For example, when recounting the day that the mob attacked his ancestral home in the village of Choti, my informant Sanchit agitatedly recalled how his father's driver had set fire to their home. Similarly, when Pooran Chand recalled the attack on the evacuation convoy carrying his family from their village of Lakki Merwat to Bannu, he also remembered that his aunt had been abducted by a local Pathan who was known to their family. This man had previously approached their family to ask for her hand in marriage, but Pooran Chand's grandparents had refused.

I am also reminded of the story of Kishori Raj, an informant I interviewed for my MPhil thesis (Kohli 2015: 25–26). While talking about communal violence, Kishori Raj too had insisted that the violent mobs that had terrorised Dera Ghazi Khan had come from outside. Yet, he also recalled an incident when he ran into a violent mob and was saved only by the timely intervention of his student.

> I was a teacher in Choti town. I would go there every Friday and Saturday and there, there was a person called Bhagwandas Ram from whom I had just claimed my dues. Later I realised that I had forgotten my wallet at his place. When I went to recover my wallet, I ran into the mob.... But one of my students was part of the mob.... So he told them that this is my teacher, don't do anything to him. Then they told me to go to Kot Chutta, a nearby village, because riots had broken out here. But for a moment they had raised their axe [to strike]. But my student said 'Hey! This is my teacher! Don't do anything to him' so it isn't that there weren't good people there. There were good people. It is because of him that I survived. (Kishori Raj quoted in Kohli 2015: 25)

I have recounted these stories here because of the specificity of the violence that they depict. That is, the violence of the Partition was both strange and familiar, at the same time. That people's friends came to their rescue and helped them in whatever way they could even as others turned on them. In contrast to the seemingly random chaos of this specificity, the fantasy of Partition violence as the action of 'outsiders' seeks purely to other the violence. It implies that the violence and those who caused it somehow belonged outside society itself. There is no reckoning with the violence of our past to be found here, just its avoidance.

There is a theodicical quality to this narrative of violence as purely an action of 'outsiders'. It hopes to preserve a sense of *punjabiyat* (Punjabiness) or Indianness, of *insaniyat* (humanity). Thus, this reminds us that even as the *nomos* of plural-Punjab (and with it India) collapsed, it nevertheless endured briefly, among the ashes. But, perhaps what this narrative – or fantasy – actually conceals is a sense of guilt, an implicit acknowledgement of the un-neighbourliness of some relations. Perhaps, this image of 'perfect' neighbours actually conceals the imperfection of these relationships.

After all, the othering of violence in this manner results in the annihilation of local histories of conflict. The fact that Kishori Raj's student stopped a mob from lynching him cannot merely be explained away as the conscionable act of a 'good' person; this student was after all part of a violent mob. Rather, this story might be read as the evocation of a local history. It references the socio-cultural context of South Asia where traditionally one's teachers were revered like one's ancestors. Therefore, what Kishori Raj's story evokes is a local history of interpersonal relations. We see this even in Pooran Chand's story, where the 'abduction' of his aunt was not just a random act of violence. Rather, it was the tactical use of ethnonational violence for the fulfilment of unrequited desire. Similarly, I suspect, Sanchit's driver's arson attack might be indicative of a silenced local history of class conflict.

I suspect the latter not on the basis of mere conjecture, but based on my past research on the Partition. In my MPhil thesis, I had drawn attention to the Hindu practice of untouchability against Muslims (Kohli 2015). Although my thesis had focused on the memories of survivors of Dera Ghazi Khan, the Hindu practice of untouchability against Muslims was widely prevalent in much of South Asia at the time. I had used memories of untouchability to argue that in this region, ethnonationalism predated the Partition. That is, the Partition did not result in the spontaneous outburst of newly discovered nationalist passions, but was the result of long-simmering antagonisms. However, my allusion to long-simmering antagonisms should not be misinterpreted as support for the ancient hatreds or clash of civilisations style of discourse. The antagonisms that I am referring to here, specifically concern the intersections of class, religion and caste. And while these intersections predate the Partition, they were made antagonistic by the quasi-feudal *zamindari* system that the British colonial policy of indirect rule upheld. What made these previous conflicts different from the Partition was the latter's pursuit of racial and ethnic homogeneity.

Contrary to nostalgic recollections of the pre-Partition period as one of unrivalled sectarian harmony, the reality was far more complex. While pre-Partition South Asia did embody a far more plural culture than it does today, it was also an oppressively hierarchical quasi-feudal society. As my informants were always quick to remind me, in Punjab, the majority of zamindars were Hindu. Bhanwarilal, one of my key informants, described this social dynamic as follows:

> Hindus were in minority. Muslims had the majority. If we could stay there and dominate, we did it only because we were financially strong. From the agricultural point of view we were strong. Because we owned the land. They would work for us. If they needed money, they would come and take it from us. They would take it on interest. We would give them money on interest. So that is why we were dominant.

In this way, Hindu zamindars possessed a significant amount of power and privilege in relation to most Muslims. Far from a paradise of syncretism, the pre-Partition period was also one where Hindu zamindars dominated much of the countryside through their ancestral capital: land, money and debt. These rigid hierarchical relations comprise a local history whose antagonisms were accelerated and brought to fruition by the Partition. That is, not all of Partition violence can be explained away as the result of ethnonationalist passions. The class conflict created due to the practice of untouchability, the indebtedness of Muslim peasants and workers, and years of servitude also had their part to play in the specific incidents of violence that some informants remember. I evoke this history of the structural violence perpetrated by Hindus to further problematise the binary classification of victim and perpetrator.

Therefore, what is necessary in histories of the Partition is greater attention to such local histories that, in the writing of history, have been overshadowed by the Partition. Here, Nonica Datta's (2009) work on the Partition proves instructional. In *Violence, Martyrdom and Partition*, Datta records the oral testimony of Subhashini (1914–2003). Subhashini was a prominent woman in the Haryana circle of Arya Samaj and served as the head of the Kanya Gurukul in Khanpur, Haryana: a well-known institution devoted to the education of rural women. This is an astonishing testimony because Subhashini remembers 1942 (the year of her father's murder by Muslim Rangars), and not 1947, as a rupture. Subhashini's father Phool Singh (later known as Bhagat Phool Singh) was a prominent Jat leader and Arya Samaj activist in his lifetime (N. Datta 2009).

Subhashini simultaneously mourns and celebrates 1947. She celebrates it as the year when her Jat community avenged her father's death. In 1947, the Jats of Haryana carried out a carefully planned programme of ethnic cleansing. By the time the dust had settled most Muslims had either been killed, forced to flee to Pakistan or been forcibly converted to Hinduism. Datta observes that in Subhashini's memory, 'Partition was preordained to avenge her father' (5). But, simultaneously, in scattered recollections of the piles of dead bodies of Muslims she saw in 1947, she also quietly mourns the death and destruction unleashed by the Partition.

However, Datta shows that the Jats' ethnic cleansing of Muslims was unconnected to the Partition. Datta documents a history of conflict between the pastoral nomadic communities of Muslims and settled Hindu Jat peasants. But this conflict was a recent invention. Going back in history, the Jats and pastoralists had worked together to resist British rule in 1809 and again in 1824 (N. Datta 2009). She traces the beginning of the conflict to British colonial policies that took away the political, cultural and grazing rights of the Muslim pastoralists, thus bringing them into conflict with Jat peasants. Datta's work adds much needed specificity to the documentation of Partition violence. Moreover, the broad contours of a conflict between settled peasants and pastoral nomads that is exacerbated by colonial policies of land use and thereby leads to genocidal violence has echoes with other global contexts such as the Rwandan genocide (Mamdani 2012).

Similarly, in addition to adding specificity to the spatial distribution of violence in Sultanpuri during the 1984 pogroms, Das (2007) also observes how some of the violence on the ground unfolded due to motivations entirely different from those implied by the reductive lens of religious conflict. For example, Das recounts the story of a woman whose husband took advantage of the 1984 pogroms to murder the Sikh man she had been having an affair with (158).

Paying attention to the specificity of violence as it unfolds on the ground problematises essentialist understandings of the Partition and other episodes of ethnocidal violence. Recognising the tactical use of violence in these contexts follows the prescription of Herzfeld's (2005) critique of Anderson (1983) and Gellner's (1983) 'top-down' theorisations of nationalism. Herzfeld (2005: 6) argues that by not grounding their account of nationalism within the everyday life of the average citizen, Anderson and Gellner assume that 'ordinary people have no impact on the form of their local nationalism: they are only followers'. Instead, locating the agency of the individual within a larger account of ethnonationalist violence, one acknowledges them as thinking social actors while also recognising a deadly but 'tactical' (de Certeau 1984) quotidian appropriation of nationalism and its violence.

The essentialist understanding of Partition violence as little more than a violent convulsion of conflicting religious nationalisms also erases subaltern Hindus – Dalits and Scheduled Castes – from the scene. After all, the Hindu-fold is merely an illusion that struggles to hold a number of antagonistic castes and religious communities together (van der Veer 1994). The Dalit experience of the Partition has remained one of Partition literature's more glaring oversights.

Urvashi Butalia (2000: 235) was among the first to point to this absence and famously observed that Partition history's focus on religion had rendered many others – such as the Scheduled Castes or Dalits – invisible, leaving them 'virtually untouchable even in the writing of this history'. Butalia extends the metaphor of 'untouchability' to imply immunity from the violence of the Partition. Through the testimony of her sole Dalit informant Maya Rani, Butalia (234) posits that as 'untouchables' Dalits found themselves positioned ambiguously in relation to the violence of the Partition; they were neither anyone's allies, nor enemies.

However, Gyanendra Pandey (2009) wonders how Dalits might be considered to have enjoyed a 'bizarre immunity' when they also became refugees as a result of the Partition. Pandey points to the displacement and exile of Dalits as an example that Dalits were far from 'untouched'. Similarly, Ravinder Kaur (2007) has documented the discrimination faced by Dalits in the rehabilitation process. Kaur's work argues against the common-sense idea that traumatic experiences lead to the disintegration of social hierarchies. Rather, Kaur observes how these hierarchies were preserved and reproduced by the Indian state through the rehabilitation process. This was done not just through the establishment of separate camps for caste-Hindu and Sikh, and Dalit refugees but also in the difference of capital expended on their rehabilitation. Dalits received very little per capita in comparison to caste-Hindus and Sikh refugees[6] (Kaur 2007).

Conclusion

In this chapter, I have examined how violence as a narrativising frame (Feldman 1997) involves the delineation of the boundaries of national community (G. Pandey 2001). Violence is always remembered as having occurred 'outside' the community, thus involving the implicit view of the community as a pre-existing homogenous whole. Yet, this homogeneity – like the imagination of a single, homogenous Hindu-fold – is a mask that conceals internal contestations. It is in reference to the latter that I have detailed some examples of the local histories of conflict, as well as the Dalit experience of the Partition. These are examples problematise such abstractions.

This discussion is tangentially related to my earlier discussion of silence, trauma and healing. I have critiqued the use of the trauma label not because I believe that the Partition was not a traumatic experience. Rather, my argument is that 'trauma' as a moral statement on suffering (Fassin and Rechtman 2009) implies an automatic ascription of victimhood. I have used ethnographic examples from my own fieldwork and those of others to argue that the ascription of victimhood requires careful attention to the specificity of a particular context. Victimhood in the context of the Partition is a particularly vexing issue given the structural privilege of upper-caste Hindus as well as the retributive aspect of the violence itself.

Urvashi Butalia (2000), Menon and Bhasin (1998), Gyanendra Pandey (2001) and Veena Das' (2007) ethnographic work on the plight of women during the Partition further problematises any discussion of victimhood. These feminist examinations of the Partition were driven the desire to unsilenced memories of gendered violence while exploring narrative frames that went beyond the Hindu–Muslim–Sikh narrative. This body of work disputes the authenticity of male-centred narratives that present the deaths of women relatives as a voluntary sacrifice. Through a polyphonous retelling of the Thoa Khalsa incident (among others), Butalia (2000) and Menon and Bhasin (1998) show that these women did not die these deaths voluntarily, but were instead often coerced and shamed into accepting murder by their male relatives as 'martyrdom'. Additionally, they also draw attention to the unreliable aspect of memory by documenting how their informant Bir Bahadur Singh (a survivor of Thoa Khalsa) insists on remembering his very-much-still-alive mother as a 'martyr' (Menon and Bhasin 1998; G. Pandey 2001). Das (2007: 34) subsequently built on this foundation to describe the Partition as a 'war of fathers'.

This body of work is especially noteworthy for producing a nuanced account of victimhood and violence. That is, while these caste-Hindu and Sikh men might be considered 'victims' of communal violence as religious minorities facing genocidal violence in their neighbourhoods, they were also simultaneously perpetrators of gendered violence within their own communities. Thus, given the myriad specificities involved, one cannot easily speak of trauma and victimhood in the context of the Partition. To simply remember the Partition through the voices of its survivors does not constitute reckoning with this complex past.

How might we then remember the Partition amid the intertwining of the violence in our past and present? In the two chapters that follow, I explore how nostalgia for the pre-Partition past uncomfortably sits beside a visceral *ressentiment*.

Notes

1 I have deliberately omitted any further biographical details about this informant in order to preserve his anonymity.

2 A long wooden stick, similar to a staff.

3 A form of martial art (often associated with Sikhs) that comprises a style of stick fighting. In battle, sticks may often be substituted with swords.

4 A translation of *Hindu phir bhi dab ke rehta hai.*

5 *Punjabiyat* translates to Punjabiness and expresses a certain idea of the warmth, hospitality, comradery and passion that is said to be intrinsic to relationships by and with Punjabi people.

6 For anyone interested in the Dalit experience of the Partition beyond my brief discussion here, Sen (2012) is a great starting point. Here I have primarily focused on the literature on the Punjabi Dalit experience.

8
Remembering Partition in the Time of Fascism

In this chapter, I explore the idea of 'healing' further. The two stories that I present in this chapter – Gangaram and Pooran Chand's – involve the juxtaposition of nostalgia and bigotry, often treated as contradictory perspectives. Both of them had revisited Pakistan following the Partition and had a number of close friends and acquaintances there. On the surface, their stories seemed to be exemplars of peace and reconciliation. Yet, even as they expressed a deep attachment with the place of their birth, they swore vengeance on Muslims. Although they fondly remembered the bonhomie of their visits across the border, they articulated a firm belief in the ideology of Hindu nationalism. I use these stories to reflect on the imprint of Hindu nationalism on these narratives and wonder how we might evaluate 'healing' in this context. Ultimately, both these stories explore what it means to inhabit a history that is not only alive but also unfinished.

Gangaram's Story

I met Gangaram for the first time in February 2018, through Bhanwarilal. They had known each other for quite some time through their involvement in the All-India Mianwali District Association. Gangaram, like Bhanwarilal, also hailed from Mianwali. Gangaram was born in March 1935 and was 12 years old at the time of the Partition. His family had owned a vast amount of agricultural land and a clothes shop in Mianwali. His family moved to Jalandhar in March 1947, in response to Punjab's March riots.

By early August, when the situation appeared deceptively calm, his family left him in Jalandhar (as a precaution) and moved back to Mianwali to resume their business. However, by the end of the month the violence had escalated significantly leaving them no choice but to move to Jalandhar for good. Eventually his family decided to settle in Delhi and started a business. When I met Gangaram, he was living in north Delhi. As the oldest son of his father, he had taken over the family business and now owned three shops in different parts of the city.

Gangaram walked into my project like a breath of fresh air. By February 2018 I had begun to feel varying levels of disinterest and disgust towards some of my informants. Until I met Gangaram, all of the informants I had met were fairly Islamophobic. But Gangaram seemed different. His story seemed like a fairy tale of hope and reconciliation. For example, he had visited Pakistan 22 times since 1992. Between 1992 and 2018 he had made a trip to Pakistan almost every year and had cultivated a vast network of friends across the border. I also learned that the people who had occupied his ancestral home following the Partition had later allowed him to build a small two-bedroom unit for himself on the same plot. As a result, whenever he visited Pakistan he stayed in an apartment of his own, on his ancestral land. While he clarified that his ownership of the apartment was largely symbolic, it was nevertheless a powerful symbol of reconciliation, of having learned to live with a border neither had chosen.

Consequently, he also received a regular flow of guests from Pakistan. Anytime someone from Mianwali visited India for Urs[1] or medical reasons, Gangaram would host them and offer them every bit of help that they needed. I witnessed this first-hand when in May one of his friends from Mianwali came to Delhi for a major surgery. Gangaram sponsored their visa, hosted the family in his own house and drove them to and from the hospital. I barely got a glimpse of Gangaram during this period as he devoted his entire time to helping his friends.

Gangaram's hospitality and solidarity were well known across the border. He showed me clippings from Pakistani newspapers that had published brief features on him. The articles documented Gangaram's attachment to his birthplace and his frequent visits to Mianwali. One clipping also made note of the fact that Gangaram had monetarily sponsored the construction of a classroom in an all-girls school in

Mianwali. Among the people of Mianwali, Gangaram was something of a local celebrity. An Urdu book authored by a Mianwali historian[2] on the famous 'sons' of Mianwali included a brief biography of Gangaram. Gangaram's biographical vignette was written in a deeply personal tone, like an affectionate letter from a close friend. It addressed him as Lala – the endearing yet respectful title used by the people of Mianwali – and constantly switched between addressing him in the first and third person, a sign of familiarity in Hindi/Urdu. Here is a brief excerpt from the book:

> You left sitting on top of your belongings on the roof of a truck. But *Lala's* soul got left behind in Mianwali. This is why he remained incomplete even after reaching *Hindustan*. And now he looks for excuses to return to Pakistan….
>
> Even today he wears a white *salwar-kameez* and a boski[3] *salwar-kameez*. He wears the traditional Mianwali sandals. He speaks the Saraiki of Mianwali with his family in India. He has kept a thick-thick moustache. Half the Mianwali *biradari* [brotherhood or community] is as close as siblings to him. Even today he comes to Mianwali. Even today he only brings 2–3 clothes for himself and the rest of his luggage – which is substantial – is filled with precious gifts for his friends. In Mianwali he distributes gifts like sweets.
>
> The respect that the people of Mianwali have for him in their hearts is no less than that one might have for a famous personality. When you come from Delhi you bring laughter and a liveliness spreads. Somewhere someone is arranging for your food and drinks. Elsewhere big musicians like Tahir Saqi are called to a local stage to perform in your honour. Every individual wishes that you will become their guest. (Excerpt read aloud by Gangaram; translation mine; emphasis added)

The book's reference to Gangaram's ethnic attire is noteworthy. In my fieldwork I found that Gangaram was the only one of his generation (that I encountered) who still dressed in the full Mianwali ethnic attire. Whenever I met him, Gangaram was always turned out in a *salwar-kameez* and a turban.[4] His attire along with his thick handlebar moustache evoked the image of a zamindar patriarch of a bygone age.

Gangaram had adopted the attire in 2002, during his nephew's wedding. That was also shortly after his father's passing. Appearing at the wedding in full ethnic attire – as the oldest male relative on the groom's father's side of the family – Gangaram had symbolically assumed the role of his family's reigning patriarch.

Gangaram had also received some attention in the Indian press. He showed me the photocopy of an article in a Hindi newspaper that was headlined 'The Scent of the Soil of His Motherland Beckons Him to Pakistan'. Gangaram also remembered being interviewed for television by an NDTV reporter in Lahore in 2006. The Indian cricket team's 2006 tour of Pakistan had led to a brief thaw in relations, inspiring hope for peace between the rival South Asian nuclear powers. Like a number of other Indian travellers, Gangaram had used the cricket series as a pretext to visit Pakistan with his family. It was during that visit that Gangaram had met Imran Khan (known at the time primarily as a legendary cricketer) and taken a photograph with him.

That February when we first met, Gangaram had been planning yet another month-long trip to Pakistan. He had just received his visa and begun collecting gifts for his friends. The confirmation of his visa had produced a wave of enthusiasm among his friends in Pakistan. One of them had even published the itinerary of his trip in an Urdu newspaper in Pakistan. Gangaram proudly showed me a photograph of the newspaper clipping on his phone. Other friends of his, whom he introduced to me over the phone, told me that they had planned a grand welcome for him. Abdulsattar Khan, a Lahore-based senior advocate, said he planned to greet him at the railway station with a small motorcycle cavalcade. Others had begun planning feasts and parties in his honour. Gangaram also had a list of weddings to attend. Each year he received a number of wedding invitations – some that even listed him as an RSVP contact (a symbolic honour more than anything else) – and he regarded attending these an important duty as an elder of this community.

During our initial meetings, Gangaram and I had several heartwarming conversations about hatred and belonging. When I cautiously shared with Gangaram my observations about the latent Islamophobia of Partition survivors, he said that he found this hatred irrelevant in his own life. He said that the Partition was something that had happened in the past and, while his family had been displaced because of it, no one had died. He contrasted his family's experience with those of other families who had suffered much more and reasoned that those who had lost close friends and kin feel more passionately about the Partition.

Spending time with Gangaram at his shop and his home, I learnt that his family strongly disapproved of his links with Pakistan. Gangaram and his wife Meghana often argued about his frequent trips to Pakistan. Although, based on my experience of my parents' divorce, I suspected the friction between them ran much deeper. To me, Pakistan appeared to be just one among many triggers in a generally fractious marriage. Gangaram's enthusiasm for Pakistan never failed to annoy Meghana. She would often punctuate Gangaram's experiences of travelling around Pakistan with Islamophobic jibes. She said she found the full-bearded appearance of Muslim men terrifying and felt physically repulsed by the *burqa*. She claimed that Muslims were dirty and had no concept of hygiene. In these moments, Gangaram always disagreed with her, countering her arguments with a wealth of personal experiences. He would always emphasise the love and respect that people had for him across the border.

Whenever I visited Gangaram's house, I found myself caught in the crossfire of such arguments. My interest in his forthcoming trip and the tacit support that that implied provoked vociferous denunciations from Meghana, Aditya (his son) and Bhanwarilal. They all saw Gangaram's love for Mianwali as an irrational obsession. Yet implicit in these arguments was the age-old question of belonging and community: the afterlife of the Partition. One such exchange went as follows:

Bhanwarilal [*loudly, with sarcasm*]: Delhi is so big, tell me which person is getting a fit to see Gangaram? Tell me this? Gangaram is the only one who has the wish to see [Pakistan].

Gangaram [*quietly*]: No there are many....

B: Tell me this, which person of Mianwali has gone there? You show me.

Meghana: It is an obsession without any reason.

B: *Arre*, I have asked in the Mianwali *biradari*, now you are quiet but I know how many people of the Mianwali *biradari* have gone there, till today.

G: Two-four some....

B: Aside from Gangaram no one has gone. Gangaram has gone. Gangaram's family has gone.

M: Went forcefully.

B [*sarcastically, to Gangaram's son*]: Come *rajkumar* [prince], honour the man!

G [*turning away from them to talk to me*]: Last Holi [festival], people had specially come from Multan for Holi. Sent them visa, as a sponsor, they celebrated Holi right here.

M [*bitterly*]: They only need a place to stay, this is why they keep praising you.

G: But that everywhere, [*speaking louder and faster*] they have only one place to stay, I have a hundred.

M: Who else have they got but you?

G [*shouting*]: I have a hundred places to stay.

While Gangaram's words and actions indicated that to him there was no difference between his Indian and Pakistani relationships, his family clearly disagreed. The heart of these arguments was the way in which Gangaram imagined his national belonging, his *watan*. In Hindi/Urdu, the word *watan* is synonymous with 'nation', 'ethnicity', 'country', and 'birthplace', all at once. I use the word *watan* here because of the way that it more accurately captures the ambiguity between these words, an ambiguity that is fundamental to the post-Partition identity of survivors. For Gangaram, his Indian citizenship went beside his view that Mianwali was his *watan*.

This was something I explored in a conversation with his son, Aditya. During one of these arguments about whether Gangaram should proceed with his trip to Pakistan, Aditya rhetorically asked me why Gangaram felt the need to keep going back despite having already been there so many times. When I mentioned Gangaram's love for his *watan* and his friends, Aditya mentioned Gangaram's advancing age. 'Love, but he has reached an age as well. 20 times he has.... We say go somewhere else, for sightseeing,' Aditya replied.

'Look now, what can be a better place to go to than your own *watan*, you tell me,' I replied poetically.

'But this is the *watan* now,' Aditya observed in a genteel tone.

'But if you ask him this, he will probably say that Mianwali is his *watan* too,' I replied impulsively. At this point, we turned to him and retold this conversation to Gangaram. He loudly exclaimed, 'That's it', smiled and gave me a high-five.

Numerous times during our interactions, Gangaram told me that even today he still considers Pakistan his *watan* and the people of Mianwali his *watani* (co-nationals). He told me that the first time he visited Mianwali, he made his friends stop their car at the district's border so he could bow his head to the soil, to pay homage. 'When the border of Mianwali zilla came, so Mianwali starts there, there I stopped to do *pranam*.[5] I bowed my head to the soil, *bhai* now we have reached our zilla.'[6]

He said that going across the border is always easier than coming back. When returning from Pakistan, it all comes back to him, the fact of his displacement, the border, the Partition. Gangaram said that while saying goodbye, they do not greet each other. Their farewells are peppered with the silence of stifled tears. He said:

Now when we go, we meet with happy hearts. On the way back....
Always harder than going. Very difficult. Although we have no blood
relation there, there is no Hindu there, but it is our culture, our land,
our own place where we played, the place of our father-grandfather-
great-grandfather, the place of their ancestors. Although there
[Mianwali] all the young blood is there but whenever ... a sadness
takes over. [*Pause.*] Mianwali zilla is very big, very big.... It reminds me
of the full scene of the fighting and killing, how people were becoming
refugees and leaving. Like we also left like that.... The heart does ache.

Gangaram's words display a deep attachment to the land of his birth along with a rare recognition of the syncretic culture that predated the Partition. He describes this attachment by continuously invoking the 'soil' (or 'land') as a sacred symbol. This symbolism recurs in a bucket list wish that he confided in me. Gangaram said that he hoped to die in Mianwali. He said that even the people of Mianwali had told him that they prayed that whenever death came for him – in the due course of life – that it would find him in Pakistan so that they might bury him in his ancestral city. They had told him that they would build him a memorial-like gravesite and light a candle on it every Thursday night. He confided that this is what he wanted for himself too, so that his body could be returned to the soil of his birth.

When Meghana and Aditya overheard him say this, they were horrified. Meghana insinuated that this meant that 'the Muslims' wanted to kill him while his son scoffed and remarked, 'They won't build anything.' Aditya even threatened to steal and hide Gangaram's passport, to prevent him from ever travelling again. Later that day when we were bidding our goodbyes, Gangaram pulled me aside and gave me a peek into his Nehru jacket's breast pocket. 'I keep my passport with me all the time so they can't do anything,' he explained. He winked mischievously and showed me the freshly stamped Pakistani visa before returning it to his pocket.

During those initial weeks of our acquaintance, Gangaram and I bonded over our shared appreciation for our Pakistani heritage. Noticing our shared 'obsession' with Pakistan, on more than one occasion, Meghana compared me to her husband, calling us a bunch of 'wandering souls', in jest. There was a mischievousness to my friendship with Gangaram. As someone who had similarly faced the scorn of my extended family for my 'ill-advised' closeness to my Pakistani friends in Dublin, I could instinctively relate to the antagonistic dynamics of Gangaram's family. Gangaram's friction with his family also struck me as proof of the genuineness of his affection for Pakistan.

Yet, upon spending more time with him, I saw that these thoughts coexisted with his passion for Hindu nationalism. After we had exchanged phone numbers on WhatsApp, Gangaram began to forward me Hindu Right propaganda. One of the texts he forwarded warned of the demographic threat that Muslims pose to 'Hindu India' (Figure 8.1).

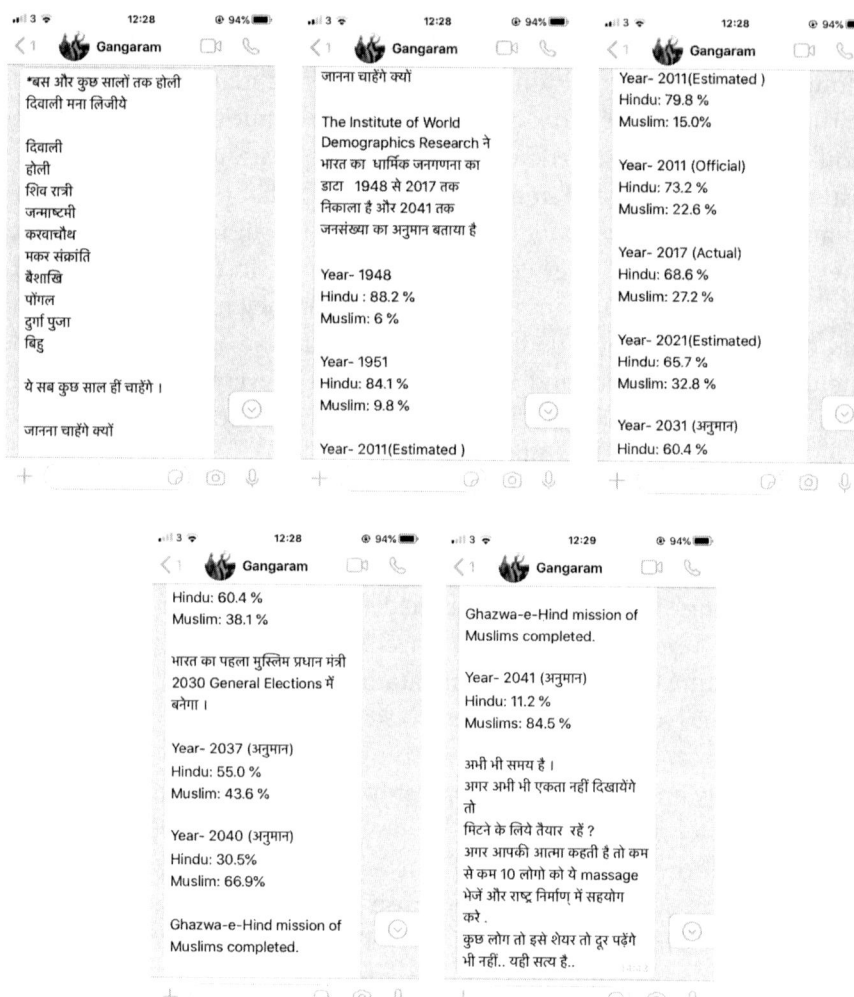

Figure 8.1   Screenshots of Hindu Right propaganda texts forwarded by Gangaram
Source: Author.

This text message begins with an ominous warning telling Hindus that they must celebrate their festivals now as these will no longer be celebrated in the future. The text alleges that 'the Institute of World Demographics Research has released religious demographic data for India from 1948 to 2017 and have estimated the population for 2041'. Displaying a biopolitical obsession with population figures, the message consistently fabricates and overestimates the population of Muslims until the year 2017. The message thereafter projects an incremental increase of India's Muslim populations. It warns that with India's Muslim population at 38.1 per cent, India will elect its first Muslim prime minister in the year 2030. The text predicts 2040 as the year when India's Muslims will outnumber its Hindus and labels this dubious landmark as the completion of the 'Ghazwa-e-Hind mission' or the total conquest of India. The text ends with another ominous warning:

> There is still time. If you will still not show unity then get ready to be wiped out? [*sic*] If your soul says so then forward this massage [*sic*] to at least 10 people and contribute to nation building. Forget sharing, some people will not even read it.. [*sic*] This is the truth.. [*sic*]

This text message evokes a Hindu nationalist version of the Great Replacement conspiracy theory. It alleges a Muslim conspiracy to capture India's democracy by somehow outbreeding Hindus. It implicitly constructs Hindus as a disunited and weak community that is sleepwalking into a demographic trap.

Another text message that Gangaram forwarded alleged that Mohammad Ali Jinnah, Jawaharlal Nehru and Sheikh Abdullah were in fact half-brothers and the illegitimate sons of Motilal Nehru. I have mentioned this conspiracy theory at various times in my book. In the Hindu Right ecosystem, this conspiracy theory is dubiously credited to M. O. Mathai. Mathai was Jawaharlal Nehru's private secretary during the latter's term as prime minister. Mathai is also believed to have had an affair with Indira Gandhi, a rumour often used to paint the Nehru–Gandhi family as a nest of decadence and corruption. The text message Gangaram forwarded attempts to provide a citation for its details by including the link to a Google search on M. O. Mathai (Figure 8.2).

Our communication over WhatsApp marked a dramatic change in our conversations. As I began to increasingly engage him in political conversations, I realised that Gangaram truly believed in these discourses. Gangaram was an enthusiastic supporter of Modi and the BJP, and a firm believer in the ideology of Hindu nationalism. Before any major state legislative election, Gangaram would send me messages asking me to pray for the BJP, vote for them (if I could) and implore me to forward

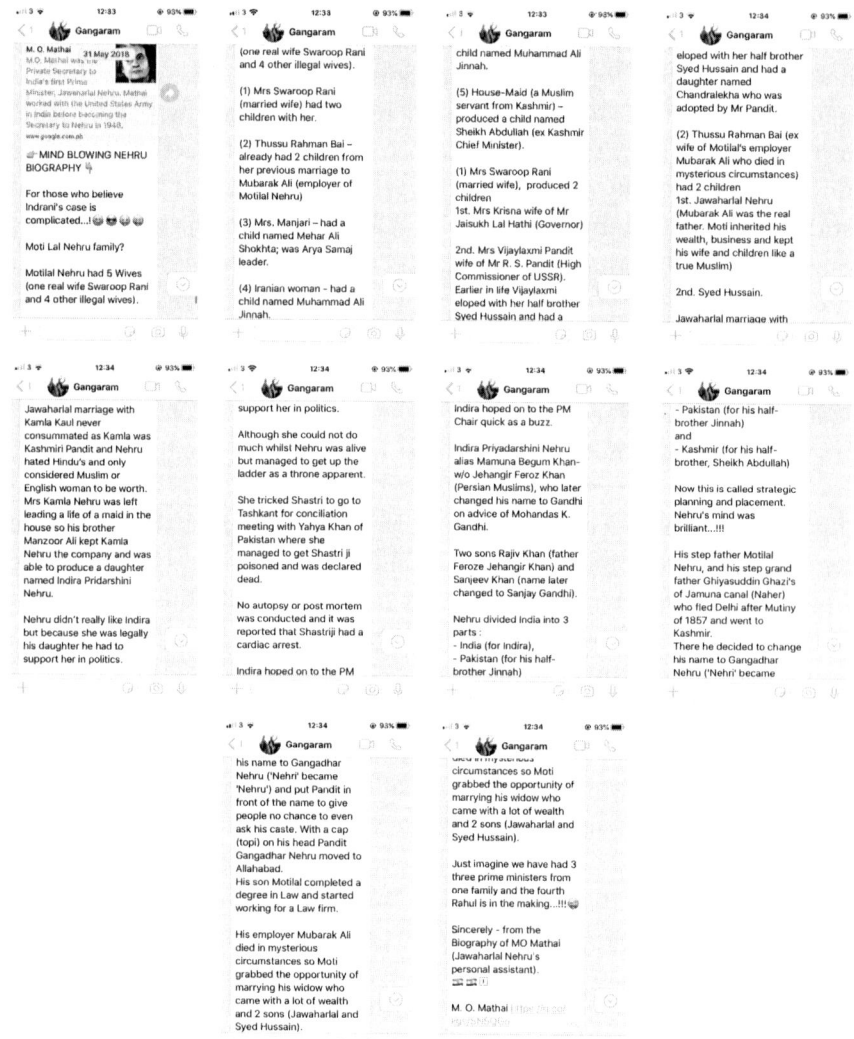

Figure 8.2 Screenshots of a forwarded text message from Gangaram. The text details a popular Hindu Right conspiracy theory about the 'true' genealogy of Nehru and Jinnah.

Source: Author.

the message to 'all my friends'. Whenever the BJP won an election, Gangaram would send me messages congratulating 'the nation' on the victory and optimistically celebrating the forthcoming period of 'development' and 'progress'.

Gangaram also believed that the Congress was a party for Muslims that had historically held India back through a combination of 'minority appeasement', corruption, ineptitude and sabotage. He was particularly vitriolic towards Jawaharlal Nehru. But his discourses on Nehru were often self-contradictory. Gangaram held Nehru's unwillingness to share power as the primary reason for the Partition. Yet, he also believed that Motilal Nehru had conspired the Partition in order to split South Asia into independent fiefdoms for his three illegitimate sons. Both these discourses sought to understand the Partition through the rhetoric of blame; blame that was always squarely placed on the Nehru family and by extension, the Congress party. In the same vein, Gangaram lamented the Partition and wondered why Hindus and Muslims could not have been allowed to live in peace, the way they had been living for centuries previously.

However, Gangaram also often contradicted himself by expressing his support for the RSS and the two-nation theory. Responding to my accusations of the role of RSS ideologue V. D. Savarkar in opining the two-nation theory, Gangaram described the RSS as a necessary force. 'Of course we believe in the Two-Nation Theory,' he stated vociferously. Gangaram spoke at length about the 'humanitarian work' that the RSS had done during the Partition, such as running soup kitchens for refugees at railway stations and 'protecting' Hindus during riots.

Gangaram did not perceive the dissonance in his own rhetoric on the Partition. Gangaram's belief in the two-nation theory was a direct contradiction of his earlier insistence on the Partition as an unnecessary evil and a failure of Nehru's politics. His faith in the RSS and the two-nation theory was couched in the familiar discourses of Hindu nationalism. Like many of my other informants, he too recounted a history of Hindu victimhood, a history comprised of hundreds of years of oppression and atrocities at the hands of Muslims. 'What else is their history?' he asked rhetorically, implying that the history of Muslims is nothing but a history of violence. 'Ghori came 18 times', he said, in a reference to Mahmud of Ghori's raids into Punjab and north India. 'How many times they looted Somanatha Temple! What else did they even do, this Ghazni, Aurangzeb, Khilji, whatever?' In imputing the violence of a few medieval rulers onto the Muslims of today, Gangaram was merely regurgitating the rhetoric of the BJP.

My counter-argument that the sacking of temples was not confined to Muslim rulers alone but was instead a regular part of all medieval warfare in South Asia (Eaton 2000) was roundly dismissed by Gangaram. 'Only you don't believe this history. Are the rest of us idiots? Are the television people idiots? Everyone believes this history,' he taunted me. In this post-truth era, belief was clearly of paramount importance to the epistemology of history. When I kept quiet in response to this, Gangaram went on to link this 'history' of Muslim oppression to another familiar discourse of Hindu nationalism: the lust of Muslim masculinity.

Returning to the Partition, he spoke about how roughly 500–600 Hindu women had been kidnapped during Pakistan's attack on Srinagar in 1947. 'What atrocities did they not do on them…,' he mourned. 'In our Mianwali there is a village called Harnoli. There they did so many atrocities. There was a family there, they came to Gurgaon later. They threw 18 women of their own family into a well, themselves, with their own hands.' Gangaram was practically shouting at me at this point. Gangaram had mentioned this family before, back when I had first asked him how he is able to maintain such good relations across the border despite the pain and suffering of the Partition. Back then, he had contrasted his family's relative lack of suffering with this family's.

'Eighteen!' he repeated. 'You ask us why our heart burns, ask them how much their heart burns.' An awkward silence hung between us for a time. I did not know how to respond to his last comment. I felt a complex mixture of emotions that ranged from disgust at his opinions to guilt for having disrespected his suffering. Gangaram, for his part, had a lot more to say and continued speaking. He insisted that all Muslims should be made to leave India. 'Kill them, drive them out of here,' he declared. He argued that they should all be sent to Pakistan because they may live here but their hearts are always with other Muslims. In doing so, he repeated a line that is spoken all too often across India, that Muslims may live in India but their sympathies will always lie with Pakistan.

In an exasperated tone, I asked him, 'So what is your solution for all this? Do you want a Pakistan for Hindus, I mean a country like Pakistan only for Hindus?' My usage of Pakistan here was meant to critique Hindu nationalism's dream of an ethnically pure nation by comparing it to its own understanding of its bitter enemy. Instead, Gangaram let the penny drop.

'We in fact want this to be a Hindu Rashtra [state]. We want to remove this nonsense of secularism from the constitution. We want Article 370 [Jammu and Kashmir's Special Provisions] to be removed so Hindus can build houses there.' Gangaram went on to add that he wanted the BJP to return to power in 2019 with a two-thirds majority in Parliament and in three-fourths of all the state legislatures so that they may have the numbers to rewrite the constitution. 'We do not believe in this constitution,' he declared firmly.

Not only did the BJP go on to win the 2019 election handsomely, in August 2022, a section of Hindu seers and 'scholars' announced that they are working on a draft constitution for their Hindu Rashtra (*Hindustan Times* 2022). The draft constitution proposes shifting India's capital to Varanasi (Modi's parliamentary constituency and a city of great religious significance to Hindus) and the cancellation of the voting rights of all Muslims and Christians.

Getting progressively worked up, he continued, '*Hindustan* anyway belongs to Hindus only. Why have so many of them [Muslims] been left behind?' He noted that on the other hand, 'No Hindu families are left in Mianwali today but there are so many Muslims left in India.' 'When they do not have any love for *Hindustan*, no love for Hindus so why have they been left here? This is the most treacherous community. You cannot trust them. They only betray you,' he declared.

Utterly disillusioned and disappointed with him, I said, 'You are saying such horrible things. I never expected this from you. You have so many friends in Pakistan, you have been there so many times. If you hate them so much why do you even go there?'

He shrugged and replied, 'Among Muslims, the 5% that are literate are fine. The rest 95% are useless fanatics. I only go to Pakistan to meet my friends. The friends I have from that time, with whom I have maintained relations, I only go to meet them. I do not have any love for Pakistan.'

In this way, Gangaram was one of the most complicated people I encountered during my fieldwork. His relationship with Mianwali (a relationship that was undoubtedly one of love and warmth) sat dissonantly beside his *ressentiment* for Muslims and 'secularism'. On the one hand, his attachment with Mianwali was so deep that he routinely fought with his family to maintain his links with Pakistan. The latter came to a head in April 2018, when Meghana's knee replacement surgery forced Gangaram to indefinitely postpone his trip to Pakistan. While Gangaram chose to stay in Delhi to take care of Meghana, he did so almost begrudgingly. In turn, he was subjected to Meghana and Aditya's taunts.

Sometimes his attachment with Mianwali made him express views that might even be considered 'anti-national' by the BJP's own yardstick of patriotism. In August 2018, when we last met, Gangaram was once again contemplating a trip to Pakistan. He was elated by Imran Khan's victory in Pakistan's 2018 general elections. The reason, he explained, was that Imran Khan too was from Mianwali. By going over there at this time, he wanted to celebrate the victory of his successful *watani* (co-national).

Another time, while discussing India's 1971 war with Pakistan, he remarked that the Pakistani General A. A. K. Niazi who had surrendered to the Indian Army in Dhaka was also from Mianwali. This led to an interesting, almost treasonous exchange about honour and respect:

Gangaram: He is from the proper city. That Bangladesh fellow [*lowers voice*] is from our Mianwali. There was a book on our Mianwali. In that there was a chapter on General A. K. Niazi, he wrote.... Harish Chander Lakdha wrote that on the one hand we are delighted that we have conquered Bangladesh, but on the other hand there is a thing in our heart that a General from our Mianwali who is a Pathan had to surrender. [Own opinion] Instead of surrendering had he shot himself he would have been considered a big martyr. Now he lost all respect in Mianwali. Had he shot himself so then killed in battle....

Interviewer [PK]: Have you ever met?

G: Not him but his son-in-law, yes. His son-in-law lives in South Africa. Johannesburg. He lives there.

PK: So his honour was completely destroyed after the surrender?

G: This is the thing.... The 93,000 prisoners that were taken.... The loss of honour was bound to happen. If he had not surrendered then,

then many would have died. On the one hand he did well, saved the lives of so many people, but on the other hand the name of Mianwali city got tarnished. *Bhai,* look he surrendered despite being a Pathan. It would have been better had he shot himself, who would have known in the fighting, who shot him. This line I remember he had written on this. [Quoting] Although we were delighted with our victory, 93000.... [*Breaks off.*]

PK: But we are also sad....

G: That a man from our city had to surrender. And being a Pathan he dishonoured Mianwali.

The complexity of such an exchange where he laments the alleged dishonouring of Mianwali even as he celebrates India's victory in a war captures the way Gangaram's discourses routinely fell outside neatly homogenising nationalist discourses. Yet, despite inhabiting this space of ambiguity, Gangaram was fully committed to the ideology of Hindu nationalism. He was completely enamoured by Modi and the BJP. I had seen the BJP's campaign material (a BJP-printed scarf and flag) at his house and also been on the receiving end of his habitual forwarding of Hindu Right propaganda on WhatsApp. That part of him was genuine too.

How might we then understand this complexity? How might we make sense of this apparent ideological schizophrenia? How might we remember the Partition through this seemingly dissonant haze? It is helpful, at this point, to turn to Pooran Chand's story for its similarity to Gangaram's.

Pooran Chand's Story

Pooran Chand is by now a familiar figure in this book. Pooran Chand was one of my key informants. I have written about him at length in Chapter 1 and mentioned the story of his aunt's abduction in Chapter 7. During my fieldwork in Faridabad, Pooran Chand and I came to develop a grandparent-like relationship. He was an incredibly thoughtful and articulate man. Incidentally, among his community – the other elderly men with whom he shared walks and chats in Rose Garden – he was known for being quiet and circumspect. Pooran Chand and I had happened to bond over our shared experience of having been immigrants.

In the 1980s, at the height of the Iran–Iraq war, Pooran Chand had spent five years working in Libya and Iraq. Throughout his life, Pooran Chand had worked in the Indian Road Construction Corporation, a public sector company. But in his final years of service, he had been offered the opportunity to work in Libya and had seized it. His one-and-a-half-year-long stint in Libya was followed by a three-and-a-half-year-long deputation to Iraq. He described his time in Saddam Hussein's Iraq as the 'golden years' of his life. We would often sit together in Rose Garden and trade stories of our travels abroad. I loved spending time with him and would try to meet him almost every week. Over the course of time we spent together, Pooran Chand and I developed an honesty of rapport that went far beyond what I had with the average informant.

Pooran Chand's experience of the Partition was rife with violence. His family had been a wealthy zamindar family in the NWFP village of Lakki Marwat. Following the announcement of the NWFP's inclusion in Pakistan, tensions rose to a fever pitch. As sporadic incidents of violence broke out across the countryside, the army began to evacuate Hindus and Sikhs to the big cities of Bannu and Dera Ismail Khan, from where they could ultimately be put on buses and trains to India. It was in September 1947 that their village was evacuated. Pooran Chand's family had sent him to Bannu a week before their planned evacuation.

However, the army convoy that the rest of his family was travelling in was attacked just outside Lakki Marwat. Unfortunately, part of Pooran Chand's family happened to be in that part of the convoy that bore the brunt of the offensive. Pooran Chand's paternal grandmother received a bullet wound just above her eye (she lost her eyesight in one eye as a result) while his aunt (father's sister) was abducted. The attack forced the army convoy to retreat to Lakki Marwat.

When Pooran Chand's family finally reached Bannu, he learned that his father and grandmother were not among them. They had decided to stay behind to look for his aunt. 'My *dadi* was all bandaged up, but she is a mother. So she tried a lot,' Pooran Chand said. His grandmother and father pleaded with the local SP (superintendent of police). Pooran Chand remembered that though the SP was a Muslim, he gave their case fair treatment. The SP gathered intelligence on the whereabouts of Pooran Chand's aunt. As I have written previously in Chapter 7, his aunt was abducted by a man who was known to their family. The SP then organised a meeting of the local Pathans and pleaded with them to return the woman to her family. The Pathans did not agree to this. Pooran Chand said that they too were zamindars and presented a united front. Negotiations ensued and a compromise was reached. It was agreed that a public hearing would be held in the presence of the DC, SP, and Pooran Chand's grandmother and father. It was here that his aunt would be given an opportunity to choose whom she wanted to stay with. A day before the hearing, the DC and SP seized the Pathans' guns and organised a brief private meeting between Pooran Chand's aunt and grandmother. Pooran Chand said that this meeting was particularly important as his family was afraid that his aunt's abductors might intimidate or deceive her into choosing them. On the day of her hearing, Pooran Chand's aunt publicly renounced her abductors and chose to go to India with her family. The DC and SP acted swiftly and whisked the family away to the relative safety of Bannu. From there, they arranged for Pooran Chand's aunt and grandmother to fly to Ambala, all before the abductors could plot any sort of revenge.

All of this took a number of months and Pooran Chand was reunited with them only in January 1948. Meanwhile Pooran Chand himself had to endure an agonisingly long wait for evacuation from Bannu. In Bannu, their entire extended family cramped into the home of a relative. The first evacuation train from Bannu was scheduled to run on 14 December 1947. While Pooran Chand's aunt and uncle were allotted a place on that train, Pooran Chand himself along with most of his family was scheduled to travel on 16 December. On the 14th, when Pooran Chand accompanied his aunt and uncle to the railway station to bid them farewell, the policeman overseeing the boarding informed them that the train only had space left for one more person. His aunt and uncle pushed him ahead and put him on the train. Pooran Chand choked up as he remembered the moment. 'It was not my number. But what of that, everyone wants that their child should go [safely]: The train from Bannu terminated at Maddi Indus. From there he changed another train until he finally reached Kurukshetra, a full two days ahead of the rest of his family.

Despite the violence and desperation that characterised his final memories of the Frontier, Pooran Chand still experienced a deep attachment with the land. This was visible in his fondness for movies and literature that featured the Frontier and Afghanistan. His nostalgia along with my interest in the Frontier meant that between us, we managed to somehow connect even the most inconsequential small talk to Bannu. One afternoon, while we were enjoying the faint December sunshine in Rose Garden, Pooran Chand began to talk about the health benefits of sun-bathing and Vitamin D. He then told me the story of an Afghan Hindu refugee who had settled in Faridabad. This man had developed a troublesome skin condition and his doctor had advised regular, moderated sun-bathing as a cure. When I showed an interest in the man's Afghan heritage, Pooran Chand spoke at length about these subsequent migrations. Some Hindu families had used their familial links to migrate to Faridabad in the 1960s, while other Hindus and Sikhs from Afghanistan had migrated to India in the '80s and '90s, as a consequence of the Soviet invasion and subsequent Taliban regime. Using family visas and refugee status, many of them had ultimately acquired Indian citizenship through naturalisation. Later, Pooran Chand even introduced me to some of them.

However, talking about subsequent migrations from the Frontier led to further recollections about Bannu. Pooran Chand spoke at length about Bannu's military importance to British domination over the nearby Pashto tribes and Afghanistan. He revealed that the British would use regular aerial bombardment and raids to project their power over these rebellious hill tribes.

In this vein, he unexpectedly began to recount an essay by Rabindranath Tagore (2002), called 'Civilization and Progress'. In it, Pooran Chand recalled, Tagore had contested common-sense ideas of progress and civilisation through two brief vignettes. One vignette recounted a true incident where a British bomber pilot's plane malfunctioned forcing him to crash-land in the very same Frontier tribal areas that he had just been bombing. Although the pilot was captured by a Pashto tribe, he was treated as an honoured guest and later safely escorted to a nearby British cantonment. The second vignette recounted a story from Tagore's own life. Tagore had once found himself driving through the Bengali countryside in a car whose engine was prone to overheating and needed to be frequently cooled with water. Tagore found that although water was scarce in the countryside, the villagers he encountered were always generous in sharing it. However, once he reached the suburbs of Calcutta (where piped water was relatively abundant), he noticed that people began to charge him money for the water he needed. Through these vignettes, Tagore sought to contrast the exploitativeness and brutality inherent in modernity (as signified by the British army and the city of Calcutta) with the warmth and hospitality of the countryside.[7] Pooran Chand considered this essay one of the most memorable pieces of writing he had ever read.

By New Year, I had traced this essay of Tagore's (2002) to his book *Talks in China* and procured a copy of it. One January afternoon, I showed up to Rose Garden with this book and presented it to Pooran Chand. He choked up with emotion as he took the book from me and started leafing through it. 'If I had my glasses with me I would read it,' he said. When I told him the book was intended as a gift for him, he declined and told me to keep it for myself. I opened the book to 'Civilization and Progress' and showed him the essay. He held the page close to his eyes and squinted at it until he could finally read the title. He asked me whether I had read it and I replied that I had, and complimented him on the sharpness of his memory. He said that he remembered this essay vividly. He had first come across it while studying for his faculty of arts (FA) degree. 'Some words are such that they remain in your heart,' he remarked nostalgically.

This simple gesture began a conversation that continued for many months. Over the course of several meetings, he told me the story of how he had tried his best to keep in touch with the Frontier in the 1950s. Pooran Chand said that between 1953 and 1955, while he was pursuing his FA in Delhi, he would go to the Delhi Public Library. In those days, one could apparently find Pakistani newspapers in the public library, including the English daily *Pakistan Times*. 'I used to go there to read *Pakistan Times*, because we were from there, so just to get an idea of what is happening there these days, what is the news, like that,' Pooran Chand recalled. One day, while reading the newspaper, he came across the advertisement of an Urdu newspaper printed in Bannu called *Halal-e-Noh* (New Life). Pooran Chand does not remember how he did it (whether it was mentioned in the advertisement itself), but somehow, he managed to get the address of the editor of *Halal-e-Noh* and sent him a letter.

> I am quite deft with letters. So I wrote to him that this is how it is, I am from Bannu and now I am studying in Delhi and it was nice to see a mention of Bannu and your paper. In his reply, the editor started regularly sending me copies of *Halal-e-Noh*. So now that paper started coming to my house. And I kept reading it till the time it kept coming. Then something happened and the government banned the import and export of newspapers. Back when *Halal-e-Noh* used to come, so one time I even sent in an article. So just like how I had to write essays for my FA-BA, so like that I wrote an essay in Urdu: 'Science vs Progress'. Meaning, the benefits of science, like technology and all, that I broadly wrote and the drawbacks of science like bombs and all that, the loss of lives, that, like that. In that I had used a reference of Tagore also. So I wrote the essay and sent it to them and it got published also. Back then, at that time, I did not have the awareness so I did not save a copy. And now I do not even know if I can get that copy from somewhere or not. But this I wanted to tell that I had written an Urdu essay that was published in Bannu which had a reference to Tagore's *Civilization and Progress*.

In addition to his beautifully serendipitous correspondence with *Halal-e-Noh*, Pooran Chand had also made contact with the Pakistan High Commission and expressed an interest in receiving governmental literature. 'Back then embassies of all countries would send material for free. Interest was rare so if someone wrote them a postcard saying they want to know more about Pakistan, or Bannu, or Soviets, they would start sending material for free,' Pooran Chand explained. As a result he would also receive reading material in Pashto (his mother tongue) and Urdu. This was his way of keeping in touch with his *watan*.

Just as a random conversation about Vitamin D had started a whole conversation on Pooran Chand's attempts at keeping in touch with his homeland, discussing the works of Tagore revealed a powerful cultural symbol in Pooran Chand's life. Tagore's (2005) short story *Kabuliwala* (The Man from Kabul) – first published in 1892 – was one of Pooran Chand's favourite stories. He had first read the story when he was in college and had felt drawn to it ever since. When its Hindi movie adaptation released in 1961 (also titled *Kabuliwala*), he saw it twice in Delhi's famous Delite Cinema.

Tagore's *Kabuliwala* is a beautifully bittersweet story of filial love. In it, Rehman (the titular Kabuliwala) strikes up an unlikely friendship with Mini (pronounced min-knee), the 5-year-old daughter of a middle-class aristocratic writer (a character based on Tagore himself). Rehman is a Hazara man from Afghanistan. He leaves behind a 5-year-old daughter of his own to earn a living as a travelling fruit vendor. Living alone in Calcutta, hawking his wares in the often-times hostile neighbourhoods of upper-caste Bengalis, Rehman encounters Mini, a girl who reminds him of his own daughter back home. Rehman befriends her by offering her fruits and pistachios. Mini and Rehman come to share a beautifully filial bond. But, when Rehman receives news of his own daughter's illness, he prepares to return home. However, while collecting his debts from the neighbourhood, Rehman has an altercation that ends in him stabbing the other man. Rehman is arrested and spends the next eight years in jail. When he returns to the author's home following his release, he meets a much older Mini, getting dressed for her wedding. And though the author recognises Rehman, Mini seems to have no recollection of him. Heartbroken, realising that even his own daughter might not recognise him, the Kabuliwala bids them farewell, returning to Afghanistan.[8]

Pooran Chand described the story to me in great detail and told me to watch the movie. He recounted how the Pathans of the Frontier were colloquially referred to as Kabuliwalas in passing. He said that when he saw the movie, he had liked it so much that he had started calling his niece Mini. And, when her sister was born, he had taken to calling her Tini (pronounced tin-knee). Pooran Chand said that the thing he loved the most about the movie was Manna Dey's famous song 'Aye Mere Pyaare Watan' (O my beloved nation). As he said this, he spontaneously broke into song, singing the well-known couplet, 'Ae mere pyaare watan, aye mere bichhde chaman, tujhpe dill kurbaan' (O my beloved nation, O my parted land, I dedicate my heart to you). Pooran Chand's voice fluttered and wavered as he tried to hold the tune despite the obvious lump in his throat. 'Manna Dey did not make too many good songs after that,' he remarked as he continued humming the tune.

In the movie, Rehman's Afghan friends sing the song in a bout of nostalgia. The movie's music video constantly switches back and forth between close-ups of Rehman's (played by Balraj Sahni) nostalgic face and wide-angle shots of the Afghan–Frontier landscape. The song – which was specifically written for the movie – refers to Rehman's abandoned *watan* (Afghanistan or the Frontier) and not to the India in which the movie released. However, this song has lingered in the zeitgeist besides other popular pieces of nationalistic music. But, in Pooran Chand's emotional rendition of it, I could glimpse the Kabuliwala pining for his abandoned homeland.

Like Gangaram, Pooran Chand too had revisited Pakistan. In 2007, Pooran Chand and a friend of his (now deceased) had travelled to Pakistan together. Crossing the border via the Samjhauta Express train ('Reconciliation Express'), they had first reached Lahore and then continued onward to Bannu and Lakki Marwat. While revisiting Lakki Marwat, Pooran Chand had run into Sadiq, the grandson of his maths teacher. 'I did not recognise him, but he recognised me,' Pooran Chand said. Despite the fact that the two were practically strangers to each other, a warm friendship developed between them. Sadiq took them to his home and hosted them for the rest of their time in Pakistan.

While in Lakki Marwat, Pooran Chand had even revisited his ancestral house. He said that his house was now occupied by another family. When I asked him if he had gone inside, he said, 'No. Although the people who were with me said if you say we'll talk to the people inside and get it open, but I said no.' When I asked him why, he did not reply. An awkward silence weighed upon us then, the weight of 70 years of unfinished history.

Following Pooran Chand's trip, Sadiq had also visited India a couple of times. Sadiq had used the Urs of Ajmer Sharif to spend time with Pooran Chand and his family here. The two still kept in regular touch. In fact, on more than one occasion, Pooran Chand received a phone call from Sadiq while we were hanging out in Rose Garden.

During his visit to Pakistan, Pooran Chand had also helped reunite Chetan with his long-lost uncle. I had written about Chetan in Chapter 1 while recounting the history of NIT Faridabad. Chetan's uncle (mother's brother) had chosen to convert to Islam and stayed behind in Bannu. He owned a vast amount of agricultural land there. However, since their migration to India, the rest of Chetan's family had lost touch with his uncle. When Chetan had heard of Pooran Chand's plans to go to Pakistan, he had written his uncle a letter and handed the sealed envelope to Pooran Chand. There was no address on it, just the man's old Hindu name. Yet, against all odds, in Bannu, Pooran Chand ran into an elderly gentleman who recognised the old Hindu name. Pooran Chand translated Chetan's letter into Urdu, enclosed Chetan's Indian address and phone number and sent it along. A few days after Pooran Chand returned from Pakistan, Chetan received a call from his uncle. And then, after more than 60 years of separation, Chetan's mother finally spoke to her long-lost brother.

Yet, the sweetness of these stories lived beside Pooran Chand's belief in Hindu nationalism. In one of the first discussions we ever had about politics, Pooran Chand told me that he believed that Article 370 should be removed from the Indian Constitution. He believed that Article 370 – the constitutional article which until August 2019 granted the state of Jammu and Kashmir special status within the Indian Union – was the only roadblock to peace in the valley. He felt that the article should be removed so that Hindus, especially retired Hindu army officers, could buy land in Kashmir and settle there.

The abolition of Article 370 along with Article 35A (that empowers the state of Jammu and Kashmir to define its permanent residents and restrict the ownership of private property to residents) is a cause that the BJP and the Sangh Parivar have long championed, one that they ultimately achieved in August 2019. The Hindu Right visualise the abolition of these constitutional provisions as necessary steps to enable large-scale demographic changes in the Muslim-majority Kashmir valley. Thus, in supporting the abolition of Article 370 and linking it to large-scale Hindu migration into the valley, Pooran Chand was vocally supportive of Hindu settler-colonialism in Kashmir.

Similarly, Pooran Chand believed in the Hindu Right's version of Indian history as a series of 'Muslim' invasions and occupations. In this vein, he hoped that the Supreme Court would award the disputed site of the erstwhile Babri Masjid to Hindus, and that in time a grand Ram Temple would be built there.

However, even as he supported some of the BJP's core Hindu nationalist agendas, he also felt ashamed of the beef lynchings that had become routine by 2018. He even admitted that these acts of 'cow vigilantism' were impossible without the tacit support of the government of the day. Pooran Chand also acknowledged that Hindus too consumed beef regularly.

Similarly, by virtue of the time he had spent in the Middle-East, Pooran Chand had a more nuanced view of the post-9/11 world order. Unlike many of my other informants he did not believe that Muslims were inherently prone to terrorism or that countries with a Muslim majority were condemned to chaos. Instead, he had a grudging admiration for the 'efficiency' and 'social freedoms' of Saddam's Iraq, especially the lack of street crime and the high prevalence of women in the work-force at the time. On numerous occasions he lamented that the US had ruined Iraq and Libya through its military interventions.

Yet, despite breaking ranks with the Hindu Right on some of these subjects, Pooran Chand also espoused faith in a de-facto majoritarianism. In a conversation where I critiqued the Modi government's sectarian impulses, Pooran Chand countered by reminding me that the government of the day enjoys the majority and support of the people. The opposition cannot expect the government to function by their values, he said. When I reminded him that secularism is not only a constitutional principle but also a humanitarian value, he dismissed me by saying, 'These values have been created by those who are against this government. The opposition cannot be in opposition and still dictate terms.' Democracy is rule by the majority and the majority has elected Modi and this government to do the job, he reminded me.

In defence of this majoritarian doctrine, he turned his attention to the Middle East and argued that in 'Muslim countries' the head is always Muslim. 'Show me one Muslim country whose head is from the minority. Iraq has 15% Christians but still their President has always been Muslim,' he argued. Everywhere it is the majority that rules, he observed, 'and now Hindus have also awoken to this realisation'. This idea that by embracing the BJP's naked majoritarianism the Hindu has 'awoken' is part of how India's turn to Hindu nationalism is experienced by its supporters as a veritable revolution.

Pooran Chand was also extremely critical of the Congress' soft-Hindutva. In Rahul Gandhi's frequent temple visits during the Gujarat state legislature elections of 2018, he implicitly saw a vindication of Hindu nationalism. Pooran Chand rhetorically asked:

> And why should Hindus not vote for BJP? Who knows what Rahul Gandhi is? Is he a Christian, is he Muslim, is he Hindu, what is he? Till today he has never been to a temple but now that elections are on, he is touring temples. His mother! Who knows what [religion] she is?

Pooran Chand saw the Congress' soft-Hindutva as nothing but an opportunistic, electoral facade. If anything, Rahul Gandhi's temple-hopping campaign appeared to reify the hegemony of Hindu nationalism, firmly establishing the primacy of religion discourse within politics.

'The majority of this country accepts this. In democracy it is the will of the majority that prevails,' Pooran Chand continued. Responding to recent political commentary, he said that it was not right of the opposition parties to allege that the majority is stupid. They know what they want and they have voted for this government, he reminded me. And then, he prophetically observed, 'This government is not going to go away so soon. They will stay a while.'

Pooran Chand also denied the violence inherent in Hindu nationalism. As he saw it:

> Violence is not in the nature of Hindus. In fact it is not in our blood. Those are just one or two incidents, like Babri Masjid [demolition], or Mumbai riots and blast. It is some anti-social elements. These are one or two, they are not the norm. All this is not in the blood of Hindus.

When I disagreed and argued that at the moment Hindus seem very aggressive and fanatical, he justified this as a response to a history of the oppression of Hindus.

This is because they [Hindus] have been oppressed. First by Mughals, then by Congress. Hindus have been oppressed and now they have risen up. Hindus are 88% in this country, but Congress has done nothing for Hindus. Earlier it was a government of the 12%.

[*Pause.*]

During Partition, RSS had a major role. During Partition, RSS helped our people a lot. Saved us from attacks, fought back, gave food, found houses. These Congressi only talk. Now that Pranab Mukherjee [former Indian president and influential Congress leader] has accepted the invitation of the RSS so they have made a ruckus over that. *Arre bhai*, at least listen to him, what he wants to say. They are not capable of giving sacrifices. When the 1962 war happened in the mountains [Himalayas], there our soldiers' corpses were lying in the cold. Government could not retrieve their dead bodies. Even Indira Gandhi had refused.[9] Then 500 volunteers of RSS had gone and retrieved them. In fact it is not in their blood to give sacrifices. Only us, Hindus, can give sacrifices for the nation.

It is unclear whom he specifically means when he says, 'they are not capable of giving sacrifices'. Coming right after his critique of the Congress, one would assume that the 'they' refers to the Congress. However, in his final sentence, he contrasts this 'they' with all Hindus, implying that the 'they' includes not just the Congress but the '12%' religious minorities (a reference to Muslims) whom he believes the Congress is representative of.

However, despite his faith in the 'activism' of the RSS during the Partition, Pooran Chand's view of the organisation as a whole was far more complex. In August 2018, towards the very end of my fieldwork, Pooran Chand gave me a copy of the RSS weekly magazine *Panchajanya*. This particular edition of the magazine contained some Partition survivor narratives, as it commemorated the 71st anniversary of India's Partition and Independence. 'This has something about Partition. I thought this might help you. You can write about these in your study,' he said as he handed me the magazine. He flipped through it, showing me some of the stories. He said that some of these were interesting, but he had not read them completely. And then, his voice dropped to a whisper as he added, 'There is a man who comes here. He's an RSS *pracharak* [member]. He gave it to me. This magazine is of the RSS. So it will have some of the RSS ideas but you can ignore them. Today's RSS is not that organisation.'

When I asked him what he meant by that, he said that during the Partition, volunteers of the RSS had done real social service. 'They gave Hindus batons! Before that Hindu homes did not have weapons.' He clarified that in the Frontier some families had owned licensed arms for protection from Kabaili [tribal raiders] but that largely people had no weapons. Pooran Chand stressed that back then, there was a need for the RSS. '[Back] Then Hindus needed protection. Muslims were committing many atrocities. This is a different time now. These days Muslims are not doing anything,' he admitted. He contrasted the RSS volunteers of old with their contemporaries. According to him, the old volunteers were freedom fighters who were prepared to take blows on their body, were prepared to die for their country and community. By contrast, he saw the volunteers of today as fanatics and blamed them for indoctrinating Hindus and spreading hatred. 'Now they only talk about Hindu–Muslim. Only spread hatred. They are turning Hindus into fanatics,' he said.

Critiques of the current dispensation were also voiced in other ways. For example, while discussing the death of celebrated left-wing journalist Kuldip Nayar in August 2018, Pooran Chand and some of his other friends in Rose Garden lamented the decline in the quality of Indian journalism. Despite being largely supportive of Modi and BJP, many of them joined in the chorus exclaiming, 'These days all of them [journalists] are bought and sold'. This critique was somewhat surprising considering that vast sections of the Indian media are quite visibly in bed with the BJP government. Pooran Chand contrasted the 'friendly' journalists of today with Kuldip Nayar's courageous reportage during the Emergency of 1975–1977. They remembered him as someone who would often voice inconvenient truths.

However, my most enduring memory of Pooran Chand is of a conversation we had in February 2018. We were taking a half-round of the Rose Garden together when he unexpectedly remarked, 'My life, to tell you the truth, there is a sadness. All this that happened, I had become a sadist [*sic*] then.' Although he used the word sadist what he actually meant to say was sad or depressed. He explained that in the years immediately following the Partition, looking at how life was like here, he had become depressed. 'I was just sad, never really laughed fully,' he said. When I asked him whether it was the Partition that had caused this, he nodded and said, 'One does get affected. Once that leaves an imprint it becomes difficult. After that I became a secluded, separatist [*sic*], silent-type, even now I don't talk much. Even today I don't speak a lot. So all these things, just gloomy type....' He let those words hang momentarily. When I encouraged him to speak further, he added, 'When someone's smile is not natural, and you see that it is not natural, mine was just like that. I would see others and do the same but it was not the same. My mind got affected *na*.' I had noticed his sombre disposition; I had seen his weak smiles and heard his half-hearted laughter. And even though he had bared his heart to me, none of that had alleviated the melancholy he observed in himself. I do not think anything could. Some ruptures are beyond healing.

My field notes tell me that the last time I met Pooran Chand was on 25 August 2018. Feeling a lump in my throat, I had said something silly like, 'You're going to remember me a lot'. I remember his voice cracking as he just told me to call him once in a while. I promised I would, but in the four years since, I never did. I have never been good with goodbyes. Somehow it just felt easier this way.

Notes

1   Every year, India grants a certain number of visas to Pakistani nationals so that they might visit India's prominent Sufi *dargah*s for the religious celebrations. The Urs of Khwaja Moinuddin Chisti (in Dargah Sharif, Ajmer), Nizamuddin Auliya (in Nizamuddin Dargah, Delhi) and that of Amir Khusro (also Nizamuddin Dargah, Delhi) are among the most prominent Urs. These Urs attract crowds in excess of 100,000 people and are a potent symbol of interfaith unity.

2   Details anonymised.

3   A kind of silk that is spun using the traditional Chinese method of silk-weaving. Due to the fact that it was incredibly rare to find boski silk in

Mianwali before Partition, the fabric is prized by the people of that generation. Its rarity and price meant that the fabric was also a symbol of wealth and success.

4   The Mianwali turban is different from a Sikh turban.

5   A gesture of reverential or religious salutation.

6   The Hindi word for district that is also colloquially used as a synonym for 'area' or 'region'.

7   Tagore occupies an interesting place in anti-colonial and nationalist thought. Poulomi Saha (2013: 1) writes, 'Tagore models in his speeches and writing a locally rooted globalism, committed to a universal humanism and an avowed love of country, and it takes a form that is explicitly neither nationalist nor cosmopolitan'. In many of his writings, such as his 1916 novel *Home and the World* (*Ghare-Baire*) his philosophy is best described as one seeking to negotiate local attachment with global engagement. In this way, Tagore's nostalgia for country sat beside his refusal to endorse Bengali anti-colonial nationalism (1). Tagore's politics involved a steadfast repudiation of *all* nationalisms. Tagore saw nationalism as 'one of the most powerful anaesthetics that man has invented' (Tagore quoted in Saha 2013: 4). Saha thus concludes, 'While Tagore was anti-nationalist, he neither identified as cosmopolitan nor did he imagine such an outlook to be the answer to the quandary of factionalism and Empire' (14).

8   This famous short story of Tagore has been the subject of much critique and reflection. On the one hand, Tagore's representation of the simple-minded, honest but passionate Pathan through the character of Rehman is reflective of the racist stereotypes of Afghan and Pathan people. Seen in this light, Rehman often resembles a racist caricature. However, the story's lingering appeal lies in its universal themes, its focus on filial love being the foremost. A professor of history at James Madison University, Shah Mahmoud Hanifi argues that Tagore's *Kabuliwala* presents a snapshot of South Asian history that raises 'good questions about the cultural place of the Kabuliwala, the location of Afghan identity in relation to the Indian identity, or identities, and how these communities take shape through various migratory and mobility-based practices over the longue duree' (Hanifi quoted in Finnigan 2018). In this sense, Rehman's selling of dry fruit documents economic and migratory ties between Afghanistan and India; ties that are

themselves folded within a larger South Asian history of migration, trade and cultural exchange (Hanifi quoted in Finnigan 2018).

9   This is a vexing reference (possibly even a slip of tongue) since Indira Gandhi only became prime minister in 1966. It was her father, Jawaharlal Nehru, who was in power at the time of India's 1962 war with China.

9

Healing, Victimhood and *Ressentiment*

Nostalgia and *Ressentiment*

As I have stated previously, there is a tendency within the musealisation and oral historical work on the Partition to conflate Partition survivors' nostalgia for their homeland with a refutation of bigotry. The ethnographic vignettes I have discussed in the previous chapter contain a number of nuances that problematise this assumption. In the vignettes of both Gangaram and Pooran Chand, we see that their nostalgia for their birthplace sits beside their Islamophobia and faith in majoritarian doctrines. This is most visible in Gangaram, whose frequent visits to Pakistan and warm relations with people in Mianwali sharply contrast his vitriolic outbursts in subsequent conversations. How might we make sense of these narratives?

One possible explanation for this might be found in James Scott's (1990) idea of hidden transcripts. Scott understands all human behaviour as a series of carefully crafted performances, as a compilation of public and hidden transcripts. According to Scott, both those in power and their subordinates perform public and hidden transcripts. In Scotts' reckoning, a public transcript is an 'open interaction between subordinates and those who dominate' (2). For the dominated, Scott sees hidden transcripts as an everyday form of resistance and an essential part of revolutions and insurrections. Hidden transcripts are not just 'speech acts' but also 'a whole range of practices'. Scott sees the border between the public and the hidden transcript as a 'zone of struggle between dominant and subordinate' rather than a solid wall frozen in space and time. In that sense, the hidden transcript is not 'secret' per say but one that is performed among a 'restricted public', a carefully selected audience (14).

There is some relevance of hidden transcripts to Gangaram's story. After all, Gangaram's contrasting perspectives could be seen as the oscillation from a public to a hidden transcript. We might regard his secular and reconciliatory posturing among his Pakistani friends as a public transcript that he enacts in contrast to the hidden transcript he revealed to me after we had become more familiar with each other. Thus, Gangaram's Islamophobic outbursts and text messages might be seen as a hidden transcript revealed to a 'restricted public' (14). This would partly explain why it took me some time to access that side of Gangaram.

However, the application of hidden transcripts to this context is also problematic for a number of reasons. While Scott's theory defines public and hidden transcripts as the result of unequal power relations, Gangaram's relations with his friends in Pakistan cannot be understood through the reductively binary categories of 'dominant' and 'subordinate'.

Furthermore, Susan Gal (1995) critiques Scott's discussion of power by arguing that his use of the categories 'dominant' and 'subordinate' constitutes a broad generalisation. Moving from analyses of the narratives of slave masters and slaves in the United States to British colonialists and their subjects in Burma, among others, Scott traverses the globe through space and time at a breakneck speed. Scott does not pay sufficient attention to the particular contexts of the historical and ethnographic evidence he references (Gal 1995). Despite some fundamental similarities, the power relations that organised slavery in the United States were quite different from those that structured the British Empire. The result is a detemporalised and decontextualised understanding of power.

Furthermore, Gal critiques Scott's description of public transcripts. The issue is twofold. First, Scott does not sufficiently define the term 'public'. In reducing the idea of public to a question of one's audience and thereby of a specific model of first-hand witnessing, Scott articulates a Western ideological construct that relies on the 'separation of language from a face-to-face situation' (417). Gal locates this ideological construct within the decontextualisation of language through print. Scott's uncritical use of 'public' evades any discussion of alternative publics. If 'public' pertains only to the fact of having an audience, then hidden transcripts too must have their publics and with it, power imbalances and struggles within the 'restricted publics' of these subordinate groups. Scott pays no attention to this and instead presents dominant and subordinate groups as neatly juxtaposed homogenous groups.

Second, Scott describes public transcripts as performances. As Gal argues, the view that one's public transcript is a 'performance' implies that it is by definition unauthentic. She notes that in seeing acting as something that is 'imposed' on the weak – as a fact of their subordination – Scott implies belief in the idea of an 'authentic self'. This is problematic because it implies that this 'authentic self' is 'betrayed' (or concealed) by performance (411).

This dichotomy involves an implicit heirarchisation. The hidden transcript is by definition considered the 'truer' transcript due to the very fact that it must be *hidden*. By contrast, the public transcripts (of both the subordinated and dominant) conceal their respective 'authentic selves' by acting out a script. Therefore, if I were to argue that Gangaram and Pooran Chand's Islamophobia somehow comprises a hidden transcript, then, I would also be implying that their hatred for Muslims was a more 'authentic' emotion than their nostalgia for their birthplace.

However, these ethnographic vignettes suggest that the truth is far more complex. Stories of the correspondence both men have maintained with their birthplace suggest that their yearning for their birthplace (their nostalgia) is as authentic an emotion as their Islamophobia. In Gangaram's case this is further complicated by the fact that he routinely defied his family and close friends in order to maintain this correspondence. Gal (1995: 412–413) captures some of this complexity when she writes:

> More generally, the expression of contradictory opinions by a single speaker, in different contexts, is not necessarily evidence of dissembling or inauthenticity.... But these contrasting stances cannot be classified as posed versus genuine; they are evidence of the coexistence of deeply felt yet contested discourses.

While Gal's argument leaves the question of hypocrisy unanswered,[1] her larger argument, that the charge of inauthenticity against one or the other set of discourses involves a denial of specificity, still holds. The real challenge of ethnography here then is to understand how nostalgia and hatred coexist in the lives of Partition survivors. These are not contradictory discourses as much as they are articulations of the struggle for the reconciliation of the past with the present, the search for healing.

As I have argued in Chapter 6, oral history has a tendency to present remembrance as a singularly healing act. However, the act of remembrance does not serve as an end in itself. For its survivors, remembering the Partition is part of the articulation for their demand for justice, for revenge. Ultimately, to engage with the full complexity of Partition survivor narratives is to confront the terrifying possibility that revenge might be the only 'healing' they desire.

We see this expressed in similar shades in the narratives of Gangaram and Pooran Chand. For example, Gangaram laments the Partition and its violence, celebrates his links with the people of Mianwali but still expresses frustration at the fact that a number of Muslims were 'left behind' in India. The latter also complicates his feelings about the Partition, making him simultaneously express faith in the biopolitical logic of Partition and the two-nation theory. As a result, Gangaram opposes the Partition when talking about his friends in Pakistan but supports it while talking about Muslims in India. We see a similar struggle play out in Pooran Chand's testimony when he details the efforts he made to keep in touch with Bannu, through literature. Although he recognises the deep psychological imprint that the violence of the Partition has left on him, he is still cynically supportive of the current majoritarian dispensation. While he acknowledges the violence of Hindu nationalism (beef lynchings, the demolition of the Babri Masjid and radicalisation of Hindus by the RSS) in spades, he nevertheless sees Modi's rise to power as an 'awakening'. He recognises Modi's government as an enabler of sectarian violence, yet he feels that history necessitates this majoritarian mobilisation. So what is it that they ultimately yearn for?

During her fieldwork on the Partition, Nonica Datta (2017) noted a similar contrast in the discourses of the celebrated Punjabi writer Amrita Pritam. As stated previously, Amrita Pritam was a survivor of the Partition. The horrific sectarian violence that engulfed Lahore forced her to relocate to Faridabad in 1947. Datta's work records Pritam's memories of isolation and helplessness as she struggled to find her feet in the newly independent nation. Datta is particularly drawn to the way Pritam describes India's Independence as a tragedy:

> For Amrita, 'this *takseem* (division) happened on very *maslui* (weak) foundation'. As she says repeatedly that when she heard of Partition, she thought it was a temporary madness. She did not think that it would continue. It was a storm of hatred, which was not properly managed, she said. 'It too shall pass. It cannot last for long. We will return. Later, all hell broke loose'. The questioning of freedom in 1947 continues: 'What kind of *azadi* [freedom] and at what cost are we gaining?' The dilemma remains, 'If Partition had happened on religious grounds, then why did so many people remain in *Hindustan*…? More than half the Muslims are here. On what basis was it done?' She also points out that 'ironically, Hindus could not stay there [Pakistan], and here [India] Muslims could remain. There is democracy here. It was very difficult.' (N. Datta 2017: 75)

What is striking here is that Amrita Pritam – a secular, feminist writer – also wonders why India was left with a large population of Muslims while Hindus and Sikhs were almost entirely ethnically cleansed from Pakistan. Yet, she also laments her own displacement from Lahore and is similarly mournful of the relationships the Partition interrupted. Pritam's discourses are similar to Gangaram's and Pooran Chand's who, in their respective vignettes, similarly wonder why so many Muslims were 'left behind' after the Partition.

This discourse constructs India's Muslim population as some kind of 'human residue' left behind by the Partition. All three speakers, in different ways identify 'democracy' and 'secularism' as the reasons for this. This is brought out starkly in Amrita Pritam's quote above when she says that 'Hindus could not stay there [Pakistan], and here [India] Muslims could remain. There is democracy here. It was very difficult' (75). The lamentation here is against a perceived inequality of suffering, that 'we' suffered more than 'them'. In having retained some of its Muslim population, India – because of its 'democracy' – is implicitly seen as the loser of the Partition. The presence of this 'proximate enemy' also symbolises the Partition's unfinished nature. In other contexts, this inequality of suffering is also often cited as proof of the 'peace-loving' and 'weak' nature of Hindus. To its speakers, the issue here is not violence per se, but the inequality of death, suffering and misfortune.

Such discourses grapple with the unfair distribution of misfortune as much as they struggle with the debris of nation-building. This unresolved history demands resolution not merely through a form of theodicy but also through 'justice', reparations and revenge. That is, opposing the Partition while speaking of the intimate but simultaneously espousing the logic of the Partition when confronted with the larger themes of politics and history, they show a yearning for reconciliation and healing. That is, this discourse is a conflicted articulation but an authentic yearning for reconciliation nevertheless. I use the word 'reconciliation' here to refer to the hope for an end to an unfinished history, a resolution, whatever that end might be. This is one interpretation I offer.

It is this that makes Gangaram's call for the complete ethnic cleansing of Muslims from India seem like the completion of a process. He aspires to genocide because to him it appears like the resolution to an unfinished history. This is not to argue that the aspiration to resolution makes this any less of a genocide. But, to him and my other informants, the complete ethnic cleansing of Muslims did not appear to be an act of unprovoked mass-murder. Rather, it was seen as the necessary resolution to an unfinished history, and the turn to Hindu fascism, the very first step of the 'awakening'. Genocide is not purely murder here, it is justice.

There is, however, a second interpretation I want to offer. In the way that my informants' nostalgia for their abandoned homeland goes beside their desire for revenge (their *ressentiment*), there is also the confluence of two different strains of nostalgia: restorative nostalgia and reflective nostalgia. Here, their reflective nostalgia – one that prompts reflection on feelings of loss (Boym 2001: 41) – meets the internalised restorative nostalgia of Hindu nationalism. Where the former is evocative of the wounds of the past, the latter posits the 'restoration' of the ancient glory of Hinduism – through the establishment of the Hindu Rashtra (nation state) – as just reparations for this loss. To diagnose the reflective nostalgia of Partition survivors as evidence of their lack of hatred would be to miss the forest for the trees. That is, this nostalgia for the intimate is itself folded within a larger nationalist, restorative nostalgia that posits genocide and fascism as the remedy to a historically conceived victimhood.

Genocide and fascism as justice – as the revenge of the non-violent Hindu – also follows the logic of karma. It cites a laundry list of historical injustices by Muslims – the Partition being the latest – to establish their guilt. Having established guilt, it articulates the logic of *like begets like* to vow to do to them what was allegedly previously done to Hindus. This formulation mobilises a karmic theodicy of violence. This 'action-reaction' thesis – albeit one that casts a long eye over history – weaponises the theodicy of karma to sanction violence against the 'other'. Ultimately, mobilising memories of the violence of Muslims during the Partition, this discourse justifies the violent Hindu nationalism of today.

This theodicy of violence is rendered meaningful by the articulation of a historically conceived victimhood. Remembrance, in this context, is not purely an act of 'healing' as imagined by the practitioners of Partition oral history. Rather, history is remembered strategically. The history of the Partition (and beyond) is remembered to establish their own status (and that of all Hindus) as the eternal victims of history. It is against this victimhood – this feeling of having been wronged – that they articulate the demand for justice through the discourses of Hindu nationalism. The justice they seek is that of revenge, an eye for an eye. Healing, as it is implicitly aspired to in this context, is not the kind of reconciliatory forgiveness that is often imagined. Rather, the healing aspired to by Partition survivors is an expression of the primal desire for blood in exchange for blood.

Victimhood forms an important part of this discourse and it is therefore important to deconstruct it in some detail. I have previously stated that the uncritical use of the word trauma flattens the field of victimhood. By treating all survivors of the Partition as innocent traumatised victims, it thereby perpetuates an implicit denial of the violence of and within one's own collectivity. I return to the theme of victimhood here to elucidate its larger moral and political claims.

Building on the work of Nietzsche, Robert Horwitz (2018) argues that the claim to group victimhood is located in the feeling of *ressentiment*. As stated previously, *ressentiment* refers to thinly veiled feelings of unsatisfiable jealousy and hatred. Nietzsche theorised *ressentiment* as the way in which a 'sufferer' searches for a cause for their suffering (Olick 2007). This basic idea is expressed through Weber's (1965: 110) understanding of *ressentiment* as a form of 'theodicy of the disprivileged' (also see Olick 2007: 157). *Ressentiment* is therefore hatred with a moral content, triggered by jealousy and anger at the fact of one's own dispossession. However, *ressentiment* is not just empty anger. It is a hatred that is specifically directed at those who are held responsible for one's misfortune/suffering.

In Chapter 4, I have previously mentioned the *ressentiment* visible in my informants' discourses on Independence. This was starkly visible in the way that my informants' asked what, if anything, they had received from India in lieu of their 'sacrifices'. While some, like Bhanwarilal and my granduncle Om Prakash, visualised reparations in material terms, for others like Jogesh and Kishore, reparations involved, at the very least, being granted the symbolic status of 'freedom fighters'. Yet, all of these demands for reparations were articulated alongside a deeply felt jealousy of those who were seen to have not suffered. We see a similar expression of *ressentiment* in Amrita Pritam, Gangaram and Pooran Chand's discourses above as their remarks on India's Muslims are partly located in feelings of jealousy. Their anger at the perceived inequality of suffering is also a jealousy of the latter's perceived lack of suffering.

Robert Horwitz (2018: 554) notes that 'victimised groups stand not simply for their own wounds and innocence, but for something larger … the mission to secure fundamental justice, or some other grand calling'. In his discussion of victimhood, Horwitz draws a distinction between the kind of group victimhood that characterises the American far-right and the state-centred national discourse of victimhood characteristic of Nazi Germany. He argues that most nineteenth and twentieth-century victimhood centred on the nation state drew on the sacrifices of soldiers. Soldiers are seen as victims on behalf of the nation, and their sacrifices are considered redemptive for themselves and the nation.

I find this distinction between group and state victimhood irrelevant in the Indian context as the group victimhood of my informants collapses into a national victimhood by virtue of the fact that to them, their group *is* the nation. The additional fact of the Hindu nationalist capture of the Indian government furthers erases the distinction between the Indian state and the Hindu collective. Victimhood, in this context, springs from the soldiers and freedom fighters who died in service of the nation, as well as co-religionists who have been killed in acts of 'Muslim aggression' during the Partition, and beyond. Victimhood, therefore, springs from anyone who is seen to have died in defence of or due to their membership of the Hindu nation.

We see a clear example of this in Pooran Chand's comment in Chapter 8 when he moves from calling Mughals and the Congress party oppressors of Hindus, to extolling the RSS' 'sacrifices' during the Partition, to the Congress' alleged inability to retrieve the dead bodies of Indian soldiers who died in the 1962 war with China. Pooran Chand finishes this by saying, 'In fact it is not in their [Muslims/Congress] blood to give sacrifices. Only us, Hindus, can give sacrifices for the nation.' In doing so, Pooran Chand establishes a clear genealogy of sacrifice stretching from medieval times to the Partition (including the 'sacrifices' of the RSS volunteers) to the dead soldiers of 1962, all the while presenting the 'minority-appeasing', liberal elite of the Congress as traitors to the Hindu nation. Here it is relevant to recall my discussion in Chapter 4, of the sacrifice and martyrdom bestowed on the dead of the Partition as a form of theodicy in service of the Hindu nation. Memories (real and imagined) of the 'sacrifices' of kith, kin and co-religionists during the Partition motivate this feeling of Hindu victimhood, demanding revenge as justice. Thus, hatred and the aspiration for genocide are presented as a mission in pursuit of a fundamental justice.

Horwitz identifies suffering and the *ressentiment* that springs from it, as central to the way hatred is presented as an appeal for justice and a claim to moral goodness. He writes:

> Suffering became constitutive of self-understanding and produced a moral code validating hatred of the evil enemies who caused the suffering.... The resentful are no longer actors per se; rather they are defined passively by their victimhood. They become active only in their hatred of their purported oppressors. Their hatred is the mark of their moral goodness.... *Ressentiment* is the feeling, victimhood the status. (Horwitz 2018: 555)

Ressentiment also manifests itself in the feeling of having been oppressed and marginalised, in the everyday affairs of the nation state. It is articulated in the view that 'unworthy others' might be 'unjustly favoured' over the 'deserving' members of one's community (555). The latter along with the trenchant individualism of neoliberalism also motivates a critique of affirmative action and similar policies of positive discrimination aimed at addressing systemic inequality. Affirmative action, in this context, is understood as a 'cynical use of government' by the 'other', as a 'triumph of illegitimate clientelist politics' (564). It is seen as the product of a self-serving alliance between minorities and liberal elites or 'minority-appeasement'. As Horwitz writes:

> Policies designed to address systemic privilege are perceived as engaging in unwarranted entitlement that violates the traditional presumed ethic of individual merit, hard work and color-blindness. The critique of victimhood shifts the debate from the structures of power that inscribe inequality to the question of personal character. (565)

Here, it is relevant to recall my discussion of my informants' discourses around hard work in the immediate aftermath of the Partition, in Chapters 2 and 3. My informants were always careful to emphasise that they were 'hard-workers' rather than 'refugees'. While my informants sanctified their hard work as a national sacrifice, this discourse was also a karmic justification of their middle-class, upper-caste Hindu privilege. Furthermore, it invoked national character – their inherently hard-working nature – as a form of predestination.

Using stories of hard work while underplaying the role of the state's welfare schemes in the rehabilitation of Partition refugees, my informants would profess the supposedly uniquely resilient character of the Punjabi community. In the process, they also sought to legitimise the fortune of their privilege. Such narratives would be interspersed with claims of the inherent backwardness of lower-caste Hindu communities (such as Dalits, OBC and SC) and Muslims. Such discussions would move the debate from the structural inequalities perpetuated by the caste system to a victim-blaming discourse that would attribute the generational poverty of these communities to their lack of street-smartness and hard work: *purusharth*. We observed a clear example of this in Rajaram's sexist and casteist observations in Chapter 5. Rajaram alleged an inherent 'backwardness' in a community of slum-dwelling Assamese/Bangladeshi Muslims by pointing to the fact that 'their women' collected and traded scrap paper for a living.

In the electoral realm, this feeling of *ressentiment* is articulated through the perception that the Congress party is a party of the Muslims. As stated previously in the Introduction, the feeling that the post-Independent Indian state has been captured by minorities and 'minority-appeasing' liberal elites, and is wielded against the 'meek' Hindu majority, forms a major part of Hindu nationalist discourses (van der Veer 1994). During my fieldwork, remarks that the last 60 years of Congress-led rule was the 'Raj of Muslims' were routine. This political victimhood that *ressentiment* perpetuates then presents Hindu fascism as a necessary 'awakening'. Therefore, when framed against a sense of historical victimhood, Hindu nationalism acquires an emancipatory façade, promising liberation from liberal elites and treacherous minorities. To its supporters, the goal of an ethnically pure Hindu nation seems like a project of justice.

What I have identified as *ressentiment* here has been relatedly described by Arjun Appadurai (2017) as 'democracy fatigue'. Appadurai theorises democracy fatigue as a syndrome where democracy itself is seen as an obstacle to national progress. A classic example of this discourse was on display recently in the words of the NITI Aayog CEO Amitabh Kant. On December 8, speaking at an event hosted by the right-wing publication *Swarajya* magazine, the government think-tank CEO declared, 'Tough reforms are very difficult in the Indian context, we have too much of democracy.... You needed political will to carry out these reforms (mining, coal, labour, agriculture) and many more reforms still need to be done' (*The Hindu* 2020). Contemporaneous with the escalating farmer protests across the country – organised in response to neoliberal agricultural 'reforms' – Amitabh Kant's comments seemed particularly tone-deaf. However, his words express the ethos of democracy fatigue in a refreshingly honest manner.

In the context of the memories of the Partition, democracy fatigue manifests itself in the sentiment that India's unfinished Partition – due to the presence of Muslims – is a failure of democracy. Consequently,

Hindu nationalism's aspiration for an 'end' to this 'unfinished' Partition necessitates the elimination of minorities and the 'democracy' that is seen to protect them. In this way, the 'fascism of the streets' and of high-office (Appadurai 2021) combine to fulfil the desire for justice: for genocide and fascism. Thus, by removing all physical and material trace of its proximate enemy, Hindu fascism ultimately hopes to complete that which was left 'unfinished' in 1947.

The Difficulty of Remembrance

Krishna Sobti once famously said that 'Partition was difficult to forget but dangerous to remember' (Sobti quoted in Butalia 2000: 283). To paraphrase Shakespeare, the dilemma at hand is that of: to remember or not to remember. In this book, I too have grappled with this dilemma. While the suffering of the Partition makes it necessary to remember, the *ressentiment* of Partition survivors and religious nationalism makes it dangerous to do so. As I have shown in this book, memories of the Partition feed into Hindu nationalist discourses inspiring the turn to a form of retributive fascism. Urvashi Butalia too grappled with this dilemma in her work. In reference to Krishna Sobti's aforementioned comment, Butalia (2000: 283) wrote:

> But does this mean then that we must not remember it? Over the years, despite many uncertainties, I have become increasingly convinced that while it may be dangerous to remember, it is also essential to do so – not only so that we can come to terms with it, but also because unlocking memory and remembering is an essential part of beginning the process of resolving, perhaps even of forgetting.

I agree with Butalia on the *need* to remember. As Milan Kundera (1999: 4) famously wrote, 'The struggle of man against power is the struggle of memory against forgetting'. But the larger question this raises is *how* we might go about remembering the Partition. However, Butalia thoughtfully acknowledges the fact that to the Hindu nationalist gaze, memories of the Partition serve as 'proof' of the allegedly inherent brutality of Muslims. Butalia notes that the RSS took up the issue of

'Hindu honour' with gusto even in the 1940s. For example, in the 29 December 1949 issue of its magazine, *The Organiser*, the RSS compared the rape and abduction of Hindu and Sikh women during the Partition to Alauddin Khilji's thirteenth-century sacking of Chittor. The article titled 'Pakistan the Sinner: 25,000 Abducted, Thousands Sold' ran as follows:

> For the honour of Sita, Sri Ram warred against and destroyed Ravana, when filthy Khilji besieged Chitoor [*sic*] its thousands of women headed by Rani Padmini all clad in *gerua* [saffron] saris, mounted the funeral pyre smiling ere the *mleccha* [impure] could pollute a drop of the noble Hindu blood. Today, when tens of hundreds of Hindu women are spending sorrowful days and nights in Pakistan, the first free government of the Union of Indian Sovereign Democratic Republic has nothing but a whimper. (*The Organiser* quoted in Butalia 2000: 145)

Butalia notes that such commentary on the rape and abduction of Hindu and Sikh women by Muslim men was part of *The Organiser*'s regular reportage and, formed the backdrop against which accusations that Pakistan was a 'barbaric', 'uncivilised' and 'lustful' nation were raised (145). Furthermore, the violence of the Partition is seen as a continuation of Khilji's 'Muslim invasion'. As stated previously, accessing such historical and cultural narratives of victimhood and sacrifice forms an important part of the discourse of sacrifice as a form of theodicy.

Panchajanya, the RSS mouthpiece that Pooran Chand brought to my attention towards the end of my fieldwork, continued this discourse. The magazine's 19 August 2018 edition built on this discourse of Hindu victimhood to remember stories of the Partition as the RSS' finest hour. The headlines of the oral historical vignettes in this edition ranged from 'Had the Sangh [RSS] not been there, we would not have crossed the border' (Bhargava 2018), 'The *swayamsevaks* [RSS volunteers/cadre] were filled with endless courage' (Mishra 2018a), 'The *swayamsevaks* stood their ground in every situation' (Mishra 2018b), 'We are indebted to the Sangh that the people of our village survived' (A. Kumar 2018a), 'We found stability in our lives due to the help of the *swayamsevaks*' (A.

Kumar 2018b), 'Muslims crossed all limits of barbarity' (Mishra 2018c), 'Hindus would not have survived without the Sangh' (Mishra 2018d) and 'The *swayamsevak*s supported the army' (Mishra 2018e). These headlines and stories clearly present the Partition as the RSS' golden hour of service to the (Hindu) nation.

For Butalia, the solution to this dilemma lay in editing out the hate speech of her informants whilst acknowledging the violence and bigotry of the Indian state and ethnonationalist organisations. In the late 1990s, this seemed a workable comprise. It allowed survivors the space to remember, mourn and vent, while drawing attention to some of the ways in which the violence of the Partition was embedded within political and cultural crosscurrents. Other oral history projects, including the 1947 Partition Archive, have followed Butalia's lead in this.

But much has changed since the 1990s. A generation since Butalia (2000) and Menon and Bhasin's (1998) pioneering work, the spectre of Hindu fascism dominates India's politics and institutions in a way it never has at any other point in Indian history. This radical transformation of the very character of the Indian republic necessitates a radical rethinking of the task of (oral) history-writing.

Editing out hate speech – no matter how vitriolic and problematic – in the current context risks remembering the Partition purely through the rose-tinted glasses of nostalgia. Such heavily editorialised narratives fail to tell the 'true' stories of the survivors they quote. I suspect that the latter furthers the (*res-*)sentiment among many survivors that *their history* has remained untold, that the 'true story' of the Partition still remains unheard and unspoken, 'suppressed' and 'repressed'. This is also politically problematic for it distracts attention away from the Partition's silent, enabling presence in the mass support enjoyed by the BJP. In this time of Hindu fascism, remembering the Partition must entail confronting the Hindu nationalism of Partition survivors.

There is a strange entangling of temporality in Hindu nationalism's use of the Partition. Hindu nationalism's aspiration for a violent 'end' to the 'unfinished' business of 1947, imagines a future that is the past. Consequently, the suffering of the past, the Partition, ominously looms over us portending our future – of the suffering that awaits our society should the Hindu nationalist project run its course. In this strange liminal present where the future that is aspired to is the past, and the past an ominous foretelling of our future, it becomes imperative to confront those cultural and political processes that threaten to take us both forwards and backwards to 1947. The looming spectre of fascism makes it imperative to expose the violence and fascism in our midst – in our homes and social circles – and to see these in concert with the 'fascism of the streets' (Appadurai 2019, 2021) and of high office.

Under the Modi regime, the Hindu nationalist reading of Partition history has been acknowledged through subtle winks and nods, and even in parliamentary proceedings. In July 2018, while defending his ruling coalition against a no-confidence motion, Prime Minister Modi made a vexing reference to the Partition. He countered the Congress' allegations against the misrule of his own government by pointing to the Congress' history of misrule (*Hindustan Times* 2018). Modi equated the Congress' 2014 decision to bifurcate the state of Andhra Pradesh to the Partition of India. Modi said:

> This is not the new for you. You divided India–Pakistan during independence. Today also we are facing problems. You have divided Andhra Pradesh also like this. If you had taken them into confidence, these problems would not have happened. But you thought nothing about this. (Narendra Modi quoted in *Hindustan Times* 2018)

Meanwhile, the BJP has sought to present its unconstitutional actions in Jammu and Kashmir as the 'unshackling' of the state from 'vested interest groups' (*The Hindu* 2019a). In Parliament, BJP leaders Amit Shah, Jitendra Singh (minister of state) and Jugal Kishore Sharma (MP representing the constituency of Jammu) blamed the de facto 1948 Partition of Jammu and Kashmir on Nehru (Vincent 2019). Invoking the bogeys of 'corruption', 'nepotism' and 'Partition', the BJP has presented its Hindu nationalist project in the Kashmir Valley as one of 'development' and 'liberation'. The discourse was set by Prime Minister Modi who in a series of tweets, celebrated the passage of Jammu and Kashmir Reorganisation Act 2019, along with constitutional amendments to Articles 370 and 35A, as a 'momentous occasion' that promised a 'new dawn' and a 'better tomorrow' as the people of the state had been finally freed from the 'shackles' of 'vested interest groups' (*The Hindu* 2019a).

Meanwhile, on 11 July 2019, the RSS and BJP organised a rally on the subject of 'overpopulation' which was attended by the Union Minister Giriraj Singh (*The Print* 2019). Speakers at the rally warned of the 'overpopulation' of Muslims and spoke of a conspiracy to 'capture' and 'Islamise' India (Matra 2019a, 2019b). They also warned that as the population of Muslims rises, they will demand a 'second Partition' of India (*The Print* 2019).

Therefore, all through their eight years in government, the BJP has consistently used the power of high office to acknowledge the Hindu Right's understanding of the Partition. My point in recounting these parliamentary proceedings and supplementary discourses, is to show how the history and memory of the Partition has been consistently co-opted in pursuit of a fascist agenda. Irrespective of the censorship of hate speech in oral history archives, memories of the Partition continue to inspire a fresh cycle of ('retributive') genocidal violence. All that oral history's censorship accomplishes is an ignorance of how these memories inspire contemporary majoritarian mobilisations.

Throughout my fieldwork, I was haunted by the guilt that I might in fact be aiding and abetting the ideological grassroots work of Hindu nationalism. Through this discussion, I do not mean to imply that we must stop studying violence, or stop studying histories that the far-right targets with its disinformation campaigns. However, a possible answer might lie in paying more attention to the kinds of people whose stories we choose to tell. The Partition survivors that I interviewed, and that most oral historians seem to interview, are mainly upper-caste, middle-class Hindus. If the telling of their narratives seems to reify a regime of truth, then that has much to do with their positionality. Sucheta Mahajan (2011: 286) warns against oral histories that draw from a 'restricted social stratum' for their tendency reproduce 'community myths'. This is our cue to pay more attention to the narratives of those who are not as privileged, such as the working class, Dalits and Adivasis.

Unfortunately, this realisation comes too late for the study of the Partition. The last generation of Partition survivors is dying and by the middle of this decade, almost all of them will have passed on. The imprint of death is already visible on recent oral histories of the Partition, such as Aanchal Malhotra's (2017) work on 'material memory'. As survivors are lost to the mists of time, we begin to interrogate inanimate objects for the stories they might tell. Yet, even this carries the imprint of caste and class. What stories shall we tell of those whose life was their sole material possession?

There is an additional methodological point to be made here. Because most oral history is based on one-off life-history interviews, oral historians are not embedded long enough in the lives of their informants to observe many of these specific entanglements between politics and memory. My experience with my informants underscores the need for participant observation. My patient, persistent presence in their everyday lives allowed me an insight into the specificity of their memories, including their myriad contradictions and complexities. One-off interviews simply cannot achieve this. What is needed therefore is less oral history and more ethnography, but specifically, ethnography that draws on participant observation and is reflexively critical of the epistemology of memory.

What does it mean then to remember the Partition in the time of fascism? It means that we remember the Partition as a portent or warning of the future that awaits us. It means understanding nationalism's rationalisation of violence through its call to absolute conformity and homogeneity. It means observing the role of a fascist ideology as a form of theodicy of death and suffering. It means interrupting these established theodicical understandings of 'sacrifice' and 'martyrdom'. It means deconstructing ideas of national community implicit in narratives of violence. But most of all, remembering the Partition in the time of fascism means recognising that the suffering my ancestors experienced in the past is what India's minorities are experiencing today. Rather than ignore the fascism that thrives on the victimhood of the Partition, we must use these memories to express solidarity towards those being similarly oppressed today.

Perhaps in drawing this lesson from the Partition we might finally move closer to forgetting it. By forgetting, I do not mean forgetting the Partition itself but perhaps, moving past the impassioned ethnonationalism it feeds. However, this appears highly unlikely at the moment. But, if we must continue to remember the Partition in the present, let us do so as part of an actively anti-fascist politics, one that expresses solidarity towards all such victims of genocidal and structural violence.

Note

1   Gal avoids any engagement with the possibility of contradicting discourses being a product of hypocrisy. This appears to be a glaring blind spot in her critique. Here, Scott offers some clarity as his idea of hidden transcripts already accounts for hypocrisy as a product of power relations. Hypocrisy might be seen as a consequence of the acting that is 'imposed' on the weak, as a fact of their domination. For the powerful, hypocrisy is an inevitable consequence of the masks they must wear in public in the performance of their hegemony. Here, Michel de Certeau's (1984) idea of 'tactics' is more appropriate. Although de Certeau does not specifically theorise hypocrisy, a de Certeau-ian understanding of hypocrisy would see it as a tactical appropriation of discourse in pursuit of one's self-interest.

Conclusion
Field Notes on Global Authoritarianism

Victimhood, *Ressentiment* and the Crisis of Meaning

One of the most significant contributions this book makes to the field of Partition Studies is its analysis of the discourse of *purusharth* and suffering as a form of sacrifice. My discussion of this discourse offers important insights into the politics of self-making. Older ethnographies of the Partition such as G. Pandey (2001), Butalia (2000), Menon and Bhasin (1998), Das (2007) and N. Nair (2011) show that while Partition survivors resented politicians and identified their lust for power as the cause of their suffering, the notion of personal suffering as a form of sacrifice for the nation was yet to be articulated. So when did this shift occur? Understanding this requires a brief examination of the history of Hindu politics in Punjab alongside the events and afterlife of the Partition.

The transition to a Hindu nationalist identity among Punjabi refugees was not straightforward. This has a lot to do with the pre-Partition demography, social structures and dominant politics of Punjab which tended to be assemblages of multiple communities. The kinship system of *biraderi* functioned as the beating heart of the local community in Punjab. Derived from the Persian word *birader* (brother), *biraderi* is a system of patrilinear kinship that is common to the Hindus, Muslims and Sikhs of West Punjab (Anjali Roy 2019). While *biraderi* denotes a broad descent group that includes all those among whom common descent can be traced in the paternal line across the generations, the boundaries, form and size of specific *biraderi*s were products of their social and political contexts (Gilmartin 1994).

Although *biraderi* provided the foundation for the imagination of the 'nation-as-family' in Punjab (Gilmartin 1994; Anjali Roy 2019), the shift to nationalist thinking was partly a consequence of colonial policies of land use and broader shifts in Indian politics. Predictably, the rivers of Punjab feature prominently in this story, providing the land its name (and thereby identity) – a composite of the Persian words *panj* (five) and *ab* (river) – and functioning as the locus of wider socioeconomic exchanges.

David Gilmartin (2015b) has compared the Indus canal system to the printing press as the facilitator of the imagination of a broader community that could transcend the social constraints of a community based on real physical contact. Participation in this integrated and engineered river basin environment provided individual irrigators with a frame for the imagination of 'a common community of action upon nature' (Gilmartin 2015b: 199). Gilmartin argues that this 'vision that, though mediated by engineers, had the power to resonate with the structure of new nationalist imaginings'. The symbolic and material cohesiveness of the Indus irrigation system was preceded by the Land Alienation Act, 1900, which enabled the visualisation of a single socioeconomic class of landowners. This legislation ultimately enabled the pro-gentry and pro-landlord politics of the Unionist Party (199). Building on existing assemblages of 'tribe', *biraderi* and village community, these developments alongside the progression of the anti-colonial movement substantially enabled the imagination of broader communities based on class, religious and ultimately (ethno-)national identities.

Neeti Nair's (2011) work shows that during these early nationalist imaginings and class consolidations, the 'national' and 'communal' had still not solidified. Nair writes, 'The nation was seen in a starkly Hindu idiom, as well as explicitly including members of other religious communities' (49). Her historiography of Hindu politics in Punjab documents a rich tradition of religiously informed anti-colonial protests. Nair argues that despite the existence of communal tensions – both on the ground and in high politics – in the 1930s and 1940s, Partition was still not inevitable.

The complexity of Punjab's pre-Partition politics lies in the fact that even as these ambiguities existed in high politics and subaltern discourse, some Hindus were vocally supportive of Partition, even as others opposed it (N. Nair 2011). Such conflicting visions of ethnic, religious and national community were borne out in the vibrant presence of the Brahmo Samaj, Arya Samaj, Hindu Mahasbha and RSS within Punjab's complex milieu of Hindu politics – all this aside from the presence of the Muslim League, Akali Dal, Unionist Party, Congress and other prominent organisations and political parties representing Muslim, Sikh and other configurations of religious, caste, class and ethnic interests. Thus, Ayesha Jalal (1998: 2183) asserts that Punjab, with its inversion of the all-India majority–minority equation – with Hindus and Sikhs in a minority and Muslims in a majority – was at the 'centre-stage of the struggle between nationalism and imperialism'.

The ambiguities and specificities of Punjab's identity politics are also evident in the narratives of survivors. Survivors of the Partition remember their disbelief at the violence, their forced migration and even the permanence of their displacement. For example, my granduncle Om Prakash remembered his grandfather's disbelief at the suggestion of a permanent transfer of population. 'My grandfather did not agree.... He said I have seen life, so it has never before happened that the population itself is exchanged and that you'll never come back' (Om Prakash quoted in Kohli 2015: 27). Nair's informants – as well as many of my informants – remembered hoping for a return to their ancestral homes once the violence had abated; some held on to this hope till as late as 1948. These hopes were ultimately dashed by India's enactment – and subsequently Pakistan's reciprocation – of a permit system to stop the back-flow of refugees (Zamindar 2007). As a hard-border and harsh visa regime took shape, it became apparent to all that the Partition and its displacement could not be undone.

The cataclysmic events of the Partition began a decisive shift towards an explicitly Hindu national identity in high politics and quotidian life. As stated previously, the violence of the Partition involved a visceral demarcation of new national boundaries (G. Pandey 2001) – its violence branding the insignia of religious identity onto the bodies of its victims and survivors. As the narratives of my informants show, the fact of their suffering was a stark reminder of the religious and national identity they had been bequeathed.

While the Partition had excluded them from Pakistan, their assimilation into post-Partition India took time. As I have stated previously, the narratives of Partition survivors reveal a memory of unbelonging in those initial years in India. Arriving destitute in a land that was largely foreign to them – nevertheless one in which they were said to belong – Partition survivors were treated with fear, suspicion and indifference. This is visible in Chapter 1 where Pooran Chand remembers the Frontier Refugees' contestations with the state. Similarly, Thakar Daas remembers being seen as a 'Muslim' and 'habshi' (barbarian) by the Hindus of north India. My granduncle Om Prakash and other informants remembered being advised to wear a *kara* to distinguish them as allies to the Hindu and Sikh mobs of Delhi; apparently they looked just like Muslims in their *salwar kameez* (ethnic attire).

As stated previously in Chapter 2, in the years immediately following the Partition, Partition survivors were seen as 'outsiders' and 'refugees' – as *sharanarthi*. To the survivors, this label implied lack of agency, controllability, docility and even femininity (Anjali Roy 2019). Instead, Partition survivors argued – and continue to assert – that they are *purusharthi* (hard-workers) who have earned their place within the new nation through their hard work and entrepreneurial cleverness. Ravinder Kaur's (2007) work shows that even an older generation of Partition survivors was reluctant to claim a refugee identity and to acknowledge the support offered by the state. Anis Kidwai's (2011) Partition memoirs note that some Punjabi newspapers objected to the description of Punjabi refugees as *sharanarthi*. The counter-argument being that they saw themselves as those who labour, as *purusharthi* (Kidwai 2011; also see Anjali Roy 2019: 202). In Lucknow, refugees constituted themselves into the '*Purusharthi* Merchant Association' while protesting for the allotment of shops in the years following the Partition (Anjali Roy 2019: 124). Through this hyper-masculine invocation of the term *purusharth*, Partition survivors sought to re-establish pride, honour and agency.

Here, the use of the Sanskrit word *purusharth* is itself revealing of a deeper political–cultural–linguistic shift that had been set in motion at the end of nineteenth century by the proliferation of the reformist Arya Samaj movement. Anjali Gera Roy (2019: 193–194) explains:

The Hindu Punjabi experienced a schizophrenic split in identifying with the Indian nation through his allegiance to the Hindu nation, which demanded disidentification with Punjabi identity, appropriated in the construction of Sikh religious identity. The privileging of the Hindu ethnoreligious over Punjabi ethnolinguistic identity demands a closure of overlapping, flexible, polysemous religious boundaries of Punjab and fluid religious practices to the adoption of a closed, unified, fixed, sanatani [orthodox] Hindu identification with the pantheon of Hindu gods who were overshadowed by the mixed saints of Punjabi villages.

Roy argues that in Punjab, the Arya Samaj's Sanskritisation drive focused on assimilating upper- and middle-class Hindus into mainstream Hinduism. This differed from other Indian regions where Sanskritisation was pursued by Dalits and lower-caste Hindus in pursuit of upward social mobility. In Punjab, the Arya Samaj's reformist return to Vedic rituals and its rejection of the Sanatan Dharam's (orthodox religion) idolatry appealed to upper-caste Punjabi Hindus as an effective response to Islamic and Sikh critiques of Hinduism's mysticism, superstition, casteism and anthropomorphism (Anjali Roy 2019). Sweeping Punjabi society at the end of the nineteenth century, the Arya Samaj movement had Sanskritised large sections of middle- and upper-class Punjabi Hindus. This provided the silent foundation for a subsequent explicit identification with Hindu nationalism and the Hindu-fold following the displacements of the Partition.

The emergence of the *purusharthi*-martyr discourse of self-making is consonant with a larger political–cultural–linguistic shift towards Hindu nationalism. The use of Sanskrit words such as *purusharth* is a product of dual positionality: the positionality of my informants as upper-caste Hindus and that of Hindu nationalism as an ideology of Brahmanical supremacy. Martyrdom and sacrifice are a key part of the latter. Thomas Blom Hansen's (2021) recent book examines how sacrifice constitutes a veritable political theology in the Indian context, featuring prominently in the philosophy of Hindu nationalism and in a ritualistic sense (as renunciation and self-sacrifice) in Gandhian non-violence.

In the post-Partition context, Hindu nationalism as ideology and discourse is particularly successful because it functions as a form of theodicy. It transcends individual and group differences, allowing for the political and cultural assimilation of Punjabi Hindus into the fabric of the new, implicitly Hindu nation. Additionally, by consecrating the death and suffering of kith, kin and co-religionists as 'martyrdom' and a 'sacrifice' to the Hindu nation, it transcends the 'uselessness' of their suffering. As a form of theodicy, Hindu nationalism reimagines such 'useless' suffering (Levinas 1988) and 'bad' death (Seremetakis 1991) as suffering *for* the nation, rather than as ambiguous futile suffering *on the way* to the nation.

The later shift from purely a discourse of *purusharth* to one of *purusharth* as a form of sacrifice is substantially motivated by a visceral feeling of *ressentiment*. Unaddressed over decades, Partition survivors' resentment towards political elites – who are characterised by their moral culpability for and indifference to the suffering of Partition survivors – has matured into the visceral *ressentiment* we have seen in this book. As a form of theodicy of the 'disprivileged' (Weber 1965: 110), *ressentiment* provides a diagnosis of the causes of suffering while voicing a demand for justice and reparations.

Finding its companion and equal in Hindu nationalist narratives of historical victimhood, it places the suffering of the Partition within a larger history of Hindu victimhood. As I have stated in Chapters 2 and 3, the *purusharthi*-martyr discourse condemns not only Muslims and the political elites who are seen to have caused their suffering but also those who are seen to have not suffered or unfairly benefitted from their hard work and sacrifices and its effect on the subsequent prosperity of the Hindu nation. In this way, they critique caste-based reservations and the various ways in which the liberal state is seen to be held hostage by liberal elites and hostile minorities.

Building on a perceived historical victimhood – one that is both constitutive and characteristic of the Hindu nation – Hindu nationalist discourses on the Partition articulate the demand for material (see Part II) and symbolic reparations (see Part III). *Ressentiment*, in this context, disguises the violence of Hindu nationalism as 'self-defence', 'retribution' and ultimately 'justice'.

Thus, remembering the Partition involves a persistent dialogue with the racial and ethnic borders of the post-Partition nation state. It is this that I have drawn attention to by asking what it means to remember the Partition in the time of fascism. This question observes not only the centrality of the Partition's memory within the politics of Hindu nationalism but also the reimagination of the past in India's Hindu fascist present. It expresses the specificity of the entanglement of a past that is reinterpreted and made politically relevant by the present and a present regime that is legitimised by a victimhood and *ressentiment* drawn from the past (Connerton 1989). Ultimately, I have used hermeneutic political anthropology to contextualise politics within the cultural crosscurrents from which they originate and that gives them meaning to the public.

In concluding this book I want to return to my discussion of victimhood and *ressentiment* to delineate its relevance to the global rise of authoritarianism. Underlying the emergence of the latter is a persistent crisis of meaning that is characteristic of what has become known as 'the Post-Truth era' (Mair 2017).

Jeffrey Olick (2007) observes that the idea of *ressentiment* – that past suffering necessitates reparations – can be said to underlie modern understandings of trauma and the humanitarian idea. Nietzsche (1989: 127) understood *ressentiment* as a consequence of the fact that 'every sufferer instinctively seeks a cause for his suffering' (also see Olick 2007: 156). Nietzsche's theorisation was a precursor to and inversion of Weber's understanding of theodicy as the justification of 'good fortune' as 'legitimate fortune' (see Chapter 2). Nietzsche branded *ressentiment* the 'fullest realization of slave morality'. Olick explains:

> Nietzsche points out, there is a close connection in German between the words for *guilt* (*Schuld*) and for *debt* (*Schulden*). The sense of guilt that slave morality foists on the world (*'bad conscience'*) developed in relation to the idea that every injury has its equivalent and that it can, in some way, be paid back, an idea rooted in the contractual, material relationship between creditor and debtor. (156)

For Nietzsche, this 'memory of injury' (trauma?) is inhibitive to progress particularly for the victim who is held hostage by their past and its psychic wounds. An individual suffering from *ressentiment* becomes an 'angry spectator of all that is past' and 'cannot break time's covetousness' (Nietzsche quoted in Olick 2007: 156). *Ressentiment* also simultaneously burdens the perpetrator by making them subject to 'illegitimate' moral claims. Nietzsche was unequivocal in his denunciation of claims for reparations, redress and regret as thoroughly illegitimate. According to him, such a politics 'seek[s] a compensation that will never be adequate' while making itself a 'slave' to an unchangeable past. The illegitimacy of *ressentiment*, for Nietzsche, lies in its deceit, in the way that it disguises revenge, anger and jealousy as 'justice'. For Nietzsche, *actual* anger and hatred are infinitely more moral due to the honesty of their expression (156).

Today, Nietzsche's extreme moralisation of the politics of reparation and humanitarianism would be regarded as a form of 'virtue signalling'. Virtue signalling refers to a narcissistic, self-righteous and moralising discourse that denigrates another's politics while establishing a dubious moral high ground for the speaker. While I do not agree with Nietzsche's virtue signalling, I do agree with his recognition of the inadequacy of reparations as redressal for human suffering. After all, when dealing with death and suffering on the scale of something like the Holocaust or the Partition, how does one put a price on adequate reparations? How might we ever hope to compensate these survivors for the death of their kith and kin, for the pain of displacement, for the interruption of a social world?

But, in the case of the Partition, survivors do articulate a price. They demand the restoration of their former wealth and privilege; they demand the status of 'freedom fighters' and 'martyrs' to the nation; and they demand the genocide of their 'racial enemy' as retribution for past suffering: *an eye for an eye and a tooth for a tooth*. However, having engaged with the suffering and trauma of Partition survivors, we can also understand their *ressentiment*.

For example, when Bhanwarilal mourns the suffering of the Partition and demands reparations, we can empathise with his pain and recognise its 'humanity'. Our empathy with his *ressentiment* in this context is located in our acknowledgement of the humanitarian ideal underlying it – a connection between *ressentiment* and humanitarianism that Nietzsche and Max Scheler too have observed before us (Olick 2007). In demanding adequate compensation for their suffering and displacement, my informants articulate the familiar discourse of human rights.

Yet, at the same time, given that Bhanwarilal and my other informants legitimise retributive genocide and Hindu fascism as reparations for the Partition, this very same empathy with their suffering is experienced as a troubling dissonance. Genocide and fascism – anti-humanitarian to their core – here seem to draw on the very same politics of reparations that underlies the international human rights regime. Where I, and other left-leaning academics, would generally be in favour of reparations for slavery and colonialism, here, the very same discourse appals us. The victimhood of Partition survivors implores us to take cognisance of their *ressentiment* even as their support for retributive violence unsettles and disgusts us.

This conflicting emotional response along with the deliberate disinformation and reflexive revisionism by Hindu nationalist organisations and their supporters in this context comprises the crisis of meaning in this context. Ultimately, as we deconstruct narratives of violence and memories of the pre-Partition period, we find ourselves wondering who is a victim and who the aggressor.

The relevance that this question acquires has much to do with how we treat suffering and victimhood in society. Kleinman, Das and Lock (1997) remind us of the social dimension of suffering. Not only is suffering fundamentally a 'social experience', but that suffering also has 'social use' (ix–xi). In this way, suffering – as experience, memory, representation and politics – not only is intimately connected to existing cultural idioms of interpretation and expression (see Chapter 4) but also has political uses. As Kleinman, Das and Lock write, 'collective suffering is also a core component of the global political economy. There is a market for suffering: victimhood is commodified' (xi).

The commodification of collective suffering and the victimhood derived from it feeds into the efficacy of a larger politics of victimhood. One of the most prominent qualities of the politics of victimhood is that it somewhat paradoxically claims an apolitical space for itself (Jeffery 2006). As Laura Jeffery and Mattei Candea write, 'Victimhood can be a prime way of suspending or attempting to suspend the political through an appeal to something non-agentive and "beyond" or "before" politics, such as poverty or suffering'. Victimhood attempts to secure a political space that is paradoxically based on the negation of the political, posturing as a neutral position allegedly based on a higher moral claim (Jeffery and Candea 2006: 289).

Given victimhood's implicit posturing as apolitical, Laura Jeffery (2006) has described victimhood as an 'anti-politics machine'. Here,

Jeffery builds on James Ferguson's (1994) argument that the international development industry and its discourses constitute an 'anti-politics machine' that deliberately depoliticises deeply political questions around accountability and resource allocation. By focusing on the depoliticising nature of the politics of development, Ferguson (1994) argued that the act of and claims to depoliticisation are in fact deeply political in themselves.

Victimhood – furthered by *ressentiment* – as an 'anti-politics machine' (Jeffery 2006) compounds the crisis of meaning, in this context. On a basic level, the victimhood of Partition survivors leads practitioners of Partition oral history to frame their informants as passive, innocent witnesses of a horrific past, rather than as active and intelligent political subjects who 'tactically' (de Certeau 1984) marshal discourses of trauma, victimhood and violence to articulate a deeply political memory of the Partition (Raychaudhuri 2019). On a secondary level, this larger discourse of Hindu victimhood significantly depoliticises the violent politics of Hindu nationalism, packaging its call for 'revenge' as an apolitical demand for justice, as even 'national interest'. Framed against the victimhood of the Partition, a Hindu fascist state (with the ethnic cleansing it implies) does not appear as an act of violence or oppression but as the logical, *reasonable* completion of the Partition – the deliverance of the promised nation.

This clever appropriation of the discourses of victimhood by powerful groups and states is one of the defining features of the ongoing post-truth era. Combined with carefully organised disinformation campaigns, they muddy the waters sowing confusion such that sifting 'fact' from 'fiction' becomes a difficult task in itself. As discourses based on appeals to emotions and beliefs (of rhetoric that 'tells it like it is') resonate deeply with the general populace, we appear to transcend 'truths' and 'facts' – the allegedly stable foundations of 'modern', 'scientific' society.

Yet that is only one level on which the crisis of meaning operates. The cleverness of discourse results in a deep mismatch between the rhetoric that one hears and the actions one observes. Not only do 'facts' appear irrelevant to debates, but words themselves do not seem to mean what they should (Trend 1995). Speaking in an interview with *The Hindu*'s Social Affairs editor G. Sampath, social activist and Magsaysay

Award winner Aruna Roy eloquently summarised this crisis of meaning in the Indian context. Roy said:

> But today, the 'emergency' is with doublespeak: the rhetoric talks about what you like to hear but the substance goes against everything you value. In this kind of nebulousness, it is always more difficult to get people together because many hear only the rhetoric. (Aruna Roy quoted in Sampath 2018)

Roy's mention of the Emergency is a reference to the Indira Gandhi era. From 1975 to 1977, Indira Gandhi invoked the 'Emergency' provisions of the Indian constitution, suspended the legislature and the fundamental rights of citizens and continued to rule by fiat. Gandhi's actions were a desperate bid to cling to power following the Allahabad High Court's 1975 verdict disqualifying her election to the Lok Sabha (lower house of the Indian Parliament) on the grounds of minor election malpractice. This was followed by a Supreme Court order forbidding Gandhi from voting in Parliament until her appeal of the aforementioned verdict had been resolved. During this period, Gandhi also found herself besieged by the rising popularity of nationwide protests led by opposition leader Jayprakash Narayan with the support of a united opposition front which prominently included the Hindu Right (Ramachandra Guha 2017).

In comparison to the 'transparency' of Indira Gandhi's declaration of authoritarianism, Modi's authoritarian regime has been characterised by an undeclared 'emergency'. Under the last seven years of Modi's rule the space for dissent and resistance has shrunk even as Modi and some of the top leaders of the BJP have paid lip service to the ideals of democracy and liberty. A nationwide spate of bovine-related lynchings has normalised violence and discrimination against Muslims and Dalits, with the indifference and tacit cooperation of state institutions (see Chapter 6).

As democracies embrace 'strong men' and as fascism is increasingly packaged as 'justice' and 'national progress', politics has become a minefield of dissonance. What increasingly seems to take its place is a fatigue with democracy (Appadurai 2017) that while scapegoating and vilifying minorities mouths a defence of its hate speech as 'free speech'.

As words dissolve into empty rhetoric, political discourse has been consumed by ontological, phenomenological and epistemological crises. We can no longer trust the meanings of words, the intentions of political actions nor even our own 'knowledge' of these processes.

Perhaps the clearest example of this has been the Modi government's enactment and defence of the CAA. As a law that links Indian citizenship to religion – an unprecedented legal development – the CAA is animated by the silent enabling presence of the memory and *ressentiment* of the Partition. However, the rhetoric and events surrounding the law present something of a case study in authoritarianism and post-truth. In the following section I detail some of these contestations around the CAA and then move on to draw broad conclusions regarding the crisis of meaning, the global rise of authoritarianism and the task of anthropology amidst these cataclysmic processes.

The CAA and the Ghost of the Partition

The CAA is a problematic law in that it links Indian citizenship with religion to fast-track citizenship appeals for 'illegal migrants' from six religious communities – Hindus, Sikhs, Jains, Buddhists, Parsis and Christians – from the neighbouring countries of Afghanistan, Bangladesh and Pakistan (Regan, Gupta and Khan 2019). The law accepts citizenship claims on the broad assumption that all of these groups face religious persecution in their originating countries. In doing so, the Act exempts these individuals from being prosecuted for 'illegal' migration. Meanwhile, all Muslims – including those belonging to persecuted communities in the neighbourhood such as the Ahmadiyas and Rohingyas – are excluded from the protections offered under this Act (Regan, Gupta and Khan 2019).

As a legislation that explicitly links Indian citizenship to religion, the CAA serves as the foundation stone of the Hindu Rashtra envisioned by the Hindu Right. Consequently, Appadurai (2019) has dubbed the CAA 'the loudest dog whistle by a ruling party since Indian independence, intended to declare Muslims as open game for any form of degradation and destruction'. The brutal lynching of over 50 Muslims and the burning of hundreds of Muslim homes and businesses during the four-day anti-Muslim pogrom in north-east Delhi in February 2020 (Ellis-Petersen 2020; Kamdar 2020; *Indian Express* 2020b) has proved the prescience of Appadurai's words.

The CAA is a curious piece of legislation in that it explicitly mentions only the three Muslim-majority states in India's neighbourhood: Afghanistan, Bangladesh and Pakistan. The focus on these three states is interesting considering that India also shares a land border with China and Myanmar and a sea border with Sri Lanka. Since Independence, India has also received refugees from these three countries. Between 1982 and 1987, India received 134,000 Sri Lankan Tamil refugees, comprising India's largest refugee population on record (Nath 2016). Tibetan refugees (officially designated as 'foreigners') number roughly 80,000 people (Purohit 2019). India's most recent refugee community, the Rohingyas, are estimated at about 40,000 people, with at least 16,500 recognised by the UN refugee agency (Ganguly 2019).

Contrary to the reality of the flow of undocumented migration in South Asia, the CAA somewhat revealingly focuses only on the three Muslim-majority states in this region. While the BJP has argued that the CAA is meant to give persecuted minorities citizenship, the Act neither mentions persecution (religious or otherwise) nor provides a legal definition for the purposes of jurisprudence. The Act merely defines a set of people whom it exempts from the category of 'illegal migrant', provided they entered the country before 31 December 2014 (Bhat 2019). Kundu and Mohanan argue that by creating different channels whereby citizenship can be sought on the basis of one's religion and country of origin, the CAA is inherently discriminatory. Instead of offering a reasonable justification for this discrimination (Kundu and Mohanan 2020), the Act only offers a crude generalisation that is neither grounded in reality nor consistent with its stated purpose (Bhat 2019).

However it is through the latter that we are provided an invaluable glimpse into the Hindu nationalist worldview. Although the CAA does not offer an explicit definition, it nevertheless articulates its makers' implicit understanding of religious persecution. By singling out six non-Muslim minorities in the only three Muslim-majority states in India's immediate neighbourhood, the CAA implicitly understands religious persecution as the 'normative function' of a Muslim-majority population. The CAA imagines religious persecution as something that affects *only* non-Muslim minorities in Muslim-majority states.

In doing so, the law envisions a Hindu India besieged by a fanatical Muslim horde. Standing alone in a deeply hostile neighbourhood, Hindu India is seen as an island of freedom and democracy in a sea of darkness. BJP leader and former chief minister of Gujarat Vijay Rupani said as much when in support of the CAA, 'Muslims can go to any of 150 countries, but there is only one country for the Hindus, and that is India' (NDTV 2019). Such discourses present India as the last refuge for Hindus, the lone bulwark of human rights and democracy for Hindus in South Asia.

Creating the perception that the Hindu (and by extension Hindu India) is in danger normalises a violent Hindu nationalism as the antidote to this problem. These discourses also feed off the Hindutva version of Indian history as a series of foreign invasions and occupations (see Introduction). This narrative of victimhood is crucial to presenting the violence of Hindutva as a form of reasonable self-defence, the 'action' to a 'reaction' (see Chapter 7). In the process, we see a larger politics of victimhood actively depoliticising the field, making a discriminatory and unconstitutional citizenship law seem a legitimate and necessary piece of legislation motivated by a higher moral concern for human rights in India's immediate neighbourhood.

In parliament, the BJP has sought to defend this law by reference to the Partition and the Nehru–Liaquat Pact of 1950. Both Amit Shah and Narendra Modi have sought to present the CAA as a correction of the failures of the Nehru–Liaquat Pact (Habib 2020), as an explicit attempt to complete the unfinished work of the Partition.

The Nehru–Liaquat Pact was a bilateral treaty signed between India and Pakistan in 1950 in response to persistent reports of religious persecution against Hindus in East Pakistan. This was followed by rioting in Kolkatta. This retributive pattern of violence was a continuation of the violence of the Partition (Daniyal 2019). The Pact provided a framework for the treatment of minorities in both countries (*Indian Express* 2019). It comprised a bilateral commitment by both parties to safeguard the minority communities within their territories, guaranteed them complete equality of citizenship such as equality before the law, freedom of movement, freedom of speech and worship, equality of opportunity and the right to serve in the armed forces and civil services. Significantly, the Pact formally untethered India and Pakistan from the concerns of religious minorities in the other's territories by stipulating that minorities must henceforth look to *their own* governments for the redressal of their grievances (*Indian Express* 2019). The Pact also allowed refugees to return in order to sell the properties they had left behind (Habib 2020).

However, Hindu nationalists have long held that the Nehru–Liaquat Pact was an unnecessary concession to Pakistan (Daniyal 2019). S. P. Mookerjee and K. C. Neogy (leaders of the Hindu Mahasabha and members of Nehru's cabinet) had resigned over their opposition to the Pact. They believed that military intervention and the complete annexation of East Pakistan was the only acceptable solution to the problem. Mookerjee was also in favour of the complete and forceful deportation of Muslims from India (Daniyal 2019).

Exhuming the ghost of the Partition, the BJP has argued that the CAA was necessitated by the fact that Pakistan and Bangladesh had not implemented the Nehru–Liaquat Pact. Prime Minister Modi and Home Minister Amit Shah were both quoted justifying the CAA as a correction of the Nehru–Liaquat Pact. Additionally, they argued that the CAA could not be seen as discriminatory because through the Nehru–Liaquat Pact, 'secular Nehru' too had considered India as a natural safe haven for persecuted Hindu and Sikh minorities (*Financial Express* 2019; *Outlook* 2020a). Habib (2020) has criticised the BJP's attempt to link the CAA to the Partition and Nehru–Liaquat Pact as a 'misleading but also a blatant falsification of history'.

The BJP has continuously countered the claim that the CAA is a sectarian law by claiming that the law is in fact meant to provide Indian citizenship to persecuted refugees. Internationally as well as domestically (in an affidavit filed before the Supreme Court), Modi's regime has defended the CAA as a matter of internal policy and as 'a reinstatement of Indian ideals of secularism, equality and fraternity', respectively (Sagar 2020). If the government and its leaders are to be believed, the CAA is a legislation that hopes to uphold human rights and, to enfranchise refugees and undocumented migrants.

A further layer of nebulousness in all this is that while in the past the BJP has consistently linked the CAA to a pan-India NRC, it disavowed these very same connections in response to the massive anti-CAA protests. The NRC is a proposed national citizenship verification exercise that would require those arbitrarily deemed as 'doubtful' citizens to appear before the state to prove their citizenship using identity documents, birth certificates, and even family lineage (where applicable).

Since the 2016 state elections in Assam, the BJP has presented the CAA and NRC combine as the 'final solution' to the alleged problem of 'infiltration' from Bangladesh (Gohain 2016). During the 2019 general elections, Amit Shah consistently vowed to eject 'illegal migrants' from the country and presented the NRC as the appropriate instrument to achieve that goal (BBC 2019). Shah also consistently linked the NRC to the CAA, making his intentions to target only Muslims clear as day. For example, in an 11 April speech, Shah said, 'We will ensure implementation of NRC in the entire country. We will remove every single infiltrator from the country, except Buddha [*sic*], Hindus and Sikhs' (Venkataramakrishnan 2019).

Shah reiterated this message on 23 April 2019 where in an oft-quoted (and memed) dialogue he exhorted his listeners to understand the chronology of the CAA and NRC. Shah said, 'First the CAB [Citizenship (Amendment) Bill] will come. All refugees will get citizenship. Then NRC will come. This is why refugees should not worry, but infiltrators should. Understand the chronology'. Shah repeated the message through his Twitter handle on 1 May 2019 as he tweeted, 'First we will pass the Citizenship Amendment bill and ensure that all the refugees from the neighbouring nations get the Indian citizenship. After that NRC will be made and we will detect and deport every infiltrator from our motherland' (Venkataramakrishnan 2019).

Hitherto Shah and the BJP's messaging was consistently clear. While the NRC would identify 'anti-national' 'intruders' (those without appropriate documents), the CAA would provide Hindus, Sikhs, Buddhists, Parsis, Jains and Christians with an additional chance at citizenship through naturalisation, a failsafe (Anand 2019). The sole exclusion, Muslims, would be deported or incarcerated long term in detention centres, consequently disenfranchising Muslims en masse across India.

However, following the massive anti-CAA protests – which were led by all sections of society and also replicated globally (Acharjee 2020; Deol 2020) – Modi and the BJP changed tack. In an attempt to confuse and pacify, Modi claimed that there had been no discussion of a pan-India NRC. Addressing a rally in Delhi on 22 December 2019, Modi said:

> After the formation of my government, from 2014 till this day, I want to tell the 130 crore citizens of the country, there has been no discussion on the word NRC. There hasn't even been any talk [about it]. Only, after the Supreme Court said so, it [the NRC] had to be done for Assam. What are you talking about? Lies are being spread. (Prime Minister Narendra Modi quoted in Anand 2019; Mathew and Rajput 2019)

Ironically, it was Modi's own statement that was a blatant lie. Although the ongoing NRC in Assam (one that is specific to that state) has emerged out of the Assam Accord of 1985 and been resumed by the Supreme Court of India (Anupama Roy 2019), the BJP, under Modi and Shah, was quick to turn the NRC into a regional and national electoral issue (Kundu and Mohanan 2020). This is due to the effectiveness of the discourse.

The spectre of undocumented migration from Bangladesh serves as an effective dog whistle for larger Hindu nationalist demographic anxieties. Using rumours, disinformation and dubious readings of the 2011 religious census (*Financial Express* 2015), the BJP and right-leaning academics such as Udayon Misra (2016) have assumed a direct correlation between the rise of Muslims in Assam and undocumented migration from Bangladesh (Gohain 2016). BJP leaders have alleged that anywhere between 20 and 80 million 'illegal' Bangladeshi migrants currently reside across India. This despite the fact that the Indian government has gone on record to admit that it has no official figures for the number of Bangladeshi migrants in India (BBC 2020). Moreover, recent data released by India's Border Security Force and National Crime Record Bureau have shown that since 2017, more undocumented migrants have been caught leaving for or returning to Bangladesh than entering India (Vijaita Singh 2020).

If my detailed exposition on the CAA and NRC leaves my readers feeling confused, disoriented and fatigued, then that is something of a deliberate performative element of my discussion of the crisis of meaning. It is through this strategy of deliberate obfuscation through rhetoric, rumour, dog whistles, misinformation and double-speak that the BJP has been successful in deflating some of the opposition to the CAA and its larger Hindu fascist project. Where in other times this Nuremberg-like legislation that writes Hindu supremacy into law might have been met with an immediate loss of confidence in the prevailing regime, the CAA has been met with opposition, yes, but also confusion, disinterest and even celebration.

This was visible especially in the aftermath of the Delhi pogrom of February 2020, an anti-Muslim pogrom that was a violent reactionary Hindu nationalist response to the anti-CAA protests (I. Ahmad 2020). The violence in north-east Delhi was instigated by BJP leader Kapil Mishra and openly executed by organised mobs of Hindutva 'activists' with the complicity of the police (Bedi 2020; Dwivedi 2020; *Hindustan Times* 2020). However, under the direction of the BJP-controlled Home Ministry, the Delhi Police has worked tirelessly to present the anti-CAA protestors as the 'real' conspirators of the pogrom. The result is that the very pogrom that disrupted and killed the anti-CAA movement is now being paradoxically blamed on the leaders and organisers of this movement (Lalwani 2020; Pasha 2020).

A similar campaign of misinformation and defamation was staged against India's protesting farmers. These protests began on a national scale in November 2020 in response to the passage of three controversial farm laws that threatened to significantly shrink the incomes of farmers and usher in a corporate takeover of Indian agriculture. Farmers marched on Delhi on 27 November 2020 and were halted at the city's borders through brutal police repression (A. Pandey 2020). The ensuing year-long siege was a carnival of resistance.

However, rather than take notice of the concerns of farmers, the Modi government, backed by a pliant electronic media, went on an information blitz aimed at presenting the new laws as long-pending 'reforms' that would significantly improve the lives of Indian farmers

(Bal 2020). The government also sought to undermine the legitimacy of the protests by portraying the large presence of Punjabi farmers as evidence of the movement's Khalistani affiliation. Ultimately, the strength and perseverance of the protests – along with the cloud they threatened to cast over state elections in Punjab and Uttar Pradesh – forced the government to withdraw the farm laws. Yet even as Modi conceded defeat, he lamented that he had been 'unable to convince farmers' (Ellis-Petersen 2021), posing as a patronising patriarch who had failed to reason with his misled children.

But, what do these mass movements and their encounters with the quagmire of post-truth politics have to do with the anthropologist? Everything.

A Crisis of Meaning! Post-Truth! But What's New?

So how does one make sense of all this? How does one read through the layers of nebulousness, these claims and counter-claims to victimhood? But also, is it not natural for politicians to lie? What makes *this* crisis different? And, is this crisis of meaning – this era of post-truth – unique to our times?

In the enduring resonance of the affective registers of 'belief' and 'faith' in the post-truth era, a Weberian might read further posthumous validation of Weber's (1965, 2013) life work. After all, Weber's core thesis combined political-economic sociology with the sociology of religion to observe patterns of religious thought within the 'modern' processes of nationalism and capitalism. According to Weber the genesis of capitalism drew heavily on Protestant ethics.

Within the post-truth era's crisis of meaning, we can observe the resonance (or resurgence) of claims to 'faith' and 'belief' that distinctly smack of the theological. The resemblance is heightened by the religious nature of the nationalisms of our times, be it Modi's Hindu nationalism or Trump and Bolsonaro's evangelical white nationalism. Authoritarian regimes and movements in other global contexts such as Poland, the deep states of the Middle East (including Israel), Turkey, Sri Lanka and Myanmar, to name a few, can be similarly characterised by a visibly religious strain of ultra-nationalism. In other contexts, such as the UK, where religious nationalism does not explicitly characterise conservative discourse, a particular strain of 'secular' cultural Christianity is nevertheless implicit.

Indeed, just as the 'traditional' appears to be salient within the 'modern', so too the crisis of meaning appears to be salient within the rise of authoritarianism. German philosopher Edmund Husserl (1970) appears to have been among the earliest to have raised the spectre of the crisis of meaning through his book *The Crisis of European Sciences and Transcendental Phenomenology: An Introduction to Phenomenological Philosophy* (Učník 2016). Writing in 1936, Husserl was concerned about the rise and consolidation of fascism in Europe, particularly in Germany. Husserl saw the rise of fascism as the victory of 'irrationalism' in the heart of Europe: a 'modern' society with a tradition of 'rational inquiry' (1). By announcing a perceived crisis of meaning, Husserl sought to draw attention to the problem of how the principles of 'objectivity' and 'rationality' that appeared to drive scientific progress seemed to gain so little purchase in other areas of society. As L'Ubica Učník frames it, the key problem occupying this crisis of meaning and Husserl's thought was 'the question of what constitutes knowledge and how objective knowledge relates to the meaning of the world and human subjective existence' (2).

In anthropology, this line of reflexive questioning has manifested in a persistent epistemological crisis that we now know as the crisis of representation. The crisis of representation has sought to problematise the epistemology of anthropology by asking to what degree anthropological truths may be considered 'real' truths (Maynard and Cahnmann-Taylor 2010). The crisis of representation emerged in the 1980s through the work of James Clifford (1986), Johannes Fabian (2002) and George Marcus and Michael Fischer (1986). Clifford (1986), in particular, drew attention to ethnography's lack of representativeness due to its tendency to produce abstractions and partial truths far detached from the lived experience of its subjects (also see Stanley 1996). Similarly, Fabian (2002) argued that anthropology's 'schizochronic' use of time was to blame for its 'othering' and unrepresentative representations. The anthropologist's figurative detachment, Fabian argued, hierarchically distances the anthropologist from their subject in place and time. It places the anthropologists and their readers in a detached, privileged timeframe while confining the 'other' to the past, a 'stage of lesser development' wherefrom the 'other' can be studied in its 'natural' and 'primitive' state (Bunzl 2002: xi). Fabian (2002) directly connected this tendency to anthropology's colonial past, and consequently, the history of unequal power-relations between researchers and their informants.

How might we then understand these crises? Or better yet, how might we subvert and overcome them? How do we as anthropologists show up for work amidst the epistemological, ontological and phenomenological crises that characterise the discourse of our times? There are two levels on which I propose to address these questions.

The first of these is by deconstructing a certain sense of surprise that comes across in the academic 'discovery' of these crises. For example, at the heart of Husserl's (1970) announcement of the crisis of meaning lies a certain surprise at the discovery of 'irrationality' within 'rational', 'modern' Europe. It is Husserl's inability to reconcile fascism with European modernity that leads him to proclaim this crisis. However, as I have shown in this book, fascism (and religious nationalism) is a product of modernity that adopts, co-opts and appropriates the sciences and technologies of modernity as much as it draws on a nostalgic imagination of history and tradition.

Therefore, if Husserl is unable to reconcile the rise of fascism with European modernity, then that has much to do with a certain colonial, Euro-American imagination of Europe and its place in the world. It is this conception of European modernity that Aimé Césaire (1972) eloquently admonished in his seminal essay *Discourse on Colonialism*. Césaire saw Nazism as the logical end-point of European modernity and the colonial encounter. For Césaire, fascism was merely colonialism done at home, in Europe.[1] Thus, seen in another light, the crisis of meaning at least partly appears to be a product of the shattering of self-aggrandising, narcissistic notions of one's own perceived modernity. Here, we would do well to heed Bruno Latour's (1993) reminder that *We Have Never Been Modern*.

To clarify, I am not arguing that the crisis of meaning is not real, but rather that a substantial strain of academic discourse on it goes no further than a myopic exclamation of surprise at the dissonant shattering of a particular Euro-American conception of Western modernity: a shock at the realisation of the incompleteness of the West's 'modernity'. As the rise of authoritarianism with its regime of post-truth and democracy fatigue takes hold in allegedly 'healthy' Western democracies (Appadurai 2017), they are forced to confront the 'irrationality' that self-conceptions of modernity disguise. As a racist demagogue wins the US presidential election while boasting of having 'grabbed pussies'; as he enjoys the unconditional support of his base while propounding a political culture of nepotism, unaccountability, bigotry and scapegoating; the 'modern' West is forced to confront its own 'tribalism'. This is one level at which the crisis of meaning feels jarring.

My identification of Eurocentrism in the academic response to the crisis of meaning is also tangentially evocative of Lila Abu-Lughod's (1991) critique of the crisis of representation. Abu-Lughod critiques the crisis of representation for the lack of attention Marcus and Fischer (1986) give to the issue of positionality. Abu-Lughod (1991) argues that anthropological truths are not only *partial truths* but also *positioned truths*. The crisis of representation neglects to consider the different dialogical complexities that confront 'halfie', native and feminist anthropologists in the field. Assuming a complete separation between the self that studies and the 'other' that is studied, much of the crisis of representation discourse is based on a Euro-American conception of anthropology and its practitioners.

Much like with the crisis of meaning, here too, Eurocentrism inhibits analysis, producing the partial diagnosis of a real problem. Yet, at the core of this pervasive Eurocentrism lies an essentialist view of the world. I am specifically drawing attention to essentialism in this context, to link this discussion back to Marilyn Strathern's (1992) critique of the impoverishment of the Euro-American imagination of 'society'. As stated previously in Chapter 7, Strathern has shown that the Euro-American idea of society is built on the imagination of homogeneity such that national societies are analogised to a single individual body. Homogenous, undifferentiated and held to be static over time, these big imagined collectivities rely on the logic of essentialism (Strathern 1992). This is as true of nation states that marshal history and archaeology to present themselves as eternal facts (Balibar 1992; Herzfeld 1992) as it is of religious communities (van der Veer 1994; Thapar 1996, 2015) and even imaginative conceptions of geography such as the ideas of 'Europe', 'America' and the 'West' (Said 1978; Wolf 1982).

Therefore, for the anthropologist working amid the world's authoritarianisms, its crisis of meaning and the crises within their own discipline, an increased attention to the specificities of one's context appears the only way out, a stormy crossing through the heart of the epistemological muddle as de Certeau (1984) would have it (Highmore 2007). The task of the anthropologist then is to unsettle the essentialisms of our time, rigorously challenging the masks that hide the particularities of our reality. This is as much a call to do better anthropology as it is born out of the imperative to make sense of violence.

This is what I have done in this book. By wading directly into starkly polarised debates on nationalism and belonging, I have used the memories of the Partition as a springboard for the examination of these urgent political and epistemological contestations in the South Asian context. Chief among these has been my problematisation of the Hindu-fold. Through a detailed examination of my informants' memories of violence along with relevant historical and ethnographic literature on South Asia, I have drawn attention to the shifting boundaries of the Hindu-fold (see Chapter 7). Drawing on the work of Das (2007), Feldman (1997), Misri (2014) and G. Pandey (2001), I have shown how the Hindu-fold is performed, sustained and maintained through the generous use of violence – violence that serves simultaneously as a call to arms and a warning to enemies and non-participants (Banaji 2018; Sarkar 2002).

The anti-essentialist direction of my research is also influenced by Arjun Appadurai's (1998) insights on the connections between 'vivisectionist violence' and globalisation (see Introduction). Appaduraiposits 'vivisectionist violence' as a response to the 'uncertainty' of globalisation. The modern state, with its technologies of population management and large-scale identities, disappears the individual within these broad, abstract labels (Appadurai 1998). Against this uncertainty – to essentialise that which seems fluid, fragile, unstable and thereby 'pollutable' (Douglas 1984) – this kind of gory, proximate, bodily violence seeks to establish a gruesome form of certainty: 'dead certainty'. It seeks to locate and stabilise in the body of the 'other' that which globalisation unsettles in society (Appadurai 1998: 919; also see Ghassem-Fachandi 2010).

Additionally, in the case of Hindu nationalism, it is the essentialism of a timeless, victimised Hindu nation that gives *sense* to its *ressentiment*. It is only when one imagines the Hindu nation as a timeless monolith victimised by its racial and ethnic 'other', the Muslim nation, that the contemporary violence of Hindu nationalism makes sense. It is only when an essentialised conception of the Muslim collectivity is held as the 'other' and oppressor of a similarly essentialised Hindu collectivity that revenge against Muslims anywhere in the present for the 'sins' committed by Muslims anywhere in the past *makes sense* (Sarkar 2002). For the Hindu nationalist, revenge emerges as a 'mobile concept' that dissolves temporality. As Tanikar Sarkar writes:

> [T]he Muslim of today embodies all past offences and future threats that have been allegedly committed and could be committed. Therefore, revenge may be taken on any Muslim anywhere for anything that any Muslim could do or [has] done.... Even Muslims of the past must pay for what Muslims of the present are doing, just as Muslims of the present are paying for the past. (2874)

Thus, as Sarkar's stark summation of the logic of the 'retributive' violence of Hindu nationalism shows, it is the imagination of an eternal, essentialised Hindu collectivity – alongside a similarly essentialised Muslim collectivity – that gives *sense* to this discourse. However, as Peter van der Veer (1994) has shown, Hinduism and Islam – as religions, collectivities and communities – are mere illusions that mask diverse and often contradictory religious discourses, traditions, sects and castes. Van der Veer's (1994) work demonstrates Hinduism and Islam (and similarly other religions) for the illusions that they are – abstracted large-scale labels that loosely hold together a remarkably diverse constellation of racial and ethnic groups, as well as spiritual traditions and cosmologies. Attack this essentialism and you destroy the very foundation that foregrounds the imagination of these nations: these abstractions. Here, I would also include the *nomos* – whose failings require rationalisation through theodicy – as another one of these abstractions that needs challenging.

Framed against this context, the anthropologist's problematisation of the common-sense essentialisms of our times becomes a powerful tool for the mobilisation of an effective anti-fascist politics. An explicitly anti-essentialist ethnography in this context not only speaks truth to power but also provides an account of violence – as I have done – that pays attention to the specificities of violence, including those violent acts considered 'not violence'.

The second and final level on which I wish to engage with the crisis of meaning is by sketching its relation to the limits of ethnonationalism. In her book *Hindu Wife, Hindu Nation*, Tanika Sarkar (2010) draws our attention to the limits of 'communalism' (ethnonationalism). Sarkar writes that it is important to remember that ethnonationalism – or the politics of hate in general – cannot articulate its authentic and specific agenda. The agenda is to redraw the boundaries of religious identity and national community in exclusively antagonistic and vindictive terms. Sarkar argues that due to the explicitly violent nature of this project, hate can never identify itself as such. She concludes that 'deprived of the exact words of its enterprise, it can only live as a parasite' (272).

Because it can only exist as a parasite on the margins of discourse, this kind of politics needs the conditions of post-truth in order to flourish. Unable to articulate that to which it truly aspires, its leaders instead create, settle for and depend on disinformation, dog whistles and euphemisms to spread their message of hate and violence. They are forced to disguise their calls to mass incarceration, violence and genocide as reactions to economic concerns or as 'reasonable concerns' surrounding immigration and 'overpopulation'. This is why the language of economic nationalism has become the far-right's most trusted tactic, one that has consequently yielded rich electoral dividends. This crisis of meaning, this period of post-truth then is deliberately created and nurtured by a politics of hate that despite thriving under democracy fatigue nevertheless finds itself unable to express that which is truly in its heart.

Disinformation, confusion and equivocation then are as much a deliberate strategy as they are an inability to fully air the *true* nature of one's political project, lest it trigger a definitive backlash. This is because the minute hate and violence identifies itself for what it is, and so it loses its ability to survive in this nebulous popular 'democratic' form.

Seeing their blood-stained hands for what they are, people are likely to recoil from it in disgust, enough of them anyway to disrupt the careful electoral arithmetic that manufactures the far-right's slim electoral majorities.

While the reader might interpret this as a form of theodicy – one that expresses an undying faith in the innate goodness of humanity – disgust at the violence of one's collectivity is not without historical precedent. The resounding cries of 'Never Again' that followed the revelation of the full extent of the Holocaust and American disgust at the revelation of the violence of their own troops during the Vietnam War are some examples of how the public revelation of violence – revelations that force reflection on one's own complicity in the suffering of others – can overturn public support for regimes and wars.

In the Indian context, the aftermath of Mahatma Gandhi's assassination in 1948 shows that India too is capable of being disgusted by Hindu nationalism. Gandhi's assassination by the Hindu nationalist terrorist Nathuram Godse provoked a state-led period of disgust at the violent nationalism of the RSS. The entrenchment of the narrative that Hindu nationalism (or communalism) was not nationalism can be seen as one of the most enduring consequences of this event. In Delhi, where the assassination occurred, the event significantly deescalated violence (Menon and Bhasin 1998; Ramachandra Guha 2018). As large crowds gathered to mourn and witness Gandhi's funeral procession, India and Pakistan were briefly forced to confront the human cost of extreme nationalism (Ramachandra Guha 2018). An unfortunate and unintended consequence of this was the suppression of the memory of the Partition. Too shameful to be shared, too painful to be confronted, the violence and the suffering of the Partition were temporarily consigned to silence, overshadowed by a greater – and narratively simpler – 'national trauma' (Debs 2013).

With the CAA and NRC, the BJP appears to be fast approaching the limits of its ethnonationalist discourse. So close to achieving the Hindu fascist state it has always dreamed of and yet unable to clearly articulate its dream, the BJP is forced to play the long game of a gradual creeping fascism. While the CAA and NRC combination clearly articulated the ruling party's fascist designs, the massive nationwide anti-CAA movement showed that it was too much too soon. As stated previously, the unexpected strength of the movement forced Modi to deny the link between the two policies (Anand 2019). Under pressure to back down and yet unable to do so, the BJP found itself caught between satisfying the bloodlust of its hard-core supporters while also somehow convincing its moderate followers as well as an increasingly united opposition of the goodness of the law's intentions. The result was a post-truth prime minister caught in a web of his own lies and inconsistencies. For a brief period between December 2019 and February 2020, Modi seemed to have been cornered. The recent success of the year-long Farmer Protests has definitively shown that Modi and the BJP can be forced to retreat.

Writing in *The Washington Post* in December 2019, Rana Ayyub (2019b) was among those journalists and observers who wondered if India's anti-CAA movement could be a 'tipping point' against authoritarianism in India. Author and journalist Kapil Komireddi stuck out his neck to argue that since '[i]n 2014 India was the first democratic country to succumb to this wave of populism … now India will be the first country that will show the way to reclaim democracy from the clutches of these thugs' (Komireddi quoted in Ellis-Petersen 2019).

Although India is far from finding its way out of authoritarianism, Komireddi's prophecy appears to have been indirectly realised in the United States. On 25 May 2020, George Floyd, a 46-year-old African-American resident of Minneapolis was publicly lynched by officers of the Minneapolis Police Department (*New York Times* 2021). Floyd's murder unleashed a veritable revolution with massive Black Lives Matter protests and marches sweeping the United States, reviving a long-running debate on police brutality and racial injustice (Johnson 2020). Braving COVID-19 lockdowns and brutal police repression, a critical mass of American people (especially black women) stood their ground asking for police reforms and an end to institutionalised racism. Trump's racist and insensitive response to the protests (as well as his mishandling of the COVID-19 pandemic) served only to fuel public anger against his administration.

This wave of Black Lives Matter protests that swept the United States in the summer of 2020 closely resembled the anti-CAA protests but with one crucial difference: unlike in India, Black Lives Matter protests were six months before rather than *after* the national election. The literal and symbolic feeling of asphyxiation experienced by large sections of society in Trump's America – which these historic protests articulated – transformed the 2020 American Presidential election into an existential fight. This (rightful) anger at and fear of the possibility of another four years of a poorly disguised white supremacist administration was expressed at the ballot box through a historic mandate for Joe Biden. The Biden–Harris ticket received the highest votes ever garnered by a ticket in American history and received as much as 87 per cent of the black vote (Albright 2020).

Although Trump has been voted out of office, 'Trumpism' persists. All that his electoral defeat appears to have achieved is the United States' return to 'some semblance of imperial "normalcy"' (Arundhati Roy 2021). With over 70 million votes cast in his favour (Renkl 2020), Trump was far from the unpopular demagogue many of us wished he were. Emboldened by the size of his mandate despite his comprehensive loss, Trump's lame-duck period was something of a case study in the limits of ethnonationalism. Unable to announce the coup he wished he could, the Trump campaign's desperate bid to cling to power was restricted to filing numerous unfruitful legal challenges based on a blatantly false narrative of a 'stolen' election (Rutenberg, Corasaniti and Feuer 2020). After all, for a politics whose idols constitute a veritable pantheon of the 'losers' of history – the Confederacy and Nazi Germany – one loss could never have sufficed!

Trump's most audacious attempt at a coup – publicly inciting a crowd of his supporters to storm the US Capitol Building – triggered a massive backlash from even within a section of his own party and support base (Parker, Dawsey and Rucker 2021; BBC 2021). Cornered, defeated, globally discredited as a would-be-dictator and having been impeached a historic second time (BBC 2021), Trump was forced to disavow any links to the storming of the Capitol. Treating the would-be-insurrectionists with kid gloves, the furthest Trump could go was to say that he empathised with them and that they must stand down (Parker, Dawsey and Rucker 2021). Deprived of the words to articulate his deepest ambitions, unable to take credit for or openly praise his supporters for championing his cause, the attempted Trump insurrection has remained restricted to a dubious victimhood narrative of a 'stolen' election. This does not make their attempts any less of a coup, but it is somewhat revealing that for all of his purported popularity, Trump cannot actually call his coup a coup, nor claim direct credit for the storming of the Capitol.

In the Trump universe and the conspiracy theories that orbit it, digitally manipulated content has sought to attribute the violence in the Capitol to 'anti-social elements' and 'antifa' (Reuters 2021). Why is this necessary? Why does the 'historically popular', 'unconditionally supported' Trump feel the need to attribute his supporters' attempted coup to their pariahs? The answer lies in Sarkar's (2010) idea of the limits of ethnonationalism. Although Trump's complicity in the violence was clear as day, the limits of the discourse prohibit him from *actually* taking credit for it. Caught between wanting to satisfy the blood-lust of their most radical esoteric supporters while also pacifying the shocked and alarmed moderates within their own ranks, Trump and the Republican Party could neither deny the logic of their violence nor claim credit for it.

However, Sarkar's (2010) idea of the limits of ethnonationalism must not be seen to portend the inevitable failure of this politics. This is not what this idea or my discussion of it is meant to do. I am not discussing the limits of fascism to provide hope or comfort. Rather, understanding that even the most popular 'democratic' authoritarianisms have limits helps better understand the dialogical complexities within which they operate. It is hoped that such academic analyses might feed into better anti-fascist thinking (Arendt 2017).

If there is any encouraging sign to be read in all this, it is this: the fact that the BJP – despite its popularity and Parliamentary majority – is forced to manufacture consent through disinformation, confusion and obfuscation shows that it is still far from acquiring a complete hegemony. And every major national protest movement, be it the anti-CAA movement or the Farmers' Protests, forces Modi to show his hand. As a cornered Modi regime is forced to abandon the veneer of democratic consent altogether, it will have also destroyed the very same nebulousness that allows it to thrive amid a fragmented, distracted and confused electorate. Ultimately, this is perhaps the only way out of post-truth, a classic insurgent strategy that forces fascism to reveal itself. Force the fascists to show their hand and hope that our better instincts prevail.

India: A Global Innovator

In conclusion, I want to return to Kapil Komireddi's observation about India having been among the first to succumb to this ongoing wave of authoritarianism (Ellis-Petersen 2019). Komireddi's words echo those of Appadurai (2019), who has similarly argued that India – courtesy Modi's Hindu nationalism – 'is not only following a global swing to the authoritarian right, it is an innovator'. That is, India has emerged as not only a conscientious student but also a global innovator of authoritarianism. Moving beyond Eurocentric analyses that see Modi as a student of Trump, Putin or Marine Le Pen, Hindu fascism must be seen as the global innovator that it is. In these analyses of global authoritarianism, it is important to challenge these orientalist perspectives that see the Orient as following in the footsteps of the Occident. The Orient is the master of its own will – in this case, fascism.

These connections are open for all to see. In Hindu nationalism's conception of India as the lone democracy in a hostile neighbourhood – implicit in the CAA – one can see echoes of the Zionist visualisation of Israel as an 'oasis in the desert'. We see an acknowledgement of the similarities between these discourses in a joint statement that Narendra Modi and Israeli Prime Minister Benjamin Netanyahu published in the *Times of India* in 2017 upon the conclusion of Modi's Israel visit. The joint statement refers to Indian–Israeli ties as a 'natural partnership', implies geopolitical similarities and identifies 'terrorism' as one of the common challenges facing both these countries (Modi and Netanyahu 2017). Islamophobia does not just divide, it also unites. Moreover, in recent times, India has adopted the Israeli doctrine of 'collective punishment' when dealing with its minorities and dissenters. This was visible in India's nearly six-month long internet shutdown – the longest in a 'democracy' – in the former state of Jammu and Kashmir (Schultz and Yasir 2020), as well as in the BJP-led UP government's repression of anti-CAA protests, which included the use of rampant police brutality, arbitrary detentions, hefty fines for the alleged destruction of public property and the 'sealing' of the properties of organisers and their communities in an effort to 'recover damages' (*Times of India* 2019; *Livemint* 2020; *Outlook* 2020b).

Relatedly, Ann Kingsolver and Annapurna Pandey (2019) have drawn attention to the similarities between Modi and Trump's economic nationalism (see Introduction). This similarity that begins in the slogans itself, Modi's 'India First' alongside Trump's 'America First' – as pointed out by Indian-American comedian Hassan Minhaj on his show *Patriot Act* (2019) – also extends to the level of policy (Kingsolver and Pandey 2019). Both Modi and Trump seek to boost domestic manufacturing of nationalistically branded goods while offering up their country's marginalised workers to global markets. The main difference between them is that while the Indian strategy is aimed at attracting multinational corporations to shift their manufacturing to India by promising them a skilled workforce, the United States has put emphasis on domestic consumption but lowered tax incentives for businesses (14).

The similarities between Hindu nationalists and American white nationalists are not merely coincidental. The Modi–Trump 'bromance' is something of a global phenomenon. This includes praise for Modi from former Trump aide Bannon, according to whom Modi is the leader of a 'global revolt' based on 'Reaganesque principles' (George 2016). On 22 September 2019, at the 'Howdy Modi' mega-rally in Houston, Texas, Trump and Modi ominously shared a stage (*Al Jazeera* 2019b). Addressing hysterical crowds of Indian-Americans, Modi broke with diplomatic convention to endorse Trump for re-election by thundering a clumsy paraphrasing of his own 2014 election slogan, 'Ab ki baar Trump sarkar' (This time, a Trump administration) (Lakshman 2020).

The Modi government has also made overtures to far-right politicians in Europe and Brazil. Brazilian President Jair Bolsonaro was India's official chief guest at the 2020 Republic Day (26 January) celebrations (*Indian Express* 2020a). In October 2019, India also hosted a controversial delegation of far-right MEPs (*Al Jazeera* 2019a). Their visit included a photo-op with Prime Minister Modi as well as a trip to Kashmir. This was two months after India had stripped Jammu and Kashmir off its autonomy, downgraded it to a union territory and bifurcated the former state. Kashmir was also reeling from an unprecedented telecom shutdown, a total internet shutdown, massive troop deployment and a near complete paralysis of the local economy (*Al Jazeera* 2019a). In this climate it was vital for the government to push the narrative of normalcy in Kashmir. Hosting these far-right MEPs in friendly interactions where they parroted the BJP's narrative of normalcy was meant to reassure domestic audiences about the situation in Kashmir and reinforce India's supposedly robust global standing.

The bonhomie between the far-right MEPs and Modi's government seemed to underscore their ideological similarities (and compatibility). Aadita Chaudhury has observed that while an alliance between European and American white nationalists and the Hindu Right seems impossible on the surface, there are significant historical and cultural connections between the two. German Nazis in the 1930s endorsed the idea that ancient India's sophisticated Sanskrit-speaking civilisation had been created by a common Indo-European ancestor: the Aryan race (Chaudhury 2018). This idea was in itself a product of orientalism (Thapar 1996), meant to resolve the anomaly of an advanced ancient oriental society by attributing its 'progress' to the 'racially superior' occident (Chaudhury 2018).

While the Hindu-Aryan myth has been a part of the Indian (Hindu) nationalist consciousness since the nineteenth century (Thapar 1996), it was Savitri Devi (born Maximiani Portas) – a Frenchwoman, mysticist and card-carrying Nazi – who used Aryan race theory to establish political and philosophical linkages between the Nazis and Hindu nationalists (Goodrick-Clarke 2000). For Savitri Devi, Hinduism was not just a religion but also the only living example of 'Aryan heritage'. She saw Hinduism as an ally in her goal to oppose the 'casteless', 'decadent' 'egalitarian' philosophies of the Abrahamic religions. It was in this context that Devi's ideas found traction in the strongly upper-caste Hindu nationalist circles of the Hindu Mahasabha and the RSS (43). For example, RSS Chief M. S. Golwalkar's (1939) autobiography expressed admiration for Hitler and Nazi Germany's persecution of the Jews.

However, in the present, it is India's advancing Hindu fascism that offers American and European far-right leaders important lessons on political strategy. Aadita Chaudhury has argued that 'Modi demonstrates to European white nationalists the possibilities and means of implementing authoritarian values and policies within the scope of secular, liberal and multicultural democracies'. Like Modi's Hindu nationalism, far-right leaders in Europe and the United States lament multiculturalism as the loss of a 'pristine', 'authentic' culture while harnessing nostalgia for a glorious past marked by racial homogeneity and/or supremacy (Chaudhury 2018).

However, in identifying these connections and similarities – historical and contemporary – I am not implying some kind of elaborate global fascist plot to take over the world. As Arjun Appaduria (2017) has observed, while many of these leaders and their politics connect and resemble each other, the connections are largely the result of accidental and partially overlapping ambitions, visions and strategies.

This contemporary wave of authoritarianism is located in the modern nation state's lack of sovereignty over its national economy. The relentless march of globalisation with its diffuse supply chains makes it impossible for the modern nation state to exercise complete control over its economy. In such a world, where economic sovereignty as the foundation of national sovereignty has become tenuous, states and leaders have turned towards cultural sovereignty. Thus, one finds economic anxieties are expressed as cultural and demographic anxieties, as fears around immigration, 'overpopulation' or 'demographic replacement' (Appaduria 2017). This is as much the use of a dog whistle necessitated by the limits of ethnonationalist discourse (Sarkar 2010), as it is a politics responding to the transformations of globalisation. The result is the complete eclipse of the nation (and nationalism) by the state, the shift towards statism (Appadurai 2021).

Ultimately, in this book I have used the memories of the Partition as the broad cultural canvas upon which I have tracked transformations of politics and power. Conducting fieldwork in the shadow of Modi's India and the normalisation of his Hindu nationalism, I have used these memories of violence, displacement and suffering to understand the discourses of Hindu nationalism. In the process, the ethnographic evidence I have presented has wider application across a myriad global contexts similarly reeling under the assault of this ongoing wave of global authoritarianism. The theory and conclusions of my book offer important conceptual tools for a deeper understanding of such patriarchal fascist regimes who worship the demagogues of our times – these daddy-like 'sons of the soil' whose individual fortitude symbolises the strength of the nation itself.

As they reach the final page of this book, readers may be drawn to wonder what the future holds for us. Does it offer hope for salvation? Or, does it promise nothing but more misery, oppression and suffering? Having studied India's embrace of Hindu nationalism closely, I am inclined to offer no hope or words of comfort. Rather than coin theodicies that promise the downtrodden political left that they may someday *inherit the Earth* – theodicies that may also soothe us into blissful passivity – I would like to conclude by quoting a poem Aamir Aziz during the anti-CAA protests.

> And you may kill us but we will become ghosts and write,
> We will write all the evidence of your crimes,
> And if you write jokes from the courts,
> We will write justice on the streets and walls,
> The deaf will hear us, we will speak so loudly,
> The blind will read, we will write so clearly,
> You may write the black lotus, we will write the red rose,
> You may write oppression on the land,
> Revolution will be written on the sky.
> Everything will be remembered.
> Everything will be remembered. (Aziz 2020; translation mine)

Note

1 In a lighter vein, we may regard the authoritarianisms of our time as colonialists whom the COVID-19 pandemic has forced to work from home.

Glossary

Adivasi	A term used to refer to the indigenous or 'tribal' people of South Asia.
Article 35A	A former article of the Indian constitution that conferred on the state legislature of Jammu and Kashmir the power to define its 'permanent residents' and to grant them special rights and privileges. This article was abrogated through the passage of the Jammu and Kashmir Reorganisation Act, 2019.
Article 370	A former article of the Indian Constitution that gave special status to the state of Jammu and Kashmir. This article was abrogated through the passage of the Jammu and Kashmir Reorganisation Act, 2019.
Arya Samaj	A Hindu nationalist cultural organisation that began as a monotheistic reformist movement within Hinduism. It was founded in 1875 by Dayananda Saraswati. The Arya Samaj strictly prohibits idol worship and believes in the idea of one creator God called 'Om'. Arya Samaj also believes the Vedas (a collection of ancient Sanskrit texts said to be the product of an ancient oral tradition) to be the ultimate source of knowledge. The Arya Samaj was also the first to introduce conversion into Hinduism as it aimed to consolidate the Hindu-fold by

converting Hindus 'back' from other religions (van der Veer 1994). Historically, the Arya Samaj has also supported cow protectionism and has close ideological links to the Rashtriya Swayamsevak Sangh (RSS) and Bhartiya Janata Party (BJP) (van der Veer 1994; Gundimeda and Ashwin 2018). In this way the organisation has played a critical cultural role in the creation of a Hindu nationalist consciousness (Gundimeda and Ashwin 2018).

azaadi	freedom
BJP	An acronym for the Bhartiya Janata Party or 'National People's Party'. The party was founded on 6 April 1980 by L. K. Advani and Atal Bihari Vajpayee. The BJP is India's foremost Hindu nationalist political party and has been in power since 2014. The BJP along with the RSS and Vishwa Hindu Parishad (VHP) comprises an important part of what is commonly referred to as the Sangh Parivar.
boli	language or dialect
brahmachari	a celibate ascetic
CAA	An acronym commonly for India's Citizenship (Amendment) Act, 2019. Passed in December 2019, this controversial amendment to India's citizenship laws grants Hindu, Buddhist, Sikh, Parsi, Jain and Christian minorities residing in the neighbouring states of Afghanistan, Bangladesh and Pakistan Indian citizenship through naturalisation provided they entered the country before 31 December 2014.
Chacha	father's brother
chowk	a traffic circle or roundabout
Dadi	paternal grandmother
Dalit	The word 'Dalit' means 'broken' or 'oppressed'. It is a word that has been appropriated by lower-caste Hindus – castes that are considered as 'untouchable' – as a powerful label of

	self-identification. Dalits are also alternatively referred to as Scheduled Castes, 'untouchables' or Harijan (men of god). Also see Scheduled Caste.
dera	settlement or colony
habshi	barbarian or savage
Hindutva	Coined by Hindu nationalist ideologue V. D. Savarkar, the term 'Hindutva' means Hindu-ness. Predictably, the politics of Hindutva comprises a Hindu supremacist nationalist ideology. In Hindi, Hindu nationalism is called Hindutva. This book often uses these terms interchangeably.
jauhar	A South Asian, Hindu practice of collective self-immolation of women – often assisted or coerced by male relatives – to avoid 'defilement' when facing certain defeat and capture in war. 'Martyrdom' by 'suicide' was seen as an 'honourable' death – one that also precluded the possibility of enslavement, sexual assault, forced marriage or any other form of humiliation at the hands of the enemy. Also see *sati*.
kara	A simple metal bracelet worn by most Sikhs. It is a sacred symbol and a sign of one's religiosity.
karam ke phal/ karmon ke phal	the fruits of one's deeds
Karva Chauth	A Hindu ritual observed by married women where they observe a fast from sunrise to sunset to pray for their husband's long and prosperous life.
Masi	mother's sister
mleccha	The word means 'foreign' or 'impure' and is specifically used by Hindus as a racial slur against Muslims.
muhajir	The term used in Pakistan to describe Muslims who migrated from India during the Partition. The word has religious connotations as the *muhajirun* are said to have been the first converts to Islam and emigrated with Prophet Mohammed from Mecca to Medina during the Hijra.

Nana	maternal grandfather
Nani	maternal grandmother
nazm	A genre of Urdu poetry that is often written in a rhyming verse; comparable to a sonnet.
NPR	An acronym that stands for 'National Population Register'. It is a census-like list of all individuals residing within the Indian state. This is the first step for the compilation of the proposed all-India National Register of Citizens'.
NRC	An acronym that stands for 'National Register of Citizens'. The National Register of Citizens uses the data of the NPR to compile a definitive list of Indian citizens. The process requires 'genuine' citizens to submit legal proof of their Indian citizenship through either 'proper' descent or naturalisation. While an acrimonious NRC drive is currently unfolding in the Indian state of Assam, a pan-India NRC has also been proposed by the BJP in order to identify and detain 'illegal immigrants'.
OBC	An acronym that stands for 'Other Backward Castes'. This is the legal term used by the Government of India to identify a number of socially and economically disadvantaged castes. This should not be confused with Scheduled Caste.
punjabiyat	A famed *nomic* idea of the inherent warmth, hospitality and friendliness of Punjabi people.
purusharth	Sometimes also spelt as *puruṣārtha*. An important concept within Hindu philosophy that defines the ethics and morals of hard work. As a philosophy that emphasises the benefits that accrue from diligent and sincere work, it is closely related to the idea of *karma*.
Ramayana	This along with the Mahabharata comprises the core of popular Hindu mythology. The Ramayana narrates the life of Lord Ram, a major deity within the Hindu religion and the politics of Hindu nationalism. Like the Mahabharata, the Ramayana

	constitutes an important treatise on culture, politics, statecraft and ethics. There are numerous versions of the Ramayana written in a variety of South Asian and South-East Asian languages.
RSS	An acronym that stands for the 'Rashtriya Swayamsevak Sangh' or 'National Volunteers Organisation'. The RSS is a paramilitary Hindu nationalist organisation that aspires to an ethnically pure Hindu nation state. The organisation is inspired by and closely resembles inter-war European fascist organisations such as the Hitler Youth. It was founded on 27 September 1925 by K. B. Hedgewar. The RSS is the forebear and titular leader of the Sangh Parivar.
Sangh Parivar	A *parivar* or 'family' of Hindu nationalist organisations. This 'family' of organisations gets its name from the 'Sangh' (organisation) in the name of the RSS. The Sangh Parivar includes Hindu nationalist political parties such as the BJP, 'cultural organisations' such as the VHP, Bajrang Dal and RSS and student organisations such as the Akhil Bharitya Vidhyarthi Parishad (ABVP) or the All-India Student Council.
sati	The now-outlawed Hindu ritual of burning alive a widow on her husband's funeral pyre.
satsang	A small religious (or spiritual) congregation that sings devotional songs and discusses scripture.
Scheduled Caste	Often abbreviated as SC, Scheduled Caste is the legal term that the Government of India uses for Dalit or 'untouchable' castes, granting them access to affirmative action policies.
Scheduled Tribe	This is the term used by the Government of India for legally recognised and protected indigenous communities. Also see Adivasi.
seva	In Sikh religious discourse, the performance of *seva*, or altruistic service, is the path to salvation. Interestingly, *seva* is the root word for *swayamsevak*

	(volunteer) in the name of the RSS. In the context of Hindu nationalism, *brahmachari seva* (altruistic service in the mould of a celibate ascetic) is believed to lead to the salvation of the Hindu nation.
sharan/sharanarthi	refuge
tandoor	a traditional South Asian clay oven
The Jammu and Kashmir Reorganisation Act, 2019	Signed into law on 9 August 2019, this constitutional amendment changes the constitutional status of the erstwhile state of Jammu and Kashmir. It abrogates the special status and powers conferred on the state under Articles 35A and 370 while also bifurcating the former state into the twin union territories of Jammu and Kashmir and Ladakh.
Urs	Urs is a festival that marks the death anniversary of a Sufi saint in South Asia. These spiritual celebrations are attended by Hindus, Muslims and Sikhs.
varnashramadharma	*Varnashramadharma* is the system of Brahmanical order that connects a Hindu person's caste (*varna*) to the duties and responsibilities (*shrama* and *dharma*) they must fulfil in life (B. Singh 2020). It promises a theodicical justification for the caste system.
VHP	An acronym that stands for Vishwa Hindu Parishad (Universal or World Hindu Council). It was founded in 1964 by M. S. Golwalkar, S. S. Apte and Swami Chinmayanand. The VHP constitutes an important part of the Sangh Parivar. The VHP positions itself as a movement that seeks to consolidate Hindu spiritual and religious discourse within a common platform. Transnationalism constitutes an important part of the VHP's cultural and political activities as it seeks to unite a single global Hindu-fold (van der Veer 1994). However, despite the cultural and spiritual veneer of the organisation, its involvement in pogroms and violence against minorities is well documented (van der Veer 1994; Mathur 2014).

watan   In Hindi or Urdu, depending on the context, *watan* can mean either 'nation', 'ethnicity', 'country' or one's 'birthplace'.

zamindar   A landowner or landlord, specifically one who leases their land to tenant cultivators. The term implies wealth as well as caste and class privilege.

References

1947 Partition Archive. (2011). *The 1947 Partition Archive*. https://www.1947partitionarchive.org/. Accessed 25 May 2020.

Abu-Lughod, L. (1991). 'Writing against Culture'. In *Recapturing Anthropology: Working in the Present*, edited by R. G. Fox, 137–154. Santa Fe: School of American Research Press.

Acharjee, S. (2020). 'England, Germany, Switzerland: Anti-CAA Protests Break Barriers, Shake the World'. *India Today*, 16 January 2020. https://www.indiatoday.in/india/story/caa-protest-world-students-international-foreign-modi-india-1637241-2020-01-16. Accessed 14 August 2020.

Ahmad, I. (2020). 'Violence after Violence: The Politics of Narratives over the Delhi Pogrom'. *The Polis Project*. https://www.researchgate.net/publication/340548697_Ahmad_Irfan_2020_Violence_after_Violence_The_Politics_of_Narratives_over_the_Delhi_Pogrom_The_Polis_Project. Accessed 24 April 2020.

Ahmad, M. (2018). 'BJP Leader in Front, Hindu Ekta Manch Waves Tricolour in Support of Rape Accused in Jammu'. *The Wire*, 17 February 2018. https://thewire.in/politics/hindu-ekta-manch-bjp-protest-support-spo-arrested-rape-jammu. Accessed 20 July 2020.

Ahmad, R. (2018). 'Renaming India: Saffronisation of Public Spaces'. *Al Jazeera*, 12 October 2018. https://www.aljazeera.com/indepth/opinion/renaming-india-saffronisation-public-spaces-181012113039066.html. Accessed 18 June 2019.

Ahmed, M., dir. (2015). *A Thin Wall*. USA: Surbhi Dewan. https://vimeo.com/ondemand/athinwall. Accessed 25 April 2018.

Ahsan, S. (2018). 'Junaid Khan Lynching: Fight Started over Seat, Caste Abuses, Says Punjab and Haryana High Court'. *Indian Express*,

17 April 2018. https://indianexpress.com/article/cities/delhi/junaid-khan-lynching-fight-started-over-seat-caste-abuses-says-punjab-and-haryana-high-court-5140058/. Accessed 2 June 2020.

Aiyar, S. (1995). '"August Anarchy": The Partition Massacres in Punjab, 1947'. *Journal of South Asian Studies* 18 (1): 13–36.

Al Jazeera (2019a). 'Why Europe's Far Right Supports India on the Kashmir Issue'. 3 November 2019. https://www.aljazeera.com/indepth/features/europe-supports-india-kashmir-issue-191102184856242.html. Accessed 4 January 2020.

——— (2019b). '"Howdy, Modi!": Trump Attends Indian PM's Rally in Houston'. 22 September 2019. https://www.aljazeera.com/news/2019/9/22/howdy-modi-trump-attends-indian-pms-rally-in-houston. Accessed 10 January 2020.

Albertson, T. (2009). *The Gods of Business: The Intersection of Faith and the Marketplace*. Los Angeles, CA: Trinity Alumni Press.

Albright, C. (2020). 'Black Voters Drove Joe Biden's Victory – and Have Offered This Country a Reboot'. *The Guardian*, 10 November 2020. https://www.theguardian.com/commentisfree/2020/nov/10/black-voters-drove-joe-biden-victory-reboot-2020. Accessed 11 November 2020.

Ali, A. (2007). *Twilight in Delhi*. New Delhi: Rupa Publications India.

Ambedkar, B. R. (2014). *Annihilation of Caste: The Annotated Critical Edition*. With an introduction by A. Roy. London: Verso.

Anand, J. (2019). 'Pan-India NRC Was Never on the Table, Says PM Modi'. *The Hindu*, 22 December 2019. https://www.thehindu.com/news/cities/Delhi/pan-india-nrc-was-never-on-the-table-says-narendra-modi-at-delhi-rally/article30372096.ece. Accessed 22 August 2020.

Anderson, B. (1983). *Imagined Communities: Reflections on the Origin and Spread of Nationalism*. London: Verso Books.

Ankit, R. (2019). 'In the Hands of a "Secular State": Meos in the Aftermath of Partition, 1947–49'. *Indian Economic and Social History Review* 56 (4): 457–488.

——— (2020). 'Bureaucracy, Community, and Land: The Resettlement of Meos in Mewat, 1949–50'. *Journal of Social History* 54 (1): 306–329.

Apoorvanand. (2018). 'Junaid's Lynching and the Making of a "New India" Beyond Recognition'. *The Wire*, 22 June 2018. https://thewire.in/society/junaids-lynching-and-the-making-of-a-new-india-beyond-recognition. Accessed 31 May 2020.

Appadurai, A. (1996). *Modernity At Large: Cultural Dimensions of Globalization*. London: University of Minnesota Press.

—— (1998). 'Dead Certainty: Ethnic Violence in the Era of Globalization'. *Development and Change* 29 (4): 905–925.

—— (2017). 'Democracy Fatigue'. In *The Great Recession*, edited by H. Geiselberger, 1–12. Cambridge, UK: Polity Press.

—— (2019). 'A Syndrome of Aspirational Hatred Is Pervading India'. *The Wire*, 10 December 2019. https://thewire.in/politics/unnao-citizenship-bill-violence-india. Accessed 20 August 2020.

—— (2021). 'How to Kill a Democracy'. *Social Anthropology* 29 (2): 303–310.

Arendt, H. (2017). *The Origins of Totalitarianism*. London: Penguin Books.

Arnimesh, S., and N. Pandey. (2020). 'BJP's List of Dynasts Is Only Growing Longer, It Now Includes at Least 11% of Its MPs'. *The Print,* 22 July 2020. https://theprint.in/politics/bjps-list-of-dynasts-is-only-growing-longer-it-now-includes-at-least-11-of-its-mps/465476/. Accessed 20 September 2020.

Ayyub, R. (2019a). 'India's Supreme Court Endorses Right-Wing Vision Relegating Muslims to Second-Class Citizens'. *Washington Post*, 11 November 2019. https://www.washingtonpost.com/opinions/2019/11/11/indias-supreme-court-endorses-right-wing-vision-relegating-muslims-second-class-citizens/. Accessed 09 August 2020.

—— (2019b). 'India's Protests Could Be a Tipping Point against Authoritarianism'. *Washington Post,* 18 December 2019. https://www.washingtonpost.com/opinions/2019/12/18/indias-protests-could-be-tipping-point-against-authoritarianism/. Accessed 19 December 2019.

Aziz, A. (2020). 'Sab yaad rakha jayega by Aamir Aziz' [Everything will be remembered by Aamir Aziz]. https://www.youtube.com/watch?v=PHk_5gEXDY0. Accessed 15 January 2020.

Bacchetta, P. (2000). 'Sacred Space in Conflict in India: The Babri Masjid Affair'. *Growth and Change* 31 (2): 255–284.

—— (2019). 'Queer Presence in/and Hindu Nationalism'. In *Majoritarian State: How Hindu Nationalism Is Changing India*, edited by A. P. Chatterjee, T. B. Hansen and C. Jaffrelot, 375–396. New York: Oxford University Press.

Bagchi, J., and S. Dasgupta, eds. (2003). *The Trauma and the Triumph: Gender and Partition in Eastern India*. Kolkata: Stree.

Bal, H. S. (2020). 'Cultivating Deception'. *The Caravan*, 26 December 2020. https://caravanmagazine.in/agriculture/modi-response-farmers-colonial-rhetoric. Accessed 27 December 2020.

Balibar, E. (2002). 'The Nation Form: History and Ideology'. In *Race Critical Theories*, edited by P. Essed and D. T. Goldberg, 86–106. London: Blackwell.

Banaji, S. (2018). 'Vigilante Publics: Orientalism, Modernity and Hindutva Fascism in India'. *Javnost – The Public* 25 (4): 333–350.

Banerjee, M. (2003). 'Partition and the North-West Frontier: Memories of Some Khudai Khidmatgars'. In *The Partitions of Memory: The Afterlife of the Division of India*, edited by S. Kaul, 30–73. Delhi: Permanent Black.

Basham, A. L. (1954). *The Wonder That Was India: A Survey of the Culture of the Indian Sub-Continent before the Coming of the Muslims*. London: Sidgwick and Jackson.

Basso, K. (1970). '"To Give Up on Words": Silence in Western Apache Culture'. *Southwestern Journal of Anthropology* 26 (3): 213–230.

——— (1988). '"Speaking with Names": Language and Landscape among the Western Apache'. *Cultural Anthropology* 3 (2): 99–130.

——— (1996). *Wisdom Sits in Places: Landscape and Language among Western Apache*. Albuquerque: University of New Mexico Press.

Bauman, Z. (1989). *Modernity and the Holocaust*. Cambridge, UK: Polity Press.

——— (1992). *Mortality, Immortality and Other Life Strategies*. Cambridge, UK: Polity Press.

——— (1997). *Postmodernity and Its Discontents*. Cambridge, UK: Polity Press.

——— (2002). 'Holocaust'. In *A Companion to Racial and Ethnic Studies*, edited by D. T. Goldberg and J. Solomos, 46–63. Oxford: Blackwell Publishing Ltd.

BBC (2011). 'Eleven Sentenced to Death for India Godhra Train Blaze'. 2 March 2011. https://www.bbc.com/news/world-south-asia-12605659. Accessed 27 May 2020.

——— (2012). 'Gujarat Report Says MP Ehsan Jafri "Provoked Murderers"'. 11 May 2012. https://www.bbc.com/news/world-asia-india-18031124. Accessed 22 July 2020.

—— (2018). 'India Police "Sorry" for Lynching Photo'. 22 June 2018. https://www.bbc.com/news/world-asia-india-44572406. Accessed 18 July 2020.

—— (2019). 'NRC: Amit Shah Vows to Eject Illegal Migrants from West Bengal'. 1 October 2019. https://www.bbc.com/news/world-asia-india-49890663. Accessed 10 August 2020.

—— (2020). 'India and Bangladesh: Migration Claims Fact-Checked'. 21 February 2020. https://www.bbc.com/news/world-asia-india-51575565. Accessed 23 August 2020.

—— (2021). 'Trump Impeached for "Inciting" US Capitol Riot in Historic Second Charge'. 14 January 2021. https://www.bbc.com/news/world-us-canada-55656385. Accessed 15 January 2021.

Bedi, A. (2020). 'Who Is Kapil Mishra? BJP Leader Being Blamed for Delhi Riots Had Once Called Modi ISI Agent'. *The Print*, 26 February 2020. https://theprint.in/india/who-is-kapil-mishra-bjp-leader-being-blamed-for-delhi-riots-had-once-called-modi-isi-agent/371226/. Accessed 15 August 2020.

Behar, R. (1996). *The Vulnerable Observer: Anthropology That Breaks Your Heart*. Boston: Beacon Press.

Benjamin, W. (2006). *On the Concept of History: Selected Writings, Vol. 4*. Translated by H. Zohn. Cambridge, MA: Harvard University Press.

Berger, P. L. (1967). *The Sacred Canopy: Elements of a Sociological Theory of Religion*. New York: Open Road Integrated Media.

Berger, P. L., B. Berger and H. Kellner. (1974). *The Homeless Mind: Modernization and Consciousness*. London: Pelican Books.

Bevan, R. (2006). *The Destruction of Memory: Architecture at War*. London: Reaktion Books.

Bhalla, A., ed. (1994). *Stories about the Partition of India, Vols. 1–3*. New Delhi: Indus.

—— (2006). *Partition Dialogues: Memories of a Lost Home*. Delhi: Oxford University Press.

Bharadwaj, P., and R. A. Mirza. (2019). 'Displacement and Development: Long Term Impacts of Population Transfer in India'. *Explorations in Economic History* 73 (July): 1–26. https://doi.org/10.1016/j.eeh.2019.05.001.

Bhargava, A. (2018). 'Sangh na hota toh paar nahin karr paate seema' [Had the Sangh not been there, we would not have crossed the border]. *Panchajanya*, 13–19 August 2018, 8.

Bhat, M. M. A. (2019). 'The Constitutional Case against the Citizenship Amendment Bill'. *Economic and Political Weekly* 54 (3): 1–6.

Bourdieu, P. (1986). 'The Forms of Capital'. In *Handbook of Theory and Research for the Sociology of Education*, edited by J. Richardson, 241–258. London: Greenwood Press.

Boym, S. (2001). *The Future of Nostalgia*. New York: Basic Books.

Brass, P. R. (2003a). *The Production of Hindu–Muslim Violence in Contemporary India*. London: University of Washington Press.

——— (2003b). 'The Partition of India and Retributive Genocide in the Punjab, 1946–47: Means, Methods, and Purposes'. *Journal of Genocide Research* 5 (1): 71–101.

Briggs, C. L. (1986). *Learning How to Ask: A Sociolinguistic Appraisal of the Role of the Interview in Social Science Research*. Cambridge: Cambridge University Press.

Bunzl, M. (2002). 'Foreword to Johannes Fabian's *Time and the Other*: Syntheses of a Critical Anthropology'. In *Time and the Other: How Anthropology Makes Its Object*, edited by J. Fabian, vii–xxxii. New York: Columbia University Press.

Butalia, U. (2000). *The Other Side of Silence: Voices from the Partition of India*. London: Duke University Press.

Butt, K. M., and B. Ahmed. (2016). 'Demand for Saraiki Province: A Critical Analysis'. *Journal of Political Science* 34 (1): 1–19.

Castaing, A. (2018). 'Poetics of Pain: Writing the Memory of Partition'. In *Partition and the Practice of Memory*, edited by C. Mahn and A. Murphy, 155–171. Cham: Palgrave Macmillan.

Césaire, A. (1972). *Discourse on Colonialism*. Translated by Joan Pinkham. New York: Monthly Review Press.

Chadha, G., dir. (2017). *India's Partition: The Forgotten Story*. UK: BBC Two. Available from BBC iPlayer. Accessed 19 December 2019.

Charis, S. (1994). *Vaisnavism: Its Philosophy, Theology and Religious Discipline*. Delhi: Motilal Banardidass Publishers.

Chatterjee, P. (1993). *Nationalist Thought and the Colonial World: A Derivative Discourse*. London: Zed Books.

——— (2002). 'Editor's Introduction'. In *The Small Voice of History: Collected Essays*, edited by R. Guha, 1–17. New Delhi: Permanent Black.

——— (2004). *The Politics of the Governed: Reflections on Popular Politics in Most of the World*. New York: Columbia University Press.

Chatterji, J. (1999). 'The Making of a Borderline: The Radcliffe Award for Bengal'. In *Region and Partition: Bengal, Punjab and the Partition of the Subcontinent*, edited by I. Talbot and G. Singh, 168–202. Oxford: Oxford University Press.

——— (2014). 'Partition Studies: Prospects and Pitfalls'. *Journal of Asian Studies* 73 (2): 309–312.

Chattha, I. A. (2009). 'Partition and Its Aftermath: Violence, Migration and the Role of Refugees in the Socio-economic Development of Gujranwala and Sialkot Cities, 1947–1961'. Unpublished PhD thesis, University of Southampton. https://eprints.soton.ac.uk/366712/1/Ilyas%2520PhD-E-Thesis.pdf. Accessed 26 July 2019.

Chaudhury, A. (2018). 'Why White Supremacists and Hindu Nationalists Are So Alike'. *Al Jazeera*, 13 December 2018. https://www.aljazeera.com/indepth/opinion/white-supremacists-hindu-nationalists-alike-18121214461 8283.html. Accessed 5 January 2020.

Chopra, Y., dir. (1961). *Dharmputra*. Film. India: B. R. Films.

Clifford, J. (1986). 'Introduction: Partial Truths'. In *Writing Culture: The Poetics and Politics of Ethnography*, edited by J. Clifford and G. E. Marcus, 1–26. London: University of California Press.

Cohn, B. S. (2000). 'Representing Authority in Victorian India'. In *The Invention of Tradition*, edited by E. Hobsbawm and T. Ranger, 165–210. Cambridge: Cambridge University Press.

——— (2010). *An Anthropologist among the Historians and Other Essays*. Delhi: Oxford University Press.

Collins, L., and D. Lapierre. (1975). *Freedom at Midnight*. New York: Avon Books.

Connerton, P. (1989). *How Societies Remember*. Cambridge: Cambridge University Press.

Cowasjee, S., and K. L. Duggal. (1995). *Orphans of the Storm: Stories of the Partition of India*. New Delhi: UBS.

Crehan, K. (2011). 'Gramsci's Concept of Common Sense: A Useful Concept for Anthropologists?' *Journal of Modern Italian Studies* 16 (2): 273–287.

Dalrymple, W. (1993). *City of Djinns*. New Delhi: Bloomsbury Publishing India.

Damousi, J. (2001). *Living with the Aftermath: Trauma, Nostalgia and Grief in Post-war Australia*. New York: Cambridge University Press.

Dandekar, D. (2019). 'Zeba Rizvi's Memory-Emotions of Partition: Silence and Secularism-pyar'. *Contemporary South Asia* 27 (3): 392–406.

Daniel, E. V. (1996). *Charred Lullabies: Chapters in an Anthropography of Violence*. Princeton: Princeton University Press.

Daniyal, S. (2019). 'The Nehru–Liaquat Pact Failed Refugees from Bangladesh – But So Would the Citizenship Bill'. *Scroll*, 11 December 2019. https://scroll.in/article/946454/the-nehru-liaquat-pact-failed-ref-ugees-from-bangladesh-but-so-would-the-citizenship-bill. Accessed 18 August 2020.

Das, V. (1997). 'Sufferings, Theodicies, Disciplinary Practices, Appropriations'. *International Social Science Journal* 49 (4): 563–572.

——— (2007). *Life and Words: Violence and the Descent into the Ordinary*. London: University of California Press.

Datta, A. B. (2019). '"Useful" and "Earning" Citizens? Gender, State, and the Market in Post-colonial Delhi'. *Modern Asian Studies* 53 (6): 1924–1955.

Datta, N. (2009). *Violence, Martyrdom, and Partition: A Daughter's Testimony*. Delhi: Oxford University Press.

——— (2017). 'Reframing Partition: Memory, Testimony, History'. *South Asia Chronicle* 7: 61–94. https://edoc.hu-berlin.de/bitstream/han-dle/18452/19506/04%20-%20Focus%20-%20Datta%20-%20Reframing%20Partition.%20Memory%2c%20Testimony%2c%20History.pdf?sequence=4&isAllowed=y. Accessed 29 August 2018.

Datta, V. N. (1986). 'Panjabi Refugees and the Urban Development of Greater Delhi'. In *Delhi through the Ages*, edited by R. Frykenberg, 442–460. Delhi: Oxford University Press.

de Certeau, M. (1984). *The Practice of Everyday Life*. Berkeley: University of California Press.

Debs, M. (2013). 'Using Cultural Trauma: Gandhi's Assassination, Partition and Secular Nationalism in Post-independence India'. *Nations and Nationalism* 19 (4): 635–653.

Deccan Herald (2019). 'India–Pakistan Partition: Films Which Depict the Divide'. 15 August 2019. https://www.deccanherald.com/national/ajit-doval-quits-sco-meet-as-pakistan-uses-map-showing-jk-ladakh-and-junagadh-as-part-of-its-territory-888034.html. Accessed 10 November 2020.

Deol, T. (2020). '"Inconsistent with India's Constitution" – San Francisco 6th US City to Denounce CAA-NRC'. *The Print*, 23 July 2020. https://

theprint.in/world/inconsistent-with-indias-constitution-san-francisco-6th-us-city-to-denounce-caa-nrc/466694/. Accessed 14 August 2020.

Desai, M., dir. (1960). *Chhalia*. Film. India: Subhash Pictures.

Devi, P. (2009). 'Theories of Causation in Indian Philosophy: An Analytical Study'. Unpublished PhD thesis, Gauhati University. https://search-proquest-com.jproxy.nuim.ie/docview/1789629144?accountid=12309. Accessed 29 December 2019.

Devji, F. (2013). *Muslim Zion: Pakistan as a Political Idea*. Cambridge, MA: Harvard University Press.

Dhillon, G. S. (2010). 'Martyrdom in Sikhism'. *Sikh Courier International* 57 (109): 35–37.

Drew, C. (2017). 'International Law in 1948'. Unpublished paper presented at 'International Law and the State of Israel: Legitimacy, Exceptionalism and Responsibility', University College Cork, 31 March–1 April 2017.

Dorn, W. A., and S. Gucciardi. (2011). 'The Sword and the Turban: Armed Force in Sikh Thought'. *Journal of Military Ethics* 10 (1): 52–70.

Douglas, M. (1984). *Purity and Danger: An Analysis of Concepts of Pollution and Taboo*. London: Routledge.

——— (1994). *Risk and Blame: Essays in Cultural Theory*. London: Routledge.

Dube, P. R. (2015). 'Partition Historiography'. *Historian* 77 (1): 55–79.

Dwivedi, S. (2020). '"We'll Be Peaceful Till Trump Leaves," BJP Leader Kapil Mishra Warns Delhi Police'. NDTV, 24 February 2020. https://www.ndtv.com/delhi-news/bjp-leader-kapil-mishras-3-day-ultimatum-to-delhi-police-to-clear-anti-caa-protest-jaffrabad-2184627. Accessed 14 August 2020.

Eaton, R. M. (2000). 'Temple Desecration and Indo-Muslim States'. *Journal of Islamic Studies* 11 (3): 283–319.

Ellis-Petersen, H. (2019). 'India: Largest Protests in Decades Signal Modi May Have Gone Too Far'. *The Guardian*, 20 December 2019. https://www.theguardian.com/world/2019/dec/20/india-largest-protests-in-decades-signal-modi-may-have-gone-too-far. Accessed 3 January 2020.

——— (2020). 'Inside Delhi: Beaten, Lynched and Burnt Alive'. *The Guardian*, 1 March 2020. https://www.theguardian.com/world/2020/mar/01/india-delhi-after-hindu-mob-riot-religious-hatred-nationalists. Accessed 14 August 2020.

——— (2021). 'Indian PM Narendra Modi to Repeal Farm Laws after Year of Protests'. *The Guardian*, 19 November 2021. https://www.

theguardian.com/world/2021/nov/19/indian-pm-narendra-modi-to-repeal-farm-laws-after-year-of-protests. Accessed 20 November 2021.

Fabian, J. (2002). *Time and the Other: How Anthropology Makes Its Object.* New York: Columbia University Press.

Faiz, F. A. (2017). *The Colours of My Heart: Selected Poems.* Translated by Baran Farooqi. New Delhi: Penguin.

Fareed, R. (2018). 'Kashmir Rape Case: The Girl, Her Family and the Accused'. *Al Jazeera*, 16 April 2018. https://www.aljazeera.com/indepth/features/india-asifa-rape-killing-girl-family-accused-180416070659470.html. Accessed 21 August 2020.

Fassin, D., and R. Rechtman. (2009). *The Empire of Trauma: An Inquiry into the Condition of Victimhood.* Translated by Rachel Gomme. Princeton: Princeton University Press.

Feldman, A. (1997). 'Violence and Vision: The Prosthetics and Aesthetics of Terror'. *Public Culture* 10 (1): 24–60.

Fenech, L. E. (1997). 'Martyrdom and the Sikh Tradition'. *Journal of the American Oriental Society* 117 (4): 623–642.

Ferguson, J. (1994). *The Anti-Politics Machine: 'Development', Depoliticization, and Bureaucratic Power in Lesotho.* Minneapolis: Minnesota University Press.

Financial Express (2015). 'Narendra Modi Govt Releases Religious Census, Muslim Population Rises 24 pct in India'. 22 January 2015. https://www.financialexpress.com/india-news/narendra-modi-reveals-religious-census-muslim-population-rises-24/33530/. Accessed 18 July 2020.

——— (2019). 'Citizenship Law Amendment Was Part of Nehru–Liaquat Pact, But Never Implemented: Amit Shah'. 17 December 2019. https://www.financialexpress.com/india-news/citizenship-law-amendment-was-part-of-nehru-liaquat-pact-but-never-implemented-amit-shah/1796694/. Accessed 18 August 2020.

Finlay, A. (2004). 'Me Too: Victimhood and the Proliferation of Cultural Claims in Ireland'. In *Nationalism and Multiculturalism: Irish Identity, Citizenship and the Peace Process*, edited by A. Finlay, 131–156. Hamburg: Lit Verlag.

Finnigan, C. (2018). '"The Kabuliwala Represents a Dilemma Between the State and Migratory History of the World" – Shah Mahmoud Hanifi'. *South Asia @ LSE*, 29 October 2018. https://blogs.lse.ac.uk/southasia/

2018/10/29/the-kabuliwala-represents-a-dilemma-between-the-territorial-ethos-of-the-nation-state-and-the-migratory-history-of-the-world-professor-shah-mahmoud-hanifi/. Accessed 22 July 2020.

Foucault, M. (2002). *The Order of Things: An Archaeology of the Human Sciences*. 3rd ed. London: Routledge.

—— (2019). *Discourse and Truth and Parrēsia*. Translated by Nancy Luxon. London: The University of Chicago Press.

Frankish, T., and J. Bradbury. (2012). 'Telling Stories for the Next Generation: Trauma and Nostalgia'. *Journal of Peace Psychology* 18 (3): 294–306.

Frykenberg, R. E., ed. (1986). *Delhi through the Ages*. Delhi: Oxford University Press.

Fukuyama, F. (1992). *The End of History and the Last Man*. New York: The Free Press.

Gal, S. (1995). 'Language and the "Arts of Resistance"'. *Cultural Anthropology* 10 (3): 407–424.

Gandhi, R. (1986). *Eight Lives: A Study of the Hindu–Muslim Encounter*. New York: State University of New York Press.

Ganguly, M. (2019). 'Rohingya Refugees Caught Between India and a Hard Place'. *The Diplomat*, 2 February 2019. https://thediplomat.com/2019/02/rohingya-refugees-caught-between-india-and-a-hard-place/. Accessed 18 August 2018.

Gaonkar, D. P., ed. (2001). *Alternative Modernities*. London: Duke University Press.

Gellner, E. (1983). *Nations and Nationalism*. Oxford: Blackwell Publishing Ltd.

George, V. K. (2016). 'Bannon Linked Modi Win to "A Global Revolt"'. *The Hindu*, 17 November 2016. https://www.thehindu.com/news/international/Bannon-linked-Modi-win-to-%E2%80%98a-global-revolt%E2%80%99/article16643923.ece. Accessed 4 January 2020.

Geva, R. (2014). 'The City as a Space of Suspicion: Partition, Belonging and Citizenship in Delhi, 1940–1955'. Unpublished PhD thesis, Princeton University. https://dataspace.princeton.edu/handle/88435/dsp01vq27zq64s. Accessed 23 April 2022.

Ghatak, R., dir. (1965). *Subarnarekha*. Film. India: Radheshyam Jhunjhunwala.

Ghassem-Fachandi, P. (2010). 'Ahimsa, Identification and Sacrifice in the Gujarat Pogrom'. *Social Anthropology* 18 (2): 155–175.

Ghosh, V., ed. (2013). *This Side, That Side: Restorying Partition.* New Delhi: Yoda Press.

Gillis, J. R. (1994). 'Memory and Identity: The History of a Relationship'. In *Commemorations: The Politics of National Identity,* edited by J. R. Gillis, 3–24. Princeton: Princeton University Press.

Gilmartin, D. (1994). 'Biraderi and Bureaucracy: The Politics of Muslim Kinship Solidarity in 20th Century Punjab'. *International Journal of Punjab Studies* 1 (1): 1–29.

——— (2015a). 'The Historiography of India's Partition: Between Civilization and Modernity'. *Journal of Asian Studies* 74 (1): 23–41.

——— (2015b). *Blood and Water: The Indus River Basin in Modern History.* Oakland: University of California Press.

Godse, G. (2015). *Why I Assassinated Gandhi?* Delhi: Farsight Publishers and Distributors.

Gohain, H. (2016). 'Assam Election Results: A Rejoinder'. *Economic and Political Weekly* 51 (36): 1–4.

Golwalkar, M. S. (1939). *We or Our Nation Defined.* Nagpur: Bharat Publications.

Goodrick-Clarke, N. (2000). *Hitler's Priestess: Savitri Devi, the Hindu Aryan Myth, and Neo-Nazism.* New York: New York University Press.

Government of India. (2019a). *The Jammu and Kashmir Reorganisation Act, 2019.* New Delhi: The Gazette of India. http://egazette.nic.in/ WriteReadData/2019/210407.pdf. Accessed 8 January 2020.

——— (2019b). *Citizenship (Amendment) Act 2019.* New Delhi: The Gazette of India. http://egazette.nic.in/WriteReadData/2019/214646.pdf. Accessed 8 January 2020.

Government of National Capital Territory of Delhi. (2020). *Dr N. C. Joshi Memorial Hospital.* http://health.delhigovt.nic.in/wps/wcm/connect/ DOIT_NCJMH/ncjmh/home. Accessed 6 December 2020.

Greenwood, A. (2019). 'Authority, Discourse and the Construction of Victimhood'. *Social Identities* 25 (6): 746–758.

Guha, Ramachandra. (2017). *India after Gandhi: The History of the World's Largest Democracy.* New Delhi: Picador India.

——— (2018). *Gandhi: The Years That Changed the World, 1914–1918.* Delhi: Penguin Books.

Guha, Ranajit. (2002a). *History at the Limit of World-History.* New York: Columbia University Press.

———— (2002b). *The Small Voice of History: Collected Essays*. New Delhi: Permanent Black.

Gundimeda, S., and V. S. Ashwin. (2018). 'Cow Protection in India: From Secularising to Legitimising Debates'. *South Asia Research* 38 (2): 156–176.

Gupta, H., dir. (1961). *Kabuliwala*. Film. India: Bimal Roy and Leela Desai.

Habib, I. (2020). 'CAA-NRC and Its Misleading Historical Context'. *Indian Express*, 2 January 2020. https://indianexpress.com/article/opinion/columns/caa-nrc-and-its-misleading-historical-context-6196201/. Accessed 18 August 2020.

Halbwachs, M. (1992). *On Collective Memory*. Translated by Lewis A. Coser. Chicago: The University of Chicago Press.

Hamilakis, Y. (2007). *The Nation and Its Ruins: Antiquity, Archaeology, and National Imagination in Greece*. Oxford: Oxford University Press.

Hansen, A. B. (2002). *Partition and Genocide: Manifestation of Violence in Punjab, 1937–1947*. New Delhi: India Research Press.

Hansen, T. B. (2021). *The Law of Force: The Violent Heart of Indian Politics*. New Delhi: Aleph Book Company.

Hasan, M. (1995). *India Partitioned: The Other Side of Freedom*. New Delhi: Roli Book.

Hashmi, R. S., and G. Majeed. (2014). 'Saraiki Ethnic Identity: Genesis of Conflict with State'. *Journal of Political Studies* 21 (1): 79–101.

Herzfeld, M. (1992). *The Social Production of Indifference: Exploring the Symbolic Roots of Western Bureaucracy*. Chicago: The University of Chicago Press.

———— (2005). *Cultural Intimacy: Social Poetics in the Nation-State*. London: Routledge.

Highmore, B. (2007). 'An Epistemological Awakening: Michel de Certeau and the Writing of Culture'. *Social Anthropology* 15 (1): 13–26.

Hill, K., W. Seltzer, J. Leaning, S. J. Malik and S. S. Russell. (2008). 'The Demographic Impact of Partition in the Punjab in 1947'. *Population Studies* 62 (2): 155–170.

Hindustan Times (2018). 'No-Confidence Motion: Modi Slams Congress, Equates Andhra Pradesh Bifurcation to India–Pakistan Division'. 21 July 2018. https://www.hindustantimes.com/india-news/no-confidence-motion-modi-slams-congress-equates-andhra-pradesh-bifurcation-to-

india-pakistan-division/story-5JuVEZWoETgRgZkHkYL8GN.html.
Accessed 20 June 2020.

———— (2020). 'Inflammatory Slogan at Union Minister Anurag Thakur's Election Meeting in Delhi'. 28 January 2020. https://www.hindustan times.com/cities/inflammatory-slogan-at-union-minister-s-election-meeting-in-delhi/story-gEQrnqiLEMRFsY4oYMOEDL.html. Accessed 15 August 2020.

———— (2022). '"Hindu Rashtra" Draft Proposes Varanasi as Capital Instead of Delhi'. 13 August 2022. https://www.hindustantimes.com/india-news/seers-prepare-constitution-of-hindu-rashtra-101660332478751. html. Accessed 14 August 2022.

Hobsbawm, E. (2000). 'Introduction: Inventing Traditions'. In *The Invention of Tradition*, edited by E. Hobsbawm and T. Ranger, 1–14. Cambridge: Cambridge University Press.

Horwitz, R. (2018). 'Politics as Victimhood, Victimhood as Politics'. *Journal of Policy History* 30 (3): 552–574.

Husserl, E. (1970). *The Crisis of European Sciences and Transcendental Phenomenology: An Introduction to Phenomenological Philosophy*. Translated by David Carr. Evanston: Northwestern University Press.

India Today (2016). 'Why Is Gurgaon Now Gurugram? A Brief History of the City'. 13 April 2016. https://www.indiatoday.in/education-today/gk-current-affairs/story/why-gurgaon-is-now-gurugram-317728-2016-04-13. Accessed 10 July 2019.

———— (2019). 'When Donald Trump Called PM Modi Father of India'. *India Today*, 25 September 2019. https://www.indiatoday.in/india/story/when-donald-trump-called-pm-modi-father-of-india-1602819-2019-09-24. Accessed 21 December 2019.

Indian Express (2019). 'Explained: The Nehru–Liaquat Agreement of 1950, Referred to in the CAB Debate'. 12 December 2019. https://indian express.com/article/explained/explained-what-was-the-nehru-liaquat-agreement-of-1950-referred-to-in-the-cab-debate-6162191/. Accessed 18 August 2020.

———— (2020a). 'Explained: Ahead of Bolsonaro's Visit on Republic Day, a Look at India–Brazil Ties'. 20 January 2020. https://indianexpress.com/article/explained/explained-brazil-president-is-chief-guest-at-republic-day-heres-how-india-brazil-are-connected-6222996/. Accessed 14 January 2021.

—— (2020b). 'Week after Delhi Violence, Death Toll Climbs to 53; 654 FIRs Registered, Say Police'. 5 March 2020. https://indianexpress.com/article/cities/delhi/delhi-violence-death-toll-6301079/. Accessed 14 August 2020.

Jain, L. C. (1998). *The City of Hope: The Faridabad Story*. New Delhi: Concept Publishing Company.

Jain, S., and A. Sarin. (2018). 'Setting the Stage: The Partition of India and the Silences of Psychiatry'. In *The Psychological Impact of the Partition of India*, edited by S. Jain and A. Sarin, 1–11. London: Sage.

Jalal, A. (1985). *The Sole Spokesman: Jinnah, the Muslim League and the Demand for Pakistan*. Cambridge: Cambridge University Press.

—— (1998). 'Nation, Reason and Religion: Punjab's Role in the Partition of India'. *Economic and Political Weekly* 33 (32): 2183–2190.

Jeffery, L. (2006). 'Victims and Patrons: Strategic Alliances and the Anti-Politics of Victimhood among Displaced Chagossians and Their Supporters'. *History and Anthropology* 17 (4): 297–312.

Jeffery, L., and M. Candea. (2006). 'The Politics of Victimhood'. *History and Anthropology* 17 (4): 287–296.

Johnson, D. (2020). 'The George Floyd Uprising Has Brought Us Hope. Now We Must Turn Protest to Policy'. *The Guardian*, 30 June 2020. https://www.theguardian.com/commentisfree/2020/jun/30/black-lives-matter-protests-voting-policy-change. Accessed 26 August 2020.

Kabir, J. A. (2013). *Partition's Post-Amnesias: 1947, 1971 and Modern South Asia*. New Delhi: Women Unlimited.

Kala, A., and A. Sarin. (2018). 'The Partitioning of Madness'. In *The Psychological Impact of the Partition of India*, edited by S. Jain and A. Sarin, 12–32. London: Sage.

Kamdar, M. (2020). 'What Happened in Delhi Was a Pogrom'. *The Atlantic*, 28 February 2020. https://www.theatlantic.com/ideas/archive/2020/02/what-happened-delhi-was-pogrom/607198/. Accessed 15 August 2020.

Kamra, S. (2008). 'Partition and Post-Partition Acts of Fiction: Narrating Painful Histories'. In *Partitioned Lives: Narratives of Home, Displacement and Resettlement*, edited by A. G. Roy and N. Bhatia, 99–115. New Delhi: Pearson Longman.

Karmi, G. (2015). *Return: A Palestinian Memoir*. London: Verso.

Kaur, R. (2007). *Since 1947: Partition Narratives among Punjabi Migrants of Delhi*. New Delhi: Oxford University Press.

Kesavan, M. (2019). 'An All-India NRC Would Turn Citizens Into Supplicants'. *The Telegraph*, 23 November 2019. https://www.telegraphindia.com/opinion/an-all-india-nrc-would-turn-citizens-into-supplicants/cid/1721575?ref=author-profile. Accessed 17 October 2020.

Khan, Y. (2017a). *The Great Partition: The Making of India and Pakistan*. 2nd ed. London: Yale University Press.

———— (2017b). 'Why Pakistan and India Remain in Denial 70 Years On from Partition'. *The Guardian*, 6 August 2017. https://www.theguardian.com/world/2017/aug/05/partition-70-years-on-india-pakistan-denial. Accessed 25 May 2020.

Khwaja, A. I., P. Bharadwaj and A. R. Mian. (2009). 'The Partition of India: Demographic Consequences'. *International Migration*. https://epod.cid.harvard.edu/publications/partition-india-demographic-consequences. Accessed 19 August 2019.

Kidwai, A. (2011). *In Freedom's Shade*. New Delhi: Penguin Books India.

Kingsolver, A., and A. D. Pandey. (2019). 'Economic Nationalism in the US and India: Comparing Strategies and Impact'. *Economic and Political Weekly* 54 (23): 1–6.

Kleinman, A., V. Das and M. Lock. (1997). 'Introduction'. In *Social Suffering*, edited by A. Kleinman, V. Das and M. Lock, ix–xxvii. London: University of California Press.

Kohli, P. (2015). 'Denial within Nostalgia: An Oral History of the Partition Accounts of the Indian Derawal Community'. Unpublished MPhil thesis, Trinity College Dublin.

Koonz, C. (2003). *The Nazi Conscience*. Cambridge: Harvard University Press.

Krafft, T. (1993). 'Contemporary Old Delhi: Transformation of a Historical Place'. In *Shahjahanabad/Old Delhi, Tradition and Colonial Change*, edited by E. Ehlers and T. Krafft, 93–119. Bonn: Franz Steiner Verlag Stittga.

Kuhn, T. S. (1996). *The Structure of Scientific Revolutions*. 3rd ed. London: The University of Chicago Press.

Kumar, A. (2018a). 'Sangh ke reeni hain hamare gaon ke zinda bacche log' [We are indebted to the Sangh that the people of our village survived]. *Panchajanya*, 13–19 August 2018, 14.

———— (2018b). 'Swayamsevakon ne maddad ki toh aaya jeewan main stay-itwa' [We found stability in our lives due to the help of the *swayamsevak*s]. *Panchajanya*, 13–19 August 2018, 16.

Kumar, R. (2020). 'Kathua, Unnao, Hathras: The Government's Hall of Shame'. *The Wire*, 2 October 2020. https://thewire.in/women/kathua-unnao-hathras-the-governments-hall-of-shame. Accessed 18 October 2020.

Kumari, A. (2013). 'Delhi as Refuge: Resettlement and Assimilation of Partition Refugees'. *Economic and Political Weekly* 48 (44): 60–67.

Kundera, M. (1999). *The Book of Laughter and Forgetting*. Translated by Aaron Asher. New York: Harper Perennial Modern Classics.

Kundu, A., and P. C. Mohanan. (2020). 'Citizenship (Amendment) Act: How Do We Move Forward?' *Economic and Political Weekly* 55 (12): 1–5.

Lakhani, S. (2017). 'A Boy Called Junaid'. *Indian Express*, 2 July 2017. https://indianexpress.com/article/india/faridabad-lynching-train-beef-ban-a-boy-called-junaid-4731198/. Accessed 4 June 2020.

Lakshman, N. (2020). 'Trouble Lurks Behind the Bilateral Bonhomie'. *The Hindu*, 27 February 2020. https://www.thehindu.com/opinion/lead/trouble-lurks-behind-the-bilateral-bonhomie/article30925385.ece. Accessed 26 July 2020.

Lalwani, V. (2020). 'Delhi Riots: In WhatsApp Group to Support Protests against CAA, Vibrant Debates about Strategy'. *Scroll*, 11 August 2020. https://scroll.in/article/969951/delhi-riots-in-whatsapp-group-to-support-protests-against-caa-vibrant-debates-about-strategy. Accessed 15 August 2020.

Laskar, R. H. (2018). 'Radical Sikh Groups Want Vatican Status for Golden Temple, PM's Apology for Operation Blue Star'. *Hindustan Times*, 27 February 2018. https://www.hindustantimes.com/india-news/radical-sikh-groups-want-vatican-status-for-golden-temple-pm-s-apology-for-operation-blue-star/story-u0AptG11mNGh5XWjTp30uK.html. Accessed 1 March 2018.

Latour, B. (1993). *We Have Never Been Modern*. Translated by Catherine Porter. Cambridge, MA: Harvard University Press.

Levinas, E. (1988). 'Useless Suffering'. In *The Provocation of Levinas: Rethinking the Other*, edited by R. Bernasconi and D. Wood, 156–167. London: Routledge.

Leys, R. (2000). *Trauma: A Geneaology*. Chicago: The University of Chicago Press.

Livemint (2020). 'UP Won't Accept Anarchy, Claims Will Be Collected from Anti-CAA Rioters for Damaging Property: Adityanath'. 19 August 2020.

https://www.livemint.com/politics/news/yogi-says-claims-will-be-collected-from-anti-caa-rioters-for-damaging-property-115978111 68842.html. Accessed 20 August 2020.

Mahajan, S. (2011). 'Beyond the Archives: Doing Oral History in Contemporary India'. *Studies in History* 27 (2): 281–298.

Mahn, C., and A. Murphy, eds. (2018). *Partition and the Practice of Memory.* Cham: Palgrave Macmillan.

Mair, J. (2017). 'Post-truth Anthropology'. *Anthropology Today* 33 (3): 3–4.

Malhotra, A. (2017). *Remnants of a Separation.* Noida: Harper-Collins Publishers.

Mamdani, M. (2012). 'What Is a Tribe?' *London Review of Books* 34 (17): 20–22.

Manto, S. H. (2012). *Manto: Selected Short Stories.* New Delhi: Random House.

Manto, S. H., and J. Ratan. (1985). 'Black Marginalia: Saadat Hasan Manto's "Siyah Hashiye"'. *Indian Literature* 28 (1): 21–36. http://www.jstor.org/stable/24158444. Accessed 20 March 2018.

Marcus, G., and M. Fischer. (1986). *Anthropology as Cultural Critique: An Experimental Moment in the Human Sciences.* Chicago: The University of Chicago Press.

Mathew, L., and A. Rajput. (2019). 'PM Narendra Modi: No Talk of NRC at All, Lies Being Spread about Detention Centres'. *Indian Express*, 23 December 2019. https://indianexpress.com/article/india/pm-naren-dra-modi-citizenship-amendment-law-nrc-bjp-campaign-delhi-6179940/. Accessed 24 December 2019.

Mathur, C. (2014). 'The Indian State, the Diasporic Hindu Right and the "Desire Named Development"'. In *Enacting Globalization: Multidisciplinary Perspectives on International Integration*, edited by L. Brennan, 13–19. London: Palgrave Macmillan.

Matra, A. (2019a). 'BJP Rally Calls for Check on Muslim Population, Twitter Reacts'. *The Quint*, 15 July 2019. https://www.thequint.com/elections/social-dangal/bjp-rally-calls-for-a-check-on-muslim-population-twit-ter-reacts. Accessed 20 July 2019.

——— (2019b). 'Don't Stoke False Fear of Muslims Taking Over India, Says Twitter'. *The Quint*, 17 July 2019. https://www.thequint.com/elections/social-dangal/dont-stoke-false-fear-of-muslims-taking-over-india-says-twitter. Accessed 20 July 2019.

Mavelli, L. (2016). 'Governing Uncertainty in a Secular Age: Rationalities of Violence, Theodicy and Torture'. *Security Dialogue* 47 (2): 117–132.

Mayaram, S. (1997). *Resisting Regimes: Myth, Memory and the Shaping of a Muslim Identity*. Delhi: Oxford University Press.

Maynard, K., and M. Cahnmann-Taylor. (2010). 'Anthropology at the Edge of Words: Where Poetry and Ethnography Meet'. *Anthropology and Humanism* 35 (1): 2–19.

McClintock, A. (1995). *Imperial Leather: Race, Gender and Sexuality in the Colonial Context*. New York: Routledge.

McLeod, W. H. (1992). 'The Sikh Struggle in the Eighteenth Century and Its Relevance for Today'. *History of Religions* 31 (4): 344–362.

Menon, R., and K. Bhasin. (1998). *Borders and Boundaries: Women in India's Partition*. New Brunswick: Rutgers University Press.

Messick, B. (1987). 'Subordinate Discourse: Women, Weaving, and Gender Relations in North Africa'. *American Ethnologist* 14 (2): 210–225.

Mishra, A. (2018a). 'Vilakshan veerta se bhare swayamsevak' [The *swayamsevak*s were filled with endless courage]. *Panchajanya*, 13–19 August 2018, 9.

——— (2018b). 'Harr paristithi main date rahe swayamsevak' [The *swayamsevak*s stood their ground in every situation]. *Panchajanya*, 13–19 August 2018, 11.

——— (2018c). 'Mussalmanon ne barbarta ki haddein paar karr di' [Muslims crossed all limits of barbarity]. *Panchajanya*, 13–19 August 2018, 17.

——— (2018d). 'Sangh na hota toh nahin bachte Hindu' [Hindus would not have survived without the Sangh]. *Panchajanya*, 13–19 August 2018, 20.

——— (2018e). 'Swayamsevak ne diya sena ka saath' [The *swayamsevak*s supported the army]. *Panchajanya*, 13–19 August 2018, 23.

Misra, U. (2016). 'Victory for Identity Politics, Not Hindutva in Assam'. *Economic and Political Weekly* 51 (22): 1–7.

Misri, D. (2014). *Beyond Partition: Gender, Violence and Representation in Postcolonial India*. Chicago: University of Illinois Press.

Modi, N., and B. Netanyahu. (2017). 'Hand in Hand into the Future: Indian PM's Visit to Israel Reflects How the Two Countries Are Working Together on Many Fronts'. *Times of India*, 4 July 2017. https://timeso findia.indiatimes.com/blogs/narendra-modis-blog/hand-in-hand-into-the-future-indian-pms-historic-visit-to-israel-reflects-how-the-two-countries-are-working-together-on-many-fronts/. Accessed 3 January 2020.

Mufti, A. (2007). *Enlightenment in the Colony: The Jewish Question and the Crisis of Postcolonial Culture.* Princeton: Princeton University Press.

Nair, N. (2011). *Changing Homelands: Hindu Politics and the Partition of India.* London: Harvard University Press.

Nair, S. (2017). 'The Meaning of India's "Beef Lynchings"'. *The Atlantic,* 24 July 2017. https://www.theatlantic.com/international/archive/2017/07/india-modi-beef-lynching-muslim-partition/533739/. Accessed 7 June 2020.

Nanda, J. (1948). *Punjab Uprooted: A Survey of the Punjab Riots and Rehabilitation Problems.* Bombay: Hind Kitabs Limited.

Nandy, A. (1990). 'The Politics of Secularism and the Recovery of Religious Tolerance'. In *Mirrors of Violence,* edited by Veena Das, 69–93. Delhi: Oxford University Press.

——— (1991). 'Hinduism Versus Hindutva: The Inevitability of A Confrontation'. *Times of India,* 18 February 1991. http://southasia.ucla.edu/social-life/various-articles/hinduism-versus-hindutva/. Accessed 24 November 2020.

——— (1997). 'The Twilight of Certitudes: Secularism, Hindu Nationalism, and Other Masks of Deculturation'. *Alternatives* 22 (2): 157–176.

——— (2007). *An Ambiguous Journey to the City: The Village and Other Odd Ruins of the Self in the Indian Imagination.* New Delhi: Oxford University Press.

Naqvi, T. (2012). 'Migration, Sacrifice and the Crisis of Muslim Nationalism'. *Journal of Refugee Studies* 25 (3): 474–490.

Nath, A. (2016). 'The Ignored Plight of Sri Lankan Refugees in Tamil Nadu'. *India Today,* 9 June 2016. https://www.indiatoday.in/india/story/sri-lankan-refugees-tamil-nadu-plight-camps-war-13168-2016-06-09. Accessed 2 July 2020.

NDTV (2017a). 'The Train That 16-Year-Old Junaid Took Is a Horror on Wheels'. https://www.youtube.com/watch?v=NNsry2Cdmiw. Accessed 4 June 2020.

——— (2017b). 'No Witnesses for Junaid Khan's Murder, CCTV of Bikers a New Lead'. https://www.youtube.com/watch?v=pEcT7rAZJwI. Accessed 4 June 2020.

———— (2019). '150 Countries for Muslims, Hindus Only Have India, Says Vijay Rupani'. 24 December 2019. https://www.ndtv.com/india-news/vijay-rupani-says-150-countries-for-muslims-hindus-only-have-india-2153952. Accessed 18 August 2020.

———— (2022). 'Bilkis Bano's Rapists Are "Brahmins, Have Good Sanskar": BJP MLA'. 18 August 2022. https://www.ndtv.com/india-news/bilkis-banos-rapists-are-brahmins-have-good-sanskar-bjp-mla-3266193. Accessed 27 August 2022.

News18 (2019). 'Year after Garlanding Jharkhand Lynching Accused, Jayant Sinha Reveals BJP Paid Their Legal Fees'. 3 May 2019. https://www.news18.com/news/india/year-after-garlanding-jharkhand-lynching-accused-jayant-sinha-reveals-bjp-paid-their-legal-fees-2127471.html. Accessed 20 July 2020.

New York Times (2021). 'What We Know About the Death of George Floyd in Minneapolis'. 12 January 2021. https://www.nytimes.com/article/george-floyd.html. Accessed 14 January 2021.

Nietzsche, F. (1989). *On the Genealogy of Morals*. Translated by W. Kauffman and R. J. Hollingdale. New York: Vintage Books.

Nihalani, G., dir. (1988). *Tamas*. Film. India: Blaze Entertainment Pvt Ltd.

Nora, P. (1989). 'Between Memory and History: Les Lieux de Memoire'. *Representations* 26 (April): 7–25.

———— (1992). 'General Introduction: Between Memory and History'. In *Realms of Memory: Rethinking the French Past*, edited by P. Nora, 1–20. New York: Columbia University Press.

Ohri, R. (2019). 'Six Convicted, One Acquitted in Kathua Rape Case; Sentencing Shortly'. *Economic Times*, 11 June 2019. https://economictimes.indiatimes.com/news/politics-and-nation/kathua-rape-case-verdict/articleshow/69720996.cms?from=mdr. Accessed 20 July 2020.

Olick, J. (2007). *The Politics of Regret: On Collective Memory and Historical Responsibility*. New York: Routledge.

Ortner, S. B. (1972). 'Is Female to Male as Nature Is to Culture?' *Feminist Studies* 1 (2): 5–31.

———— (1973). 'On Key Symbols'. *American Anthropologist* 75 (5): 1338–1346.

Outlook (2020a). '"Was Pandit Nehru Communal?" Modi Quotes First PM To Defend Citizenship Law'. 6 February 2020. https://www.outlookindia.com/website/story/india-news-was-pandit-nehru-communal-modi-quotes-first-pm-to-defend-citizenship-law/346870. Accessed 18 August 2020.

—— (2020b). 'UP CM's Nod to Tribunals to Recover Damages for Property Destruction During Anti-CAA Protests'. 18 August 2020. https://www.outlookindia.com/newsscroll/up-cms-nod-to-tribunals-to-recover-damages-for-property-destruction-during-anticaa-protests/ 1918405. Accessed 19 August 2020.

Özsu, U. (2014). *Formalizing Displacement: International Law and Population Transfers*. Oxford: Oxford University Press.

Page, D. (1982). *Prelude to Partition: The Indian Muslims and the Imperial System of Control, 1920–1932*. New Delhi: Oxford University Press.

Pai, S., and S. Kumar. (2018). *Everyday Communalism: Riots in Contemporary India*. New Delhi: Oxford University Press.

Pandey, A. (2020). '"It Is Developing as a Mass Movement": Farmers' Protest Finds Support across Society'. *The Caravan*, 13 December 2020. https://caravanmagazine.in/agriculture/farmer-protest-developing-as-mass-movement. Accessed 13 December 2020.

Pandey, G. (1990). *The Construction of Communalism in Colonial North India*. New Delhi: Oxford University Press.

—— (2001). *Remembering Partition: Violence Nationalism and History in India*. Cambridge: Cambridge University Press.

—— (2009). 'Nobody's People: The Dalits of Punjab in the Forced Removal of 1947'. In *Removing Peoples: Forced Removal in the Modern World*, edited by R. Bessel and C. B. Haake, 297–319. Oxford: Oxford University Press.

Pandey, V. (2018). 'Allahabad: The Name Change That Killed My City's Soul'. BBC, 7 November 2018. https://www.bbc.com/news/world-asia-india-46015589. Accessed 2 August 2019.

Parker, A., J. Dawsey and P. Rucker. (2021). 'Six Hours of Paralysis: Inside Trump's Failure to Act after a Mob Stormed the Capitol'. *Washington Post*, 12 January 2021. https://www.washingtonpost.com/politics/ trump-mob-failure/2021/01/11/36a46e2e-542e-11eb-a817-e5e7f8a 406d6_story.html. Accessed 15 January 2021.

Pasha, S. (2020). 'Delhi Police Chargesheet Misses Key Fact: Riots Killed the Anti-CAA Protest'. *The Wire*, 18 June 2020. https://thewire.in/rights/ delhi-police-chargesheet-riot-media-coverage. Accessed 15 August 2020.

Patriot Act. (2019). 'Indian Elections: Patriot Act with Hasan Minhaj'. https://www.youtube.com/watch?v=qqZ_SH9N3Xo. Accessed 19 August 2020.

Pinney, C. (2018). *Lessons from Hell: Printing and Punishment in India*. Mumbai: The Marg Foundation.

Portelli, A. (1998). 'What Makes Oral History Different'. In *The Oral History Reader*, edited by R. Perks and A. Thomson, 63–74. London: Routledge.

Pritam, A. (2009). *Pinjar: The Skeleton and Other Stories*. Translated by Khushwant Singh. New Delhi: Tara Press.

Puri, K., pres. (2017). *Partition Voices*. Radio program, BBC Radio 4, August 2017. https://www.bbc.co.uk/programmes/b090rrl0. Accessed 10 July 2022.

—— (2019). *Partition Voices: Untold British Stories*. London: Bloomsbury Publishing.

Purohit, K. (2019). 'After 60 Years in India, Why Are Tibetans Leaving?' *Al Jazeera*, 21 March 2019. https://www.aljazeera.com/indepth/features/60-years-india-tibetans-leaving-190319231424509.html. Accessed 18 August 2020.

Rajagopalan, M. (2011). 'Postsecular Urbanisms: Situating Delhi within the Rhetorical Landscape of Hindutva'. In *The Fundamentalist City? Religiosity and the Remaking of Urban Space*, edited by N. AlSayyad and M. Massoumi, 257–282. London: Routledge.

Rajghatta, C. (2019). 'Steve Bannon: As a Nationalist, Modi Was a Trump before Trump'. *Times of India*, 14 July 2019. https://timesofindia.india-times.com/world/us/steve-bannon-as-a-nationalist-modi-was-a-trump-before-trump/articleshow/70210775.cms. Accessed 4 January 2020.

Ray, M. (2008). 'Growing Up Refugee: On Memory and Locality'. In *Partitioned Lives: Narratives of Home, Displacement and Resettlement*, edited by G. A. Roy and N. Bhatia, 116–145. New Delhi: Pearson Longman.

Raychaudhuri, A. (2009). 'Resisting the Resistible: Re-writing Myths of Partition in the Works of Ritwik Ghatak'. *Social Semiotics* 19 (4): 469–481.

—— (2012). 'Demanding the Impossible: Exploring the Possibilities of a National Partition Museum in India'. *Social Semiotics* 22 (2): 173–186.

—— (2019). *Narration South Asian Partition: Oral History, Literature, Cinema*. New York: Oxford University Press.

Razdan, P. (2017). 'Ballabgarh Lynching: Man Who Allegedly Stabbed Junaid Khan on Train Arrested'. *Hindustan Times*, 11 July 2017. https://www.hindustantimes.com/delhi-news/ballabgarh-lynching-man-who-allegedly-stabbed-junaid-khan-on-train-arrested-from-maharashtra/story-QqD3PIWT6PcMXalBVITvZP.html. Accessed 2 June 2020.

Regan, H., S. Gupta and O. Khan. (2019). 'India Passes Controversial Citizenship Bill That Excludes Muslims'. *CNN*, 17 December 2019. https://edition.cnn.com/2019/12/11/asia/india-citizenship-amend-ment-bill-intl-hnk/index.html. Accessed 16 July 2020.

Renkl, M. (2020). '71 Million People Voted for Trump. They're Not Going Anywhere'. *New York Times*, 9 November 2020. https://www.nytimes.com/2020/11/09/opinion/trump-biden-nation-divided.html. Accessed 3 April 2023.

Reuters (2021). 'Fact Check: News Report Saying Antifa Took Responsibility for Storming Capitol Is Digitally Altered'. 7 January 2021. https://www.reuters.com/article/uk-factcheck-news-report-antifa-altered/fact-check-news-report-saying-antifa-took-responsibility-for-storming-capitol-is-digitally-altered-idUSKBN29C2ZF. Accessed 15 January 2021.

Ricoeur, P. (1970). *Freud and Philosophy: An Essay on Interpretation*. Translated by Denis Savage. London: Yale University Press.

Riggs, E., and Z. R. Jat. (2016). 'The 1947 Partition of India and Pakistan: Migration, Material Landscapes, and the Making of Nations'. *Journal of Contemporary Archaeology* 3 (2): 121–294.

Roth, M. (2012). *Memory, Trauma, and History: Essays on Living with the Past*. New York: Columbia University Press.

Roy, Anjali G. (2019). *Memories and Postmemories of the Partition of India*. London: Routledge.

Roy, Anupama. (2009). *The Caste Question: Dalits and the Politics of Modern India*. London: University of California Press.

—— (2010). *Mapping Citizenship in India*. New Delhi: Oxford University Press.

—— (2019). 'The Citizenship (Amendment) Bill, 2016 and the Aporia of Citizenship'. *Economic and Political Weekly* 54 (49): 1–13. https://www.epw.in/journal/2019/49/perspectives/citizenship-amendment-bill-2016-and-aporia.html. Accessed 30 July 2020.

Roy, Arundhati. (2021). 'Arundhati Roy: Our Battle for Love Must Be Militantly Waged – and Beautifully Won'. *Scroll*, 30 January 2021.

https://scroll.in/article/985529/arundhati-roy-our-battle-for-love-must-be-militantly-waged-and-beautifully-won. Accessed 10 February 2021.

Rutenberg, J., N. Corasaniti and A. Feuer. (2020). 'Trump's Fraud Claims Died in Court, but the Myth of Stolen Elections Lives On'. *New York Times*, 26 December 2020. https://www.nytimes.com/2020/12/26/us/politics/republicans-voter-fraud.html. Accessed 10 January 2021.

Sagar. (2020). 'The Government's Disingenuous Defence of the CAA and NRC in the Supreme Court'. *The Caravan*, 10 April 2020. https://caravanmagazine.in/law/the-governments-disingenous-defence-of-caa-and-nrc-in-the-supreme-court. Accessed 11 November 2020.

Saha, P. (2013). 'Singing Bengal into a Nation: Tagore the Colonial Cosmopolitan?' *Journal of Modern Literature* 36 (2): 1–23.

Sahni, B. (2001). *Tamas*. Translated by Bhisham Sahni. New Delhi: Penguin.

Sahni, P. (2003). 'Batwara: Partition and the City of Amritsar'. Unpublished PhD thesis, Massachusetts Institute of Technology. https://dspace.mit.edu/handle/1721.1/70371. Accessed 29 July 2019.

Said, E. (1978). *Orientalism*. London: Routledge and Kegan Paul.

Salim, A., ed. (2003). *Lahore 1947*. Lahore: Sang-e-Meel Publications.

Sarkar, T. (2002). 'Semiotics of Terror: Muslim Children and Women in Hindu Rashtra'. *Economic and Political Weekly* 37 (28): 2872–2876.

——— (2010). *Hindu Nation, Hindu Wife: Community, Religion, and Cultural Nationalism*. Bloomington: Indiana University Press.

Sathyu, M. S., dir. (1974). *Garam Hawa*. Film. India: Ishan Arya, M. S. Sathyu and Abu Siwani.

Schäuble, M. (2014). *Narrating Victimhood: Gender, Religion and the Making of Place in Post-war Croatia*. New York: Berghahn Books.

Schultz, K., and S. Yasir. (2020). 'India Restores Some Internet Access in Kashmir after Long Shutdown'. *New York Times*, 26 January 2020. https://www.nytimes.com/2020/01/26/world/asia/kashmir-internet-shutdown-india.html. Accessed 20 August 2020.

Scott, J. C. (1990). *Domination and the Arts of Resistance: Hidden Transcripts*. New Haven: Yale University Press.

Scroll (2019). 'Kathua Case: Jammu Court Orders FIR against Investigators for Allegedly Torturing Witnesses'. 23 October 2019. https://scroll.in/latest/941426/kathua-case-jammu-court-orders-fir-against-investigators-for-allegedly-torturing-witnesses. Accessed 20 July 2020.

Seervai, H. M. (2005). *Partition of India: Legend and Reality*. 2nd ed. London: Oxford University Press.

Sen, D. (2012). 'Caste Politics and Partition in South Asian History'. *History Compass* 10 (7): 512–522.

Seremetakis, N. C. (1991). *The Last Word: Women, Death and Divination in Inner Mani*. London: The University of Chicago Press.

Sharma, A. K. (2011). *A History of Educational Institutions in Delhi, 1911 to 1961*. New Delhi: Sanbun Publishers.

Sharma, V. (2009). 'Inherited Memories: Second-Generation Partition Narratives from Punjabi Families in Delhi and Lahore'. *Cultural and Social History* 6 (4): 411–428.

Simko, C. (2012). 'Rhetorics of Suffering: September 11 Commemorations as Theodicy'. *American Sociological Review* 77 (6): 880–902.

Singh, B. (2020). 'Aspects of Sikh Axiology: Three Essays'. *Sikh Formations* 16 (4): 448–464.

Singh, J. K. (2019). 'Negotiating Ambivalent Gender Spaces for Collective and Individual Empowerment: Sikh Women's Life Writing in the Diaspora'. *Religions* 10 (11): 598–614.

Singh, K. (2004). *A History of the Sikhs: Volume 1, 1469–1838*. New Delhi: Oxford University Press India.

—— (2009). *Train to Pakistan*. Gurgaon: Penguin Books.

Singh, S. (2018). 'No-Confidence Motion: In Speech, PM Narendra Modi Sets Agenda for Upcoming Polls, Points to Attack Congress'. *Firstpost*, 21 July 2018. https://www.firstpost.com/politics/bypolls-to-one-lok-sabha-seat-and-56-assembly-seats-to-be-held-on-3-and-7-nov-announces-ec-8862741.html. Accessed 2 February 2020.

Singh, Valay. (2020). 'As Modi Launches Ram Temple Construction, Fears of "New Republic"'. *Al Jazeera*, 5 August 2020. https://www.aljazeera.com/news/2020/8/5/as-modi-launches-ram-temple-construction-fears-of-new-republic. Accessed 5 December 2020.

Singh, Vijaita. (2020). 'More Migrants Returning to Bangladesh, Shows BSF Data'. *The Hindu*, 15 December 2020. https://www.thehindu.com/news/national/more-migrants-returning-to-bangladesh-shows-bsf-data/article33338577.ece?homepage=true. Accessed 15 December 2020.

Sinha, J. B. P. (2002). 'A Cultural Frame for Understanding Organisational Behaviour'. *Psychology and Developing Societies* 14 (1): 155–166.

Sontag, S. (1978). *Illness as Metaphor*. New York: Farrar, Straus and Giroux.

Spear, P. (1952). *India, Pakistan and the West*. London: Oxford University Press.

Srinivas, M. N. (1966). *Social Change in Modern India*. London: University of California Press.

Stanley, L. (1996). 'The Mother of Invention: Necessity, Writing and Representation'. *Feminism and Psychology* 6 (1): 45–51.

Strathern, M. (1992). *After Nature: English Kinship in the Late Twentieth Century*. Cambridge: Cambridge University Press.

——— (1999). *Property, Substance and Effect: Anthropological Essays on Persons and Things*. London: The Athlone Press.

Swift, J. (2003). *Gulliver's Travels*. London: Penguin Books.

Tagore, R. (2002). *Talks in China*. New Delhi: Rupa Publications.

——— (2005). *Selected Short Stories*. Translated by William Radice. 3rd ed. London: Penguin Books.

Talbot, I. (2006). *Divided Cities: Partition and Its Aftermath in Lahore and Amritsar*. Karachi: Oxford University Press.

Talbot, I., and G. Singh. (2009). *The Partition of India*. Cambridge: Cambridge University Press.

Thapar, R. (1996). 'The Theory of Aryan Race and India: History and Politics'. *Social Scientist* 24 (1–3): 3–29. https://www.jstor.org/stable/3520116. Accessed 17 February 2020.

——— (2009). 'The History Debate and School Textbooks in India: A Personal Memoir'. *History Workshop Journal* 67: 87–98. http://www.jstor.org/stable/40646211. Accessed 5 May 2018.

——— (2015). *Somanatha: The Many Voices of a History*. London: Verso Books.

The Hindu (1951). 'Hospital Named after Badshah Khan'. 7 June 1951. https://www.thehindu.com/todays-paper/tp-miscellaneous/tp-others/dated-june-7-1951-hospital-named-after-badshah-khan/article2793 8890.ece. Accessed 19 December 2017.

——— (2017a). 'Hard Work Is More Powerful than Harvard: Modi'. 1 March 2017. https://www.thehindu.com/elections/uttar-pradesh-2017/hard-work-more-powerful-than-harvard-narendra-modi/article173 87381.ece. Accessed 21 December 2019.

——— (2017b). 'Junaid Lynching: Main Accused "Confessed" to Crime, Say Police'. 9 July 2017. https://www.thehindu.com/news/national/other-states/junaid-lynching-main-accused-confessed-to-crime-say-police/article19245913.ece. Accessed 4 June 2020.

—— (2018). 'Crimes against Dalits Increased by 6 Percent between 2009 and 2018: Report'. 11 September 2018. https://www.thehindu.com/news/national/report-flags-increase-in-crimes-against-dalits/article 32584803.ece. Accessed 23 November 2020.

—— (2019a). 'J&K Reorganisation Bill Passage Momentous Occasion: Narendra Modi'. 6 August 2019. https://www.thehindu.com/news/national/jk-reorganisation-bill-passage-momentous-occasion-narendra-modi/article28838574.ece. Accessed 6 July 2020.

—— (2019b). 'One Who Is Not Proud of Trump Praising Modi May Not Consider Himself Indian: Minister'. 25 September 2019. https://www.thehindu.com/news/national/those-not-proud-of-trump-calling-modi-father-of-the-nation-dont-consider-themselves-indians-jitendra-singh/article29507536.ece. Accessed 21 December 2019.

—— (2020). '"Reforms Are Difficult as India Has Too Much of Democracy," Says NITI Aayog CEO'. 8 December 2020. https://www.thehindu.com/business/Economy/reforms-are-difficult-as-india-has-too-much-of-democracy-says-niti-aayog-ceo/article33281237.ece. Accessed 14 December 2020.

The Print (2019). 'MP Giriraj Singh Blames Muslims as He Calls for a Law to Control Population'. https://www.youtube.com/watch?v=UnGuY2eFQr8. Accessed 14 September 2019.

The Wire (2022). 'Bilkis Bano – "Merely Because Act Was Horrific, Is Remission Wrong?": SC Poses Query, Issues Notice'. 25 August 2022. https://thewire.in/law/bilkis-bano-remission-supreme-court-ajay-rastogi. Accessed 27 August 2022.

Tikekar, M. (2005). *Across the Wagah: An Indian's Sojourn in Pakistan*. New Delhi: Promilla and Co. Publishers & Bibliophile South Asia.

Times of India. (2018a). 'RSS Can Prepare an Army within 3 Days: Mohan Bhagwat'. 12 February 2018. https://timesofindia.indiatimes.com/india/rss-can-prepare-an-army-within-3-days-mohan-bhagwat/articleshow/62877231.cms. Accessed 18 October 2020.

—— (2018b). 'Union Minister Jayant Sinha Garlands 8 Lynching Convicts, Faces Opposition Flak'. 8 July 2018. https://timesofindia.indiatimes.com/india/union-minister-jayant-sinha-garlands-8-lynching-convicts-faces-opposition-flak/articleshow/64901863.cms. Accessed 20 July 2020.

—— (2019). '2 Days after Yogi Adityanath's Warning, UP Seals Assets of "Rioters"'. 22 December 2019. https://timesofindia.indiatimes.com/

india/2-days-after-yogi-adityanaths-warning-up-seals-assets-of-rioters/ articleshow/72920784.cms. Accessed 19 August 2020.

Times Now (2018). 'Union Minister Giriraj Singh Predicts Another "Partition" in 2047, Calls for a Law to Curb Population'. 17 September 2018. https://www.timesnownews.com/india/article/giriraj-singh-predicts-partition-in-2047-bjp-bharatiya-janata-party-leader-calls-for-a-law-to-curb-population/285595. Accessed 21 August 2020.

Trend, D. (1995). *The Crisis of Meaning in Culture and Education*. London: University of Minnesota Press.

Tuncel, T. K. (2014). 'A Review of the Social Memory Literature: Schools, Approaches and Debates'. *Uluslararasi Suçlar Ve Tarih* 15: 77–124.

Učník, L. (2016). *The Crisis of Meaning and the Life-World: Husserl, Heidegger, Arendt, Patočka*. Athens: Ohio University Press.

van der Veer, P. (1994). *Religious Nationalism: Hindus and Muslims in India*. London: University of California Press.

——— (2014). *The Modern Spirit of Asia: The Spiritual and Secular in China and India*. Oxford: Princeton University Press.

Venkataramakrishnan, R. (2019). 'Who Is Linking Citizenship Act to NRC? Here Are Five Times Amit Shah Did So'. *Scroll*, 20 December 2019. https://scroll.in/article/947436/who-is-linking-citizenship-act-to-nrc-here-are-five-times-amit-shah-did-so. Accessed 22 August 2020.

Verdery, K. (1996). *What Was Socialism, And What Comes Next?* Princeton: Princeton University Press.

Vincent, P. L. (2019). 'Historians Contest Amit Shah's Vallabhbhai Patel Narrative'. *The Telegraph*, 12 August 2019. https://www.telegraphindia.com/india/historians-contest-amit-shahs-vallabhbhai-patel-narrative/cid/1697506. Accessed 12 August 2020.

Virdee, P. (2013). 'Remembering Partition: Women, Oral Histories and the Partition of 1947'. *Oral History* 41 (2): 49–62.

——— (2018). *From the Ashes 1947: Reimagining Punjab*. New York: Cambridge University Press.

Weber, M. (1965). *The Sociology of Religion*. Translated by Ephraim Fischoff. London: Methuen & Co. Ltd.

——— (2005 [1930]). *The Protestant Ethic and the Spirit of Capitalism*. London: Routledge.

——— (2013). *From Max Weber: Essays in Sociology*. London: Routledge. E-book, Maynooth University Library website. http://ebookcentral.

proquest.com/lib/nuim/detail.action?docID=1111791. Accessed 24 March 2020.

White, H. (1966). 'The Burden of History'. *History and Theory* 5 (2): 111–134.

——— (1984). 'The Question of Narrative in Contemporary Historical Theory'. *History and Theory* 23 (1): 1–33.

Wilkes, T., and R. Srivastava. (2017). 'Protests Held Across India after Attacks against Muslims'. Reuters, 28 June 2017. https://in.reuters.com/article/india-protests/protests-held-across-india-after-attacks-against-muslims-idINKBN19J2C3. Accessed 7 June 2020.

Wilkinson, I. (2013). 'The Problem of Suffering as a Driving Force of Rationalization and Social Change'. *British Journal of Sociology* 64 (1): 123–141.

Wilkinson, I., and A. Kleinman. (2016). *A Passion for Society: How We Think about Human Suffering*. Oakland: University of California Press.

Wilson, H. S. (2002). 'Salvation in World Religions: An Evolving Christian Understanding'. *Mission Studies* 19 (1): 108–136.

Wolf, E. R. (1982). *Europe and the People Without History*. Berkeley: University of California Press.

Wolpert, S. (2006). *Shameful Flight: The Last Years of British Empire in India*. New Delhi: Oxford University Press.

Young, J. E. (1988). *Writing and Rewriting the Holocaust: Narrative and the Consequences of Interpretation*. Indianapolis: Indiana University Press.

——— (1993). *The Texture of Memory: Holocaust Memorials and Meaning*. New Haven, CT: Yale University Press.

Yuval-Davis, N. (2003). *Gender and Nation*. London: Sage Publications.

Zamindar, V. F. (2007). *The Long Partition and the Making of Modern South Asia: Refugees, Boundaries, Histories*. New York: Columbia University Press.

Index